Post-Traumatic J

Stephanie N. Arel • Shelly Rambo
Editors

Post-Traumatic Public Theology

Editors
Stephanie N. Arel
Boston University
Stamford, Connecticut, USA

Shelly Rambo
Boston University
Boston, USA

ISBN 978-3-319-82148-1   ISBN 978-3-319-40660-2 (eBook)
DOI 10.1007/978-3-319-40660-2

© The Editor(s) (if applicable) and The Author(s) 2016
Softcover reprint of the hardcover 1st edition 2016
This work is subject to copyright. All rights are solely and exclusively licensed by the Publisher, whether the whole or part of the material is concerned, specifically the rights of translation, reprinting, reuse of illustrations, recitation, broadcasting, reproduction on microfilms or in any other physical way, and transmission or information storage and retrieval, electronic adaptation, computer software, or by similar or dissimilar methodology now known or hereafter developed.
The use of general descriptive names, registered names, trademarks, service marks, etc. in this publication does not imply, even in the absence of a specific statement, that such names are exempt from the relevant protective laws and regulations and therefore free for general use.
The publisher, the authors and the editors are safe to assume that the advice and information in this book are believed to be true and accurate at the date of publication. Neither the publisher nor the authors or the editors give a warranty, express or implied, with respect to the material contained herein or for any errors or omissions that may have been made.

Cover illustration: Cover image © Marc Casas Borras / EyeEm/Getty Images

Printed on acid-free paper

This Palgrave Macmillan imprint is published by Springer Nature
The registered company is Springer International Publishing AG
The registered company address is: Gewerbestrasse 11, 6330 Cham, Switzerland

Acknowledgments

This volume was inspired by the tenacity and the indefatigable energy of the first responders to the events of April 15, 2013, in Boston, Massachusetts. The Boston Marathon bombing affected the Boston community deeply and motivated us to gather a group of theologians together to address the public impact of theology on the trauma and suffering happening before our eyes. A powerful discussion ensued. It blossomed into the essays contained in this volume. The text would not have come to fruition without the steadfast support of the Center for Practical Theology at Boston University School of Theology. Miracle Ryder provided substantial support of another kind, assisting us in logistics, project management, and organization of the initial meeting and so enabled this rewarding collaboration. Several Boston University graduate students devoted significant time and energy to the project at different stages. We thank Kathryn House, Ashley Anderson, and Kaitlyn Martin. Burke Gerstenshlager had an initial vision for this work, and his check-ins were instrumental in bringing us to Palgrave. Phil Getz and Alexis Nelson provided generous support throughout the process.

Contents

1. Introduction — Shelly Rambo — 1

2. War Bodies: Remembering Bodies in a Time of War — Willie James Jennings — 23

3. Trauma, Reality, and Eucharist — Bryan Stone — 37

4. Running the Gauntlet of Humiliation: Disablement in/as Trauma — Sharon V. Betcher — 63

5. The Trauma of Racism and the Distorted White Imagination — Dan Hauge — 89

6. "Serving the Spirit of Goodness": Spiritual and Theological Responses to Affliction in the Writings of St. John of the Cross and Louise Erdrich — Wendy Farley — 115

7 Elegy for a Lost World 135
   Mark Wallace

8 The Virtual Body of Christ and the Embrace
   of those Traumatized by Cancer 155
   Deanna A. Thompson

9 Examining Restorative Justice: Theology, Traumatic
   Narratives, and Affective Responsibility 173
   Stephanie N. Arel

10 9/11 Changed Things: The (Post-Traumatic)
   Religious Studies Classroom 193
   Katherine Janiec Jones

11 "La Mano Zurda with a Heart in Its Palm":
   Mystical Activism as a Response to the Trauma
   of Immigration Detention 217
   Susanna Snyder

12 Taking Matter *Seriously*: Material Theopoetics in
   the Aftermath of Communal Violence 241
   Michelle A. Walsh

13 Traumas of Belonging: Imagined Communities
   of Nation, Religion, and Gender in Modernity 267
   Susan Abraham

Afterword 291

Appendix: Images 301

Index 303

LIST OF FIGURES

Fig. 12.1 The Louis D. Brown Peace Institute's Traveling Memorial Button Project, bottom reads: "When Hands Reach Out In Friendship, Hearts Are Touched With Joy" 244

Fig. 12.2 *A Peace Institute Survivor's Sandplay Example.* Sandplay performed by a participant following a visit with her son's murderer in jail. In the picture, the participant indicates she is reflecting on self through the figure placed by the mirror. She also indicates she is reflecting on reconciling the perpetrator's innocent child self with the horrific action in which he had later engaged through her placement of other figures in the tray. Struggles with experiences of anger, "evil" or "othering," suffering, and trauma in tension with the survivor's belief in the Peace Institute's peace principles of forgiveness and justice are expressed in material theopoetic form through her play with material objects in the sand and the metaphoric excess of poetic and affective meaning suggested 247

Contributors

Susan Abraham is Associate Professor of Theological Studies at Loyola Marymount in Los Angeles. Her teaching and research explores postcolonial and feminist theological practices invigorating contemporary communities of faith. She is the author of *Identity, Ethics, and Nonviolence in Postcolonial Theory: A Rahnerian Theological Assessment* (Palgrave Macmillan, 2007) and co-editor of *Shoulder to Shoulder: Frontiers in Catholic Feminist Theology* (Fortress, 2009). Her publications and presentations weave practical theological insights from the experience of working as a youth minister for the Diocese of Mumbai, India, with theoretical perspectives from postcolonial theory, cultural studies, and feminist theory. Ongoing research projects include issues in feminist theological education and formation, interfaith and interreligious peace initiatives, theology and political theory, religion and media, global Christianities, and Christianity between colonialism and postcolonialism.

Stephanie N. Arel is currently a postdoctoral fellow at the Institute for the Bio-cultural Study of Religion at Boston University. She holds a certificate in trauma modalities for clinical treatment from the New York Institute for the Psychotherapies, and recently served as a fellow on the Intercontinental Academia on Human Dignity, hosted jointly by Hebrew University and Bielefeld University. She is the author of *Shame, Affect Theory, and Christian Formation* also published with Palgrave in 2016.

Sharon V. Betcher is an independent scholar, writer, crip philosopher and farmer living on Whidbey Island, Washington. She is the author of two academic manuscripts, *Spirit and the Politics of Disablement* (Fortress, 2007) and *Spirit and the Obligation of Social Flesh: A Secular Theology for Global Cities* (Fordham, 2014) as well as theological essays within multiple anthologies worked through the critical lenses of ecological, postcolonial and disability studies theory. She is a regular columnist for *Whidbey Life Magazine*.

Wendy Farley received her Ph.D. from Vanderbilt University in 1988. After 28 years of teaching at Emory University, she will direct Spirituality Studies at San Francisco Theological Seminary. Her teaching and research interests include women theologians, religious dialogue, classical texts, contemporary ethical issues, and contemplative practices. Her most recent books include *The Thirst of God: Contemplating God's Love with Three Women Mystics* (2015) and *Gathering Those Driven Away: A Theology of Incarnation* (2011).

Daniel Hauge is currently a doctoral student in Practical Theology at Boston University School of Theology. He has received an STM from Boston University and an MDiv from Regent College. His research takes an interdisciplinary approach to analyzing whiteness in the church and society, integrating critical whiteness studies, developmental and social psychology, and liberation theology

Willie James Jennings is Associate Professor of Systematic Theology and Africana Studies at Yale Divinity School. His recent book, *The Christian Imagination: Theology and the Origins of Race*, is now a standard text being read in seminaries, colleges, and university courses in a variety of disciplines. He recently completed a commentary on the book of Acts. He is currently at work on a book about creation.

Katherine Janiec Jones (Trina) is the Associate Provost for Curriculum and Co-Curriculum and an Associate Professor of Religion at Wofford College in Spartanburg, S.C. Prior to joining Wofford's faculty in 2006, she served as Assistant Professor of religion for four years at Transylvania University in Kentucky. Her current research interests revolve around cross-cultural philosophy of religion and fostering interreligious competency and engagement within a liberal arts context. She is currently working on a book project focusing on the role of myth, ritual, and symbol in the public performance of femininity.

Shelly Rambo is Associate Professor of Theology at Boston University School of Theology. Her research and teaching interests focus on religious responses to suffering, trauma, and violence. She is author of *Spirit and Trauma: A Theology of Remaining* (Westminster John Knox, 2010) and

Resurrecting Wounds: Living in the Afterlife of Trauma (Baylor University Press, forthcoming, 2017), which explores the significance of resurrection wounds within the Christian tradition and as it meets contemporary expressions of post-traumatic life in the broader culture.

Susanna Snyder is Assistant Director of Catherine of Siena College, and Tutor in Theology, at the University of Roehampton, London. She is also a Research Associate of the Oxford Centre for Christianity and Culture at Regent's Park College, Oxford. Her research focuses on immigration, refugees, and Christian ethics, and her work has been published in numerous journals and edited volumes. Her first monograph, *Asylum-Seeking, Migration and Church*, was published by Ashgate in 2012, and she co-edited *Church in an Age of Global Migration—A Moving Body*, published by Palgrave Macmillan in 2015. She has been involved in supporting refugees and people seeking asylum in the USA and UK since 2004.

Bryan P. Stone is the Associate Dean for Academic Affairs and E. Stanley Jones Professor of Evangelism at Boston University School of Theology. He received his Ph.D. in Systematic Theology from Southern Methodist University and his research is in the areas of theology and culture and evangelism and congregational development. Stone has written books such as *Faith and Film: Theological Themes at the Cinema* and *Evangelism after Christendom: The Theology and Practice of Christian Witness*.

Deanna A. Thompson is Professor of Religion at Hamline University in St. Paul, Minnesota. She is the author of several books, most recently *The Virtual Body of Christ in a Suffering World* (Abingdon, 2016), and she speaks and blogs about how faith and life look different viewed through the lens of stage IV cancer.

Mark I. Wallace Ph.D. graduate of The University of Chicago is Professor of Religion and member of the Interpretation Theory Committee and the Environmental Studies Committee at Swarthmore College, Pennsylvania. His teaching and research interests focus on the intersections between Christian theology, critical theory, and environmental studies. His most recent books are *Green Christianity: Five Ways to a Sustainable Future* (Fortress, 2010) and *Finding God in the Singing River: Christianity, Spirit, Nature* (Fortress, 2005). He is a member of the Constructive Theology Workgroup and co-founder of the Chester Swarthmore Learning Institute, a gathering of urban and religious leaders committed to empowering their local communities.

Michelle Walsh teaches at the School of Social Work, Boston University, USA. She is a licensed independent clinical social worker, activist, ordained as a Unitarian Universalist community minister, and holds a Ph.D. in practical theology. She is the author of *Violent Trauma, Culture, and Power: An Interdisciplinary Exploration in Lived Religion*, also forthcoming from Palgrave in 2016.

CHAPTER 1

Introduction

Shelly Rambo

In the immediate aftermath of the Boston marathon bombings, representative religious leaders across the city gather in an interfaith service to mark the tragedy. They offer carefully crafted words of comfort and guidance, as they situate the traumatic event and subsequent suffering within their traditions. They draw from the imagery of their sacred texts and reach for the promises and visions of their traditions: God heals the brokenhearted. Light will shine in the darkness. We are not alone. God is in our midst. The marathon events are placed within a wider story of God's relationship to the world. Some appeal to God's control and sovereign hand over history, while others point to the works of mercy extended in the midst of the horror, turning our eyes to the "Good Samaritans" and to the power and resiliency of the human spirit.[1] Many point to the counter-logic of faith traditions as the source of healing. The words offered are tokens of the theologies operative in the aftermath, the attempts to make meaning out of the chaos.

In nearby hospitals, chaplains gather in units to provide spiritual care. Disaster teams mobilize. The vicinity is locked down and armored vehicles move in. The two prominent local mosques receive a media barrage of camera and calls, as the religious identities of the suspects are revealed.

S. Rambo (✉)
Boston University School of Theology, Boston, USA
e-mail: srambo@bu.edu

The mosque in Cambridge comes under particular scrutiny, as leaders are now labeled "radical" and "anti-Western." Teachers at nearby Latin Rindge High School recall images of Dzhokhar Tsarnaev in their classrooms, as they try to reconcile the teen they knew with the named perpetrator. Talk of the death penalty is quick to follow Tsarnaev's imprisonment. What can render justice to such events, and what are the limits of justice? The quick links between immigration, citizenship, religious identity, and terrorism are made—the tremors of 9/11 can be felt. The soaring eagles of the MLK Jr. Statue in the background, the Boston University community gathers on Marsh Plaza in honor of Lu Lingzi, a Chinese student killed in the bombings; the cities of Shenyang and Boston are linked. The term "Boston Strong" emerges as makeshift memorials spring up, marking a space of mourning and reverence for the loss of life. Narratives begin to form about Boston's resiliency after the blast.

This snapshot account of the aftermath of trauma reveals the multilayered dimensions of tragedies like the one in Boston. Although the scene is particular to Boston, the dynamics of the aftermath and the search for meaning are shared across contexts. In her opening to the interfaith service three days after the bombing, Rev. Liz Walker notes that while the questions of evil and suffering are perennial, the events that spark our inquiry come "far too often these days."[2] Traumatic events seem more like an epidemic of culture, a norm rather than an exception. While great wisdom traditions provide long histories of inquiry, particular situations shape the questions. In our current context, the inquiries are shaped by the discourse of trauma. David Morris writes: "Over the past four decades, post-traumatic stress disorder has permeated every corner of our culture."[3] The frequency of the events is also coupled with a growing awareness that trauma can often blur the lines between one event ending and another beginning. Increasingly, when these events happen, the question of whether it was religiously motivated has also become a mark of our times, a product of the terrorist attacks on September 11, 2001. With the rise of religious fundamentalisms, religion is often not thought of as a source of healing but, instead, as a source of great harm.

This collection invites readers into the broader work of what we are calling *post-traumatic public theology*. As religions offer frameworks of meaning for living in the world, theologians continually examine those frameworks with the aim of bringing them to life in the present moment. Questions about the meaning of suffering surface. But the landscapes in which these questions arise present new challenges for religious traditions and call for new configurations of faith in the aftermath. The landscapes call for the theological work of unearthing the organic resources for healing and for identifying the points at which the logic of religious claims can be mobilized as tools for healing and harm.

This volume argues that the work of theology offers something distinctive in the aftermath. The essays in this collection map this post-traumatic religious territory. The theologian diagnoses the contemporary moment, interpreting "the present-day world and its pressing concerns."[4] But theology is also a meaning-making enterprise, a constructive and visionary endeavor. Exploring the inner life of peace-builders who work in intractable situations of conflict, Marc Gopin describes them as living in two worlds.[5] The first is the world of enmity, hatred, impasses, and division. We could call this the world *as it is*. The other is what Gopin calls the "special world," in which people reach across divisions and imagine the world *otherwise*. The special world is not separate from the first, but, rather, located within it. Gopin is interested in how persons are able to envision otherwise—how they develop this capacity when others are not able to see beyond the violence.

Here, we position the work of theology as a two worlds practice. It is the work of transfiguring the world—working between the *as is* and the *otherwise*. The visions and practices of religious traditions can assist us in this transfiguration, offering not simply the counter-logic, but the counter-movements to bring about peace: movements of compassion and justice, of resistance and resilience. What are the spiritual muscles needed to live according to the counter-logics referenced in the interfaith service? The authors in this collection operate between these worlds. They share commitments to justice and to cultural analysis as part of the work of theology. But they also unearth the resources within religious traditions to address the suffering of our times. Eyes wide open to the suffering, they propose multi-sensory engagements for transfiguring it.

Post-Traumatic

Trauma is the suffering that remains.[6] This simple definition speaks to the problem of integration that lies at the heart of traumatic experience. While definitions of trauma differ, one common denominator is the notion that traumatic experiences *overwhelm* human processes of adaptation. Because of the force of violence, symptoms emerge that reflect an inability to integrate that occurrence in the aftermath. The challenge of healing, then, is to incorporate that experience into a framework of meaning—to make sense of it, in the full-orbed meaning of sense. As intrusive memories and sensory triggers represent the difficulties of orienting oneself to life, the vision of integration is one of befriending the world again, of restoring trust and connections, and of finding avenues by which that experience can be placed in the fuller arena of one's life. Thus, the post-traumatic is the challenging territory of this work of integration.

The study of trauma is a little over a century old, with its origins in the neurological studies conducted by Jean-Martin Charcot and Sigmund Freud at the turn of the twentieth century.[7] Now a century later, the phenomenon of trauma has traveled off the psychoanalytic couch and extended into an interdisciplinary study of the effects of violence. Since the insertion of post-traumatic stress disorder (PTSD) in the Diagnostic and Statistical Manual of Mental Disorders (DSM-3) in 1980, the phenomenon of "overwhelming" experience has become a way of identifying the violent effects of living in the aftermath of violence. Cathy Caruth refers to this traumatic aftermath as the "enigma of suffering."[8] Something distinctive about traumatic response and reception emerges long after the traumatic event occurs, confounding notions of time, experience, and language. Trauma shatters interpretive frameworks. For the psychologist, historian, philosopher, and theologian interpreting experience and existence, trauma presents serious challenges to assumptions at the heart of these disciplines. If theology is a meaning-making enterprise, how does the shattering of meaning in trauma impact religious claims about lived existence?

Much of the theorizing about trauma emerged within the context of post-Holocaust studies, and analysis was often accompanied by vocabulary such as catastrophe, impossibility, ineffable, and rupture. Defined largely in terms of precipitating large-scale events, trauma was framed in terms of negations, and the emphasis was on the sheer inaccessibility of the traumatic event. As the term "trauma" became increasingly part of our working societal vocabulary, the limitations of the definition began to emerge as well. Trauma was generally marked by an event and its aftermath. But questions arose about whether situations of ongoing violence are considered traumatic. Because definitions of trauma were also generated from within a western European context, questions about whether the term translated across cultures also emerged. Along with these challenges, the symptomology of individual trauma accounted for in psychoanalysis, became recognizable outside of the psychological sphere and extended into an interdisciplinary study of suffering.

As the field of trauma studies continues to expand, the post-traumatic brings several key emphases to the "age-old" inquiries of religion. First, the post-traumatic points to a deepened awareness of the *fragility of the human*. There is an increased sense of the vulnerability of human persons to violence. One of the enigmatic aspects of trauma is the way in which the effects of violence transmit between human persons. Studies of the children of Holocaust survivors show that children can manifest symptoms of their parent's experience, even when the parent has not verbally communicated that experience to them. This intergenerational transmission of a traumatic experience exceeds explanation. It also suggests a kind of traumatic interdependence. We carry not simply the experiences that are unique to us but also the experiences of others. Judith Butler examines this phenomenon in her exploration of extreme suffering; she uses the term "precarity" to describe the constitution of persons as interdependent in how we bear suffering. She writes: "Loss and vulnerability seem to follow from our being socially constituted bodies, attached to others, at risk of losing those attachments, exposed to others, at risk of violence by virtue of that exposure."[9] Trauma studies confront us with the notion that we are constituted by the pain of others. This language of vulnerability also extends to the fragility of the earth and the planetary, as the realities of climate change and energy resourcing provide images of our wounded environment. We can speak about violence done to the earth and the consequences of exploiting resources differently when placing trauma within a broader picture of human and planetary interdependence.[10]

Robert Eaglestone notes that trauma theory draws our attention to "both our terrible strength and our utter weakness."[11] Who are we that we can wound and be so wounded? As John Thatamanil notes, each of the religions provides an analysis of the human predicament. Each outlines the human condition, posing the questions of suffering and harm and generating a path to healing.[12] In the Christian tradition, analysis of suffering is often quickly linked to the discourse of sin, guilt, and fault. Wendy Farley notes in *The Wounding and Healing of Desire*, "Classical theology and reform liturgy justifies rather than encounters suffering. Before suffering can speak or cry out, it has been steamrolled by an aggressive theology of sin and guilt."[13] She contends with the alignment of sin with suffering that is so central to the Western Christian tradition; to unhinge sin from suffering is not a rejection of Christianity but, in fact, an expression of certain strains of the Christian tradition that have often been relegated to the margins. The contemplative aspects of both the Christian and Buddhist traditions approach suffering as inherent in human life. Farley's theological work demonstrates how the practice of theologizing can yield a different view of the human—one that asserts the beauty and fragility of creaturely life.

Second, the post-traumatic signals a deepened awareness of the *limits of human cognition and language* to account for experience. Studies in trauma display a rupture in a person's ability to access memories of traumatic experience—essentially to bring experience to language, the story experience. While much emphasis had been placed on "recovering the story" of trauma, studies in trauma reveal the degree to which experiences could not be captured in language. The emerging attention to the somatic dimensions of trauma emphasizes the limits of language and points to rituals and expressions of healing that target the body. Bessel van der Kolk, a forerunner in pointing to the neurobiological studies of trauma and their implications for treatment, recognizes the body as storing past trauma. Studies of the brain signal that traumatic experiences are processed differently than others, bypassing cognitive processes and lodging in the limbic system. The effect of this is that trauma cannot be accessed primarily through recovering the story of what happened, because trauma is not processed via the frontal lobe, the linguistic part of our brain. Eaglestone comments: "we have to feel our way around, find out the shape of things."[14] This move beyond the primacy of language in trauma studies has opened up to a study of affects, what is often referred to as affect theory.[15] The focus on affects allows theorists to gesture toward the noncognitive dimensions of how we move in the world and how we take it in. This does not entail a rejection of cognition and reason, but fosters a more full-orbed interpretation of what motivates human behavior and response. Fear, anxiety, and shame are primary affects operative in the post-traumatic landscape.

What if we are motivated more by fear and anxiety than decision and choice? Political theorist, Neta Crawford, suggests that the sphere of international politics has presumed, as its starting point, a fixed conception of the human as "naturally aggressive, power-seeking, fearful and rational."[16] In her essay, "Human Nature and World Politics: Rethinking 'man,'" she asserts, instead, that aggression is only *one* aspect of our nature; cooperation and trust also play a role. Mapping out a different way of understanding the human, one that reflects a more dynamic, biological, and adaptive view, Crawford focuses on how fear can operate on an institutionalized and global level. While world operations are, in theory, governed by reason, Crawford displays something resonant with traumatic analysis: "Fear, and also anger and perceived humiliation, affect the ways people reason and react to threats: fear is a powerful source and re-enforcer of both the cognitive and motivated biases that interfere with the communication and reception of deterrent threats. Fear can become institutionalized and self-reinforcing."[17] Thus, the stakes for Crawford: "In assuming that distrust is natural, we have done little research on empathy and trust and spent too little effort in devising policies to promote trust."[18] Yet this conception does not take account, she argues, of complex affective dimensions. Although she doesn't specifically target the 9/11 moment, she suggests that politics may be operating in this post-traumatic mode. If experience in the aftermath involves the retriggering of the senses and the fight-or-flight response which puts persons "on alert," then the nature of fear and anxiety must be more fully explored, not simply as an individual phenomenon, but as an institutionalized one.

Multiple affects play out in both the personal and public spheres. James Gilligan, in his study of incarcerated men, unearthed the primacy of shame at the root of their violent behavior.[19] Their aggressive acts were, he found, attempts to overcome shame. North American society is structured around systems of punishment, in which guilt plays a primary role. But Gilligan asserts that shame is rarely addressed. The result is that violence is perpetuated within the justice system rather than addressed. Gilligan uses the story of Cain and Abel as a founding story to account for shame. Yet pride and guilt became the defining features of the human condition as narrated in Judeo-Christian thought. Without consideration of shame and fear, analysis of what drive human behavior is limited. Certain affects, then, rise to the surface in the post-traumatic landscape, and this may prompt theologians to return to primary narrations of the human condition within sacred texts.

Third, the post-traumatic points to the challenges of moving in the world in *time*. At the heart of traumatic experience is a rupture in the experience of time. Part of the challenge of understanding and integrating traumatic experiences relates to the temporal distortions at the heart of trauma; the unintegrated fragments of past violence return in the present, as if to hijack or possess it. The linear framework of past, present, and future is a way of orienting oneself in time. When this orientation is lost, what grounds persons and communities in the world?

It is also important to note that our conception of "posts," as in post-traumatic, have also been reshaped by trauma studies. What comes "after" is suddenly transformed into the question of the aftermath, which implies a persistence of what has come before instead of a clean break from it. Eaglestone conveys this reverberation of the past in the present through the term "afterwardsness."[20] Trauma not only fractures time, but also challenges our representation of it. Trauma thus provokes the rethinking of endings, endings beyond which we cannot imagine but nonetheless survive. This can be evidenced already in popular culture—fascination with zombies, dystopia, reflect the interest in envisioning the nature of life after impossible endings, after utopic visions of what the world will become. The envisioning of the aftermath has given way to visions of the afterlife—not as otherworldly or something at the end of time, but an untimed afterlife.

Within religious traditions, eschatology involves envisioning the ends toward which the religions point, including discussions of salvation and the afterlife. Different religions envision a widely different terrain—incarnation, enlightenment, and death without a "world-to-come." As religious traditions engage in discourses of the afterlife, they also exercise the capacity to imagine the future. Thus, eschatology, a speculative discourse, has often been concerned with reading the signs of the times, with predicting the future. It reflects religious traditions at their most uncertain and yet at their most imaginative. The discourse of ends is also bound up with expectations and fear, promise and anxiety. Might eschatology be the most fitting doctrine in the aftermath of trauma? What if we begin with endings?

This visionary discourse about the transformation of the world might occupy an important place in the aftermath of trauma. How will bodies be configured in the afterlife? What if the language of the afterlife were reemployed to envision the world in the aftermath? This shifts us from the territory of the aftermath to that of the afterlife and invites us to think about what forms of life can arise from death. As bodies "resurrect" in the aftermath of trauma, might theology have something to speak about the nature of life following "deaths," as it resonates with the experiences of trauma? As the question of forgiveness looms large in the landscape of traumatic survival, the nature of forgiveness might need a different linear orientation. If traumatic experience cannot be isolated to the past, then the process of forgiveness might involve a kind of on-goingness—not a definitive process or clean break, but a continuing process of reckoning with the past. As Jesus meets the disciples in the event of resurrection, there are two features that accompany his return: he identifies fear in his declaration of peace, and he speaks about forgiveness. Resurrection is about life in the aftermath, and the territory is named in relationship to the difficult challenges of post-traumatic.

This uncertainty of time inherent in trauma turns attention to space: the texture of the land, the aesthetics of skin, a trust in the palpable and not in the promissory. In *The Christian Imagination*, Willie James Jennings turns us to the soil in a different way, as he identifies the roots of modern Christian theology in the soil of colonialism.[21] Underlying Jennings' analysis is the trauma of dislocation, of being exiled from home, of being uprooted. To turn to space is to reframe memory and remembrance, not simply as a recovery of the past, but as involving an embodied regeneration of the present, involving all of the natural elements.

The post-traumatic, then, signals an increased awareness of the fragility of lived existence. It also brings the problems of time and language to bear on frameworks of meaning. As religious leaders reach into their traditions in the aftermath of tragedies, what can account for experiences in which persons and communities are unable to imagine a way forward? What are bodies doing in the aftermath, and how might religious rituals enact a different way of knowing the world, given the realities of violence? By using the term "post-traumatic" to guide our theological reflections, we are intentionally placing theology in active relationship with the medical model. We do this in order to bring the therapeutic framing of trauma—diagnosis, disorder, disease—into active engagement with religious frameworks for interpreting what medical anthropologist, Arthur Kleinman, calls "the art of living."[22] In our contemporary setting, PTSD has become more than a diagnostic label for individual suffering; it has become a way of naming the conditions of life more broadly. Richard Mollica argues that the Western medical model has displaced indigenous practices of healing and pathologized suffering in ways that disconnect communities from resources for healing.[23] The medical model is not value-neutral. In many cases, religious communities do not perceive the language of mental health as competing with the language of faith. But are the visions of healing offered by each compatible? What happens to the religious vocabularies of human and divine when placed under the therapeutic umbrella?

Public

Public events of violence often expose the fragility of existing infrastructures of support. Within the context of the USA, the aftermath of Hurricane Katrina called attention to the ongoing challenges within New Orleans that made certain persons more susceptible to the devastating effects of the hurricane. The trauma of Hurricane Katrina was not simply the impact of the storm. The effects of the storm were tied to pre-existing societal inequalities that were laid bare in the aftermath. Issues related to race and class raised questions, not only about the resources available to provide care, but also about accessibility to those resources and who has access to them. New Orleans continues to rebuild. Its failures at disaster recovery point to another variety of trauma, in which events expose the trauma of race within the USA. Events such as the shooting of Michael Brown in Ferguson, MO, Eric Garner in New York, and church members in Charlestown, SC, are being assessed not simply as isolated events of violence, but as a manifestation of a longstanding history of violence and oppression. To be "raced" in particular ways means that violence done to certain populations is given more attention than others. Not all public tragedies are weighed equally. While the event of the Boston Marathon bombings drew great attention, Rev. Liz Walker's neighborhood witnesses multiple violence deaths each year due to gang violence with little media attention.

The term "insidious trauma" was coined by Maria Root to identify a dimension of trauma that she was witnessing in her clinical work.[24] Certain populations within society are more vulnerable to external harm in *everyday* life because of an aspect of their identity (race, gender, sexual orientation, disabilities). Their movements in the world already carry with them a certain hyper-vigilance. Trauma survivors give accounts of experiencing the world as an enemy in the aftermath of a traumatic event; the clients with whom Root worked felt this hostility on an ongoing basis. Because of their marginalized status within society, their exposure to harm was a part of their everyday experience. When traumatic "events" occurred, the effects were compounded. The question of resources for healing also comes into play. The resilience of persons in the aftermath of trauma is often correlated to the existing social and economic resources available to them. Root brings the dimension of societal realities such as racism, sexism, heterosexism, and able-ism into the arena of trauma studies. In public events such as the Boston marathon bombings, asking the question of which populations are more vulnerable to harm and which have resources available in the aftermath is critical.

When public tragedies occur, it is also important to track the rhetoric of belonging and identity that quickly forms in the aftermath. The rhetoric of the interfaith service was accompanied by assertions of what it means to be a Bostonian and, in turn, what it means to be an American. If, as Crawford notes, fear is a collective affect, then public traumas will generate securing mechanisms. Who are my people? Where do I belong? The assertions of togetherness and assertions of unity, oneness, and a common humanity can also be accompanied by practices of exclusion and scapegoating.

Judith Herman's book, *Trauma and Recovery*, is recognized as something of a sacred text within the field of trauma studies. Herman's study of psychological trauma mapped out the phenomenon of trauma and a path to recovery. Yet, what is often overlooked is Herman's commitment to situating the study publicly and politically. The first chapter serves as a kind of cautionary tale, noting that trauma enters and exits public consciousness in cycles of remembering and forgetting. The study of trauma itself is subject to amnesia. The memory loss Herman points to is not a simple account of the difficulty of recovering traumatic memories of the past but of a wider "forgetting" that takes place within the public sphere. She insists that the study of suffering, of violence, is always political and public: "The systematic study of psychological trauma therefore depends upon a political movement. Indeed, whether such study can be pursued or discussed in public is itself a political question."[25]

Since the publication of Herman's book in 1992, the media plays an increasingly large role in bringing trauma into public view. Cameras are positioned on the front lines of war. Traumatic social events play across TV screens like action movies. Days of footage covered the Boston bombing, while the Internet media sites provide a steady stream and immediate access to most situations of violence. In these projected images of trauma, what do we see and what we do not see? In *Regarding the Pain of Others*, Susan Sontag posed the critical questions about the lens through which we view human suffering.[26] Does it mobilize us to action? Does it generate compassion? Or does the lens distance us? There is concern that more media coverage may inoculate viewers to the realities of violence. This is where key dimensions of public life must be highlighted: how the media presents reality, the impact of the virtual/visual, and the nature and quality of our connectedness. Judith Butler makes the important link between the frames of suffering and the value of human life. The positioning of the camera turns us to suffering, but to *whose* suffering?

The rise of social media has also transformed engagements with trauma. Social media can facilitate connections, offering a collective network of care that has not been fully conceptualized theologically. What we think of as "the public" is expanding, and tragedies are linked/ing in new ways. The viral effect of slogans such as "I Can't Breathe," "Black Lives Matter," and "Boston Strong" echo in other parts of the country and the world—linking to Newtown, to Norway, to Virginia Tech.

Theology

Theologies stand in more precarious places when we consider trauma. The post-9/11 context has changed the face of religion in the USA, especially as it is invoked in public. In the interfaith service after the Boston bombing, the specter of 9/11 was present. This means that while religious leaders are engaging the age-old questions of suffering, they are also contending with the realities of religiously motivated violence.

As we link this to the problem of the future in trauma discourse, it is important to think about the work of theology, not as providing or securing certain answers but, instead, positioning persons in a certain way in relationship to suffering. The danger is that theology will provide no guidance, on the one side, and a kind of dogmatic retrenching on the other. I want to suggest that the kind of theologizing that we witness in this volume provides what, in clinical terms, might be described as directionality. In Kaethe Weingarten's work on trauma, she maps out the vision that guides her work with survivors.[27] She uses the term "directionality" to talk about the trajectory of her sessions with clients. In working with them, she says that she is assisting them in envisioning the future. She does not predict or grab an endpoint and lead them to it. The end is not clear to either of them, she notes. Yet the session is not without direction. This work in the present with a tenuous future is a helpful guide for interpreting the work of theology in respect to trauma. Without directionality, there is despair; with directionality, resilience can replace despair. The concept of resilience infuses current studies in trauma. It pushes against the notion of healing as an endpoint and, instead, emphasizes a positioning of life in the aftermath that is much more focused on process and practice. In turn, the theologians here draw attention to the practices and pedagogies of religious traditions rather than to the articulation of beliefs and claims as theological endpoints. How does faith orient persons and communities to suffering? How might faith reposition us in the world?

Inaugurating the collection with the events in Boston and following it with reflections on the future of post-traumatic public theology highlights the extent to which we think larger interests come to bear on individual suffering. The theologian is positioned differently in publics elsewhere. Whereas Willie James Jennings begins the volume by tying war trauma to nationhood and American identity, Susan Abraham concludes by addressing themes of national identity and trauma within the context of India, post-Partition. While the volume takes seriously the US context, this conclusion points to the need for expanding the post-traumatic lens to consider the particularities of contexts in which trauma occurs. The afterword of the volume follows in the form of a conversation featuring the voices of four eminent theologians who have significantly shaped contemporary theological reflection on trauma. Due to their fundamental contributions to the field, these theologians engage in a discourse about hope, human suffering, and the role of the theologian in public spaces, completing the volume by pointing to future trajectories and contexts for post-traumatic public theology.

This collection invites readers into a deeper exploration of how trauma functions in public, acknowledging that religion is implicated in the suffering and also instrumental in alleviating it. The essays feature three important modes of doing theology: political, constructive, and practical. They focus on the *practiced* dimension of faith, deemphasizing beliefs as cognitive assertions and, instead, concentrating on the development of ways of being that are cultivated over time. They want to affirm a vision of beauty, love, and desire that gives life rather than takes it. A vision of goodness can counter the distorted logic that brings about harm. Christian claims of incarnation fundamentally affirm embodied life and call participants to protect lives. The vision of the cross and the suffering of Jesus' body, remembered by a community in the aftermath, is not a call to more suffering and trauma, but to a way of healing that moves in and through trauma. While much is shattered, the authors point to a vision of healing that withstands the force of trauma. Some bonds cannot be broken. There is a way of communing that still holds amidst the shattering of violence.

They also emphasize the *communal* and collective nature of these practices that guard against the individualism and, often, isolationism of persons and communities who have experienced trauma. Instead of merely retrieving aspects of the tradition, they work constructively to bring the resources to bear on traumatic realities. These retrievals are not, however, made without recognizing the ways in which religious traditions are complicit in trauma. In some cases, Christianity provides the supporting logic to systems that are unjust and that wield great harm. These retrievals are not naïve about the tradition nor do they vilify or defend but, instead, assess how they function in light of trauma. And although most of the essays locate their constructive elements within the Christian tradition, they begin to highlight a method of retrieval that is not restricted to a particular religion. Every religion has resources from which to draw in response to trauma, and each can learn from the other. The essays in this volume offer examples for religions to explore, within their own contexts, what it means to be human in a post-traumatic and public world.

Several essays feature the work of theology as cultural analysis. These shed light on how culture deals with trauma and how it appears—or disappears—when placed within particular narratives. The authors provide analysis about how society, particularly American society, frames suffering. When traumatic events occur within the USA, there are cultural and civic narratives that surface and ways of representing persons that deeply reflect an understanding of what it means to be an American and how a nation should function. Traumatic events delineate identity, defining "nation." Globalization and post-colonial realities make an impact on the status of nation and nationhood. As the status is more fragile, the lens of trauma is helpful for detecting who benefits from nation and what harm is done in the name of nationhood. We could call this political theology.

Willie James Jennings situates the return of military veterans within the context of a country that does not own up to its history and that continues to deny the deep contradictions that lie at the heart of its identity. He suggests that while veterans bear the diagnosis, moral injury is a shared condition. The memory work and penance required for the healing journey Christians undertake must thus include a communal "burden sharing" with the wounded veteran through a reimaging of the body of Jesus. Taking us inside the country's obsession with reality TV, Bryan Stone examines how the dynamics of watching and being watched position viewers in relationship to suffering. Although bringing suffering into public view, the dynamics of the "real" do not activate the viewer and while offering visions of individual transformation and witness, it "fits hand-in-glove with a neoliberal rationality of self-governance and self-empowerment enshrined in American individualism." He turns to Christian practices and sacraments to envision a deeper response to suffering that also has the possibility of speaking beyond the individual to the "transformation of social and political institutions."

Other essays concerned with the impact of post-colonial political and social dynamics examine how certain bodies are vulnerable to the gaze of the nation. Objectification by the nation and national discourses incurs its own particular trauma. Sharon Betcher asserts that the disabled body is a site of political violence, in which cultural scripts continually are placed on bodies. Subject to the aesthetic judgments of a culture obsessed with perfection and wholeness, disabled bodies symbolize humiliation. Yet, drawing from a tradition that locates at its center a humiliated God, Betcher recognizes that after trauma humility can "recuperate love," leading to the radical acceptance of human vulnerability. Daniel Hauge recognizes this vulnerability in the demonization of black bodies viewed through the lens of whiteness. He confronts dominant America culture, identifying that even trauma studies and treatment operate from an imaginative frame that distorts race and racism. American Christianity(ies) are implicated in this distortion, but Hague shows how black theologians center "the experience of black people under racial oppression in America as their interpretive starting point." This shift in origin permits a more accurate telling of the narrative of oppression while also engaging the notion of time.

Other essays feature constructive engagements with the Christian tradition. They show how resources within this tradition could be retrieved and reimaged in light of trauma. They point to theology as offering counter-logic to cultural or therapeutic practices. When the authors point to resources within the Christian tradition, they point to a way and not a set of beliefs. Wendy Farley claims that the Christian contemplative tradition has distinctive resources for engaging suffering: "A certain kind of faith is needed to enter into the land of affliction." Modeling this faith through explorations, two teachers, John of the Cross and Father Damien, Farley describes a way *through* suffering, that is evidenced in great spiritual teachers. They are sourced by a Great Love, goodness, and a vision of compassion. "However deeply despair and violence go," Farley writes, "the great love goes deeper." Mark Wallace reaches to sacred scriptures for its testimony to the Earth, animated and yet threatened by human abuses. From the scent of sagebrush to the visions of turquoise water and soaring falcons, he provides a sensual elegy to a communion of all living beings. He recovers a vision of Jesus who communes with the earth and draws from it materials to heal. He points to a spiritual way of connection amidst loss, of grit amidst land threatened by human greed: "There are still occasional droplets of grace within the tempest of encroaching ecocide in the biosphere." Deanna Thompson's understanding of community expanded when she entered into the experience of living with cancer. Amidst treatments, she discovered a virtual community that took the form of a CaringBridge online site. While cancer has not been understood under the rubric of trauma, Thompson connects the two and describes how this unlikely community arose, expanding her notion of the body of Christ as interpreted within the Christian tradition, while pointing to a curious phenomenon of interfaith healing.

Another set of essays takes us inside zones of trauma and shows us how the work of social engagement is challenged and expanded within these settings. College classrooms, detention centers, prisons, and trauma-response organizations become sites for rethinking how we form persons and communities for responding to trauma. Taking the context as a starting point for reflection, they re-envision what spirituality looks like within these settings, and thus, expand traditional conceptions of social justice and activism.

Amidst a growing movement of restorative justice, Stephanie Arel suggests that educators are often unaware of the ways in which trauma functions within justice settings. She begins to outline what affective attunement might look like. If those who teach about traumatic events and their affective impact are inattentive to the layers of trauma operating within the broader criminal justice system *and* also within their own experiences, then damage can be done in the name of restoration. Do principles of restorative justice, such as mutual regard and forgiveness, make persons more vulnerable to trauma, "opening up a world of shame and trauma"? Trina Janiec-Jones claims that 9/11 changed her religious studies classroom, by fundamentally refocusing how she teaches religion and how she perceives the world in which her students are immersed. Underlying her descriptions of the changing landscape of religion in the USA and the identity formation of college-students, she questions whether they will find a spirituality that can sustain them in the midst of trauma. She prompts us to re-envision classrooms as sites of activism. Drawing from her ethnographic research in immigration detention centers, Susanna Snyder discovers that activists working within this setting describe their work as rooted not only in a spiritual tradition but also in "mystical activism." The works of Soelle and Anzaldua provide a map for this blending of contemplation and activism. Snyder discovers that "mysticism can act as a powerful source of endurance for individuals, as well as providing a subversive stimulus to resistance and the fight against injustice."

Interviewing a teen whose friend was murdered in a Boston neighborhood, Michelle Walsh discovers that the aftermath practices contain spiritual wisdom that may serve as a taproot for trauma healing. Wearing a button that displays a picture of the deceased, the teen describes the loss and the sense of the continuing presence of her friend with her: the dead commune with the living. Walsh displays the rich, contextual, and intercultural texture of trauma healing work: political, prophetic, playful, and testimonial. The political and traumatic also merge in Susan Abraham's essay, where she expands practical responses to trauma into the global sphere. Abraham presses trauma theory to confront histories rising out of non-Western contexts, drawing from multiple disciplines to affirm a post-traumatic public theology that includes citizenship for the vulnerable bodies of women from India and Pakistan. Challenging categories of "religion" and "nation," and asserting that "It is traumatic to belong to nation," Abraham's essay supports a cross-cultural approach that fosters a reimagining of the ways that we speak about trauma.

In the afterword to the volume, four prominent theologians, Phillis Isabella Sheppard, Warren Kinghorn, Andrea Bieler, and Storm Swain, discuss questions that emerged from the work of compiling this text. Together they reflect on the roles they play as theologians in the aftermath of trauma. They share information about the resources they depend on to respond to trauma and reveal where they find hope in trauma's aftermath. Their joint responses recognize theologians' accountability in responding to trauma, promoting, as Andrea Bieler writes, a post-traumatic public theology that holds up hope in the public square amidst the "injustice and the precariousness of life."

Conclusion

This collection was birthed in the immediate aftermath of the Boston marathon bombing.

Years later, the effects of that event live on. With the death penalty assigned unanimously by jurors, Tsarnaev awaits his fate in federal prison. The appeals process begins. Tsarnaev's lawyers file a motion for a new and more just trial. Meanwhile, survivors of the blast continue to pursue psychological care and physical therapy, enduring operations, delayed symptoms, and additional amputations from sustained wounds that refuse to heal. These are the vestiges of trauma. Subsequent marathons have come and gone. Many of those injured have crossed the finish line, some on foot and others in hand cycles. Their bodies mark how the past makes itself present in the aftermath. As is often the case, the iconic images of the marathon and the phrase, Boston Strong, still work on us, providing definition in complex ways —trauma changes us on many levels. It affects our sense of safety and our attempts at meaning making. It connects us and divides us, altering our self-perception and our perceptions of God. Yet, while trauma truncates possibilities, it also opens new ones.

Trauma and its aftermath press theology and theologians across all religious traditions to pay attention to the recurring nature of trauma and the long, continual process of healing. We hope that the essays in this volume reflect a deep awareness of the challenges of the repetition of trauma, how trauma emerges in lives and memory over time. Theology in a post-traumatic mode requires attentiveness to the fragility of humanity, and the work here attempts to chart new territory in modeling how to develop a critical but constructive theological voice in dealing with the multiple issues that trauma raises. In an effort to negotiate tradition and practice listening to what lies beyond language and cognition, paying attention to the somatic dimensions of experience, the essays honor that one can be interrupted or affected by trauma and altered forever. But they also recognize that there are theological resources that offer understanding and new visions. Our intention ultimately is that these essays might lead to a more responsive Christian theology, while pointing to the need for more work from all religious traditions.

Notes

1. Rev. Nancy Taylor (2013) linked the communal response to bombing to the parable of the Good Samaritan in the Christian scriptures. A full account of the service can be found at: http://www.c-span.org/video/?312222-1/interfaith-service-bombing-victims-boston.
2. Rev. Liz Walker (2013). http://www.c-span.org/video/?312222-1/interfaith-service-bombing-victims-boston.
3. David J. Morris (2015) *The Evil Hours: A Biography of Post-Traumatic Stress Disorder* (New York: Harcourt Publishing Company), xii.
4. Serene Jones and Paul Lakeland (eds.) (2005) *Constructive Theology: A Contemporary Approach* (Minneapolis: Augsburg Fortress Press), 4.
5. Marc Gopin (2012) *Bridges Across an Impossible Divide: The Inner Lives of Arab and Jewish Peacemakers* (New York: Oxford University Press), 1.

6. Shelly Rambo (2010) *Spirit and Trauma: A Theology of Remaining* (Louisville: Westminster John Knox Press).
7. This history appears, in summary form, in several places: David J. Morris (2015) *The Evil Hours: A Biography of Post-Traumatic Stress Disorder* (New York: Houghton Mifflin Harcourt Publishing); Judith Herman (1992) *Trauma and Recovery* (New York: Basic Books); Bessel A. van der Kolk and Alexander C. McFarlane (eds.) (2006) *Traumatic Stress: The Effects of Overwhelming Stress on Mind, Body, and Society* (Guilford, CT: The Guilford Press).
8. Cathy Caruth (ed.) (1995) *Trauma: Explorations in Memory* (Baltimore: Johns Hopkins University Press).
9. Judith Butler (2006) *Precarious Life: The Powers of Mourning and Violence* (London: Verso), 20. She writes: "For I am confounded by you, then you are already of me, and I am nowhere without you. I cannot muster the 'we' except by finding the way in which I am tied to 'you,' by trying to translate but finding that my own language must break up and yield if I am to know you. You are what I gain through this disorientation and loss. This is how the human comes into being, again and again, as that which we have yet to know," 49.
10. Sarah Goodyear (2015) "Can Living with Long-term Drought Cause Trauma?" *The Nation*, July 21, 2015. http://www.thenation.com/article/can-living-with-long-term-drought-cause-trauma.
11. Robert Eaglestone (2014) "Knowledge, 'afterwardsness' and the future of trauma theory," in Gert Buelens, Samuel Durrant, and Robert Eaglestone (eds.) *The Future of Trauma Theory: Contemporary Literature and Cultural Criticism* (New York: Routledge), 10.
12. John J. Thatamanil (2006) *The Immanent Divine: God, Creation and the Human Predicament* (Minneapolis, MN: Fortress Press).
13. Wendy Farley (2005) *The Wounding and Healing of Desire: Weaving Heaven and Earth* (Louisville, KY: Westminster John Knox Press), 8.
14. Eaglestone, "Knowledge, 'afterwardsness' and the future of trauma theory," 10.
15. See Melissa Gregg and Gregory J. Seigworth (eds.) (2010) *The Affect Theory Reader* (Durham: Duke University Press).
16. Neta C. Crawford (2010) "Human Nature and World Politics: Rethinking 'Man,'" in K. Booth (ed.) *Realism and World Politics* (New York: Routledge), 158.
17. Crawford, "Human Nature," 173.
18. Crawford, "Human Nature," 173.
19. James Gilligan (1997) *Violence: A National Epidemic* (New York: Vintage).
20. Eaglestone, "Knowledge, 'afterwardsness' and the future of trauma theory," 11.

21. Willie James Jennings (2011) *The Christian Imagination: Theology and the Origins of Race* (New Haven, CT: Yale University Press).
22. Arthur Kleinman (2007) *What Really Matters: Living a Moral Life Amidst Uncertainty and Danger* (Oxford University Press).
23. Richard F. Mollica (2008) *Healing Invisible Wounds: Paths to Hope and Recovery in a Violent World* (Nashville, TN: Vanderbilt University Press).
24. Maria Root (1992) "Reconstructing the impact of trauma on personality," in L.S. Brown & M. Ballou (eds.) *Personality and Psychopathology: feminist reappraisals* (New York, Guilford Press), 229–265.
25. Herman, *Trauma and Recovery*, 9.
26. Susan Sontag (2003) *Regarding the Pain of Others* (New York: Picador Press).
27. Kaethe Weingarten (2004) *Common Shock: Witnessing Violence Every Day* (New York, NY: New American Library).

Bibliography

Butler, J. 2006. *Precarious life: The powers of mourning and violence*. London: Verso.

Caruth, C. (ed.). 1995. *Trauma: Explorations in memory*. Baltimore: The Johns Hopkins University Press.

Crawford, N.C. 2010. Human nature and world politics: Rethinking 'man'. In *Realism and world politics*, ed. K. Booth. New York: Routledge.

Eaglestone, R. 2014. Knowledge, 'afterwardsness' and the future of trauma theory. In *The future of trauma theory: Contemporary literature and cultural criticism*, ed. G. Buelens, S. Durrant, and R. Eaglestone. New York: Routledge.

Farley, W. 2005. *The wounding and healing of desire: Weaving heaven and earth*. Louisville: Westminster John Knox Press.

Gilligan, J. 1997. *Violence: A national epidemic*. New York: Vintage.

Goodyear, S. 2015. Can living with long-term drought cause trauma? *The Nation*, July 21. http://www.thenation.com/article/can-living-with-long-term-drought-cause-trauma

Gopin, M. 2012. *Bridges across an impossible divide: The inner lives of Arab and Jewish peacemakers*. New York: Oxford University Press.

Gregg, M., and G.J. Seigworth (eds.). 2010. *The affect theory reader*. Durham: Duke University Press.

Herman, J. 1992. *Trauma and recovery*. New York: Basic Books.

Jennings, W.J. 2011. *The Christian imagination: Theology and the origins of race*. New Haven: Yale University Press.

Jones, S., and P. Lakeland (eds.). 2005. *Constructive theology: A contemporary approach*. Minneapolis: Augsburg Fortress Press.

Kleinman, A. 2007. *What really matters: Living a moral life amidst uncertainty and danger*. New York: Oxford University Press.

Mollica, R.F. 2008. *Healing invisible wounds: Paths to hope and recovery in a violent world*. Nashville: Vanderbilt University Press.

Morris, D.J. 2015. *The evil hours: A biography of post-traumatic stress disorder*. New York: Houghton Mifflin Harcourt Publishing Company.

Rambo, S. 2010. *Spirit and trauma: A theology of remaining*. Louisville: Westminster John Knox Press.

Root, M. 1992. Reconstructing the impact of trauma on personality. In *Personality and psychopathology: Feminist reappraisals*, ed. L.S. Brown and M. Ballou. New York: Guilford Press.

Sontag, S. 2003. *Regarding the pain of others*. New York: Picador Press.

Taylor, N. 2013. Interfaith service for bombing victims in Boston. http://www.c--span.org/video/?312222-1/interfaith-service-bombing-victims-boston

Thatamanil, J.J. 2006. *The immanent divine: God, creation and the human predicament*. Minneapolis: Fortress Press.

Van der Kolk, B.A., and A.C. McFarlane (eds.). 2006. *Traumatic stress: The effects of overwhelming stress on mind, body, and society*. Guilford: The Guilford Press.

Walker, L. 2013. Interfaith service for bombing victims in Boston. http://www.c-span.org/video/?312222-1/interfaith-service-bombing-victims-boston

Weingarten, K. 2004. *Common shock: Witnessing violence every day*. New York: New American Library.

CHAPTER 2

War Bodies: Remembering Bodies in a Time of War

Willie James Jennings

In North Carolina, no one remembers easily. We are a military state. Military bases and military culture imprint our state, and now that imprint is scarred, indeed it has been scarred for quite some time, because what fills the social landscape of North Carolina are wounded veterans, those whose bodies are marked with the memories of war. They are signatures of an unclean escape from death. We who inhabit this state with them, both the geographic and the psychic state, are implicated in their very difficult work of remembering, remembering not only who they were before war, but of negotiating the memories of war that shape their present. Yet, what has become clear to me is that the challenge of that memory work is made even more tortuous by its entanglements in America's confused moral landscape.

Memory work is always crowded work. Few sites of memory work are more crowded right now than the memory work of veterans, especially those carrying what some therapists and scholars are calling moral injury. The idea of moral injury powerfully articulated in the writings of psychotherapist Jonathan Shay has emerged in recent years as a crucial hermeneutic for understanding the tortured memory work of war veterans, trying to come to terms with having transgressed their moral beliefs.[1] How does

W.J. Jennings (✉)
Yale Divinity School, New Haven, USA

one negotiate life after transgressing, not simply a moral principle, but the coherence of a moral universe? Moral injury occurs when the fabric that holds moral agency and the self together are torn asunder.[2]

Moral injury involves a remembering that is dangerous, because it carries the power of condemnation, shame, and guilt that can unleash a view of the self as irredeemable and un-reparable.[3] All remembering after participating in war is troubled, but this memory work holds an unbearable heaviness, because it is enfolded inside a theological vision of transgression and even apostasy. Those who remember from within a moral universe or a theological framework must confront the ideas that they have disobeyed a divine law of how life ought to be handled and humanity maintained or even acted in ways that imply that they have turned from the true way of God and toward evil. Moral injury draws us into a liminality that is wider and deeper than just the adjudication of particular events and morally horrendous actions or inaction. As psychiatrist and moral theologian Warren Kinghorn suggests, moral injury throws the identity of those so wounded into question.

> Soldiers who kill in ambiguous circumstances are often to themselves neither guilty nor innocent, neither victims nor perpetrators, neither heroes nor villains, but some complex amalgam of them all that is not well captured in the sound-bite conversation with which the American public has to date discussed our current wars.[4]

The theological question here is not how do we remember or even how do we remember well? The crucial question is "under what conditions do we remember?" It is the conditions that surround the memory work of veterans that I want to consider in this essay. Those conditions implicate all of us in their sorrows and require a theological intervention that draws us into a shared work of remembering with them. Veterans exist on the American social landscape as human objects to gaze upon and who evoke a range of emotions from pity to admiration, from anger to confusion. We have been taught to look in ways that create distance between us and them, a distance that increases through the growing chasm between the rich and the poor. Our military rank and file increasingly come from among the working poor so that the difference between military and civilian now more than ever mirrors the difference between the have-nots and those of means and therefore of choice. Of course, such difference also exists within the military, between those trained for leadership and who enjoy the benefits of elite military academy training and those soldiers whose bodies are weaponized and made to face the full force of warfare. We see the bodies of soldiers through lenses that separate and isolate their lives from our own and turn their stories into singular occurrences strung together by heroic gestures of sacrifice.

Their moral injury must be seen against the horizon of the seared consciousness of a country that functions in a constant state of moral injury. Unlike veterans, however, we have institutionalized ways of numbing the pain of our psychic wound and denying the reality of our moral incoherence. We function with both the denial of our deep connection to soldiers and the real implication of weaponizing human beings and telling them to kill or be killed for us. Americans rarely follow the ledger all the way down to the reality being bought with the lives of human beings. We normally stop short of true sight of that cost, settling on ambiguous and abstract ideas like freedom and democracy, when the actual matter at hand is the freedom of a corporation to operate and/or to extract natural resources from the earth unhindered by whatever people inhabit that land. What our veterans expose is the deep contradictions of America's moral landscape, contradictions that are glossed over by a hyper-patriotism that constantly exploits memory.

How does one remember horror when every work of remembering is being drawn inside the ideological uses of memory, that is, inside the nationalistic and commercial desires of the present? This production of memory is happening on top of the tortured memory work of veterans and their families trying to cope with moral injury. I write not as one who is doing the important therapeutic and/or pastoral work of working with soldiers and their families, but as a theologian watching the deployment and redeployment of their strength, and the exploitation of their suffering and pain through jingoistic sloganizing even in places that should resist such, that is, in churches and by pastors and other Christian intellectuals who have released these women and men to strange narratives of sacrifice. Their suffering is being drawn deeply into the propagandistic operation of the state. In effect, their bodies disappear in the remembering operations of the State and the market and they reappear only in psychosis inducing slogans like "Freedom is never free."

The kind of theological intervention that might aid in the soul repair of veterans and their families must first clarify and challenge the uses of memory on the American social landscape.[5] We must ask with our veterans, who wishes to remember with them, and who wishes to remember for them? Those wishing to remember for them for the purposes of statecraft and the market must be resisted. We should resist the kind of remembering that silences their voices and/or presses them to speak only in commemorative script and patriotic ritual. As Paul Connerton noted in his classic text, *How Societies Remember*, the use of commemorative ceremony and ritual fundamentally shape the present and prescribe the contours of our agency and subjectivity.[6] In this regard, veterans are often invited into a kind of remembering that renders them lifeless monuments who should be seen but never heard, even when they speak.

Secondly, together with veterans we must engage in a more systemic sense of remembering that addresses American's historical amnesia, especially in relation to war and violence. Our propensity to ignore our past hinders attempts of war wounded veterans to reconcile with their own past. Therapeutic intervention should have clear sight of our troubled historical consciousness. Pastoral intervention that intends to address moral injury needs a theological vision that draws veterans into God's own memory work. For Christians, we serve a God who remembers and invites us to enter the divine reality of remembering in ways that remind us not only of who we are but also who God has been for us and will be for us.

Whose Memory, Which Story

Americans have been cultivated in the art of forgetfulness. Historically, this was part of the tacit agreement immigrants made as they journeyed to this new world. They stripped away their immigrant past and embraced an American future that was constituted precisely in the constant abandoning of the old world narratives of life. Gone was life configured through the stories of village and field in old Europe, Asia, or Africa, and as those stories faded even in memory, so too faded the sense of participating in the on-going drama of a people. That sense of storied existence marked the path through which an individual could envision their life woven to their ancestors' journey. Broken off from those ancestral journeys, immigrants in America both crafted and were subjected to a new narration of life and identity. The American story they entered and in turn enacted worked like a cleaning agent constantly peeling away the layers of memory and the old world story and shaping a vision of citizenship bent on fantasizing the future.[7]

The ethnic past of an immigrant in America was a burden to be stripped away, because it presented an uncivilized state. Immigrants coming to the

USA from its very beginnings agreed to a twofold civilizing project, of the land and of their own bodies. Both were bound to cultivation toward Anglo existence, and any immigrant who resisted was marking a path toward failure. So, to remember an ethnic past rightly was to begin one's memory work in America as the place where the new began and the old has passed away. Such remembering is already shortsighted, being cut off from the horrors of assimilation and violence that lay at the historical foundations of becoming a citizen in the USA. The fantasy of an American present lays waste to an immigrant past that remembers beyond the geographic and temporal boundaries that conceal an American story born in violence and conquest.

Such fantasizing does strange things to the past. We Americans always do strange things with our past. History exists for us, but we thwart its work, because we narrate the past in ways that justify a present that glories in America's power and world leadership. America is a place intoxicated with narrative power. That narrative power has been overwhelming, not only for a public habituated in its performance, but also for generations of veterans who have been subjected to its life mangling affects. Veterans have been asked to narrative their lives inside of profound contradictions—honorable service inside of dishonorable wars, virtuous actions enmeshed in violence, national celebration and admiration coupled with constant neglect. Such contradictions only intensify once they reenter a civilian world that drowns their individual stories inside an American narrative that turns their lives into nothing more than illustrations of patriotism.

America's narrative power cannot be defeated, but it can be resisted. As the Swiss Reformed theologian, Karl Barth suggested, we should deny the State its pathos.[8] Writing at the beginning of the Bolshevik Revolution, Barth saw Christians caught between two equally problematic forms of narration. On the one side, he heard revolutionaries calling for the overturning of the current State and the establishment of another—a new State captured by the spirit of the times that would usher in a new liberated humanity. On the other side, he heard those he called reactionaries or legitimizers of the status quo, who imagined civilization at stake in any threats to the State. Thus, the justifications for war were bound to either of these narratives. Barth understood that the goal of those who offered these narratives was to have us chain our lives inside these master stories. His response to these narratives was simple but path breaking—starvation.

> Deprive them of their *Pathos*, and they will be starved out; but stir up revolution against them, and the *Pathos* is provided with fresh fodder.[9]

Barth suggested we starve these narratives of their pathos. Pathos, in this sense, is our emotional and psychic yielding to the drama being enacted or intimated through the master story. In our situation, the master story is of an America that enables abundant life and is therefore always worthy of sacrifice, always justified in the use of violence, and always in need of our thankfulness. The point is not to seek to defeat that master story, but to drain it of its pathos by refusing its desired effect. It is precisely this pathos that entangles the pain and suffering of veterans in a drama that strangles their individual stories. It leaves them with the Herculean task of making sense of a personal past that is crowded with American narration. America's master story denies the moral incoherence of war and thereby thwarts the grief work that should connect the struggles of veterans to a broader national struggle to reconcile our moral claims with our immoral actions. Ironically, the pathos-inducing work of patriotic narration intended to bind Americans together in a shared sense of nationhood constantly undermines the important work of binding us to our veterans in a shared sense of moral injury and responsibility for the damages of war.

This is why those who work therapeutically with veterans must be cognizant of the psychic threat posed by America's master story. They should refashion the individualistic orientation of some forms of clinical therapy and pharmacological treatment toward helping wounded soldiers separate the pathos of patriotic narration from their struggle of processing their military service. Clinical and pastoral care should also envision their reintegration as a shared reintegration of communities into *their stories* and a return into *their memories*. No veteran should be left alone with their memories. Just as we shared in their lives before their enlistment and their journeys into the theaters of violence, so too their memories are a part of us now, part of our journey. We should share in their memories not as sites of exploitation for dramatic movies or moralistic sermonizing about the cost of freedom or the horrors of war, but as co-sufferers of death's wounds and co-laborers with them, seeking to reclaim the joy of life. Thus, we must envision a memory work that is the work of whole communities and not just soldiers sequestered away in group therapy. A pastoral response to moral injury, however, must also consider the divine reality of remembering that invites all of us to memory work that participates in the life of God.

The God Who Remembers

Theologian Darrell Cole has suggested that Christian veterans of war may be helped by a renewed focus on penance and the use of extended penitential practices.[10] Warren Kinghorn agrees with this possibility and suggests that for Christians, both Catholic and Protestant, "the loss of penance often means the loss of interpersonal confession as well."[11] Both theologians are drawing on and commending what seems to have been a church practice applied to soldiers returning from war as a way to restore them to ecclesial community and communion. Even if the war aligned with the criteria for a just war, penance acknowledged the loss of life at the hands of another. How widespread and rigorously applied was this practice is a matter of debate and speculation, but its value, suggests Kinghorn and Cole, lay in orienting Christian soldiers and the entire church toward a process of confession, forgiveness, and reconciliation that might aid in soul repair for veterans. As Kinghorn notes, penance (as a part of a pastoral invention) moves…"beyond therapeutic instrumentalism."[12] This interest in penance has some promise, but it must be placed within a more substantial theological framework that grasps both the technologies of the self born of this practice and a strong Christological mediation for negotiating the work of remembering and confessing.

While Kinghorn is right to imagine a deeper set of concerns for morally wounded veterans than helping them gain basic social functioning and relief from the agony of guilt, penance as a practice would be difficult to imagine as a central means of soul repair and restoration, given its long history of creating a self locked in self interrogation.[13] Indeed, the logics of therapeutic instrumentalism grew out of the practices of confession and penance. Those practices were nurtured through the gestures of monastic life, where adherents would submit their whole lives to constant examination and interrogation. The practices of penance and confession drew heavily from the logic of obedience. As philosopher Michel Foucault noted that within the monastic frame "…obedience [was] complete control of behavior by the master, not a final autonomous state. It [was] a sacrifice of the self, of the subject's own will. This [was] the new technology of the self."[14] Along with obedience, penance and confession were also anchored in contemplation that was "the permanent contemplation of God"[15] coupled with constant self-examination. This is the generative soil on which grew modern therapeutic technique.

This is not to suggest that penance and therapeutic instrumentalism are bound together, nor am I equating penance with a form of therapeutic technique. At issue here is the self being imagined by and through penance and, more importantly, the self that must be overcome formed through military training and the crucible of war. Penitential practice may be a powerful way to intercept the self and draw personhood back toward a genuinely theological narration of life, but without consideration of the ways penitential gestures have already been part of military training, or their sorted history in regimes of subjugation, their use in attempted soul repair may prove counterproductive and harmful. We must analyze how a vision of obedience has been inculcated in soldiers through a command structure and rituals of punishment for its violation that has taught them how to evaluate their behavior, measure their performance, and, to a certain extent, judge their character. Penance in order to be made helpful must be extracted from a military ecology of obedience. As long as penitential practice is imagined on the horizon of an unexamined vision of obedience, it will reinforce the self constituted within military culture, a self already locked in constant struggle against itself over its failures to obey orders or its moral failure in obeying orders.

Penance understood rightly has its logic revealed within an economy of grace, yet its history cannot be easily extricated from masculinity constituting performances of sacrifice and chivalric displays of honor, both of which heavily mark military culture. Moreover, penitential gestures have also been intercepted by the problems of individualism that permeate religious and therapeutic practice in the west. As long as penance is offered to veterans as a form of self interrogation and self assessment, it turns their memory work into an isolated endeavor, inconsequential to the shared work of the whole people of God. Worse, it leaves wounded soldiers vulnerable to the pathos of patriotic narration and the powerful forces of the state and the market that wish to exploit their memories. More should be imagined and offered to Christians who have spilled blood in war than singular processes of penance. Our pastoral response should begin not with the soldier, but the One killed by the military. It should begin with Jesus.

Jesus is the innocent who has been killed in conflict. Yet, he has risen not in vengeance or condemnation, but in new life. He is the resurrection and the life, and he offers forgiveness from the site of his body marked by violent death. Jesus returns to the scene of violence and betrayal, that is, to a world stamped with the memories of his murder, and he remembers with us and for us, drawing our past into his future and shaping our present in his presence. In Jesus, we learn that God remembers. This is not a declaration of the divine capacities for memory, but of the communion dynamic in God's memory. We can see a glimpse of this communion dynamic in the drama of his return to his disciples after his resurrection. In John 20:19–29, Jesus enters the room with his disciples and guides them in two crucial actions that are rarely if ever joined together. First, he guides them toward touching what last they saw as a corpse while, secondly, also moving them toward a future after murder and betrayal. The memory of a dead Jesus is not erased but bound to the presence of their resurrected friend, directing them to see and touch him, and to remember with him, never without him.

It is the memory of corpses as well as bodies tortured that refreshes the wound of moral injury. The dead do not speak and their silence or their silencing cries and screams before their deaths fall on war veterans like a crumbling wall. Jesus moves toward us in the silence, never intending to speak over it, but speak to us with the silence. His words draw us to look clearly at the aftermath of violence registered in bodies and his presence is meant to sustain us as we look. This looking can be utterly overwhelming, especially in our memories where our eyes cannot shut off visual displays repeated without warning and without mercy. Jesus, however, brings mercy to memory. He knows what it is like to be with those tormented by their memories and to see in their eyes guilt, shame, and fear.

To such people, that is, to us, he offers a way to move toward a future. That future is his body. He draws those haunted by torturing memories into his peace, a peace that sustained him through death and back into life. His peace does not cover over pain but orientates life toward working with wounds. The disciples were now witness to a God who works from the site of his own wounded body turning his followers toward a mission of forgiveness and healing. Jesus renews and deepens his disciples' knowledge of life with the God of Israel. They will now live in and toward the triune God. This is the ground of God's memory work—with everything we remember, we remember a friend who returned from the dead and by the Holy Spirit says to us that death, even the deaths we have caused, is not the last word about our lives.

Jesus does not humanize the knowledge of God but shows us how the divine knowing and remembering humanizes us by bringing us into the compassion that constitutes God's knowing and remembering. As the Psalmist said, "God knows how we were made; God remembers that we are dust."[16] The disciples of Jesus are invited in the memory work of a God seeking to embrace that God's creation. The Son has come to seek and save the lost. This divine desire is, indeed, part of the remembering. God remembers what others have forgotten. The peoples destroyed by evil, the cries of anguish and pain, the injustice covered over and long forgotten, the hidden truths, the inside stories, the complexities of agency that meant that the action done was not the action intended, the man, woman, and child who each died alone and forgotten—all these things and more God remembers. The animals that no one knew, the trees that no human eyes ever saw, the bugs that flourished only in the sight of God—all these things and more God remembers. The plans, ideas, hopes, dreams, songs, poems, dances, touches, and smiles that escaped all the practices that enable us to remember, God remembers this—and more.

The Son through the Spirit invites us into this holy archeology, this holy remembering. This remembering calls a community to engage together in remembering, never releasing anyone to it as a solitary task. A soldier in memory work is embraced, even engulfed, in a church's memory work of not only their individual life, but also of the wider context of military service in America and America's troubled history of conflict and imperialism. More decisively, the memory work of a faith community finds its life in the God who remembers altogether and moves us by the Holy Spirit toward a shared exposition and shared confession. God remembers not to destroy us but to bring life at the site of death and violence. Such memory work of a church could reform identity freshly because it challenges the self created not only through the wounds of war but also through military training and patriotic narration. This work of remembering resists the painful memory myopia of individual immoral actions that hang around the neck of veterans like millstones and locks arms with them to remember again a God who knows the matter in its fullness even beyond their memory and calls them to forgiveness and life.

Such memory work reaches beyond a forensic vision of confession, forgiveness, and absolution toward a far more substantial operation of soul repair. Cole, Kinghorn, and others are right to wonder about the efficacy of forensic visions of confession and forgiveness that do not penetrate the depths of personal anguish that veterans feel over their actions in battle. Soul repair from moral injury, in this regard, requires an embodied intervention and must ensure a way to move forward in life even with torturing memories. Yet, the work of penance falls short of this goal, unless it is first imagined through the lens of the remembering body of Jesus and then the bodies of a community and finally, the body of a wounded veteran who is encircled in the work of burden sharing. Dietrich Bonhoeffer in his famed meditations on temptation delivered to a reunion of students who participated in the renegade seminary in Finkelwalde said that when we are tempted, it is the temptation of Christ.[17] In effect, there are no longer any private temptations for a Christian. They are all temptations of Christ in his body.

Such a vision of temptation seems counterfactual and against the grain of forensic individualistic visions of a singular life struggling against sin. Yet, temptation while it is a reality in each of us, it also connects us completely and intimately. Moreover, we come to our temptations through being joined to the journey of Mary's son. Jesus has seized our temptations and made them his own and has drawn us into a shared endeavor of facing temptation and a shared work of recovery from the failures to overcome sin. The greatest danger with a schema of penance, confession, and forgiveness is that it conceals this shared work and presses us to imagine individual mechanisms of restoration, each a technology of the self that we do together along parallel tracks of existence, one person's penance aligned with another person, and so on, in an assembly line of affective response to suffering. I am not accusing those scholars who have turned to penance and its related liturgical actions of suggesting such a schema. My point is the need for a vision of moral injury that is intensely communal and requires a response that turns church into a verb, where women and men join the burden of veterans as their burden and carries the weight of memory together. It is precisely this sense of a body shared that must lead the way in any pastoral invention that seeks to help women and men who have experienced too much on fields of battle and must now battle alone the fields of memory.

Notes

1. Jonathan Shay (1994) *Achilles in Vietnam: Combat Trauma and the Undoing of Character* (New York: Scribner).
2. Brett T. Litz, Nathan Stein, Eileen Delaney, Leslie Lebowitz, William P. Nash, Caroline Silva, and Shira Maguen (2009) "Moral Injury and Moral Repair in War Veterans: A Preliminary Model and Intervention Strategy," *Clinical Psychology Review*, vol. 29, no. 8, 695–706. Litz, et al., state, "Moral injury requires an act of transgression that severely and abruptly contradicts an individual's personal or shared expectation about the rules or the code of con-

duct, either during the event or at some point afterwards...This may entail participating in or witnessing inhumane or cruel actions, failing to prevent the immoral acts of others, as well as engaging in subtle acts or experiencing reactions that, upon reflection, transgress a moral code," 700.
3. Litz, et al., "Moral Injury," 698.
4. Warren Kinghorn (2012) "Combat Trauma and Moral Fragmentation: A Theological Account of Moral Injury," *Journal of the Society of Christian Ethics*, vol. 32, no. 2, 63. Kinghorn suggests that moral injury is "an injury that invades character... [and destroys]...the capacity for social trust." 59. He notes the idea of moral injury has come on the radar of the medical community and is being imagined through the same diagnostic lens as PTSD (post-traumatic stress disorder). However, moral injury, Kinghorn suggests, because it is a wound of the soul, reaches beyond a medical model of diagnosis and treatment and places a set of theological questions in front of us.
5. Rita Nakashima Brock and Gabriella Lettini (2012) *Soul Repair: Recovering from Moral Injury after War* (Boston: Beacon Press), 110–111.
6. Paul Connerton (1989) *How Societies Remember* (Cambridge: Cambridge University Press), 43–48.
7. See Neill Irvin Painter (2010) *The History of White People* (New York: W.W. Norton & Company) and Matthew Frye Jacobson (2002) *Special Sorrows: The Diasporic Imagination of Irish, Polish, and Jewish Immigrants in the United States* (Berkeley: University of California Press).
8. Karl Barth (1968) *The Epistle to the Romans* (London: Oxford University Press), 483.
9. Barth, *The Epistle to the Romans*, 483.
10. Darrell Cole (2002) "Just War, Penance, and the Church," *Pro Ecclesia*, vol. 11, no. 3, 313–328.
11. Kinghorn, "Combat Trauma," 70.
12. Kinghorn, "Combat Trauma," 67.
13. See Michel Foucault (1994) "Technologies of the Self," in Paul Rabinow (ed.) *Ethics: Subjectivity and Truth* (New York: The Free Press), 223–251; and his essay, (2013) "Right of Death and Power over Life" in Timothy Campbell and Adam Sitze (eds.) *Biopoltics: A Reader* (Durham: Duke Press), 41–60.

14. Foucault, "Technologies of the Self," 45.
15. Foucault, "Technologies of the Self," 45.
16. Psalm, 103:14.
17. Dietrich Bonhoeffer (2012) "Bible Study on Temptation, June 20–25, 1938," in Victoria J. Barnett (ed.) *Theological Education Underground: 1937–1940* (Minneapolis: Fortress Press), 386–415.

BIBLIOGRAPHY

Barth, K. 1968. *The epistle to the Romans*. London: Oxford University Press.
Bonhoeffer, D. 2012. Bible study on temptation, June 20–25, 1938. In *Theological education underground: 1937–1940*, ed. V.J. Barnett. Minneapolis: Fortress Press.
Brock, R.N., and G. Lettini. 2012. *Soul repair: Recovering from moral injury after war*. Boston: Beacon.
Cole, D. 2002. Just war, penance, and the church. *Pro Ecclesia* 11(3): 313–328.
Connerton, P. 1989. *How societies remember*. Cambridge: Cambridge University Press.
Foucault, M. 1994. Technologies of the self. In *Ethics: Subjectivity and truth*, ed. P. Rabinow. New York: The Free Press.
Foucault, M. 2013. Right of death and power over life. In *Biopolitics: A reader*, ed. T. Campbell and A. Sitze. Durham: Duke Press.
Jacobson, M.F. 2002. *Special sorrows: The diasporic imagination of Irish, polish, and Jewish immigrants in the United States*. Berkeley: University of California Press.
Kinghorn, W. 2012. Combat trauma and moral fragmentation: A theological account of moral injury. *Journal of the Society of Christian Ethics* 32(2): 57–74.
Litz, B.T., N. Stein, E. Delaney, L. Lebowitz, W.P. Nash, C. Silva, and S. Maguen. 2009. Moral injury and moral repair in war veterans: A preliminary model and intervention strategy. *Clinical Psychology Review* 29(8): 695–706.
Painter, N.I. 2010. *The history of white people*. New York: W.W. Norton.
Shay, J. 1994. *Achilles in Vietnam: Combat trauma and the undoing of character*. New York: Scribner.

CHAPTER 3

Trauma, Reality, and Eucharist

Bryan Stone

T. S. Eliot once said, "Humankind cannot bear very much reality."[1] But at least for the present, the trend toward reality television programming is firmly in place, with the format proving itself to be every bit as popular and profitable as fictional programming that features trained and highly paid actors. Of course, television and cinema have always been bound by aesthetic conventions of realism: characters are supposed to sweat when it is hot outside, and they should be bruised or their hair and clothes in disarray after a fight. But there are important differences between standard aesthetic conventions of realism, even documentary realism, and those associated with Reality TV. These differences have to do with particular visual techniques (e.g., the use of hand-held cameras, minimalist editing, or employment of raw footage) but even more with an alteration in the relationship of viewers to the television medium that is part of wider cultural dynamics and economic processes.

In the past decade, Reality TV has been largely responsible for accomplishing the transformation of television from a medium in which audiences were largely passive observers into a medium in which viewers are now given the impression of a more interactive participation by watching individuals who demonstrate an awareness of being captured on camera,

B. Stone (✉)
Boston University School of Theology, Boston, USA

© The Editor(s) (if applicable) and The Author(s) 2016
S.N. Arel, S. Rambo (eds.), *Post-Traumatic Public Theology*,
DOI 10.1007/978-3-319-40660-2_3

often documentary style, or who appear to be "looking back" at us. While the Reality TV format purports, at least implicitly, to tell the truth about our world and ourselves, what is theologically important about Reality TV is not only the truth (or the "reality") to which it claims to grant us access, but the way reality is "performed" as a spectacle and thereby "dislocated" by the destabilizing and diminishing of the distance between reality and representation.[2] That dislocation is especially critical when it comes to the way Reality TV exposes and engages suffering, pain, catastrophe, and loss through its preoccupation with narratives of personal trauma for the sake of entertainment. Through its distinctive performances of the real, Reality TV exposes what is hidden and makes public what is private, while engaging suffering and trauma through idealized modes of confession, absolution, and redemption (drawn largely from the popular discourse and conventions associated with the "recovery" movement). In this essay, I argue that while Reality TV opens up new possibilities for witnessing trauma at a cultural level, the commodification, sensationalization, and sentimentalization of trauma in Reality TV inevitably thwart the kind of empathy, solidarity, and "remaining" with trauma that is required by a healing witness to it. While Reality TV exposes and reveals, it also obscures and covers over. The essay concludes with a reflection on the Christian practice of Eucharist in light of Reality TV that attempts to take seriously what Shelly Rambo calls the "middle Spirit" between crucifixion and resurrection.

Laying Claim to the Real

Over the last two decades, television audiences around the globe have become fixated on shows that feature non-actors (offered up as "real" people) acting spontaneously in unscripted or minimally scripted situations that feature the "ordinary" and the "everyday," and that thereby lay claim to the real. Some of the earliest Reality TV shows in the USA were MTV's *The Real World*, first broadcast in 1992, and *Survivor* and *Big Brother*, both appearing in 2000. All of these are surveillance-based shows, where television viewers were invited to look in voyeuristically on groups of people living together in close proximity within exotic or artificially constructed social settings. Granted, nothing could be less connected with "reality" than a couple dozen Americans, all strangers to one another, living together for 30 days on an island in Fiji or in a house constructed on a Hollywood back-lot. But while these settings are entirely different from anything that resembles real life for most of us, the shows give viewers access to raw emotions and often spontaneous and "unmediated" drama, romance, and struggle that are captivating. Of course, the emotions and the drama are not wholly unmediated, but rather professionally edited and, at times, instigated by the producers. But precisely this interaction (and tension) between the real and the artificial construction of the real, along with an awareness by viewers of this construction, is what is so important within Reality TV, as one seeks to understand its cultural and theological significance.

One of the ways that Reality TV lays claim to the discourse of the real is by its turn to the ordinary—the ordinary person, experience, or situation—and to mundane topics such as auto and home renovation, clothing, or parenting. Even when celebrities are the main attraction, Reality TV helps us see them as ordinary, in a "behind-the-scenes" light. While this turn to the ordinary is one of the most significant and distinguishing features of realist representation in Reality TV, it is also the object of many of the criticisms related to the vulgarity of the genre. Detractors, for example, argue that our arts and entertainments should ennoble us to rise above the clichéd and banal. If the unruly, foul-mouthed, and promiscuous behavior of someone like Snooki from *Jersey Shore* is "ordinary," then our society has not only reached rock bottom, but begun digging.

Proponents of Reality TV, by contrast, champion this turn to the ordinary as the democratization, demystification, and diversification of the medium. Anyone can now be made a TV star, and we are no longer offered only what the "Hollywood elite" script for us to watch, but rather the perspectives, emotions, and behavior of people "just like us." This turn to the ordinary is consistent with the wider assumption in postmodern culture that everything and everyone, no matter how commonplace, must be made visible and public. If I have a good glass of wine before going to bed, this must be announced on *Facebook*. If I just bought a new set of Fiestaware, that too must be "tweeted," or sent out with a picture on *Instagram*. Social media ensure that the banality of our daily lives is replicated and transmitted electronically to the world.

In Mark Andrejevic's influential study of Reality TV, he asks why it is now, at this point in our history, that the drive to make oneself seen is so powerful; why, as he puts it, that "getting real – attaining authenticity – means being seen."[3] Andrejevic employs a Lacanian analysis of the relationship between voyeurism and the scopic drive in laying claim to the real that frames this phenomenon in relation to a surveillance-based economy.

Increasingly, an economy based on ever more sophisticated techniques for monitoring consumer behavior broadcasts the message that "making oneself seen" is a form of individuation and self-authentication. We are told that we can express ourselves through customized consumption – consumption that requires we make our preferences and habits known to producers. In this respect, we are invited to participate in the logic of the drive: we can attain our own "inner freedom" by submitting ourselves to ever more comprehensive forms of surveillance. This submission is portrayed not as a structural necessity of the proliferation of flexible capitalism – which requires proliferating consumption in response to enhanced productivity – but as the consumer's drive to express his or her authentic subjectivity, a subjectivity that has been stifled by the uniformity of mass society. In short, subjectification entails active submission to surveillance, which means that we don't just endure the monitoring gaze, we embrace the drive to make ourselves seen.[4]

Criticisms of Reality TV frequently focus on both the voyeurism that is enacted, on one hand, and the exhibitionism that is encouraged, on the other. If Andrejevic is right, however, both the voyeurism and the exhibitionism are but symptoms of a more fundamental participation in our surveillance by an economic order that seeks to expand our consumptive practices and in which what our eyes are offered is derived from extraordinarily close surveillance of our eyes. At the same time, as we are transformed by our media into active voyeurs and "watchers" (a more active stance), we submit to being watched. And so it is that our own unique empowerment, creativity, individuality, and freedom turn out to be but another form of submission. In a slightly different take on the Foucauldian notion of self-discipline and self-policing that take place from the standpoint of a panopticon, where we never know if and when we are being watched, ours is a culture in which we are constantly inventing and performing ourselves in the knowledge that we are *always* being watched.[5] But is this egalitarian opportunity really a form of empowerment, equality and emancipation?

Aaron Sorkin, the Academy Award winning writer of *The Social Network*, a film about Mark Zuckerberg and the creation of *Facebook*, appeared on *The Colbert Report* (aired September 30, 2010), where he called *Facebook* "a performance" rather than reality—a performance whereby we "invent ourselves" for others. If Sorkin is right, the phenomenon of *Facebook* is similar in many ways to Reality TV, with both exhibiting a distinctively postmodern relationship between watching and being watched. According to Sorkin, "socializing on the internet is to socializing, what Reality TV is to reality."[6] In a postmodern era, reality is not just something "out there" in relationship to which we order our lives rightly or not, or that we either perceive clearly or not. As with *Facebook*, the "reality" that is revealed or exposed in Reality TV is one that is performed, rather than the object of reference. Perhaps the real has always been a performance. But reality entertainment embraces this premise with gusto and lays claim to the real as something to be managed, manipulated, played with, consumed, and engaged as a means of self-expression. Sophie Van Bauwel describes this blurring of the distinction between reality and representation, between the real and the simulacrum (or hyperreal), as a "dislocation" of reality; and given that we are offered so much access to reality through our media along with a knowledge that reality is being performed and managed by our media, we experienced this duality as a "trans-reality" that can neither be accepted as reality, nor rejected completely.[7]

As Andrejevic points out, the postmodern viewing subject is well aware of how reality is performed, constructed, and even distorted by the media and wants it to be known that he or she is "no dupe." Reality TV caters to this knowledge so that it is converted into a satisfaction and complacency on the part of viewers whose media savviness about the contrivance of entertainment is precisely the means by which they submit to their formation by culture industries, and economic processes. To use Andrejevic's words, "the savvy attitude becomes a strategy for protecting artifice by exposing it... a logic that [Slavoj] Zizek describes as deception by means of the truth."[8]

Take, for example, our preoccupation with celebrities and the way they are exposed or rendered "ordinary" through Reality TV. Reality TV accomplishes a demystification of the star machine, and our gaze exerts a kind of mastery as it observes the arbitrariness inherent in the media's creation of celebrity. But the very gaze through which we exercise this mastery in watching Reality TV is, at the same time, an act of passive submission to the medium itself and to the ideal of celebrity, which is no less reinforced. In the same way, moving in the opposite direction, as we watch the ordinary person receive an artificial makeover into the celebrity mold, whether by learning "what to wear" or by winning *American Idol*, we are confirmed in our knowledge of how the whole entertainment edifice is artificial. We are even allowed to "vote" on who will become our celebrities, so that we can have an active hand in the artificiality of celebrity, while at the same time granting us the illusion of having risen above the whole thing. Reality TV, as with so many of our postmodern forms of entertainment, depends on our complacent "knowing" as a form of participation in the unreality of its reality. To quote Andrejevic, "Savviness works to inoculate capitalist culture by incorporating its self-critique into its self-propagation. It is in this respect that the savvy subject stages the scene of its submission as constitutive of its inner freedom."[9]

Reality TV's appeal to the drive to make oneself seen should be seen as part of a larger transformation in the relationship between reality and representation. If once it was easier to distinguish between the real and the imaginary or the simulated, our social experience now is one that is saturated with signs, images, photographs, videos, films, games, and other electronic applications that increasingly blur that line. We can make the artificial look real (through computer-generated imagery), but we can also make the real look artificial—indeed, that may be what Reality TV does best. Only Reality TV could take the spectacular beauty of Micronesia or the Amazon and make them look like the Tiki Room at Disneyland or the local Rainforest Café. Reality TV is part of a larger obsession, not so much with reality as with representation, with images, replicas, simulation, and the high premium we now place in our culture on the most realistic representations possible over the original or unmediated real: "Isn't this photo clear?" "Isn't the image on my high definition television perfect?" "Isn't this digitalized surround sound system amazing?" There are those who, when attending a concert or visiting an amusement park, will spend the entire time filming the experience with a video camera. Kevin Glynn points out that the technological generation or alteration of an object or experience carries with it a certain epistemological authority and yields a hyperreality that "displaces the claims of the [original or] unmediated."[10] As Glynn puts it, "whereas 'unmediated' realities once guaranteed or stood as the measure of the truth or accuracy of images, it seems that this situation has undergone something of a reversal: the electronic reproduction of an event now functions as a powerful guarantor of its actuality and its incontrovertibility."[11] One might claim that the purpose of capturing a concert on one's smart phone is so that it can be replayed later or shared with others, but while that may be true, something more is happening here. Ironically, the "reality" of the event is enhanced and authenticated as real, precisely as it is simulated, reproduced, or captured on screen. In this way, as Glynn says, drawing on the work of Jean Baudrillard, "the space of representation – the distance between sign and referent that grants each an existence independent of the other – has collapsed."[12] It might even be appropriate to interpret Reality TV as demonstrating that in a postmodern context, what we desire is not so much "the real" as "the realistic."

In contributing to and participating in a culture of surveillance wherein everything must be seen, disclosed, revealed, and exposed, Reality TV likewise enacts a new relationship between "public space" and "private space," or rather, their mutual disappearance. As Baudrillard says, "The one is no longer a spectacle, the other no longer a secret."[13] On one hand, "the most intimate processes of our life become the virtual feeding ground of the media.... Inversely, the entire universe comes to unfold arbitrarily on your domestic screen (all the useless information that comes to you from the entire world, like a microscopic pornography of the universe, useless, excessive, just like the sexual close-up in a porno film): all this explodes the scene formerly preserved by the minimal separation of the public and private."[14] In the case of Reality TV, recognizing this collapse of the public and private is essential for understanding both the way the genre lays claim to the real and the way viewing audiences interact with the television medium and frame their own personal worlds in relation to the realities outside those worlds. The collapse of the public and private in our culture, thus, becomes a critically important backdrop for considering the appeal of Reality TV's engagement with trauma and the models of transformation and redemption that come with it.

Trauma and Reality TV

Reality TV's engagement with trauma and suffering is extensive, to say the least. Participants themselves are frequently belittled, exposed, humiliated, imperiled, made to suffer, or otherwise subjected to intense emotional experiences that call up past trauma. Their performances also set up expectations between themselves and viewing audiences that extend beyond their performances. Some endure ongoing trauma after their shows have ended, with a number of Reality TV "stars" having attempted or committed suicide. In some cases, the ongoing trauma is a response to the experience of public scrutiny that accompanies newfound celebrity or to the experience of seeing oneself edited by the show's producers in such a way as to heighten personal drama.[15]

While a study of how Reality TV traumatizes its own participants (or viewers[16]) might be valuable, my focus here is on how Reality TV witnesses and engages trauma, given the ways it lays claim to the real in the context of a culture preoccupied with being seen and within a surveillance-based economy, where the relation of the public to the private is increasingly collapsed. A survey of the various sub-genres of Reality TV programming reveals a widespread preoccupation with trauma, suffering, and tragedy. These are especially prominent in the therapeutic conventions and discourse of talk shows; in police, crime, hospital, and rescue shows (*Rescue 911, Forensic Files, COPS, Trauma: Life in the E.R.*); in programs that emphasize the discipline and monitoring of physical bodies such as makeovers and other forms of life intervention (*The Biggest Loser, Extreme Makeover*); in shows that feature dating and family relationships (*Temptation Island, The Real World, Wife Swap, The Nanny*); and in elimination-based "survival" competitions (*Survivor, Big Brother, Amazing Race*). Representations of trauma in Reality TV serve as especially good case studies for analyzing and understanding Reality TV itself, for as Van Bauwel observes, "in showing fear, pain and emotion, these Reality TV programs' promise of reality is placed at the center."[17] Suffering, pain, and trauma and their accompanying emotional responses have become emblematic of the "authentic" and the "real" on screen, and so have become central to the entire Reality TV enterprise. Perhaps it is no wonder that this preoccupation with trauma has had a spillover effect on reality-based fictional programming such as crime, forensic, and hospital dramas (e.g., *CSI, The Wire, Breaking Bad, ER, Grey's Anatomy*).

In her essay, "Trauma and Screen Studies: Opening the Debate," Susannah Radstone explores the question of why trauma has become so popular today, especially in relationship to screen media. The impressive range of popular media narratives and forms given over to the disclosure of, engagement with, and response to trauma should signal to us that something significant is going on outside of more formal clinical or theoretical channels, and that trauma as a category should be explored not only from within the fields of psychology and counseling, but the discipline of cultural studies as well. Says Radstone, "I want to raise the possibility that trauma may have become a 'popular cultural script' in need of contextualisation and analysis in its own right – a symptom, the cause of which needs to be sought elsewhere."[18] Anne Roth has written similarly of "popular trauma culture" that is permeated with narratives of victimization, survival, trauma, and recovery. Roth argues that "it is precisely the question that trauma studies scholarship has left out that ought to be explored, namely how the ubiquitous notion of trauma functions in contemporary culture."[19]

In his *Post-traumatic Culture*, Kirby Farrell examines trauma within American culture "both as a clinical concept and as a cultural trope."[20] Because not everyone within that culture experiences trauma, says Farrell, "it is always to some extent a trope."[21] But that does not diminish the extent to which trauma resonates broadly.

> People may use it to account for a world in which power and authority seem staggeringly out of balance, in which personal responsibility and helplessness seems crushing, and in which cultural meanings no longer seem to transcend death. In this sense, the trope may be a veiled or explicit criticism of society's defects, a cry of distress and a tool grasped in hopes of some redress, but also a justification for aggression.[22]

The popularization of trauma is undoubtedly related to the broad currency of more recent understandings of trauma and victimhood and, according to Anita Biressi and Heather Nunn, "the diffusion of psychoanalytic discourses in contemporary culture and in particular the concept of the recoverable self."[23] Indeed, one can readily find confirmation of this in Reality TV shows ranging from confessional-style talk shows to those based on the theme of becoming a "survivor." It is remarkable, after all, that persons who have experienced trauma are so willing to go public with what are otherwise private experiences of injury, abuse, and tragedy, especially given the fact that traumatic experiences are often forgotten or buried under layers of self-protective denial. That the concept of trauma now has such powerful cultural resonance—a resonance of which Reality TV is a commanding example—signals not merely a heightened public awareness of trauma in the form of holocaust, genocide, war, catastrophe, violence, rape, and abuse, but a recognition that these may be perpetuated by silence and denial on a cultural level. That trauma has become a "popular cultural script" must be seen, at least in part, as a positive step forward. In the last half century, women's movements and advocates for veterans returning from wars have been especially prominent in leading the way by demonstrating that a full and liberative engagement with trauma requires not only clinical and personal responses but political action, cultural expression, and public voice and witness as well.[24]

At the same time, Roth (who locates the origins of trauma as a cultural discourse in Holocaust narratives that can be traced back to the famous Eichmann trials in Jerusalem in 1961)[25] argues that trauma discourse has become so sentimentalized, sensationalized, and coopted by the discourse of "recovery" in television talk shows or other forms of popular media such as "misery memoirs" that it no longer functions to empower or heal, but rather to disguise and distract. Claims Roth,

> The notion of trauma widely disseminated via the self-help industry, which is reflected and reinforced by other popular culture products, describes a psychological reaction to an experience in which a seemingly omnipotent perpetrator inflicts extreme violence on a helpless victim. Because the latter's psychological suffering continues long after the physical pain subsided, self-help literature teaches its many consumers that in order to overcome traumatizing experiences and transform weak victims into heroic survivors, the traumatic memories must be narrated.[26]

The emphasis in American culture on witness, narrative, and memory is, of course, not the problem in and of itself, as trauma studies affirm. The problem is the way both the content of that witness and the act of witnessing have been commodified within popular culture, by reducing them to what is marketable and to what can be readily consumed.

Shelly Rambo speaks of trauma as "the suffering that does not go away" and that "persists in symptoms that live on in the body, in the intrusive fragments of memories that return."[27] Likewise, Cathy Caruth speaks of trauma as "a double wound," a wound "that is not fully assimilated as it occurs" and "that cries out, that addresses us in the attempt to tell us of a reality or truth that is not otherwise available."[28] The healing of trauma, therefore, requires processes of integration, including especially the ability to give witness to one's experience and to tell one's story. This demand—or rather an adequate response to it—is clearly related to the way the private and the public are configured (or collapsed) in postmodern culture. Indeed, the prominence given to trauma in Reality TV should be seen in this light, as a cultural opening to personal experience, memory, and testimony, on one hand, and to their framing within the context of wider cultural media, narratives, memories, and histories, on the other. Relating this dialectic directly to Reality TV, Thomas Elsaesser points out:

> It is here that the media, and in particular television, have played an especially outstanding but also controversial role. In the format of the talk show, television has shaped an entire culture of confession and witnessing, of exposure and self-exposure, which in many ways – good and bad – seems to have taken over from both religion and the welfare state. In a sense, it has made trauma theory the recto, and therapeutic television (also disparagingly called

trash TV) the verso of democracy's failure to 'represent' its citizens' personal concern in the public sphere. It also points up the credibility gap of much Judaeo-Christian religion when it comes to sustain as 'healing' the rituals of mediation that used to insert the private into the symbolic order.[29]

If Elsaesser is right, Reality TV provides an example of an important cultural 'space' (one apparently no longer offered as effectively by religion) in which trauma can be witnessed and engaged (and, in fact, absorbed as 'reality'). The question, however, is whether popular media like Reality TV distort that witness and truncate that engagement in the service of entertainment. In Reality TV's performance of revealing, exposing, and uncovering, we find also a disguising and covering over that lead to forgetfulness and repression. To quote Roth,

> The media spectacles of popular trauma culture remove these experiences of victimization and suffering from their socio-political contexts by reducing them to their smallest common denominator of a body in pain. They proclaim that, no matter what happens, whether genocide or child abuse or lesser evils, there will always be a happy ending when good wins over evil, victims become survivors, and perpetrators are punished, thus teaching consumers that the socio-economic status quo need not be changed through political action. Mass media emplotments of the pain of others are thus not only unethical because they transform traumatic experiences into entertainment commodities but also because they are politically acquiescing and covertly reinforce the oppressive hegemonies of late-modern capitalism that have generated, or at least enabled, the victimization experiences.[30]

Trauma, Reality TV, and Redemption

It is not difficult to see why the role played by television in witnessing, engaging, and attempting to transform trauma is, as Elsaessar puts it, "controversial," and why Christians might wish to contest that space and to ask further about the reasons why and the extent to which popular cultural mediations have replaced those of Christianity. Christians might also do well to ask whether and to what extent they have themselves adopted, perhaps uncritically, the types of discourse, modes of engagement, aesthetic frameworks, and therapeutic conventions employed by Reality TV, and if so, whether the collapse of redemption into a therapeutic model is a loss or a gain.

In developing her theological response to trauma, Rambo follows Judith Herman in framing the study of trauma in terms of "witness" and in stressing the importance of a witnessing presence as "an essential first step to traumatic recovery" and as the only possible way a survivor can reconnect to the world.[31] Rambo's creative theological contribution is to call for Christian theologians to deepen and expand their understanding of and language used to describe redemption so that it neither rests wholly on crucifixion-centered atonement theories nor jumps entirely forward to resurrection hope as a celebration of the victory of love and life over death. When the language of Christian theology is confined to the standard linear narrative of the salvation story that moves through and then past the crucifixion to the resurrection, it is unable to speak healing to people who have experienced trauma, argues Rambo. The extreme suffering associated with trauma is not something one merely "moves past" or "gets beyond." As Rambo puts it, "Trauma is an open wound."[32]

By exploring more deeply the importance of Holy Saturday as more than just a passing of time between Good Friday and Easter Sunday, Rambo reinterprets resurrection not as a simple victory of life over death, but rather the persistence of love through and alongside death. Redemption, accordingly, may be understood in terms of remaining and survival rather than victory or conquest. As she puts it, "Redemptive love expressed in terms of sacrifice or victory – of love emptied out or love conquering – elides the truth handed over in the Johannine [farewell discourse]: love remains. But this truth is not some content but rather a process of testifying to the precarious movements between death and life."[33] Rambo focuses her theological response to trauma on this precarious (and chaotic) "middle" between crucifixion and resurrection that "disrupts a progressive narrative."[34] It is from this middle that we are able to relate to suffering in new ways:

> The middle does not yield a narrative that calls us to suffer but instead calls us to witness suffering in its persistence, its ongoingness. If viewed from the middle, redemption is about the capacity to witness to what exceeds death but cannot be clearly identified as life. Redemption finds new expression in the always here, in the persistent witness to what remains.[35]

The problems that Rambo identifies with a progressive redemption narrative in relation to trauma have their vivid counterpart in Reality TV, where the language and images of redemption and transformation abound.

Indeed, one of the ways Reality TV both performs the real and lays claim to it is its emphasis on designing, mobilizing, and effecting processes of transformation. Obviously this is the case with makeover shows focused on the transformation of one's body, face, business, wardrobe, career, town, marriage, home, pets, personality, or soul. But it may also be said that "makeover" is not just a single sub-genre within Reality TV; rather, "'making over' and transformation define the very essence of reality TV" so that Reality TV is "less about representing reality than intervening in it; less mediating and more *involving*."[36] If Reality TV illustrates the postmodern premise that reality is itself malleable and may be transformed as a kind of performance,[37] the makeover format epitomizes the popular cultural obsession with transformation and it makes a virtue of one's willingness to participate in that makeover (thereby submitting to broader forms of cultural and economic formation as well). In this respect, Reality TV is a part of a larger network of cultural technologies aimed at producing our self-discipline, such as books, podcasts, talk shows, self-help manuals, websites, and an endless sea of seminars, life coaches, and speakers.[38]

In makeover shows, participants are routinely humiliated or asked to call up past suffering or unresolved trauma in their lives as a first step in proceeding to move toward the desired transformation. These confessions, exposures, and shocking revelations attract viewers, but they rarely provide the space or time for examining the kind of integration required by the healing of trauma, not to mention the persistence of traumatic events and the enigma of their ongoingness. Audiences who look on as voyeuristic observers share virtually in the rituals of examination and judgment (including humiliation) but not necessarily in ways that cultivate patient listening, empathy, and solidarity.

Though a focus on transformation may be seen explicitly in makeover shows, it is no less a characteristic of game shows, survival shows, or any of the other most popular sub-genres of the Reality TV format, which likewise feature this preoccupation with transformation. In fact, the engagement with suffering and trauma is stepped up a notch in survival shows, where cameras track not only the struggle of the competitors, but their dramatic interactions with one another, and especially their private moments aside with the camera in the mode of the confessional. If viewer ratings are any clue, audiences clearly enjoy watching group conflict and shows that feature physical and psychological challenges, privations, rewards and punishments.[39] They also enjoy the confessions, struggles, and neuroses of individuals revealed (or exposed) alongside intra-group scheming, alliances, and conspiracies. As Biressi and Nunn say,

> The use of video diaries, to-camera monologues, shock-tactic interviewing and so on further opens up current critical debates about the shifting parameters of the public and private world. Here, for the reality TV viewer, amateur 'pop psychological' self-analysis and/or amateur or unscripted footage meld the pleasures of voyeurism with the pseudo intimacy of the therapeutic consulting room and a sense of 'democracy of feeling' (Richards 1994) which underpins emotional realism.[40]

Of course, the goal of the survival genre is the triumph of one individual over the rest of the group. To be a 'survivor' inevitably comes to mean that others won't be.

While makeover and survival shows illustrate Reality TV's attempt to engage with suffering and trauma through the wider cultural obsession with transformation, they compare neither in scope nor intensity with the work done by television talk shows. Here, a now standard set of therapeutic conventions—what Kathleen Lowney calls "dramaturgical performances"—are followed that typically begin with a retelling of the individual's story (sometimes in the mode of "confession"), often through video and images that establish the "reality"' of the story and that reveal both the inner suffering and loss, as well the ongoing cost of the trauma in the form of relational loss and family struggle, economic and job turmoil, or other repercussions.[41] These opening revelations and confessions are not only a way of establishing the reality claim, but of casting stories of redemption in terms of recovery. Many of these shows attempt to communicate the impression that "some experiences are too 'real' to be expressed by words alone and rely on guests breaking down in tears, showing signs of distress, wringing their hands or visibly trembling as physical registers of hidden damage"; moreover, they often feature "the broader talk show convention of valorizing the body and the voice as markers of an invisible reality to which only the interviewee has recourse."[42] As trauma studies help us understand, these registers and conventions are more than television devices designed simply to secure emotional responses by viewers (even if they are overly sensationalized for that purpose); rather they reveal what Rambo describes as "the challenge of witnessing to a phenomenon that exceeds the categories by which we make sense of the world."[43] What have come to be described as "trash talk TV" shows go even further, however, and resort to hyperbole by orchestrating angry and explosive reactions, violently emotional (and often physical) outbursts, and other extreme behavior among both the participants on the show and the studio audience—all of this, of course, as a way of laying claim to "the real," given the place of emotion and spontaneity as emblematic of authenticity and truth-telling in our culture.

In *Baring Our Souls: TV Talk Shows and the Religion of Recovery*, Lowney compares talk shows to revivals of a bygone era, with today's talk show hosts having become the evangelists of the religion of recovery. Indeed, it is the recovery movement, epitomized in various twelve-step programs, that, at a popular level, has come to provide both the language for talking about and the process for moving toward redemption of all kinds, including that related to trauma. Following the opening revelation or confession, the process typically includes moralizing by the host, deployment of "experts" and "exes" who offer advice and direction, the presence of or confrontation with the victimizer (though not always), and then more moralizing, as the host offers generalized and pithy life lessons in the form of sound bites – all in the context of a highly engaged studio audience that contributes to the carnival-like atmosphere in which conversion is sought and found.[44] Lowney concludes that in TV talk shows, salvation is proclaimed as a process of focusing more on our own inner healing and less on others, thereby creating a society where our moral worlds are confined to private self-fulfillment. As she puts it, "Recovery sells. The Recovery Movement, rooted in the medicalization of deviant behavior and its lay reactions that transformed medical discourse into an eclectic spiritual philosophy of introspective journeying toward the nebulous goal of 'healing one's inner self,' has become big business."[45]

As mentioned earlier, Anne Roth's criticism of popular trauma culture's endless narrations of victimization and suffering is that they tend to remove these experiences from their socio-political contexts, assert the necessity of a happy ending where good wins over evil, and transform traumatic experiences into entertainment commodities, thereby both consenting to and perpetuating the political and economic structures of oppression that either generated or enabled victimization in the first place. The resonances between Roth's cultural critique and Rambo's theological critique are important, especially where the determined movement toward a happy ending and a neat resolution of trauma is concerned—one that avoids the kind of patient "remaining" for which Rambo argues in offering a healing presence to those who have experienced trauma.

It may be that the attention given to personal trauma by Reality TV (especially talk shows) has helped inspire victims of trauma to speak out and find their own voice or to create a more informed public mobilized in the service of ending trauma and abuse. But while Reality TV programming has its historical roots in the documentary genre and, like the documentary, seeks to reveal, expose, and tell the truth, it lacks the documentary's original focus on exposing social problems or injustices, thereby bearing an implicit "call to arms," and, in keeping with the drive to be seen that I mentioned earlier, is instead oriented far more toward "the exhibition of the self and of the psyche."[46] For the most part, the focus on exhibiting the self in Reality TV (and indeed, in popular culture itself) subordinates any transformation of social and political institutions or policies to the satisfaction of a voyeuristic curiosity that situates narratives of personal trauma within the larger agenda of entertainment. Moreover, one of the most obvious but important features of the way Reality TV engages trauma is the compression of that engagement into the time-slot available for the program itself. While the experience of trauma disrupts time and disorders the memory, the therapeutic conventions of television shows are crammed into the constraints of what can reasonably be offered in 30 to 60 minutes.[47]

One of the distinguishing features of Reality TV is that it provides us access to the perspectives, emotions, and behavior of ordinary people. But while those who are depicted as victims of trauma and suffering in Reality TV may be ordinary people, it is also true that we are glad they are not us.[48] Reality TV may thus be seen as serving an ideological function that inoculates popular viewing audiences against any serious resistance to prevailing economic and political structures. If we ask what kind of transformation *of the real* or *by the real* is enacted in Reality TV, it is to be sure one that, through processes of commodification, fits hand-in-glove with a neoliberal rationality of self-governance and self-empowerment enshrined in American individualism. The type of transformations we are most likely to find in Reality TV take three primary forms: (1) private intervention or acts of charity, (2) individual accomplishment and self-improvement, often set within the context of competition, or (3) chance or lottery (often associated with the first form, as when persons benefit from the largesse of the wealthy or powerful). What we rarely find in Reality TV are models of transformation that are the product of social solidarity or collective action.

Trauma and Eucharist

One of the notable strengths of Rambo's work is that it draws attention to the possibility of new modes of engagement with trauma that have the potential for deepening our responses in ways that move beyond the focus on either crucifixion or resurrection that has characterized Christian theological discourse and that also move beyond the commodification, sentimentalization, and sensationalization of trauma discourse in popular culture. As Rambo puts it, "a testimony to the middle runs alongside narratives of redemption, revealing new theological responses to traumatic suffering and pressing the edges of redemption in search of new vocabulary and images for framing our lives."[49]

While Rambo is right to look to theological discourse for expanding ways of talking about redemption that include the middle, and while her emphasis at this point is born out of a liturgical openness and renewed attention to Holy Saturday, it is possible to reflect further on how other Christian practices and sacraments—the Eucharist, for example—might be re-imagined and how they themselves are generative in reconceiving Christian witness to trauma. If restoring trust and meaning "is not purely cognitive," as Rambo says, but "involves instead a different sense of the world,"[50] then communal practices such as sacraments may provide an important path (a set of counter-performances, if you will) for restoring the capacity of bodily reconnecting to that world.

One potentially fruitful area for exploration by practical theologians is a re-imagining of Eucharist practices that by "looking from the middle turns us to see the movements of Spirit that exceed the triumphant logic of cross and resurrection."[51] Granted, there are good reasons for not turning to Eucharistic practice in the context of trauma, given the extent to which it is a remembrance of a trauma upon which Christian identity is constituted. So, for example, the only mention of the Lord's Supper in Rambo's book is in reference to its associations with "atonement theology" and to "salvation achieved through the blood of Jesus on the cross."[52] However, rethinking Christian witness in light of trauma and a more expansive understanding of redemption can help us imagine Eucharistic practice as enacting an ongoing participation in the brokenness of Christ's body that does not merely perpetuate more broken bodies (and psyches) but that gestures toward a love that remains and heals by helping sufferers imagine a life ahead without suggesting they simply make a "clean break from the past." As Dirk Lange observes, one of the earliest recorded church documents that refer to the Eucharist, the *Didache*, makes no explicit mention of the cross but is instead focused on the sharing of bread and wine.[53] The *Didache*, says Lange, "disrupts our remembering" and thereby both disorients and reorients this communal meal.[54] Remembering the Christ event, not through the violence of the cross but through the sharing of bread and wine, serves as a departure from traumatic reenactment and brings new possibilities for healing and solidarity.

The Eucharist is an especially interesting practice to consider not only in light of trauma studies but given the discourse, performance, and aesthetics of the real that we find in Reality TV and the characteristically postmodern relationship between reality and representation and between the public and the private that is enacted in Reality TV. In response to Christ's words, "this is my body" and "this is my blood," Christians have debated for centuries how to understand Christ's presence as "real" in the Eucharist.

In the Wesleyan tradition (cf. also Lange's fascinating treatment of Luther's position), the "reality" of Christ's presence is not in the first place a referential claim about the substance of the bread and wine, but rather a performative claim. In the act of remembering (the *anamnesis*) and the invocation of the Spirit (the *epiclesis*) in the Eucharistic prayer, Christ is "*made* real" by the Spirit to those who share in the meal. Consider the words from the "Service of Word and Table" in the *United Methodist Hymnal*:

> Pour out your Holy Spirit on us gathered here,
> and on these gifts of bread and wine.
> *Make them be* for us the body and blood of Christ,
> that we *may be* for the world the body of Christ,
> redeemed by his blood.
> By your Spirit *make us one* with Christ,
> one with each other,
> and one in ministry to all the world,
> until Christ comes in final victory and we feast at his heavenly banquet.[55]

For the Wesleys, we need not be concerned about identifying the real presence of Christ as an objective, metaphysical referent, nor do we know *how* Christ is made real. [56]

> O the depth of love divine, The unfathomable grace!
> Who shall say how bread and wine God into us conveys?
> How the bread his flesh imparts, How the wine transmits his blood,
> Fills his faithful people's hearts With all the life of God!
> Sure and real is the grace, The manner be unknown;
> Only meet us in thy ways And perfect us in one.
> Let us taste the heavenly powers, Lord, we ask for nothing more.
> Thine to bless, 'tis only ours To wonder and adore.[57]

The celebration of the Eucharist here is less a cognitive remembrance of some past event and more a performance of our relationship to and reception of Christ's presence as grace. Our reception is not a complacent or passive voyeurism that looks on "knowingly," but a bodily participation in Christ (both in the sense of the involvement of our material bodies and the enactment of a new social body). Christ's presence in the meal is in some respects an absence—a presence that cannot be grasped or fully known, contained, or managed. Indeed, it is not our reception that makes Christ real: it would be better to say that our doing is also a "be it done unto us."

In a manner parallel to Reality TV's performance of the real through its turn to the ordinary, the church likewise performs the reality of Christ's body in and through a turn to the ordinary in the sharing of everyday bread and wine. At the same time, in contrast to the performance of the real as an "obscene" elevation of banality (to use Baudrillard's way of speaking), which can only be gazed on voyeuristically, the Eucharist enacts a new public space that is a mutual sharing and participation in the reality being performed. In this space, mystery is preserved, for in the sharing of the Lord's Supper, we do not master or capture the real; nor do we merely "simulate" the real, despite the fact that it is no less a spectacle than the spectacle of the real one finds in Reality TV. Rather, we participate in the real and are made the body of Christ ("we become what we eat," to paraphrase Augustine).[58] But while we touch, taste, and participate in the real and are transformed by it as "the medicine of immortality" (Ignatius of Antioch), the real always transcends us and exceeds our grasp and control. In fact, it is better to say with William Cavanaugh that "the church does not simply perform the Eucharist; the Eucharist performs the church."[59]

At the table of the Lord, there can be no voyeurs, only active participants. Likewise, in the repetition of the liturgy, the distance between reality and representation is collapsed in a way that is at once parallel and a striking contrast to what we find in Reality TV. The reality of the Christ event "returns," as Lange puts it, but as something new and uncontrollable rather than as a commodity exploited as a utility for some other end: "In the sacraments, an event – the Christ event – continually returns, but not the event we readily imagine or contrive or desire or create. Rather, and precisely, something that we can't imagine, contrive, create, even desire – something inaccessible in that beginning – returns not to condemn, not to leave us orphans, not to leave us in despair, but to hold us in death and in life."[60]

Here again, we may say somewhat paradoxically that the "presence" of Christ in the Eucharist is also an "absence," in the sense that we cannot locate, control, or define it, as it heals and restores by disrupting our memories and narratives and opening us up to new realities and possibilities. For those who have experienced trauma (as well as for those who have not), the Christ event "returns as a force that continually disrupts our usual forms of remembering and ritualizing," so that it is not the violence of the cross that is remembered or repeated in the meal, but rather, as with traumatic memory, the inaccessibility of the event.[61] As Marcia Shoop and Mary McClintock Fulkerson observe, rather than a right performance of the Eucharist somehow guaranteeing healing "results," trauma "complicates the possibilities and pathways of healing in our liturgical practices because traumatic memory is characterized by pure repetition, not by processional transformation."[62] Transformation, therefore, "is not achieved by securing a correct or complete narrative, but by making space for sporadic comprehension of the incomprehensible. Like the task of theology that seeks to assign language and description to the ineffable, healing liturgy around trauma defies full definition and demands embodied recognition."[63]

As Reality television presses its claim to the real in new ways and in new arenas of life, our lives and institutions will continue to be shaped by its influence.[64] Fred Clark, a blogger for *Patheos*, for example, has suggested that even the presidential elections are now like an extended reality TV show where "voters are not asked to choose between candidates, but between the stars of a long-running TV show."[65] Yet, the church and its practices may still provide a cultural space and time (indeed, a counter-cultural space and time) in which rituals of redemption, solidarity, and healing can take place that witness and respond to trauma without reducing that witness and response to what can be negotiated in a 30-minute time block or that fit within recovery discourse and its therapeutic conventions. In that space, the truth of suffering and its persistence is not elided in the rush to move beyond Good Friday to Easter. As Shoop and McClintock Fulkerson say, "Traumatic memory can only give way to transformative memory when we tell the truth about ourselves, as impossible as that truth may be."[66]

Gathered around the table as a people who all possess our own scars and wounds, the Eucharist is a meal in which the real is both revealed and performed as we give witness to suffering without pretending that it is redemptive, on one hand, or that it can be neatly erased, on the other. At the same time, we are formed into a people who, having touched transcendence[67] and tasted "the real," are aware not only of suffering and its persistence but bear witness to love and its remaining. Formed anew into an unprecedented social reality—the body of Christ—we are thus oriented *to* suffering in gestures of hope rather than made passive watchers or "knowing" and complacent consumers of it.

Notes

1. T.S. Eliot (1943) *Four Quartets* (Orlando: Harcourt), 14.
2. Sofie Van Bauwel (2010) "The Spectacle of the Real and Whatever Other Constructions," in Sofie Van Bauwel and Nico Carpentier (eds.) *Trans-Reality Television* (Lanham, MD: Lexington Books), 9.
3. Mark Andrejevic (2004) *Reality TV: The Work of Being Watched* (Lanham, MD: Rowman and Littlefield), 189.
4. Andrejevic, *Reality TV*, 189.
5. Anastasia Deligiaouri and Mirkica Popovic (2010) "Reality TV and Reality of TV: How Much Reality is There in Reality TV Shows?" in Sofie Van Bauwel and Nico Carpentier (eds.) *Trans-Reality Television* (Lanham, MD: Lexington Books), 73.
6. Busis, H. "Aaron Sorkin hates the Internet. Why does he keep writing about tech geniuses?" *Entertainment Weekly*, May 16, 2012.
7. Van Bauwel, "The Spectacle of the Real and Whatever Other Constructions," 9.
8. Andrejevic, *Reality TV*, 16.
9. Andrejevic, *Reality TV*, 185.
10. Kevin Glynn (2000) "Jean Baudrillard and the Policing of Obscenity," in *Tabloid Culture: Trash Taste, Popular Power, and the Transformation of American Television* (Durham, NC: Duke University Press), 48.

11. Glynn, "Jean Baudrillard," 48.
12. Glynn, "Jean Baudrillard," 49.
13. Jean Baudrillard (1983) "The Ecstasy of Communication," in Hal Foster (ed.) *The Anti-Aesthetic: Essays on Postmodern Culture* (Post Townsend, WA: Bay Press), 130.
14. Baudrillard, "The Ecstasy of Communication," 130.
15. Some have suggested that Reality TV attracts a higher percentage of persons with mental health issues or those who possess personality vulnerabilities that are easily exploited by the medium. Whether that is true or not, it is not unusual for producers and casting agents to look for extreme personalities. As Princess Banton-Lofters, a Reality TV producer, says, "I know that when I am casting, I am looking for that person who is going to shine… That could be shining in personality, shining in lifestyle or shining in just their story. But I think it's definitely changed in that (casting professionals) are probably now looking for a little bit more of the crazy" (France). Research conducted by S. Mark Young and Drew Pinsky (2006) reveals that celebrities score significantly higher than the general population when tested for narcissistic personality. Their study finds that Reality TV personalities have the highest scores within that group.
16. One of the concerns with Reality TV is that it can trigger panic attacks, flashbacks, and even more trauma by portraying survivors in emotionally charged situations that sensationalize their experiences in order to elicit reactions from the audience, for example, by showing victims revealing abuse but confronting their abusers, etc.
17. Van Bauwel, "The Spectacle of the Real and Whatever Other Constructions," 24.
18. Susannah Radstone (2001) "Trauma and Screen Studies: Opening the Debate," *Screen*, vol. 42, no. 2, 108.
19. Anne Roth (2011) *Popular Trauma Culture: Selling the Pain of Others in the Mass Media* (New Brunswick, NJ: Rutgers University Press), 4.
20. Kirby Farrell (1998) *Post-Traumatic Culture: Injury and Interpretation in the Nineties* (Baltimore: The John Hopkins University Press), 14.
21. Farrell, *Post-Traumatic Culture*, 14.
22. Farrell, *Post-Traumatic Culture*, 14.

23. Anita Biressi and Heather Nunn (2005) *Reality TV: Realism and Revelation* (London: Wallflower Press), 110.
24. See Judith Herman (1992) *Trauma and Recovery: The Aftermath of Violence – from Domestic Abuse to Political Terror* (New York: Basic Books), especially Chapter 1, where she makes the case that "the systematic study of trauma... depends on the support of a political movement," 9.
25. See also Shoshana Felman (2002) *The Juridical Unconscious: Trials and Traumas in the Twentieth Century* (Cambridge, MA: Harvard University Press), Chapter 3.
26. Roth, *Popular Trauma Culture*, 4.
27. Shelly Rambo (2010) *Spirit and Trauma: A Theology of Remaining* (Louisville: John Knox Press), 15 and 2.
28. Cathy Caruth (1996) *Unclaimed Experience: Trauma, Narrative, and History* (Baltimore: The John Hopkins University Press), 5 and 3.
29. Thomas Elsaesser (2001) "Postmodernism as Mourning Work," *Screen*, vol. 42, no. 2, 196.
30. Roth, *Popular Trauma Culture*, 4–5.
31. Rambo, *Spirit and Trauma*, 24.
32. Rambo, *Spirit and Trauma*, 6.
33. Rambo, *Spirit and Trauma*, 137.
34. Rambo, *Spirit and Trauma*, 126.
35. Rambo, *Spirit and Trauma*, 144.
36. Jack Bratich (2007) "Programming Reality: Control Societies, New Subjects and the Powers of Transformation," in Dana Heller (ed.) *Makeover Television: Realities Remodelled* (London: I.B. Tauris), 6–7.
37. Bratich, "Programming Reality," 11.
38. Laurie Oullette and James Hay (eds.) (2008) *Better Living Through Reality TV* (Malden, MA: Blackwell), 7.
39. Shows like *Survivor* and *Big Brother* are classic examples, but dozens and dozens of other shows have upped the ante like *Fear* (MTV) or *Fear Factor* (NBC), or various forms of what has been called "ambush TV" from the earlier and far less invasive (by contemporary standards) *Candid Camera* to today's *Scare Tactics*, *Punk'd*, or *Jackass*.
40. Biressi and Nunn, *Reality TV*, 5.

41. Kathleen S. Lowney (1999) *Baring Our Souls: TV Talk Shows and the Religion of Recovery* (New York: de Gruyter), 29.
42. Biressi and Nunn, *Reality TV*, 111. Other filmic and narrative devices employed to sensationalize and exaggerate the distress and debilitation that accompanies trauma are: repetition of what is said by the host ("to reinforce the immensity of events"), the close-up ("to accentuate the minutiae of... emotional facial expressions"), news headlines (to complement the interviewee's testimony), tears or hands clasped to face or breast, and the testimony of others used to corroborate and validate that of the interviewee (113–4).
43. Rambo, *Spirit and Trauma*, 31.
44. Lowney's work interestingly demonstrates how both the carnivals and the revivals of the nineteenth century are the predecessors of the modern television talk show.
45. Lowney, *Baring Our Souls*, 133–134.
46. Biressi and Nunn, *Reality TV*, 5.
47. Biressi and Nunn, *Reality TV*, 117.
48. Van Bauwel, "The Spectacle of the Real and Whatever Other Constructions," 26.
49. Rambo, *Spirit and Trauma*, 151.
50. Rambo, *Spirit and Trauma*, 162.
51. Rambo, *Spirit and Trauma*, 151.
52. Rambo, *Spirit and Trauma*, 151.
53. Dirk Lange (2010) *Trauma Recalled: Liturgy, Disruption, and Theology* (Minneapolis: Fortress Press), 9.
54. Lange, *Trauma Recalled*, 9.
55. United Methodist Church (1989) *The United Methodist Hymnal* (Nashville; The United Methodist Publishing House), 10, emphasis mine.
56. Consider also another of the eucharistic hymns written by Charles Wesley and included in the 1745 *Hymns on the Lord's Supper*:
    Come, Holy Ghost, Thine influence shed, And realize [make real] the sign;
    Thy life infuse into the bread, Thy power into the wine.
    Effectual let the tokens prove, And made, by heavenly art,
    Fit channels to convey Thy love To every faithful heart. *United Methodist Hymnal*, 281.
57. *United Methodist Hymnal*, 280–281.

58. "You will not change me into yourself like the food your body eats, but you will be transformed into me." Augustine (2001) *The Confessions of St. Augustine* (London: Francis Lincoln), 44.
59. William T. Cavanaugh (1998) *Torture and Eucharist* (Malden, MA: Wiley-Blackwell), 225.
60. Lange, *Trauma Recalled*, xi.
61. Lange, *Trauma Recalled*, 9.
62. Marcia Shoop and Mary McClintock Fulkerson (2013) "Transforming Memory: Re-membering Eucharist," *Theology Today*, vol. 70, no. 2, 153.
63. Shoop and Fulkerson, "Transforming Memory," 154.
64. Other forms of reality programming need to be explored in this context as well. For example, I have not even touched on the construction of the news, itself a significant form of Reality TV, and the implications of that construction for the way we absorb its portrayals of tragedy, war, and trauma.
65. Fred Clark (2003) "Reality TV," *Slacktivist*, accessed on October 13, 2014, http://www.patheos.com/blogs/slacktivist/2003/10/08/reality-tv-contd/.
66. Shoop and Fulkerson, "Transforming Memory," 154.
67. Cf. Mayra Rivera (2007) *The Touch of Transcendence: A Postcolonial Theology of God* (Louisville: Westminster John Knox Press).

Bibliography

Andrejevic, M. 2004. *Reality TV: The work of being watched*. Landham: Rowman and Littlefield.
Augustine. 2001. *The confessions of St. Augustine*. London: Francis Lincoln.
Baudrillard, J. 1983. The ecstasy of communication. In *The anti-aesthetic: Essays on postmodern culture*, ed. H. Forester. Port Townsend: Bay Press.
Biressi, A., and H. Nunn. 2005. *Reality TV: Realism and revelation*. London: Wallflower Press.
Bratich, J. 2007. Programming reality: control societies, new subjects and the powers of transformation. In *Makeover television: Realities remodelled*, ed. D. Heller, 6–22. London: I. B. Tauris.
Busis, H. 2012. Aaron Sorkin hates the Internet. Why does he keep writing about tech geniuses? *Entertainment Weekly*, May 16.
Caruth, C. 1996. *Unclaimed experience: Trauma, narrative, and history*. Baltimore: The John Hopkins University Press.
Cavanaugh, W.T. 1998. *Torture and EUCHARIST*. Malden: Wiley-Blackwell.

Clark, F. 2003. Reality TV. *Slacktivist*. http://www.patheos.com/blogs/slacktivist/2003/10/08/reality-tv-contd/

Deligiaouri, A., and M. Popovic. 2010. Reality TV and REALITY of TV: How much reality is there in reality TV Shows? A critical approach. In *Trans-reality television*, ed. Sofie Van Bauwel and Nico Carpentier, 65–86. Lanham: Lexington Books.

Eliot, T.S. 1943. *Four quartets*. Orlando: Harcourt.

Elsaesser, T. 2001. Postmodernism as mourning work. *Screen* 42(2): 193–201.

Farrell, K. 1998. *Post-traumatic culture: Injury and interpretation in the nineties*. Baltimore: The John Hopkins University Press.

France, L. R. 2013. Reality TV and suicide intertwine once again. CNN, October 14. http://www.cnn.com/2013/10/14/showbiz/tv/reality-tv-suicide/

Glynn, K. 2000. Jean Baudrillard and the policing of obscenity. In *Tabloid culture: Trash taste, popular power, and the transformations of American television*. Durham: Duke University Press.

Herman, J. 1992. *Trauma and recovery: The aftermath of violence – From domestic abuse to political terror*. New York: Basic Books.

Lange, D. 2010. *Trauma recalled: Liturgy, disruption, and theology*. Minneapolis: Fortress Press.

Lowney, K.S. 1999. *Baring our souls: TV talk shows and the religion of recovery*. New York: de Gruyter.

Oueletter, L., and J. Hay (eds.). 2008. *Better living through reality TV*. Malden: Blackwell.

Radstone, S. 2001. Trauma and screen studies: Opening the debate. *Screen* 42(2): 188–193.

Rambo, S. 2010. *Spirit and trauma: A theology of remaining*. Louisville: Westminster John Knox Press.

Rivera, M. 2007. *The touch of transcendence: A postcolonial theology of god*. Louisville: Westminster John Knox Press.

Roth, A. 2011. *Popular trauma culture: Selling the pain of others in the mass media*. New Brunswick: Rutgers University Press.

Shoop, M., and M.M. Fulkerson. 2013. Transforming memory: Re-membering Eucharist. *Theology Today* 70(2): 144–159.

United Methodist Church. 1989. *The united methodist hymnal*. Nashville: The United Methodist Publishing House.

Van Bauwel, S. 2010. The spectacle of the real and whatever other constructions. In *Trans-reality television*, ed. S. Van Bauwel and N. Carpentier, 23–36. Lanham: Lexington Books.

Wesley, C. 1989. In *Charles Wesley: A reader*, ed. J.R. Tyson. New York: Oxford University Press.

Young, S.M., and D. Pinksy. 2006. Narcissism and celebrity. *Journal of Research in Personality* 40(5): 463–471.

CHAPTER 4

Running the Gauntlet of Humiliation: Disablement in/as Trauma

Sharon V. Betcher

The first, now iconic image from the finish line of the 117th Boston Marathon (April 15, 2013) is seared in memory—the photo of Jeff Bauman, become in that moment double, lower limb amputee, being evacuated from the scene (Photo by Charles Krupa). In this photographic memorial as in so many other traumatic scenes, the image of the suddenly crippled body becomes stock in trade. Because this will become a "frame of war," an image soliciting our emotions as a nation,[1] and because we already see in that frame our resolve "to get him/our nation back on his/our feet" and to aggressively counter that which occasioned our indignity, we may not register the ways in which disablement is constituted by and amidst the politics of humiliation.

We have, since 9/11, begun to understand that "the single most underappreciated force in international relations is humiliation."[2] The leveling of New York City's World Trade Center Twin Towers in 2001, as well as the 2013 Boston marathon bombing were, we now surmise, acts of persons having been humiliated waging counter aggression—so as to humble a nation, its economic doctrine, to show up its vulnerability. Humiliation may be, metaphorically speaking, as sociologist Evelin Lindner puts it, "'a nuclear bomb of emotion,' perhaps the most toxic social dynamic of

S.V. Betcher (✉)
Independent Scholar, Whidbey Island, USA

our age," in terms of breaking down human relationships at the personal, social and national levels of organization.[3] When humiliated, persons may, in response, rage. That rage has often historically—as in the contemporary—targeted the flesh of the other, where it wants to leave its lasting mark.

In the 2013 bombing of the Boston Marathon, rage struck out in an act—not the least bit ironic—meant to interrupt the display of our national prowess, our "ablenationalism"—that ritual display of the healthy, athletic body as model citizen of the once again secure, even immune nation. The bombing heaps humiliation back upon the USA by crippling bodies, thus, by proving our nation's vulnerability. If those scenarios of humiliation and counter aggression have now come to be socially recognized, what tends to be overlooked are the ways in which disablement is often among the *intended* consequences of just such inter-cultural politics, the way in which persons with disabilities may be consequently forced to live in the affective cloud left by the politics of humiliation.

"Disability" names one form of the traumatic suffering that remains in the aftermath of the religious, familial and civil politics of humiliation. That is, the intentional maiming of another as retaliation for hurt experienced results in "disablement." Consider the slashing and mutilation of bodies by machete in the war between the Hutu and the Tutsis during the Rwandan Genocide and amidst the civil collapse of Sierra Leone; the acid burning of women in India; the rape of Muslim women by Bosnian Serbs; urban gang wars leaving others permanent quadriplegics (hence, the street gang named "The Crips"). In these scenes, disfigurement is used to permanently register the pain of one's own indignity in the flesh of another.[4] Amidst the politics of humiliation, disablement ensues as the intentional leveraging of bodies—often as symbolic representatives of their nation or religio-ethnic community—against their own helplessness and powerlessness, even as ways of razing social order.[5]

But might "disability"—a term culturally employed to designate the traumatically disfigured body—also emotionally return us to just such scenes? Amidst the militant politics of humiliation, the instigator attempts to level the emotional playing field and so to render the other in a permanent state of disgrace. In such arenas, disability might then be defined as "political violence performed on the body,"[6] a way of making the other "wear shame." Disability—often the intended result of politically or civilly motivated anger (and, again, as distinct from the outright killing of the other)—therefore belongs among the very local intra-personal as well as international politics of humiliation. Disability belongs, affectively speaking, to the history of the intentional maiming, scarring and dismemberment of other humans—of the ways in which we have found to land our hurt in the skin, bone, body, brain and psyche of another. And so disabled bodies in general, I am proposing as a thesis, may be read—affectively speaking (where "affect" names an emotional atmosphere, an unreflective structure of feeling, socially engendered and culturally transmitted)—to refer us back to just such scenes as transpires amidst the politics of humiliation.[7]

We cripped ones, whether taken down in trauma or articulated in evolutionary becoming, then appear against a scrim, where disability signaled a failed political, social, or religious relationship. We become exemplary of the old law yoking the body and socio-political "debt"—that ancient law rendering "injury...as payment in default"[8] (e.g., Roman law allowed creditors to dismember one's debtor or their slaves, their legal proxies[9]). If injury in that vein gives evidence of a debt un/paid, disability would seem to "invite" contempt. And the human unconscious, itself historied in ways unrecognized by Western versions of the psychological *tabula rasa*, may then come into play in ways unanalyzed in our encounters with bodies differing. Despite the ways in which medicine treats the body as but biology, bio-medicine constitutes a reductionism—an avoidance of cultural history—which may leave us unable to deal with the political affect connected with disability—humiliation, that is. The affect roused in the presence of the "disfigured" or "marked" body spreads among a populous like a contagious disease. And humiliation—"the closet dominatrix of the emotions"—holds tremendous sway over all other feelings. It has, affectively speaking, exponential staying power.[10]

Along with cultural anthropologist, Henri-Jacques Stiker, I would argue "for a continuum of effects in which one epoch's beliefs [regarding "disability"] continue to inform the practices of succeeding generations."[11] And I am asking what residual affects this history of the politics of humiliation has on how we now live with "the disabled," how we encounter and interact with the crip. In fact, cultural notions that one is "better off dead" congeal around just this cultural sense of disability, as a humiliation of embodied life (As the tractate, Sotah of the Talmud, tellingly puts it, "humiliation is worse than physical pain"). It is living with humiliation that culture construes as worse than death, sinking all experience of disablement within it—as if all disablement were exemplary of being bound and held against one's will. Insomuch as humiliation names "the willingness to desubjectify the other person, to lock the door of civilization" on him/her,[12] the category "disability" itself comes, in turn, to rehearse the politics of humiliation and thus belongs, in this doubled way, within the work of post-trauma studies.

Disability would then remain—despite the zero sum of metaphysical causation offered up by Western medicine and evolutionary science—"ghosted"[13] by this historic, if still all too contemporary social, affective politics. Those of us born with congenital alterity or immersed by medical trauma into morphological diversity may find ourselves—in the eyes of the human community—haunted by a species memory of the politics of humiliation that is obviously not in the past. Western medicine has cleansed trauma of the guilt of the gods. Yet, the human psyche—especially given how pain metaphorically appropriates the weapon ("It feels as if I'm being shot, stabbed, tortured")[14] and given that skin, thus even wound or scar, comes into view as a feeling in the presence of the other[15]—may carry a species specter. And might it not then generate, among other insecure onlookers, an affect cloud that socially marginalizes persons with impairments, that steals our futures by foreclosing desire?

Resurrection—life in the aftermath, I mean—does not erase scars, wounds, the telltale signs of torture or trauma. So how shall we live together in the bomb craters quaking still with the politics of humiliation? In the upcoming section, I elaborate my rationale for yoking disablement with the politics of humiliation, while distinguishing humiliation from shame. Then, turning toward the overtly theological, I consider the claim that "Christianity is the only major religion to have as its central event the humiliation of its God."[16] Working with insights from theologian David Tombs, Biblical scholar Klaus Wengst and Virginia Burrus, scholar of late antiquities, I think through the humiliation of Jesus as well as the resurrection of the spirit of humility within the communities formed in his memory. Humility constitutes something of a little way—a way of living with bodies that experience humiliation as an existential exposure of the flesh. Bringing that back into our contemporary world, I explore philosophical insights for living "the body unbound,"[17] turning, finally, to religious ritual for the somatic practice of cultivating a taste for life among bodies pummeled by the politics of humiliation.

Disability and the Gauntlet of Humiliation

In the immediate aftermath of an act of terrorism or warfare, the disabled body—whether of soldier, civil servant or innocent bystander—has been publicly volleyed as a symbol for the reclamation of political identity. Nationally, we are quick to shore up this gaping body, to applaud its courage, its inspiring spirit, to give it back two legs. That impulse to prosthetics has at least as much to do with national pride and the civic body symbolically overcoming humiliation as the well-being of an individual. This becomes more obvious in historical perspective: Oliver Wendell Holmes, for example, made it socially imperative to generate prostheses for those injured during the Civil War so that the young nation of America would not be seen stumping around, humiliated, before the eyes of Europe. American technology had an obligation, Holmes insisted, "to raise the coarse and vulgar to the plane of symmetry and refinement."[18] Prosthetics reclaimed virility, the symbolic power of health. Prosthetics, in other words, repaired the social wound—the wound to national dignity. Amidst such symbolic volleys, public energies can overwhelm the needs of injured persons.

For the person now living with disability, the after-effects of humiliation do not so easily resolve as a prosthetic cover-up might lead one to believe. While cripped survivors from the Boston bombing have remained in our attentive gaze over the past year (A photo journalism expose by Josh Haner on the year of recovery for Jeff Bauman garnered a Pulitzer in photo journalism in spring 2014),[19] the socio-historical in situ of Bauman's disablement will recede. In fact, most of that individual's life will be lived without the banner of public appropriation, and he will consequently live in but the cultural theater of "the disabled." As the heroics and the memorializing of rescue recede and as the nation's need for a discursive cause for retaliatory military action and its hunger for "inspiration" passes, traumatically impacted individuals navigate this second stage of the "politics of humiliation" in the public eye, without appreciative awareness. Disability, itself construed as a humiliation, now folds over and swallows up the cultural or political memory, the scene in which the traumatized was once a social player: humiliation—here now, disablement—individuates; it isolates one from the social nexus.[20]

In his memoir, *Blue-Eyed Boy*, U.S. Marine Robert Timberg recounts how the explosion of the Amphibian Tractor in which he was riding in Viet Nam left him disfigured. After processing the relief of survival and of national pride in serving his country, he notes that "The day ultimately comes when the attention diminishes, the good fellowship is no more because he is mostly alone, and he is faced with the chilling prospect of a lifetime of coping with what war has turned him into."[21] The situational history of his disablement is easily forgotten or not yet learned when the child makes obvious what the too civilly polite hide inside their chest: "Look at his face! Look at his face! Look at his face!"[22] This was as true of soldiers in antiquity as Timberg reports in the contemporary: "Not even war heroes were spared the indignity of being mocked for their disabilities," scholar Robert Garland notes, his observations ranging from ancient Athens to the Roman Republic. Garland concludes that "even in a militaristic state like Rome the disabled veteran was not universally esteemed."[23] When the disabled body is removed from the scene of historical onset within which it might have been symbolically borrowed as a hero, as an inspiring survivor against steep odds, the person will consequently need to deal with that residual cultural tendency to read disability as always itself a humiliation.

"Humiliation inheres in every nook and cranny of the normal," William Ian Miller reminds us. Then he adds a note that brings the politics of humiliation down to the flesh of each of us: "The humiliation of the perverse, of extremis, of death camps and interrogation rooms is parasitical on the usual and familiar, not the other way around."[24] Disability names an arena on the perimeter of civility, that social practice of normalcy, where we play out the politics of humiliation under the guise of reason: surely, we categorically recognize "the invalid" when we see it! Ironically, the very bodies borrowed so as to frame a discursive cause and mount a nation's aggrieved retaliation devolve in but the blink of an eye to the categorically questionable. Disability names a kind of cultural racism wherein—to borrow the words of philosopher Judith Butler—"we have already lost sight of what and who is alive."[25] And with Miller's reminder that the extremes of humiliation depend on the usual, we might wonder if learning to navigate this "old familiar" of the purportedly ontologically invalid, of the "somatically humiliated," i.e., "the disabled," might lead us to navigate the national scales of the politics of humiliation more nonviolently.

Somatic Politics

When images of trauma survivors like Bauman are no longer useful as a civic or national recruitment tool (whether as a way to produce righteous indignation or as an inspiration to act with such resilience), then "the disabled" drop into the pocket of lives already virtually lost. Cultural spectators come soon enough, as both Timberg and Garland noted even of military personnel, to count scarred, disfigured survivors as residents of the territory of "ungrievable life," life that "already inhabit[s] a lost and destroyed zone."[26] Western culture has been and remains largely ambivalent about whether a crip constitutes a truly grievable—and not just a grievous—life.[27] In this zone, even harassment and abuse do not so easily register, personally or legally, as acts of human on human injustice.[28] That happens not only in the judgment of a life born disabled, but when that traumatized person we've wanted so much to live suddenly stands up on one leg, and we must future differently together. Reading the survivable body as a corruption of nature, onlookers—even those who have been cheerleaders of the injured—now may, without personal introspection, contribute humiliation. As a political affect, the dense cloud of humiliation sends persons reeling, refusing to create a future together explicitly in terms of the survivable body. Modern visions of social futuring—that is, the demand for "wholeness," by prosthesis or medical miracle, or else the highway of social exclusion—seem not that much more malleable on this point than what we call uncivilized responses.

Persons living in the cratered aftermath, stepping into a social world rife with unconscious, even metaphysical interpretations of trauma, must daily traverse the gauntlet of humiliation. Disability, phenomenologically speaking, often transpires against an unconscious connection made between the presumed transparency of health as evidencing truth over against the contrary connection of sickness and human sin.[29] Differently said, we often unconsciously affiliate "the holy, the sacred, the safe and sound, the unscathed, the immune" with righteousness, with God[30]—to the degree that persons living with disability have not, for example, historically been welcomed to consider ordination in the Christian tradition.[31] Disability, that is, has been affectively read as showing up the "truth" of a life…even as we can (sometimes!) acknowledge how unanchored and even counterfactual this has become from the scene of life onset of disablement. Likely this interpretation of the disabled body has to do with unconscious connections made between pain and punishment, the assumption that a disabled body is a body in pain and, over against that, the use of pain by political regimes and religious discipline for "getting at the truth."[32] Against this unconscious socio-political affiliative energy-field, crips can—as theologian Rita Nakashima Brock notes regarding a racial incident: "I was ashamed to be the target of violence..." [33]—come to feel humiliated when one becomes the focus of someone else's disgust. Stepping out of the hospital doors after my own life crisis, a massive infection occasioning the amputation of my left leg, the taunt echoed from the backseat of the car cruising the strip: "What a dog! What a dog!" Humiliation as "a ritual...operates crudely by saying 'we don't want you in our sight,'" we don't want you in our world.[34]

Among the gauntlets that must be run again and again is the terminological holding pen of "the disabled." When we pronounce another person "disabled" ("disability" being a term of depersonalization), this pronouncement serves the greater public as a way of staunching "fate contagion" or contamination via social affiliation; it is a way for the public to hold itself aloof from "the humiliated," given that "humiliation is powerfully pathogenic"[35] (Affiliation with one of us crips will envelop our social associates like a miasma, will threaten their social status). Daily, crips must enter the contestation of interpretive stances in a culture that aspires to somatic transparency of the patrolled and bounded body, so as to psychically wrest the interpretation of one's self, not only from "torturer/inflicter," but also from the narrative of ablenationalism, which yokes somatic transparency with freedom from judgment.

We humans know almost primitively the anticipated behavior of the humiliated amidst this volatile, contestatory politics of the street—the bent, submissive neck; dropping the face and lowering the eyes, declining recognition thereby; moving anonymously, as if unhearing, amidst the thunder of humiliating objectifications—medical and mercenary. Terror and trauma—whether as occasion of onset or as threatening social affect—can easily take persons living with disabilities into the psychic lockdown of humiliation. Humiliation contracts and so curtails one's sense of presence; it may therefore also be felt as impotence or powerlessness. To humiliate, as biblical poetry has picked up its morphological map, is to bring low, to bend the neck. To humiliate is to mortify—to drive another person up against the psychic limits of powerlessness and the will to live. Because of the individuation of disability and/as humiliation, this will be a wearisome, lonely, soul draining, if all too daily, passage, as one admits one's vulnerability to contempt—being the national spectacle or someone's "inspiration" but momentary and too thin a base from which to make a life of a body so visibly inscribed. One loses one's taste for life now and again.

Cringing Before the Indecorous

Entering the street theater where one encounters morphological alterity, culturally habituated desire (shaped toward an appreciation of symmetry and untarnished wholesomeness) seeks to find an alternative, objectifying—if still voyeuristic—position in relation to this abject other—as an onlooker, a charitable donor, anything that "locks the door of civilization against this outcast," while still giving us a "look see."[36] For humiliation frequently fixates on what is disgustingly curious: "Humiliation involves physical processes: fluids, solids, organs, cavities, orifices, outpourings, ingestions, excrescences, spillages. Humiliation demands a soiling."[37] More summarily, the humiliating is seen as a "breach of behavioral and aesthetic propriety," concludes theorist, Wayne Koestenbaum.[38] Though interested in the breadth of cultural scenes saturated with humiliation, Koestenbaum recognizes the cultural tracks yoking it to persons living with disabilities, where bodies appear, culturally speaking, to come undone—drooling, limping, lisping.

That connection between socio-cultural humiliation and the felt egregiousness of the body coming undone is echoed in Miller's work: "The fear of humiliation…causes people to feel greater mortification for being discovered violating norms of body control and decorousness (e.g., passing gas) than for offending against more serious moral and legal norms (cheating on income tax, stealing from the workplace, adultery, betrayal). Shame occupies itself with…the moral, the religious; humiliation tends to be grounded more trivially, engaging the conventional and the decorous…[i.e., "norms of bodily presentation and public decorum"]…"[39] Incongruously, while neither shame nor criminality voids social status or, more broadly, the claim to be [a] human, the unreflective psyche reacts to what it finds humiliating in just that way. "*[T]hat triviality*" of the purported offense to bodily decorum, Miller concludes, "*seems to bear no relation to the magnitude of averseness it engenders, or to the magnitude of the vindictiveness used to remedy it.*"[40] If we recall these insights into humiliation as we move ourselves back into the ballet of the city sidewalk, notice how the onlooker freezes over, engages "a selective anesthesia" against empathic identification[41]: "This gaze doesn't see a person; it sees a scab, an offense, a spot of absence."[42]

The gauntlet, this performance of the everyday politics of humiliation, comes in this way to be literally "de-grading," eviscerating: "Finally, what is denied is…the individual's very status to have made such a claim at all"[43]—that is, to be a person, a human (hence, the not infrequent rhetorical associations made between "the disabled" and animality or "the vegetative"). While humiliation "casts a storm cloud, a constant threat" over the witnessed [here, those categorically classified as "the disabled"], humiliation transpires, more precisely, attributionally—"inside our bodies, watching."[44]

Navigating Humiliation, Our Existential Inheritance

In learning to emotionally navigate our solicitation by that "frame of war," that image which rallies our emotions toward righteous indignation and, eventually, justifying war; or, even then comparably, in performing our culturally habituated bit roles in the daily street theatre of "the gauntlet of humiliation" of/for "the disabled," we have hit upon an affective disarticulation that will create in "the civilized" the channel for such unconscious behavior —namely, "selective anesthesia"[45] or, differently said, "righteous coldness."[46] Left unexamined, these emotional occlusions create in desire a sadistic undertow and make "the politics of humiliation"—at street level as at national level—seem all too natural, instinctual. This produces a kind of rationality taken to the base and the extreme—the pleasure of torturous, excruciating, if cold, calculating observation, for example; or, comparably, of the demand for meaning ("What happened to you? What does this mean?"). In the same way that empire's tranquil certainties—mathematics, law, reason, metaphysics—"deforms and deadens the human psyche, constituting a break between the subject and the world,"[47] so, in relation to each other, we may choose to "see(…) like a state"[48]—hence, that reading of disability as "invalid"/ating. Such cold calculation anesthetizes the voice of conscience and constitutes an unethical way of living with the pulsions of humiliation.

Given that to the human psyche, the excrescences of flesh appear a greater offense than moral failure (whether crime or sin), racializing a certain population—namely, "the disabled"—to carry this offloaded anxiety of the flesh has been implicit to "reason." Yet humiliation as an existential affect is, in the space of a lifetime, unavoidable. The assured probability of humiliation catching up with all of us at some point constitutes something of our corporeal inheritance. A culture that seals itself off from "the disabled" has already sidestepped, at a foundational level, its ethical ability to act in light of the existential unwilled precariousness of life.[49]

Socio-culturally, disablement remains affectively ghosted by aesthetic, even sadistic (cold and superior because emotionally disconnected) judgments. Our hope for nonviolence, Butler consequently insists, will alternatively come from introspectively examining what these conditions—again, "selective anesthesia" and "righteous coldness" or "righteous indignation"—occlude—namely, awareness of our fundamental dependency upon anonymous others, our existential vulnerability.[50]

Resurrecting the Spirit of Humility

Crucifixion—like the photo from the finish line of the Boston Marathon—may also be a frame of war, an emotional solicitation. The narrative of a virgin assaulted by an occupying military force, that rehearsal of a degradation ceremony, might be a comparable image. But Christianity has, at certain historic junctures, suggested that there may be a way of fielding these solicitations so as to cook up, not revenge, but humility. Rather than filling with righteous indignation when solicited by "the frame of war" or even then the felt superiority of "ablenationalism" in the presence of a crip, we can—as Christian iconography might be read to encourage—sit with the wound: "To be injured means that one has the chance to reflect upon injury, to find out the mechanisms of its distribution, to find out who else suffers from permeable borders, unexpected violence, dispossession and fear..."[51] Martin Luther King, Jr. and Nelson Mandela may be the epitome of those who have in the contemporary arrived at humility as an alternative way of renegotiating the desacralization and disgracing of bodies.

Working out the alchemy of humility can be dangerous work, given that humiliation can rebound and become a catalyst for righteous and/or militaristic acts of indignation, of terrorism—that flushed feeling of strength, countering disgrace (In terms of Christianity, think of how easily this image of the crucifixion of Jesus devolved into The Crusades and anti-Semitism). Nor is there ever any surety that we have the intrapsychic resilience to cook humility from humiliation in the kiln of the soul. Christianity has but insinuated one such practicable possibility.

Mindfulness Practice

The poetry of Philippians 2 has been as pivotal for Christianity's doctrine of incarnation as the opening chapter of the Gospel of John:

> Let the same mind be in you that was in Christ Jesus, who, though he was in the form of God, did not regard equality with God as something to be exploited, but emptied himself, taking the form of a *slave*, being born in human likeness. And being found in human form, he "humiliated himself, becoming submissive to the point of death"[52]—even death on a cross.[53]

This liturgical hymn existed as a product "of the earliest post-Easter enthusiasm" before being appropriated by Paul in his letter to the Philippians.[54] Death on the cross constituted the most extreme form of humiliation and was "almost always inflicted only on the lower class."[55] Not only "the typical punishment for slaves" and therefore a deterrent against uprisings,[56] crucifixion acted as a social quarantine, since to identify oneself with the crucified was to invite the burden of socio-political contagion. If so, the hymn insinuates God's intimate knowledge of and experiential intimacy with all these aspects of humiliation. Yet, rather than just speculating about God, the hymn, biblical scholar, Karl-Joseph Kuschel, insists, "proposes a model for the attitudes that should govern the life of the Christian community."[57]

The Pauline passage does not engage in sentimentality so as to call forth the gentile virtue of servanthood. Rather the hymn situates us amidst the socio-historical politics of bodies. "The bodies of slaves populate the pages passed down to us from the centuries that witnessed the rise of Christianity....," observes Jennifer Glancy in her *Slavery in Early Christianity*.[58] And, she adds, "We know that slavery marked the body: through shaved heads, tattoos, fetters, and the visible scars of physical discipline."[59] "Slaves ran an enormously high risk of becoming crippled, bow-backed or in some other way deformed," anthropologist Robert Garland comparably notes. "Indeed a physical deformity, however mild, was," Garland concludes, "their distinguishing hallmark..."[60] Corporeal exposure so constituted the condition of slavery that the term "body" was a term of degradation specific to this historic circumstance of human enslavement: "Throughout antiquity...every level of documentation represents slaves as bodies. The writings of early Christianity are no exception."[61] If slaves were but bodies and expressly bodies disfigured, disabled, penetrated, abused, then Christianity's doctrine of incarnation inherently situates itself amidst this politics of humiliation: God became *homoousian*—that is, "of the same nature"—with the humiliated, disfigured slave. If such conditions of socio-historical humiliation are not identical with disability in the twenty-first century, nonetheless disability today—as with slavery in antiquity—names that zone where we "hit [...] up against the boundary of what we mean by being human."[62]

Humility, the Little Way of Resurrection

As the obverse of Rome's triumphal processional displays, crucifixion—a degradation ceremony—was comparably constructed as a strut of imperial power: the public humiliation of even one person is intended to "paralyze a society's willingness to resist."[63] In his essay, "Crucifixion, State Terror and Sexual Abuse," David Tombs rereads the Christian passion narratives in light of "understanding how recent Latin American regimes used terror – [...including] sexual humiliation—to create fear and promote fatalism..."[64] It is Tomb's conviction, using "the testimonies from twentieth-century Latin America [to] create hermeneutical suspicions,"[65] that "the Gospel accounts indicate a striking level of public sexual humiliation in the treatment of Jesus"[66] during the trials and scourging. Further, after torture and execution, often itself involving sexual exposure, bodies were displayed along the roadside to spread humiliation contagion. "Crucifixion was," in Tombs words, "intended to be more than the ending of life..."[67] Through "what amounted to a ritualized form of public sexual humiliation," crucifixion attempted also "to reduce the victim to something less than human in the eyes of society."[68] Such practices of humiliating the body, of stripping away dignity, Tombs explains, "'persuades' [affiliated persons] that it is better to endure injustice fatalistically rather than to resist." The quietude of the Pax Romana was affected by way of the politics of humiliation; those acts of humiliation likely also included what we hold as the narrative of Mary's pregnancy and the birth of Jesus. Militarily sponsored gang rapes, as we know to be true even in these early decades of the twenty-first century, are used to disgrace, degrade and subdue a populous. Only in respect to the public politics of humiliation does "humility" eventually become an acquired choreography, a practicable grace learned within the Christian community.

The paschal mysteries, Biblical scholar, Klaus Wengst proposed, now imagining the gospels to be training manuals, taught one to navigate just such humiliations in a spiritually composed way. Wengst authored a small book in which he—without the insights of Tombs into state torture—arrived at the thesis which the title of his book encrypts, *Humility: Solidarity of the Humiliated.*[69] Christians can, he insisted, learn to move through humiliation without triggering the retaliatory impulse and without succumbing to indignity and its mortification, without quarantining bodies differing. There are two very ready-to-hand responses to humiliation when one has become its target: (1) revenge, whether as the violent pursuit of change or to dispel the creeping spell of contamination, and (2) repressed compliance, which may snuff out the life force. The spirit of humility, that little way of resurrection—Wengst proposed—constituted a third way.

Within the Roman world, "Someone who had been crucified was...politically suspicious"[70]—a condition to which persons living with disability, even those initiated into disablement as survivors of terrorism, can also be treated. To identify oneself with the politically suspicious—namely, Jesus, in terms of Wengst's thesis—was to carry the political burden of contagion with "humility." Gesturally, far from bowing the head submissively, "the wisdom of the humble lifts their heads and seats them among the great."[71] Wengst also excavated this biblical sentiment: "Honor yourself with humility, and give yourself the esteem you deserve,"[72] these being correctives to the cowering behavior expected of those exposed to "the furnace of humiliation."[73] As Wengst himself put it, "The interruption of violence" and "the creation of solidarity" was "the humility of the poor."[74] Having exorcised from themselves the gestural behaviors of the humiliated (those choreographed patterns of lowered eyes, neck bowed, and acting as an "absence of presence"), the practice of humility opened out "an alternative public"—a public lived without horizontal violence or scattered by the centrifugal force of humiliation.

Within the Reign of God movement to which Mary and Jesus belonged, people who aspired to humility, Wengst concluded, aspired to "the vision of a community...among whom there [were] no great ones who tread on the small...and in which there [were] no small ones who had to dodge the great..."[75] Humility named "not a virtue," but the relational pattern and social dynamic for an alternative public community,[76] for a people committed to each other, economically and socially.[77] To act with humility under such fierce constraints as affected by class-structured humiliation, military intimidation and religious exclusion required the humble, both to convert themselves from the daily demeanor of humiliation and to reject the vengeful, violent, if even legal, means at the disposal of the rich and powerful. Resurrection in and through humility constituted something of a little way.

Advancing historically from where Wengst leaves us, scholar of late antiquities, Virginia Burrus, likewise tracks Christianity's productive relationship with cultural shame and humiliation. In her *Saving Shame*, Burrus moves from the debasement of slaves to the martyrlogical spectacles of torture, then (after Constantine shut down the arena) to desert asceticism and the struggle with demonic adversaries, finally returning with Symeon, the Holy Fool, to performance art on the streets of the city. Symeon, the bean-eating saint who innovated on Israel's naked urban prophets, advanced cultural critique in the urban square specifically by playing up this zone where the observing superego reacts to the excesses of flesh. Of these diverse scenes, Burrus concludes: "The early Christian martyrs and later ascetics are seen to convert the spectacle of public humiliation into glory, transforming the shaming loss of face into a novel witness of identity…,"[78] arriving thereby at "a defiant shamelessness…that retrieves dignity without aspiring to honor."[79] As stigmatizing as its dribbles and drools, its rot and reek, might have been, flesh had already—through the incarnation—been wed with divinity.[80]

Resurrection of the body, Burrus observes, spelled something like Wengst's sense of joyous humility. Resurrection did not triumph over the flesh, but constituted an acquired grace of living this ecotone of flesh with humility: "The performance of a shamed and shameless identity opens up hitherto closed spaces, challenges prevailing assumptions, and thereby creates new social and political possibilities."[81] Flesh could be—like the disfigured body of the slave—lived shamelessly, with all humility and not a little ribald humor. In retrospect, what Christian systematic theology refers to as the doctrine of incarnation appears less a story of metaphysical space-travel than inherently a social practice of psychic projection: those encountered, even if/as subject to social humiliation, are of the same nature as God. God has made a way toward solidarity by passing through just such tidal undertows of desire, such that we too may pass through.

This recuperation of humility as a practicable path in early Christianity does not make the Christian tradition in anyway immune from perpetrating the social politics of humiliation. While Wengst's and Burrus's excavations suggest that there have been practiced passages through the affective tsunami of humiliation and so insinuate that we may be able to cultivate this wisdom yet again, Christianity has also found intimate ways—as feminists have made clear in our theological denunciation of the choreography of humility to which women's bodies were forced to submit—to promulgate the conditions of humiliation. Incarnation treated as an act of infinite condescension, i.e., "humiliation and exaltation," and wherein but one God-man temporarily visited flesh, itself wholly depraved, may not make a way through humiliation, but could be the torturous site of the excruciating infliction thereof. Humiliation can be, in that vein, masochistically churned so as to enforce the precarity of female flesh. When Christianity invokes "wholeness" amidst the regime of neoliberal embodiment, presuming this to be god-like or god-willed, it may do the same in relation to persons living with disabilities.

The Body Unbound

Today "the body"—built for consumption and endlessly malleable—serves as key to citizenship amidst neoliberal globalization.[82] Flesh, even amidst the postmodern celebration of human diversity, troubles us still as we obsessively tuck its abject excess into the tidy territory of "the clean and proper self,"[83] hide its obdurate material resistance, its dependence and neediness, behind the "modesty screen" of those racialized others, "the disabled." Cultural diversity, this ideal of neoliberal globalization replacing the role of "normal" as a cultural filter, still operatively excludes persons thought of as wholly abject. Neoliberalism's vision of a universal consumer-citizen, as theorist, Lennard Davis, observes, cannot include the homeless, the impoverished, persons with end-stage cancer, the obese, the comatose, the depressed, addicted or cognitively atypical because these are at base not consumers.[84] What constitutes "humanity" still shows up over against "the invalid."

"Disability," conversely said, names the first racial interpretation of what will lie outside civilized life. That judgment, aesthetic in nature, is made upon the basis of how we feel in each other's presence. I am, for example, only so much a fallen object, that is, "disabled," as the other—prone to anxiety where the body refuses to stay territorially intact—postures her/himself over my fleshy exposure: "To be looked at is to experience a loss of power and the feeling of the play of power on the surface of the body," for "perception is," as disabilities theorist, Bill Hughes, reminds us, "a social act of social constitution."[85] Civility and disability are mutually and simultaneously co-determined in that act. "The invalidation and disfigurement of impaired bodies," Hughes continues, "arises in the mode of perception which visualizes and articulates them as strangers."[86] And there—even under the categorical auspices of purportedly benevolent medical and scientific reason—the politics of humiliation can take root. We consequently need, concludes Davis, a new paradigm—something beyond "the body," that transcendental ideal in a material mask[87]—to include disability within and among human diversity.[88]

Philosopher Judith Butler may offer a first step toward transcending this instantiation of the politics of humiliation. In her *Frames of War*, Butler skirts around insights into the politics of humiliation– the ability we have to leverage and expose the flesh of another, to bend the other's psyche over this abject zone, more emotively volatile than criminal or moral offense:

> If we accept the insight that our very survival depends not on the policing of a boundary – the strategy of a certain sovereign in relation to its territory – but on recognizing how we are bound up with others, then this leads us to reconsider the way in which we conceptualize the body in the field of politics. We have to consider whether the body is rightly defined as a bounded kind of entity. What makes a body discrete is not an established

morphology, as if we could identify certain bodily shapes or forms as paradigmatically human. In fact, I am not at all sure we can identify a human form... [T]here is no singular human form. . . [T]he body is, in certain ways and even inevitably, unbound—in its acting, its receptivity, in its speech, desire and mobility.[89]

Flesh is, as Butler recognizes, always existentially available for political power plays. Butler has been—from *Giving an Account of the Self* through *Precarious Life* and in *Frames of War*—insinuating in our presence to each other "another solicitation" beyond that to take aim—namely, an invitation "to apprehend the precarious conditions of life as imposing an ethical obligation on us."[90] In drawing our attention to this alternative, often muted call, she has simultaneously brought forth a vulnerable, interdependent "body unbound" as the conceptual core of political theory.

Butler's theoretical innovation on the political subject as "the body unbound" might have an affinity with, or even find, an experiential history in human disability. If Butler's intent is to install a politics of nonviolence prior to national borders and deeper in our social flesh than the patrolled territory of late modernity's aesthetics of "the body," critical disability studies can appreciatively receive this concept of "the body unbound" as supportive of our own endeavors "to return us to the human...in its frailty and at the limits of its capacity to make sense."[91]

Yet philosopher, Maurice Blanchot, from whom Butler herself has occasionally gleaned insights, pushed the body unbound to a wholly other, more abject dimension, which may respect other existential truths of embodiment now cordoned among "the disabled." Blanchot sets himself before Robert Antelme's account of his experience as a French political prisoner in Nazi concentration camps: "What we encounter in Antelme's experience...is...human existence...lived as lack at the level of need... [M]an [sic], ...attached in a way that must be called abject to living, ...bears this need as a need that is no longer his own need proper but as a need that is in some sense...virtually the need of everyone."[92] Subjectivity proper collapses under humiliation, given the conditions of the concentration camp; what remains, Blanchot insisted, is relation to others *at the level of the abject*. In Blanchot's words, "*The infinite that is the movement of desire passes by way of need.* Need is desire and desire becomes confounded with need..."[93] The mewling demand around which human solidarity forms constitutes the core of our humanity, which exists only collectively.[94] If we accept Blanchot's definition, then humanity begins only where or as we move through the helplessness of abject exposure without making of it a humiliation. To be sure, negotiating the affect of humiliation is an acquired grace—maybe something like learning to put bread in each other's mewling mouths. The feeding that Christians call Eucharist may also have everything to do with learning that the solidarity of humanity begins in the little way of humility, an appreciative respect for the abject aspect of humanity, a respect for yawning need, for hunger and thirst.

Resurrecting a Taste for Life

The crucifixion of Jesus belongs among the practices of state torture intended to humiliate both an individual and his/her social affiliates. Amidst the horror of crucifixion, the body cries out its paltry needs—thirst, pain, an ache for one's relations, grief at the loss of meaning. We hear nothing as profound as a pronouncement from the heavens (as was reported at Jesus's baptism, e.g.). We just witness the dribbles of yawning, needy flesh mocking our demand for miracle and meaning, for profundity. Not surprisingly then, the first Holy Saturday lasted at least 5 to 10 years, as biblical scholar, John Dominic Crossan, poetically riffs, tongue-in-check and yet deadly serious. Anyone living the Reign-of-God movement consequent to the crucifixion had a load of political, social and religious humiliation to carry. Caught in humiliation, one tended to get snagged by self-reproach. Abhorred from above, the humiliated may come likewise to abhor themselves, community collapsing under the weight of self-contempt.

If the Gospels might then have been training manuals for those living consciously in solidarity with Jesus and Mary, despite the contagion cloud clinging to these humiliated ones, then what could the liturgy of Easter affectively perform? That Pascal ritual cycle known as the Tridaeum, the three-day passage from the remembrance of state trial and crucifixion to the resurrection (set in play with the communal foot washing and the great love commandment), might well have developed, I would wager, as a ritual of the humiliated for the humiliated. The washing of baptism (or its annual renewal on Easter) suggestively insinuated the cleansing of the defiled, disgraced self, of humanity reborn—until one could stand "naked and did not blush."[95] That ritual was, however, combined with scriptural narratives, leading from creation up to resurrection (recited from Easter Eve to Easter morn, when one was baptized): these recitatives brought one into a new narration of a life, reset the ruined scaffolding of a life frame, incorporated one into an alternative, adoptive community, those knowledgeable of and unwilling to expose another to the socio-political powers of humiliation. As theologians, Rebecca Parker and Rita Brock, put it, Christians at the paschal feast "...did not move from a secular, unbelieving world into a world of faith; they moved from being subject to the powers of demons to being free of their powers."[96]

If humiliation, like other forms of trauma, also kills desire, this makes the Eastern Church's definition of salvation "as an awakening to the whole world illumined by the brilliance of divine presence," all the more intriguing.[97] In ritual today, we dress up this paschal feast thereby enticing desire—through song and color and performance—to rouse itself yet again. Resurrection knows about life in the aftermath, lives again from within the territory of trauma. Resurrection may then have more to do with the little way of resurrection—that is, of the spirit of humility. Humility—as "non-cooperation with everything humiliating" (Gandhi)[98]—admits that human life is not just a game of mastery and self-will; it admits the vulnerability, the dispossession, the exposure, that transpires in a lifetime. Humility is a supple but insistent soul-force that attempts to recuperate love for humanity, for one's self, of enemy, in the face of unwilled vulnerability.

Psychically introjecting a humiliated God can prepare Christians for our own unwilled vulnerability, for living as bodies undone. Third century theologian, Tertullian, carrying the identification of slaves with body into the remainder of flesh, put it like this: "'[God] will love the flesh which is, so very closely and in so many ways, his neighbor—although infirm..., although disordered..., although not honorable..., although ruined..., although sinful..., although condemned.'"[99] To love the flesh is to assume the courage to be within these conditions of risk, to pass through those places where desire stalls, where desire lies comatose. Death is not itself so simply a mockery of life, but humiliation is. Life is never safe from being so humiliated you could just die; but paschal song, the dance of rainbow colors, the wash of waters, the hold of community, these may entice flesh to bloom yet again.

Notes

1. Judith Butler (2009) *Frames of War: When is Life Grievable?* (London & New York: Verso), xii–xiii.
2. Thomas L. Friedman (2003) "The Humiliation Factor," *The New York Times*, November 9, 2003 (Op-Ed).
3. L.M. Hartling, Evelyn Lindner, U. Spalthoff and M. Britton (2013) "Humiliation: A Nuclear Bomb of Emotions?" in *Psicologia Politica*, vol. 46, 56 and 65.

4. Comparably, think of the use of religio-juridical shame penalties within contemporary radical Islam. See Xan Rice (2010) "Somali Schoolboy tells of how Islamists cut off his leg and hand," *The Guardian*, 20 October 2010.
5. In Sierra Leone, the Revolutionary United Front (RUF) "appears to have selected men whose maiming would most profoundly affect the social order. 'It was the goal of the rebels to take away their role...'" See Norimitsu Onishi (1999) "Sierra Leone Measures Terror in Severed Limbs," *The New York Times*, August 22, 1999, http://www.nytimes.com/1999/08/22/world/sierra-leone-measures-terror-in-severed-limbs.html?pagewanted=all. Accessed August 24, 2014.
6. Begona Aretxaga (2006) "Dirty Protest: Symbolic Overdetermination and Gender in Northern Ireland Ethnic Violence," in Ellen Lewan (ed.) *Feminist Anthropology: A Reader* (Malden, MA: Blackwell), 306.
7. Hal Kirshbaum first proposed a connection between disability and humiliation. See his (1991) "Disability and Humiliation," *The Journal of Primary Prevention* vol. 12, no. 2, 169–181. On "affect" see Lauren Berlant (2011) *Cruel Optimism* (Durham: Duke University Press), 15.
8. Judith Butler quoting Jacques Derrida (2014) "On Cruelty," *London Review of Books*, vol. 36, no. 14, 31–33.
9. Butler citing Friedrich Nietzsche, "On Cruelty," 31.
10. William Ian Miller (1993) *Humiliation: And Other Essays on Honor, Social Discomfort, and Violence* (Ithaca: Cornell). See back cover endorsement by *Speculum* of 1995 paperback ed.
11. David T. Mitchell (2009) "Foreword," in Henri-Jacques Stiker *A History of Disability*, William Sayers (trans) (Ann Arbor: University of Michigan Press), viii.
12. Wayne Koestenbaum (2011) *Humiliation* (New York: Picador), 27.
13. Phillis Isabella Shepherd (2014) Oral presentation, Boston University, School of Theology, April 12, 2014.
14. Elaine Scary (1987) *The Body in Pain: The Making and Unmaking of the World* (New York & Oxford: Oxford University Press), 13 and 15.
15. Sara Ahmed explains that "skin as a surface...is felt only in the event of being 'impressed upon' in the encounters we have with others." See her (2004) *The Cultural Politics of Emotion* (NY: Routledge), 25. Writing more specifically in regards to pain, she

notes that "The wound functions as a trace of where the surface of another entity (however imaginary) has impressed upon the body, an impression that is felt and seen as the violence of negation," 27.
16. Bruce L. Shelley (2013) *Church History in Plain Language*, Fourth Edition (Nashville: Thomas Nelson/HarperCollins Christian Publishing House), 3.
17. Butler, *Frames of War*, 52.
18. Oliver Wendell Holmes (1863) *Atlantic Monthly*, May. Quoted in David D. Yuan (1997) "Disfigurement and Reconstruction in Oliver Wendell Holmes' 'The Human Wheel, Its Spokes and Felloes,'" in David T. Mitchell and Sharon L. Snyder (eds.) *The Body and Physical Difference: Discourses of Disability* (Ann Arbor: University of Michigan Press), 74–5.
19. James Estrin (2014) "*New York Times* Wins Two Photography Pulitzers," in *Lens: Photography, Video, and Visual Journalism*, April 14, 2014, accessed September 23, 2014, http://lens.blogs.nytimes.com/2014/04/14/the-new-york-times-wins-two-photography-pulitzers/?_php=true&_type=blogs&_r=0.
20. Lisa Guenther (2012) "Resisting Agamben: The Biopolitics of Shame and Humiliation," *Philosophy and Social Criticism*, vol. 38, no. 1, 61.
21. Robert Timberg (2014) *Blue-Eyed Boy: A Memoir* (New York, Penguin), 24.
22. Timberg, *Blue-Eyed Boy*, 152.
23. Robert Garland (1995) *The Eye of the Beholder: Deformity and Disability in the Graeco-Roman World* (Ithaca: Cornell University Press), 78.
24. Miller, *Humiliation*, 10.
25. Butler, *Frames of War*, xxix.
26. Butler, *Frames of War*, viii.
27. Judith Butler raises the question "When is life grievable?" in her *Frames of War*: "Ungrievable lives are those that cannot be... destroyed, because they already inhabit a lost or destroyed zone; they are, ontologically, and from the start, already lost and destroyed, which means that when they are destroyed in war, nothing is destroyed" (xix). Butler writes with her eyes on the ongoing Israel-Palestine confrontation as well as the post 9/11 U.S. wars in Iraq and Afghanistan and with the hope that we might learn to

recalibrate grievability through recognition of our mutual vulnerability. I am wondering how "disability" construed as culturally "in/valid" has likewise been informed by the cultural rationale of "ungrievable life."
28. Butler, *Frames of War*, xix.
29. Talal Asad (1993) *Genealogies of Religion: Discipline and Reasons of Power in Christianity and Islam* (Baltimore: The Johns Hopkins University Press), 104–105.
30. Jacques Derrida (2002) *Acts of Religion* (Routledge), 42 and 70.
31. Nancy Eiesland (1994) *The Disabled God: Toward a Liberatory Theology of Disability* (Nashville: Abingdon Press).
32. Asad, *Genealogies of Religion*, 106.
33. Rita Brock and Rebecca Parker (2001) *Proverbs of Ashes: Violence, Redemptive Suffering, and The Search for What Saves Us* (Boston: Beacon Press) 51–2.
34. Miller, *Humiliation*, 10.
35. Walter J. Torres and Raymond M. Bergner (2010) "Humiliation: Its Nature and Consequences," *Journal of American Academy of Psychiatry Law*, vol. 38, no. 2, 199.
36. Koestenbaum, *Humiliation*, 27.
37. Koestenbaum, *Humiliation*, 8.
38. Koestenbaum, *Humiliation*, 48.
39. Miller, *Humiliation*, 138–9.
40. Miller, *Humiliation*, 138–9, emphasis added.
41. David B. Morris (1991) *The Culture of Pain* (Berkeley: University of California Press), 243.
42. Koestenbaum, *Humiliation*, 33.
43. Torres and Bergner, "Humiliation," 199.
44. Koestenbaum, *Humiliation*, 30.
45. Koestenbaum, *Humiliation*, 70.
46. Butler, *Frames of War*, 52.
47. Ajitpaul Singh Mangat (2011) "The Therapy of Humiliation: Towards an Ethics of Humility in the works of JM Coetzee," MA Thesis (Knoxville: University of Tennessee), 12. Online at http://trace.tennessee.edu/utk_gradthes/896. Accessed September 23, 2014.
48. James C. Scott (1999) *Seeing Like a State* (New Haven: Yale University Press).
49. Butler (2004) *Precarious Life: The Powers of Mourning and Violence* (New York & London: Verso), xviii.

50. Butler, *Precarious Life*, xii.
51. Butler, *Precarious Life*, xii.
52. This phraseology follows the translation of Virginia Burrus (2008) *Saving Shame: Martyrs, Saints and Other Abject Subjects* (Philadelphia: University of Pennsylvania Press), 45.
53. Php. 2: 5–8, emphasis added.
54. Karl-Joseph Kuschel (1992) *Born Before All Time? The Dispute over Christ's Origin* (London: SCM Press Ltd.), 259.
55. Neil Elliott (1997) "Anti-Imperial Message of the Cross," in Richard Horsley (ed.) *Paul and Empire: Religion and Power in Roman Imperial Society* (New York: Bloomsbury/T&T Clark), 168.
56. Elliott, "Anti-Imperial Message of the Cross," 170–1.
57. Kuschel, *Born Before All Time?*, 259.
58. Jennifer Glancy (2002) *Slavery in Early Christianity* (Oxford: Oxford University Press), 29.
59. Glancy, *Slavery*, 29.
60. Garland, *Eye of the Beholder*, 22.
61. Glancy, *Slavery in Early Christianity*, 29.
62. Lennard J. Davis (2014) *The End of Normal*: Identity in a Biocultural Era (Ann Arbor: University of Michigan Pres), 29.
63. David Tombs (1999) "Crucifixion, State Terror and Sexual Abuse," *Union Seminary Quarterly Review*, vol. 53, no. 1–2, 91.
64. Tombs, "Crucifixion," 89.
65. Tombs, "Crucifixion," 100.
66. Tombs, "Crucifixion," 90.
67. Tombs, "Crucifixion," 101.
68. Tombs, "Crucifixion," 101.
69. Klaus Wengst (1987) *Humility: Solidarity of the Humiliated* (Minneapolis: Fortress).
70. Wengst, *Humility*, 73.
71. Sirach 11:1.
72. Sirach 10:28–9.
73. Sirach 2:1–3a, 4b–5.
74. Wengst, *Humility*, 21.
75. Wengst, *Humility*, 2.
76. Zeph, 2:3.
77. Wengst, *Humility*, 58.

78. Burrus, *Saving Shame*, 79. Burrus does not distinguish between shame and humiliation, though I (following Koestenbaum) have.
79. Burrus, *Saving Shame*, 8.
80. Burrus, *Saving Shame*, 49.
81. Burrus, *Saving Shame*, 43.
82. Davis, *The End of Normal*, 3.
83. See Julia Kristeva (1982) *Powers of Horror*, Leon S. Roudiez (trans) (New York: Columbia University Press).
84. Ibid., 4–5.
85. Bill Hughes (1999) "The Constitution of Impairment: Modernity and the Aesthetic of Oppression," *Disability and Society*, vol. 14, no. 2, 162 and 164.
86. Hughes, "Constitution," 155.
87. Sharon Betcher (2010) "Becoming Flesh of my Flesh: Feminist and Disability Theologies," *Journal of the Feminist Studies in Religion*, vol. 26, no. 2, 107.
88. Davis, *End of Normal*, 9.
89. Butler, *Frames of War*, 52.
90. Butler, *Frames of War*, xvii.
91. Butler, *Precarious Life*, 151.
92. Maurice Blanchot (1993) *The Infinite Conversation* (Minneapolis & London: University of Minnesota Press), 133. Also quoted in Guenther, "Resisting Agamben," 73.
93. Blanchot, *The Infinite Conversation*, 133.
94. Guenther, "Resisting Agamben," 74, emphasis added.
95. Rebecca Ann Parker and Rita Brock (2009) *Saving Paradise: How Christianity Traded Love of this World for Crucifixion and Empire* (Boston: Beacon), 136–7.
96. Parker and Brock, *Saving Paradise*, 127.
97. Parker and Brock, *Saving Paradise*, 155.
98. A known quote by Gandhi.
99. Tertullian, as quoted in Burrus, *Saving Shame*, 56–7.

Bibliography

Ahmed, S. 2004. *The cultural politics of emotion*. New York: Routledge.

Aretxaga, B. 2006. Dirty protest: Symbolic overdetermination and gender in northern Ireland ethnic violence. In *Feminist anthropology: A reader*, ed. E. Lewan. Malden: Blackwell.

Asad, T. 1993. *Genealogies of religion: Discipline and reasons of power in Christianity and Islam.* Baltimore/London: The John Hopkins University Press.

Berlant, L. 2011. *Cruel optimism.* Durham: Duke University Press.

Betcher, S. 2010. Becoming flesh of my flesh: Feminist and disability theologies on the edge of posthumanist discourse. *Journal of Feminist Studies in Religion* 26(2): 107–139.

Blanchot, M. 1993. *The infinite conversation.* Minneapolis/London: University of Minnesota Press.

Brock, R., and R. Parker. 2001. *Proverbs of ashes: Violence, redemptive suffering, and the search for what saves us.* Boston: Beacon.

Burrus, V. 2008. *Saving shame: Martyrs, saints and other abject subjects.* Philadelphia: University of Pennsylvania Press.

Butler, J. 2004. *Precarious life: The powers of mourning and violence.* New York/London: Verso.

Butler, J. 2009. *Frames of war: When is life grievable?* London/New York: Verso.

Butler, J. 2014. On cruelty. *London Review of Books* 36(14): 31–33.

Davis, L.J. 2014. *The end of normal: Identity in a biocultural era.* Ann Arbor: University of Michigan Press.

Derrida, J. 2002. *Acts of religion.* New York: Routledge.

Eiesland, N. 1994. *The disabled god: Toward a liberatory theology of disability.* Nashville: Abingdon.

Elliot, N. 1997. Anti-imperial message of the cross. In *Paul and empire: Religion and power in roman imperial society*, ed. R. Horsely. New York: Bloomsbury T &T Clark.

Estrin, J. 2014. New York Times wins two photography Pulitzers. *Lens: Photography, Video, and Visual Journalism.* http://lens.blogs.nytimes.com/2014/04/14/the-new-york-times-wins-two-photography-pulitzers/?_php=true&_type=blogs&_r=0

Friedman, T. L. 2003. The humiliation factor. *The New York Times.* http://www.nytimes.com/2003/11/09/opinion/the-humiliation-factor.html

Garland, R. 1995. *The eye of the beholder: Deformity and disability in the Graeco-Roman world.* Ithaca: Cornell University Press.

Glancy, J. 2002. *Slavery in early Christianity.* Oxford: Oxford University Press.

Guenther, L. 2012. Resisting agamben: The biopolitics of shame and humiliation. *Philosophy and Social Criticism* 38(1): 59–79.

Hartling, L.M., E. Lindner, U. Spalthoff, and M. Britton. 2013. Humiliation: A nuclear bomb of emotions? *Psicologia Politica* 46: 55–76.

Holmes, O. W. 1863. *Atlantic Monthly,* quoted in Yuan, D. D. 1997. Disfigurment and reconstruction in Oliver Wendell Holmes' 'the human wheel, its spokes and felloes.' In *The body and physical difference: Discourses of disability*, ed. D. T. Mitchell, and S. L. Snyder. Ann Arbor: University of Michigan Press.

Hughes, B. 1999. The constitution of impairment: Modernity and the aesthetic of oppression. *Disability and Society* 14(2): 155–172.

Kirshbaum, H. 1991. Disability and humiliation. *The Journal of Primary Prevention* 12(2): 169–181.
Koestenbaum, W. 2011. *Humiliation*. New York: Picador.
Kristeva, J. 1982. *Powers of horror*. Trans. Leon S. Roudiez. New York: Columbia University Press.
Kuschel, K. 1992. *Born before all time? The dispute over Christ's origin*. London: SCM Press.
Mangat, A. S. 2011. The therapy of humiliation: Towards an ethics of humility in the works of JM Coetzee, MA thesis. Knoxville: University of Tennessee.
Miller, W.I. 1993. *Humiliation: And other essays on honor, social discomfort, and violence*. Ithica: Cornell.
Mitchell, D. T. 2009. Foreward. In *A history of disability*, ed. Henri-Jacque Stiker. Trans. W. Sayers. Ann Arbor: University of Michigan Press.
Morris, D.B. 1991. *The culture of pain*. Berkeley: University of California Press.
Onishi, N. 1999. Sierra Leone measures terror in severed limbs. *The New York Times*. http://www.nytimes.com/1999/08/22/world/sierra-leone-measures-terror-in-severed-limbs.html?pagewanted=all
Parker, R.A., and R. Brock. 2009. *Saving paradise: How Christianity traded love of this world for crucifixion and empire*. Boston: Beacon.
Rice, X. 2010. Somali schoolboy tells of how Islamists cut off his leg and hand. *The Guardian*. http://www.theguardian.com/world/2010/oct/20/somali-islamists-schoolboy-amputation-ordeal
Scary, E. 1987. *The body in pain: The making and unmaking of the world*. New York/Oxford: Oxford University Press.
Scott, J.C. 1999. *Seeing like a state*. New Haven: Yale University Press.
Shelley, B.L. 2013. *Church history in plain language*, 4th ed. Nashville: Thomas Nelson/HarperCollins Christian Publishing House.
Shepard, P. I. 2014. Oral presentation, Boston University School of Theology, April 12, 2014.
Timberg, R. 2014. *Blue-eyed boy: A memoir*. New York: Penguin.
Tombs, D. 1999. Crucifixion, state terror and sexual abuse. *Union Seminary Quarterly Review* 53(1–2): 89–109.
Torres, W.J., and R.M. Bergner. 2010. Humiliation: Its nature and consequences. *Journal of American Academy of Psychiatry Law* 38(2): 195–204.
Wengst, K. 1987. *Humanity: Solidarity of the humiliated*. Minneapolis: Fortress Press.

CHAPTER 5

The Trauma of Racism and the Distorted White Imagination

Dan Hauge

On April 4, 2015, North Charleston police officer, Michael Slager, fatally shot Walter Scott several times in the back. Initial reports from the North Charleston police department maintained that Officer Slager shot Mr. Scott after a struggle, during which the officer "feared for his life" and was thus compelled to use lethal force. Three days after the shooting occurred, however, *The New York Times* posted on their website, video footage recorded by a bystander, which unambiguously showed the officer firing his gun at Mr. Scott as he was running away, from a distance of at least 15–20 feet. The video also contradicted the officer's testimony that CPR was administered, by showing no effort to render emergency medical aid to Mr. Scott for at least several minutes. One day after the video was made public, the mayor of North Charleston announced that Officer Slager was being charged with murder.[1]

Within hours, this incident had become headline news on all major outlets, happening as it did within a broader context of increased national attention to the issues of racism and policing in the USA, regarding the use of deadly force against black people, specifically, and the systemic nature of racism in police brutality and harassment of people of color, more generally.[2] The story thus generated a multitude of updates, commentary, interviews

D. Hauge (✉)
Boston University School of Theology, Boston, MA, USA

© The Editor(s) (if applicable) and The Author(s) 2016
S.N. Arel, S. Rambo (eds.), *Post-Traumatic Public Theology*,
DOI 10.1007/978-3-319-40660-2_5

with family members of both the man who died and the man who killed him, and—of course—repeated playing and frame-by-frame analysis of the incriminating video. *Time* Magazine ran a cover story with a still image from the footage under the bold headline, "Black Lives Matter: This Time the Charge Is Murder," referencing the #BlackLivesMatter Twitter hashtag, which became a central rallying cry of the protest movement against racialized police violence and harassment.[3] In this context, Walter Scott's death confronted the national consciousness as yet one more instance of a white police officer killing an unarmed black man. However, the very clarity and thoroughness with which the video contradicted the officer's initial claims led several commentators to place this particular shooting in a separate category from other controversial killings of unarmed black men by police, which were not recorded and were therefore dependent on conflicting eyewitness testimony. Many emphasized the importance of the video evidence in providing the proof necessary for challenging the officer's initial account of events.[4] In this way, the cumulative effect of the media coverage actually acted to undermine analysis of broader patterns of systemic racism, by focusing on Scott's death as a singularly shocking incident.

The way in which this tragedy was presented, both in the compulsive replaying of the violent video footage and in the portrayal of the incident as a clear, "genuine" case of police wrongdoing, reveals much about the orientation and framework through which the dominant US culture (namely, the culture shaped primarily by white Americans of European descent) processes issues of racism, violence, and trauma. This orientation is dissected in Brittney Cooper's penetrating critique of the cultural reaction and media coverage of Walter Scott's killing:

> One day after Slager's arrest, Black folks are being treated to an endless replay of this murder on cable news. There is no collective sense that being inundated with video and imagery of these racialized murders of Black men by the police might traumatize and retraumatize Black people who have yet another body to add to a pile of bodies.[5]

The lack of sensitivity to black people's collective trauma is then compounded by the fact that the dominant culture consistently demands "evidence" of this shocking magnitude to genuinely consider the overwhelming testimony of people of color regarding the systemic nature of racism:

Police officers (of all races and genders) routinely act with excessive force and callous disregard toward Black people. But Black people's witness of racial atrocity is never believed on its own merits. Instead, white people need to be able to pull up a chair and watch the lynchings take place over and over again, to DVR them, fast forward and rewind through them, to smother Black pain and outrage and fear in an avalanche of cold, "rational" analysis. Meanwhile, minds rarely change.[6]

Cooper identifies a pernicious confluence of modes of oppression, in which the failure to understand or acknowledge the trauma inflicted by racism shapes well-meaning public efforts to address the issue—in this case, holding up an instance of police violence deemed sufficiently "obvious"—and does so in such a way that actually compounds the trauma. "In this cultural climate," Cooper concludes, "it will take, it seems, an ocean of Black bodies to convince white people that structural racism is a problem."[7] Taking people of color seriously, as they describe their experiences of institutional racism, is eschewed in favor of "objective" analysis of specific cases—a strategy which devalues the pain and anger experienced by those under oppression and actually requires further suffering and indignity on their part in order to function. Therefore, the very frame through which the dominant culture in America conceptualizes and narrates racial injustice gives rise, however unintentionally, to strategies that perpetuate the problem.

Racial Trauma, Therapeutic Frameworks, and Theological Critique

Current research in trauma suggests that physical and psychic violence visited upon people of color[8] by structural racism qualifies as one of the most prevalent and sustained sources of public trauma experienced in the USA up to the present day. Working from this premise, I want to examine how the dominant American culture, and therefore powerful institutions such as the mental health industry, operates from a core imaginative frame for understanding racism that is in fact a distortion, as it vastly underestimates and, in fact, obscures the degree of pervasive trauma that structural racism produces. Specifically, this imaginative frame conceptualizes racism as either (1) a series of oppressive policies in our nation's history that have been largely reformed or (2) a category of specific hateful actions committed against people of color out of conscious prejudice and malice.

What is left out in this conceptualization is the extent to which the current social order itself persists as an environment of anxiety and indignity for people of color. As Cooper explains in another essay, written just two weeks before the killing of Walter Scott, "We treat racism as though it is the contained characteristic of a specific species of human beings known as racists that lived in a prior era of American history, but have now nearly become extinct. We keep missing that racism is ideological and institutional, rather than merely individual."[9] The predominant imaginative framework for the nature of racism—generally past and generally isolated—actually distorts its true ideological and institutional nature and is not adequate to the task of diagnosing and working toward the healing of racism-based trauma. A myopic focus on individual incidents of "obvious" racism works against developing the most effective practices for healing from trauma and pursuing strategies for structural change that address the trauma's source. This framework needs to be cracked open, examined, and exposed for what it is: an idea which originates not from those who experience racism as an oppressive force, but from the perspective of those in the dominant social position and which, intentionally or not, serves the interests of keeping white people in that position.

The act of critiquing and re-envisioning cultural imaginative frameworks is a significant and crucial task, which the traditions of black liberation theology and critical race scholarship are particularly equipped to take on. By centering the experience of black people under racial oppression in America as their interpretive starting point, black theologians confront the white dominant culture with a prophetic indictment of racism as an evil saturated throughout our society—permeating our institutional systems, cultural habits, and the very imaginations of white Americans. Their account of racism as a socially constructed, deeply rooted sin against the image of God in humanity illustrates the extent of the trauma which it generates and challenges prevailing mental health paradigms for diagnosing such trauma. Using the same interpretive framework, critical race scholars then turn the lens of analysis back upon the dominant white culture itself in a way that challenges aspects of therapeutic practice. These scholars examine how white efforts to challenge racism—including the efforts of white mental health professionals to address racial trauma—often push toward closure, healing, and reconciliation in a way which can reflect an anxious attempt on the part of whites to escape our own deep implication in perpetuating racism as a systemic reality. Well-meaning therapeutic efforts which isolate traumatic events from the broader context of racist social structures actually reinforce a framework of thought that minimizes white complicity in those structures.

Both black theologians and critical whiteness scholars challenge any approaches to healing the wounds of racism which obscure general white complicity, or privilege the interpersonal therapeutic relationship over addressing racism as an oppressive system. By persistently centering black experience under racial oppression, they offer crucial insight which offers a corrective to the dominant mental health conceptualization of racial trauma and to the dominant white conceptualization of racism itself. These theological accounts expose the predominant narrative of racism described above as a failure of social imagination and compel white Americans to look more clearly at the society we have created and grapple with our implication in propagating and sustaining this ubiquitous trauma-generating environment.

Racism and Trauma: More than an Event

A small but growing body of psychological research on trauma has emphasized the need to include racist incidents and racial injustice in general as generative sources of trauma, often with the aim of providing mental health practitioners with better tools for serving people of color. Throughout the relevant literature, however, one repeatedly hears the concern that understanding and addressing the trauma caused by racism is inhibited by the diagnostic categories currently available in the field. In his extensive article, "Racism and Psychological and Emotional Injury," psychologist, Robert T. Carter, explains that "Currently, in scholarship and research, the terms *racism* and *discrimination* are used in a way that makes it difficult to connect particular types of acts or experiences with racism to specific mental health effects."[10] While studies of racial discrimination have addressed race-related stress and distress to an extent, Carter argues:

> Existing and traditional theories or assessment approaches provide mental health professionals and counseling psychologists with no guidance in recognizing the often subtle and indirect incidents of racism and discrimination, and provide little guidance in assessing the specific effects of race-based encounters that produce psychological distress and perhaps traumatic injury.[11]

Writing in 2007, Carter notes in particular that the criteria used by the DSM IV for diagnosing Post-Traumatic Stress Disorder (PTSD) do not provide an adequate framework for identifying racism as trauma, focusing as they do on specific events of physical threat or danger, which cause particular emotional distress in the moment. "The diagnosis is limited by the fact that the person's subjective perceptions are not part of the criteria, and the event that triggers the reactions must be physical and life threatening."[12]

It should be noted that the recently released DSM-5 has proposed some alterations to the criteria for PTSD that potentially enhance its ability to account for trauma generated by racism. Eligibility for PTSD diagnosis now includes cases in which a person is repeatedly exposed to details about a traumatic event, not personally experienced, or when one has learned about trauma experienced by a close friend or family member.[13] These adjustments could potentially incorporate racially based experiences of trauma, by expanding the criteria beyond a direct encounter of harm or threat and allowing for more indirect, collective traumatic experience (such as the response of Cooper to the repeated playing of the video of Walter Scott's death). However, the DSM-5 criteria do maintain an emphasis on specific events, recognizing "racism as trauma only when an individual meets DSM criteria for PTSD in relation to a discrete racist event, such as an assault."[14]

It is this emphasis on the violent, harmful event, rather than the cumulative effects of an oppressive cultural milieu, which constitutes the largest conceptual obstacle to the dominant mental health institutional culture, fully addressing racism as a source of trauma. This dominant conception of the nature of racism undergirds the institutional practices of the mental health profession to often harmful effect, both by generating inadequate diagnostic tools, and by opening the possibility of re-inscribing trauma in the therapeutic context. The dominant mental health system needs to better integrate the insight that while specific acts of physical and verbal racial violence certainly do produce traumatic effects, such acts exist within a wider context of pervasive manifestations of structural racism. Expressions of structural racism are myriad, but they include stereotyped attitudes among white people toward racial groups, modes of discourse or non-verbal cues which confer "outsider" status upon people of color, and, most significantly, the resultant barriers to social, political, and economic power that keep white people ensconced in the dominant societal position. All of this generates a general environment of alienation and indignity, which has its own distinct power to traumatize. Referencing the relevant literature, Carter notes that "environmental stimuli, rooted in either personal or structural aspects of racism, exert a deleterious effect on opportunities and access for Blacks or people of Color. These stimuli act as stressors, and any social barrier can produce reactions that create a physiological memory trace that could establish a recurring recall of race-related experiences."[15]

In their study on "Racist Incident-Based Trauma," Thema Bryant-Davis and Carlota Ocampo draw parallels between experiences of racist incidents with other experiences more widely acknowledged to be traumatic, such as rape or domestic violence. They explain in detail how aggregations of racist incidents which can seem "minor" to whites (often referred to as "microaggressions") take an extended toll on people of color:

> American racism today largely takes the form of daily minitraumas that result from out-group status and de facto segregation such as the following: being denied promotions, home mortgages, or business loans; being a target of a security guard; or being stopped in traffic. While any one of these events may seem racially ambiguous, a pattern of racist events forms across the life domains of minority citizens. This pervasive pattern requires ongoing coping and expenditures of psychic energy.[16]

Moreover, the very ambiguous nature of many of these encounters produces a state of uncertainty and vigilance among people of color, since "many target group members who live with racism live with the expectation that racism will be felt, yet they are unsure of when the incident will occur or of what type of racism they will face. Knowing neither what will happen nor how devastating the effects will be contributes to hyperarousal and anxiety."[17] Indeed, the recent attention on police brutality and killing of unarmed black people has the potential to create even greater levels of fear, anger, and complete distrust in the systems that are ostensibly supposed to provide order and security. In the current climate, the degree of hyperarousal and expectation of injustice and the energy required to cope and resist are heightened beyond what could be considered ambiguous or subtle.

Bryant-Davis and Ocampo's point here is crucial, because this "expectation that racism will be felt" is precisely the point at which many white therapists, and indeed, white people in general, can instinctively disregard and diminish the experiences and the testimony of people of color. The common accusation leveled by whites that a person of color is "playing the race card" when they attest to their experiences of racism is, at the root, a claim that felt experiences or expectations of racism cannot possibly have legitimate grounding in reality. How can one *prove* that a particular traffic stop, or rejected job application, or failure to catch a cab derives from racial animus or intent? In a particularly pernicious move, the very sense of vigilance or expectation of racism on the part of people of color is actually taken as evidence that the racism is likely not real. Rather than believe that such vigilance is a *learned* and rational response adopted out of necessity, for self-protection, many whites reflexively presume that the anxiety and expectation of racism is irrational, owing more to some pathology that is (inexplicably) inherent in people of color rather than a perfectly understandable response to experiencing repeated patterns of racist structures and incidents. Carter argues that placing racism-based trauma within the clinical category of PTSD actually reflects and perpetuates this problem, as it creates too much focus on diagnosing pathology exhibited by the person experiencing trauma in response to racism and "leaves out consideration of the acts or experiences of racism responsible for the stress or trauma that one has had to endure."[18]

These conceptual categories also have serious implications for the therapist-client relationship specifically. Janet E. Helms addresses the potential for therapists, particularly white therapists, to re-inscribe trauma due to a failure to either understand or believe reports of trauma due to systemic racial oppression:

> Therefore, if mental health professionals or researchers perceive the person of color as arrogant, opportunistic, or hypersensitive, based on racial stereotypes, then they may minimize the effect of the original assault; they might not view the traumatic event as racist or as a violation of the individual's personhood, and thus the victim of the incident is potentially revictimized.[19]

As mentioned above, the sometimes ambiguous or subtle nature of how structural racism operates means that particular incidents can be interpreted very differently depending on one's contextual experience, either living under oppression or as a beneficiary of it. For the person of color experiencing distress due to racism:

> The emotional reactions potentially are analogous to those that characterize PTSD but differ in that the catalysts for such reactions are the person's subjective experience of the events or incidents even if observers (e.g., clinicians, researchers) or perpetuators do not perceive the same events as traumatic.[20]

Because the subjective experience of the one experiencing racism is so central to establishing how a particular event is traumatic or not, the question of whether or not a person of color's emotional response expresses trauma resulting from a "genuinely" racist incident or rather an "irrational" response reflecting a personal pathology is fraught with potential for misdiagnosis and misinterpretation. In the therapeutic context, the stakes are incredibly high due to the degree of power differential between therapist and client, in that the mental health professional literally has the power to decide whether the person suffering pain and stress is a victim of trauma or not. The power disparity in the therapist's office, however, in many ways, is simply a microcosm of the corresponding disparity in the wider society. The ability to decide whether racist incidents are "really" racist or not lies predominantly in the hands of the oppressor class—who also happen to be those with the most to lose by acknowledging that trauma is being experienced. And while those with more social power—whether a mental health professional, or white people in general—may well have sincere intentions to help, and stop racism where it occurs—they inevitably engage in such work within the tenacious influence of a distorted imagination of racism's fundamental character, a narrative which minimizes the extent of the operation of racism within our social structures, and thus minimizes the trauma endemic to living as a person of color in that environment.

The way in which these clinical categories function is intertwined in the prevalent imaginative framework of what racism *is*. If racism is primarily a matter of individual harmful actions spurred on by conscious racial hatred, then the primary way to answer the question, "is there racism here?" is to ascertain the feelings and motivations of the white people involved in the incident, as well as to determine any other variables in the situation that might "better" explain what is happening. One prime example of this is the common impulse among media analysts and theorists to find any specific reason, *other* than racism, to account for the preponderance of police harassment and violence against black people in predominantly black neighborhoods. The predominant framework allows for the possibility that there may well be a small number of police officers (or public educators, or loan officers, or taxi drivers) who operate out of personal racial animosity, and might say or do hateful things that cause trauma. However, this frame does not generally understand the everyday social world as the site for innumerable "minitraumas" which generate, to varying degrees, psychically draining anxiety among most people of color.[21]

Racism according to the dominant frame must be understood as primarily past, and to the extent that it persists today, essentially rare. Studies which consistently demonstrate unconscious racial bias[22] generally make a very small dent in this conceptualization – most white Americans simply do not want to imagine the "normal" social order as functioning consistently to advantage whites and cause trauma for people of color, to the extent that guardedness and suspicion constitute a sensible response.

What is crucial to understand is how the conceptual categories within which racism is imagined and conceived are inadequate to express the reality experienced by those suffering the brunt of oppression, precisely because they have been created and shaped by those in the dominant position, namely, white researchers and practitioners. To counter this tendency, womanist psychoanalyst and theologian, Phillis Sheppard, emphasizes the need for the discipline of psychology itself to be "shaped by realities of black women's experience."[23] In her own work, developing the area of psychoanalysis known as self psychology, Sheppard argues that "we need to bring a critical lens to the way in which psychoanalytic theories often offer decontextual perspectives that ultimately serve to reproduce the very social impingements that black women work to resist."[24] Psychological categories, including those dealing with trauma, need to better account for the fact that for black women, "cultural contexts may reflect something that is less than a joyful response, and … are actually a danger to the development of a healthy black female self."[25] The reality of racial oppression as a ubiquitous trauma-generating context simply does not fit within a framework that understands trauma primarily in terms of discrete painful events that erupt out of an otherwise relatively secure and affirming social climate. The experiences of people of color must be allowed to redefine the conceptual frameworks through which the dominant culture addresses trauma and racial injustice in general.

The Theological Vision of Liberation: Expanding the Narrative of Trauma

The relationship of Christian churches to the reality of racism and movements toward justice is fraught with contradiction. From the very beginnings of colonialism, chattel slavery was instituted under the auspices of the church, fully bolstered by theological rationale and blessing. On the other hand, the movement to abolish slavery and the Civil Rights

Movement of more recent decades drew heavily from visions for justice, human dignity, and community drawn from Christian theological traditions. However, even where Christian communities today earnestly strive to work for racial justice, their efforts often reflect an underlying commitment to the dominant cultural narrative of racism. As an *Atlantic Monthly* article on one church's "racial reconciliation" initiative puts it, "for the most part, Southern Baptists still see the issue of race as a matter individual hearts and minds, not collective experience and collective policy."[26]

Black theologians and religious scholars live and work out of these inherent tensions and contradictions. James Cone articulates the fundamental difficulty in working within the Christian tradition when he declares, "By defining the problems of Christianity in isolation from the black condition, white theology becomes a theology of white oppressors, serving as a divine sanction from criminal acts committed against blacks."[27] There is a parallel between the problems Cone identifies in the discipline of theology and problems within the discipline of psychology and the mental health field. When the lived experiences, cultures, and central concerns of people of color are excluded from shaping conceptual frameworks, then these frameworks—and the institutions shaped by them—tend to serve those in the dominant position in society at the expense of marginalized peoples. Nevertheless, as Yolanda Pierce emphasizes, "much of African-American writing ... is still self-consciously about a process of faith and belief—a faith that leads to wholeness for an individual and for a community and the struggle between the rhetoric of 'slave-holding Christianity,' as Frederick Douglass terms it, and a Christianity that liberates mind and body."[28] While Christian theology has undoubtedly been wielded to oppress people of color throughout the centuries, black theologies constitute a call to liberation and wholeness for oppressed people, a call which forces the dominant culture to confront the nature and extent of trauma, which white-centered theology and society has produced.

A Failure of Imagination

A central, crucial insight of black theology, which grounds its critique of predominant theological models, involves its analysis of structural realities which generate dominant narratives and conceptual frameworks in the first place. The "predominant cultural understanding of racism" in the mental health system does not simply emerge sui generis within the culture—it is rather one particular iteration of a series of narratives throughout colonial history which have implicitly placed white interests and perspectives as a central vantage point, and which serve, at least in part, to ensure that the basic racialized social structure is not truly threatened.[29] Cone repeatedly makes the claim that the social structures that keep racial oppression in place are so extensive, so permeated throughout American society, that it is not even possible for white people to truly understand the nature of existence under racial oppression, including by extension the trauma which it produces. "It is unthinkable," he writes, "that oppressors could identify with oppressed existence and thus say something relevant about God's liberation of the oppressed."[30]

The reason for such a gulf in understanding, according to Cone, is that white theological formulations and questions are shaped through a particular social experience of privilege rather than oppression and, therefore, cannot possibly provide a legitimate conceptual framework for addressing that oppression:

> Unfortunately, American theologians ... including radicals and conservatives, have interpreted the gospel according to the cultural and political interests of white people. They have rarely attempted to transcend the social interests of their group by seeking an analysis of the gospel in the light of the consciousness of black people struggling for liberation. White theologians, because of their identity with the dominant power structure, are largely boxed within their own cultural history.[31]

While Cone is speaking here about theological paradigms for understanding the nature of the Christian gospel, and their efficacy in grounding movements toward liberation, the issue of white identity within the existing power structure has implications for how racism and trauma are conceived from within other structures, such as the mental health system. The experiential gap between white people and people of color with regard to social power is reflected in the gap in how the problems are framed, yet the preponderant tendency of white theologians and psychologists is to continue theorizing as if our frameworks automatically have universal application. "Invariably," Cone writes, "white theologians analyze sin *as if* blacks and whites represent one community [emphasis added],"[32] and this is a complaint rather than an affirmation of unity. Any assumption that white people—immersed as we are in our dominant social location—could properly understand racism-based trauma without allowing the experiences of people of color to deconstruct our assumptions, ideologies, and instinctive ways of being in the world is extremely dubious.

Willie James Jennings also traces the genealogy of dominant Christian conceptions of race, relationships, and oppression to the centuries of European colonial expansion, the enslavement of Africans, and modernist ideologies of race. He frames the issue in terms of what he calls a "diseased social imagination,"[33] in which human relationships to place and to each other are conceived primarily in individualistic modes, profoundly shaped by these destructive historical forces. Jennings begins with an anecdote of two white missionaries entering his backyard and approaching his mother and his 12-year-old self with an invitation to their church. He reflects on the inherent oddity of this endeavor, as his mother was already an important member of their own Baptist church, and the demeanor of the two missionaries, while ostensibly offering the promise of relationship and community, exhibited a formality and awkwardness which did not communicate real recognition of a mutual shared humanity. Jennings summarizes the encounter in this way:

> In the small space of a backyard I witnessed a Christianity familiar to most of us, enclosed in racial and cultural difference, inconsequentially related to its geography, often imaginatively detached from its surroundings of both people and spaces, but one yet bound to compelling gestures of connection, belonging, and invitation. Here, however, we were operating out of a history of relations that exposed a *distorted relational imagination* [emphasis added].[34]

Jennings does not specifically address the issue of trauma in this section, but his account of white efforts at "compelling gestures of connection" which fail to understand the lived realities of the people they are trying to connect with, parallels the efforts of the mainstream mental health industry to address the trauma and suffering of racism. Both are characterized by an inadequate understanding of how that trauma is experienced and the extent to which it is generated by the entire white-dominated social fabric.

Similarly, Jennings applies this critique of the dominant socio-cultural imagination to contemporary Christian movements toward "racial reconciliation," which emanate from the dominant narrative framework. Such efforts often focus on interpersonal relationships between whites and blacks and the "healing of old wounds" to the exclusion of addressing significant systemic change:

> The concept of reconciliation is not irretrievable, but I am convinced that before we theologians can interpret the depths of the divine action of reconciliation we must first articulate the profound deformities of Christian intimacy and identity in modernity. Until we do, all theological discussions of reconciliation will be exactly what they tend to be: (a) ideological tools for facilitating the negotiations of power; or (b) socially exhausted idealist claims masquerading as serious theological accounts. In truth, it is not at all clear that most Christians are ready to imagine reconciliation.[35]

One way of summarizing Jennings' concerns here is to say that movements toward reconciliation or healing require an accurate diagnosis of the factors which cause the suffering and oppression in the first place, and this applies equally to how psychologists address racism-based trauma. Systemic efforts to assist with the healing of such trauma must incorporate (among many other things) a more in-depth understanding of the depth of the comprehensive nature of structural racism, and a better understanding of white complicity in contributing to this trauma-generating environment. How can the problem of racial trauma be efficaciously addressed by an industry shaped largely by white perspectives, when most white people do not accurately envision the problem, and indeed perpetuate it through our very modes of being in the world—our discourse, our economic structures, and other institutional and cultural norms? How can a paradigm focused primarily on healing through interpersonal interactions work when the society shaped primarily by whites is an ongoing part of the problem?

Toward a Fuller Understanding of Racism and Trauma: An Assault on Humanity

Much of the work of black theologians can be viewed as telling a more accurate narrative of the nature of racial oppression, and thus of the nature of racism-based trauma. This better narrative is grounded in the centering of black experience, as well as the theological conviction of the sacred worth of the human person. This central theological concept is generally drawn from the teaching in Genesis 1:26–28 that God created humankind, male and female, in God's image. By centering the experiences of black people under structural racism, however, black theologies confront the dominant culture with the ugly truth that the trauma resulting from racism reflects an utter repudiation of the Genesis declaration, and a comprehensive assault on the value and dignity of the human person. Sheppard focuses on the experiences of black women, which "direct us to think about what it means to be human, a good creation, in a world heartbroken by sin that dehumanizes so many based on color, ethnicity, gender, class, religion, and sexual orientation."[36] This dehumanization is enacted through more "obvious" forms of racism such as physical violence and racial slurs, but it also emerges through a dominant cultural matrix of imaging and representing marginalized peoples that defines them as "different" from a white normative center. "This *otherness*," writes Sheppard, "is perpetuated through the daily experiences of projection and internalization of negative representations of 'black' and 'female.'"[37]

Cone also frames the history of racism in terms of failing to acknowledge the *imago dei* in all people: "The extermination of Amerindians, the persecution of Jews, the oppression of Mexican-Americans, and every other conceivable inhumanity done in the name of God and country—these brutalities can be analyzed in terms of the white American inability to recognize humanity in persons of color."[38] This inability has forced people of color throughout history to strategize ways of asserting what ought to be taken for granted—their basic worth as human beings. Referencing blues songs of the mid-twentieth century, Cone explains, "When an adult black male is treated like a child in a patriarchal society—with whites calling him 'boy,' 'uncle,' and 'nigger'—proclaiming oneself a 'man' is a bold and necessary affirmation of black resistance."[39] The necessity of affirming one's humanity in the face of societal opposition to that idea constitutes a form of trauma distinct from any suffering that white people in America have experienced.

This understanding of trauma—as a sustained, ongoing dehumanization produced over centuries and communicated both directly and subtly through social structures, narratives, images, and patterns of relating—constitutes a direct challenge to the dominant cultural narrative of racism and trauma. While that narrative continues to focus on the specific actions of racist cruelty, black theologians and religious scholars emphasize a more comprehensive social reality, dating back to the chattel slavery which fueled European colonization of the Americas. Drawing from African-American antebellum spiritual narratives, Pierce examines how they utilize the traditional theological concept of hell:

> [T]he hell presented in black spiritual narratives is not just an otherworldly domain; hell is a metaphor for the time spent on earth in daily physical and

psychological suffering. Like the spiritual narratives, many African-American texts question the existence of a tortured earthly life. Why is hell on earth reserved for some people and not for others? How does one cope with the daily realities of living in hell? Dire experience precipitates the need either to escape the earthly hell or transform it into something that can be understood and conquered.[40]

It is not necessary to draw any direct equivalence between the experience of black people under slavery and black experience today to affirm the potency of the "hell" imagery in describing the trauma that many experience under racial oppression today. Mass incarceration, inadequate economic opportunity, and the persistent "othering" of people of color merit such a conceptual frame, and, indeed, these phenomena are direct descendants of the oppression and suffering of centuries past. This fundamental characteristic of racial trauma—the denial of basic humanity generated through a social environment of insecurity and indignity—complicates and, indeed, thwarts any efforts to move too easily to healing or resolution. This impulse to move decisively toward closure—which often characterizes how the mental health industry functions and presents itself to the wider public—can function to trivialize the extent of suffering under social oppression. Pierce offers a poignant counter-proposal to this emphasis in her piece, "A Litany For Those Who Aren't Ready for Healing," written the day after a grand jury in Ferguson, Missouri, decided not to indict Officer Darren Wilson in the shooting death of Michael Brown:

> Let us not rush to the language of healing, before understanding the fullness of the injury and the depth of the wound.
> Let us not rush to offer a band-aid, when the gaping wound requires surgery and complete reconstruction…
> Let us not speak of reconciliation without speaking of reparations and restoration, or how we can repair the breach and how we can restore the loss…
> Let us not value a false peace over a righteous justice.
> Let us not be afraid to sit with the ugliness, the messiness, and the pain that is life in community together.
> Let us not offer clichés to the grieving, those hearts who are being torn asunder.[41]

Pierce's words reflect not only the pain of racial injustice itself, but the additional compounded pain caused by white efforts to move too quickly to a state of reconciliation and healing, without desiring to fully understand the depth and breadth of the suffering. The prevalent conception of what healing from racist incidents might look like is grounded not in a thorough understanding of the traumatic effects of sustained racism, but rather in a projection of what grieving and recovery look like within the context of the cultural affirmation and security that whites generally experience relative to other racial groups, due to their dominant social position. Any genuine attempts to diagnose and address racism-based trauma must heed Pierce's call for "reparations and restoration," which acknowledges the depths of the injustice.

Learning to Walk Humbly as a "White Problem"—Expanding Therapeutic Practice

As black theology challenges the diagnostic framework for trauma resulting from racism, the work of critical race scholars examines and exposes fundamental assumptions which undergird therapeutic methods and practices for addressing such trauma. Specifically, these theorists critique the tendency of white people to address racial oppression in ways that attempt to transcend our own complicity in the social structures that generate that oppression. Our very ways of being—our instinctive attitudes, our habitual ways of assuming power and agency, and our distorted imaginations about the nature of racism—all these contribute to the environment of white hegemony which is a pervasive, ongoing source of trauma. Critical whiteness scholar, George Yancy, specifically affirms that "Part of my objective is to have whites tarry with the question *How does it feel to be a problem?*"[42] It is one thing to endeavor to act and work toward anti-racist ends, but the more that white people try to establish our identities as "anti-racist" or as "allies" in ways that exculpate us from complicity in white hegemony, the more likely that relational habits endemic to whiteness will influence efforts to help. "The white self that *desires* to flee white power and privilege," Yancy writes, "is precisely the problematic white self of power and privilege, a white self whose desire may constitute a function of that very white power, privilege, and narcissism *ab initio*."[43] This unacknowledged power and privilege then shapes therapeutic practices, which can often minimize the role of systems in generating trauma and which focus on the role of the relationship between therapist and client in effecting healing. This focus implicitly centers the role of the therapist and, particularly in cases where the therapist is white, can overemphasize that role as the primary healing agent.

Predominant therapeutic frameworks can also overlook alternative sources for healing. One example of an important need which the predominant narrative of racism has no real category for is the need for people of color to organize their own spaces free of white presence and influence for the sake of safety and regeneration. Sara Ahmed relates an anecdote of a conference she attended which was predominantly white, but where one activist of color had organized a black caucus meant specifically for discussion among people of color. What occurred revealed much about the nature of structural racism and its effects on people of color:

> All in all, ten people came to the black caucus, four of whom identified themselves as white. The organizer handed out a description of the event that made explicit that it was for people of color. No one left after reading the description....We sat in a circle and took turns speaking about why we had come to the event. I was very uncomfortable. I had expected this time and space to be a chance to talk to other people of color. It felt as if the one space we had been given—to take a break from whiteness—had been taken away.[44]

Even the way Ahmed describes this scenario has the potential to cause discomfort among many white people, particularly as we have been shaped by the dominant white imaginative frame of what fighting racism ought to look like. Does it not mean coming together, rather than maintaining segregated spaces? Why would the very presence of white people be problematic, if they were present in order to learn, and to engage in partnership with people of color rather than wanting to stay apart? Indeed, as Ahmed's anecdote continues it is revealed that just these sorts of impulses were guiding the white people's actions:

> From the accounts offered, there were clearly different ways that white people had given themselves permission to turn up at a black caucus: being interested in questions of race; a sense of solidarity, alliance, and friendship; a desire to be at a workshop rather than a traditional academic session; a belief that race didn't matter because it shouldn't matter... What I learned from this occasion was the political labor that it takes to have spaces of relief from whiteness. I also realized the different ways that whiteness can be "occupying."[45]

The responses of the white conference-goers reflect the culturally prevalent understanding of racism which imagines "racial healing" as emerging primarily through individual and communal relationships of good will between whites and people of color, working toward a universal state of reconciliation in which the cruel actions and attitudes of the past can be forgiven and racial divisions overcome. Ahmed's language, in contrast, suggests a form of invasion, of white people entering space in which they were not wanted, however noble their intentions. Their presence, while not necessarily traumatizing, certainly produced discomfort and a sense of violation to the people of color assembled. According to the predominant white imagination, this response on the part of the people of color present does not make sense, unless the white people's intentions were somehow established to be menacing or insincere. However, the systemic nature of racism is such that an environment shaped by white cultural modes of being, white ignorance about systemic racism, white discursive habits, and all the collective trauma that white people *signify* together can generate an atmosphere and expectation of racism as described by Bryant-Clark above. In this context, the creation of spaces free of white presence is a simple necessity, providing a source of relational sustenance, encouragement, and active resistance in the face of structural racism and trauma.

Yancy's question—"How does it feel to be a problem?"—also implicitly challenges therapeutic frameworks which do not sufficiently interrogate the underlying motivations of white therapists or the power dynamics involved in serving clients of color. Much like Pierce, Yancy is critical of any white response to racism that involves a need to quickly find "hope" in order to alleviate the discomfort and disorientation that comes with having our imagined sense of the world challenged. "I encourage whites to dwell in spaces that make them deeply uncomfortable,"[46] he writes. "The unfinished present is where I want whites to tarry (though not permanently remain), to listen, to recognize the complexity and weight of the current existence of white racism, and to begin to think about the incredible difficulty involved in undoing it."[47] Just as the dominant white narrative imagines undoing racism as primarily a process of interpersonal forgiveness and restored relationship, it also often has an implicit need to place white people in the role of the primary hero—confessing the mistakes of the past, taking the necessary steps to make things right, and then riding off to fight the forces of racism everywhere on behalf of the unfortunate, "voiceless" oppressed. But the overwhelming testimony of people of color is that this narrative is ultimately damaging, demeaning, and perpetuating of the very racist system that it purports to be tearing down.

Ahmed, in her article "A Phenomenology of Whiteness," explains that such apparently well-meaning responses actually manifest a more insidious tendency among whites to position ourselves as part of the solution and extricate ourselves from complicity in the patterns of injustice: "To respond to accounts of institutional whiteness with the question 'what can white people do?' is not only to return to the place of the white subject, but it is also to locate agency in this place. It is also to re-position the white subject as somewhere other than implicated in the critique."[48] While in one sense, the desire to help combat racism and heal the traumatic wounds which it causes is certainly preferable to the alternative, this desire may also reflect an underlying selfish need, an assumption that the white subject's own moral status and desire to "help" is automatically efficacious in itself. Whatever solutions to the immense problem of racism may be possible, they require at the very least a more chastened and humble stance on the part of white people, one that unflinchingly faces the enormity of the trauma that the current social order causes, and that recognizes complicity without centering either crushing guilt or noble attempts to overcome that complicity.

These insights from critical whiteness scholars suggest that an emphasis on verifiable, individual recovery from trauma may function more to bolster the view of the mental health industry itself as an agent of healing, instead of encouraging sensitive attention to what those oppressed by racism and trauma actually require. A paradigm that better integrates the experiences and insights of clients and scholars of color would likely de-center the role of the individual therapist and place greater emphasis on healing in community as well as the need to tear down racist patterns and structures embedded in society, which generate the trauma in the first place. This does not mean that there is no possibility of white therapists effectively contributing to the healing process, or working for racial justice alongside people of color, but it does mean that greater priority must be placed upon people of color shaping the strategies and interpretive frameworks for such work. Their experiences under oppression must be the starting point for conceptualizing what racial justice and healing from racial trauma entail.

Cone frames white participation in the struggle for justice in terms of *conversion*, which is "a *radical* experience, and it ought not to be identified with white sympathy for blacks or with a pious feeling in white folks' hearts."⁴⁹ Rather, this conversion is characterized by "a radical change in life-style wherein one's value system is now defined by the oppressed engaged in liberation struggle."⁵⁰ Moreover, white people's full implication in structural racism, and our consequent inability to truly understand the oppression and trauma which it produces, means, according to Cone, that we need the black theological critique of white-dominated society for our own possibility of redemption:

> Christianity believes that the answer to the human condition is found in the event of Jesus Christ who meets us in our wretched condition and transforms our nonbeing into being for God. If that is true, then black confrontation with white racism is Jesus Christ meeting whites, providing them with the possibility of reconciliation.⁵¹

White people, be they people of faith or not, ultimately need to embrace a more troubling imaginative vision of our current social context that requires greater amounts of "tarrying" in quiet humility, listening to people of color instead of leading and embracing disorientation. It means a willingness to grant space, to recognize that our own complicity in causing pain means that the interpersonal therapeutic model may not, in fact, be what is most empowering and healing for oppressed people in their specific situation. It definitely means an approach to fighting racism that places the marginalized and oppressed at the center of the narrative, taking our cues from their diagnosis of the situation and their strategies for resistance and change.

In a way, focusing the issue of racism in terms of trauma or the "posttraumatic" may be somewhat misleading, as that language often implies a narrative of past devastating events that endure and shape the present. This is true of racism to an extent, as its entrenched, centuries-old history does indeed haunt our present. But racism is decidedly not past but a very present reality, however different its manifestations may be today than in previous generations. Indeed, the recent attention given to police violence against black bodies and racist policing policies should make it evident that even the manifestations have not changed so much as what the dominant culture generally believes. Framing racism in terms of an omnipresent trauma-generating matrix can hopefully serve to confront the distorted white imagination, which obfuscates the true nature of systemic racism and therefore works against analysis of it as a pervasive system. It is this distorted imagination, this false narrative that needs to be gradually healed and corrected by authentic listening to the experiences of people of color. The transformation will be toward a story less triumphant, more discomfiting, and less dependent on whites in a central starring role. But the new story will have the advantage of being closer to the truth and may therefore have more possibility for inspiring authentic change.

Notes

1. Michael S. Schmidt and Matt Apuzo (2015) "South Carolina Officer Is Charged With Murder of Walter Scott," *New York Times*, April 7, 2015, accessed April 18, 2015, http://www.nytimes.com/2015/04/08/us/south-carolina-officer-is-charged-with-murder-in-black-mans-death.html.
2. This attention was catalyzed to a large extent by the shooting of Michael Brown by Officer Darren Wilson on August 9, 2014, and the use of overwhelmingly militarized police force against protestors in subsequent days.
3. For an image of the *Time* cover, see "In the Latest Issue," *Time*, April 9, 2015, accessed April 19, 2015, http://time.com/3815038/in-the-latest-issue-30/. The #BlackLivesMatter hashtag was initially created by Alicia Garcia, Patrice Cullors, and Opal Tometi following the July 2013 acquittal of George Zimmerman in the killing of Trayvon Martin, although it became more popular in the context of the protest movement following the shooting of Michael Brown. See Heather Smith (2014) "Meet the BART-stopping woman behind 'Black Lives Matter,'" *Grist*, December 4, 2014, accessed April 19, 2015, http://grist.org/politics/stopping-a-bart-train-in-michael-browns-name/.
4. For one striking example, which includes Walter Scott's mother referring to the video as a "miracle," see Robert M. Sapolsky (2015) "The Miracle in the Walter Scott tragedy," *Los Angeles Times*, April 13, 2015, accessed April 18, 2015, http://www.latimes.com/opinion/opinion-la/la-ol-walter-scott-video-20150413-story.html.
5. Brittney Cooper (2015) "Black death has become a cultural spectacle: Why the Walter Scott tragedy won't change White America's mind," Salon, April 8, 2015, accessed April 18, 2015, http://www.salon.com/2015/04/08/black_death_has_become_a_cultural_spectacle_why_the_walter_scott_tragedy_wont_change_white_americas_mind/.

6. Cooper "Black death."
7. Cooper "Black death."
8. There is something admittedly problematic about the way in which I am making broad claims about how structural racism affects "people of color" while using the example of police violence against black bodies specifically. Various racial groups have distinct histories of experiences of oppression and resistance to racism, and it is important to recognize that distinctiveness while continuing to analyze how racism functions as an overarching context that harms all people of color in various ways. This essay will focus specifically on the experiences of black Americans and the analysis offered by black psychologists and theologians.
9. Brittney Cooper (2015) "We treat racism like it's going extinct. It's not," PBS NewsHour, March 23, 2015, accessed April 11, 2015, http://www.pbs.org/newshour/updates/treat-racism-like-going-extinct.
10. Robert T. Carter (2007) "Racism and Psychological and Emotional Injury: Recognizing and Assessing Race-Based Traumatic Stress," *The Counseling Psychologist*, vol. 35, no. 1, 15.
11. Carter, "Racism," 16.
12. Carter, "Racism," 33.
13. Monnica T. Williams (2013) "Can Racism Cause PTSD? Implications for DSM-5," *Psychology Today*, May 20, 2013, accessed April 25, 2015, https://www.psychologytoday.com/blog/culturally-speaking/201305/can-racism-cause-ptsd-implications-dsm-5.
14. Williams, "Can Racism Cause PTSD?"
15. Carter, "Racism and Psychological and Emotional Injury," 41.
16. Thema Bryant-Davis and Carlota Ocampo (2005) "Racist Incident-Based Trauma," *The Counseling Psychologist*, vol. 33, no. 4, 483.
17. Bryant-Davis and Carlota Ocampo, "Racist Incident," 492.
18. Bryant-Davis and Carlota Ocampo, "Racist Incident," 492.
19. Janet E. Helms, Guerda Nicolas, and Carlton E. Green (2012) "Racism and Ethnoviolence as Trauma: Enhancing Professional and Research Training," *Traumatology*, vol. 18, no. 1, 55.
20. Helms, et al., "Racism," 58.
21. Carter, "Racism and Psychological and Emotional Injury," 63, cites a study in which 96% of black respondents "reported an expe-

rience of racial discrimination in the past year that left them feeling stressed."

22. For a brief summary of such studies, see Sendhil Mullainathan (2015), "Racial Bias, Even When We Have Good Intentions," *New York Times*, The Upshot, January 3, 2015, accessed April 25, 2015, http://www.nytimes.com/2015/01/04/upshot/the-measuring-sticks-of-racial-bias-.html?abt=0002&abg=1.
23. Phillis Sheppard (2011) *Self, Culture, and Others in Womanist Practical Theology* (New York: Palgrave MacMillan), 122.
24. Sheppard, *Self, Culture, and Others*, 120.
25. Sheppard, *Self, Culture, and Others*, 119.
26. Emma Green (2015) "Southern Baptists and the Sin of Racism," *Atlantic Monthly*, April 7, 2015, accessed April 26, 2015, http://www.theatlantic.com/politics/archive/2015/04/southern-baptists-wrestle-with-the-sin-of-racism/389808/.
27. James Cone (1990) *A Black Theology of Liberation*, 20th anniversary edition, (Maryknoll, NY: Orbis Books), 9.
28. Yolanda Pierce (2005) *Hell Without Fires: Slavery, Christianity, and the Antebellum Spiritual Narrative* (Gainesville, FL: University Press of Florida), 3.
29. For two seminal treatments of the structural issues involved, see Charles W. Mills (1997) *The Racial Contract* (Ithaca: Cornell University Press), and Theodore W. Allen (1994) *The Invention of the White Race* (London: Verso).
30. Cone, *A Black Theology of Liberation*, 9.
31. James Cone (1997) *God of the Oppressed*, rev. ed. (Maryknoll, NY: Orbis Books), 43.
32. Cone, *A Black Theology of Liberation*, 107.
33. Willie James Jennings (2010) *The Christian Imagination: Theology and the Origins of Race* (New Haven, CT: Yale University Press), 6.
34. Jennings, *The Christian Imagination*, 4.
35. Jennings, *The Christian Imagination*, 10.
36. Sheppard, *Self, Culture, and Others*, 187.
37. Sheppard, *Self, Culture, and Others*, 135.
38. Cone, *A Black Theology of Liberation*, 7.
39. James Cone (2011) *The Cross and the Lynching Tree* (Maryknoll, NY: Orbis Books), 17.
40. Pierce, *Hell Without Fires*, 7.

41. Yolanda Pierce (2014) "A Litany for Those Who Aren't Ready for Healing," Reflections of an Afro-Christian Scholar, November 25, 2014, accessed April 26, 2015, http://yolandapierce.blogspot.com/2014/11/a-litany-for-those-who-arent-ready-for.html.
42. George Yancy (2012) *Look, a White! Philosophical Essays on Whiteness* (Philadelphia: Temple University Press), 174.
43. Yancy, *Look, a White!*, 173.
44. Sara Ahmed (2012) *On Being Included: Racism and Diversity in Institutional Life* (Durham: Duke University Press), 36–37.
45. Ahmed, *On Being Included*, 36–7.
46. Yancy, *Look, a White!*, 158.
47. Yancy, *Look, a White!*, 158.
48. Sara Ahmed (2007) "A Phenomenology of Whiteness," *Feminist Theory*, vol. 8, no. 2, 164–65.
49. Cone, *God of the Oppressed*, 221.
50. Cone, *God of the Oppressed*, 222.
51. Cone, *A Black Theology of Liberation*, 108.

Bibliography

Ahmed, S. 2007. A phenomenology of whiteness. *Feminist Theory* 8(2): 149–168.
Ahmed, S. 2012. *On being included: Racism and diversity in institutional life.* Durham: Duke University Press.
Allen, T.W. 1994. *The invention of the white race.* London: Verso.
Bryant-Davis, T., and C. Ocampo. 2005. Racist incident-based trauma. *The Counseling Psychologist* 33(4): 479–500.
Carter, R.T. 2007. Racism and psychological and emotional injury: Recognizing and assessing race-based traumatic stress. *The Counseling Psychologist* 35(1): 13–105.
Cone, J. 1990. *A black theology of liberation.* 20th Anniversary edition. Maryknoll: Orbis Books.
Cone, J. 1997. *God of the oppressed.* Rev. ed. Maryknoll: Orbis Books.
Cone, J. 2011. *The cross and the lynching tree.* Maryknoll: Orbis Books.
Cooper, B. 2015. Black death has become a cultural spectacle: Why the Walter Scott tragedy won't change White America's mind. *Salon.* http://www.salon.com/2015/04/08/black_death_has_become_a_cultural_spectacle_why_the_walter_scott_tragedy_wont_change_white_americas_mind
Cooper, B. 2015. We treat racism like it's going extinct. It's not. PBS NewsHour. http://www.pbs.org/newshour/updates/treat-racism-like-going-extinct

Green, E. 2015. Southern baptists and the sin of racism. *Atlantic Monthly.* http://www.theatlantic.com/politics/archive/2015/04/southern-baptists-wrestle-with-the-sin-of-racism/389808/

Helms, J.E., G. Nicolas, and C.E. Green. 2012. Racism and ethnoviolence as trauma: Enhancing professional and research training. *Traumatology* 18(1): 53–62.

Jennings, W.J. 2010. *The Christian imagination: Theology and the origins of race.* New Haven: Yale University Press.

Mills, C.W. 1997. *The racial contrast.* Ithaca: Cornell University Press.

Mullainathan, S. 2015. Racial bias, even when we have good intentions. *New York Times.* The Upshot. http://www.nytimes.com/2015/01/04/upshot/the-measuring-sticks-of-racial-bias-.html?abt=0002&abg=1

Pierce, Y. 2005. *Hell without fires: Slavery, Christianity, and the antebellum spiritual narrative.* Gainesville: University of Florida Press.

Pierce, Y. 2014. A litany for those who aren't ready for healing. Reflections of an Afro-Christian Scholar. http://yolandapierce.blogspot.com/2014/11/a-litany-for-those-who-arent-ready-for.html

Sapolsky, R. M. 2015. The miracle in the walter scott tragedy. *Los Angeles Times.* http://www.latimes.com/opinion/opinion-la/la-ol-walter-scott-video--20150413-story.html

Schmidt, M. S., and M. Apuzo. 2015. South Carolina officer is charged with murder of Michael Scott. *New York Times.* http://www.nytimes.com/2015/04/08/us/south-carolina-officer-is-charged-with-murder-in-black-mans-death.html

Sheppard, P. 2011. *Self, culture, and others in womanist practical theology.* New York: Palgrave MacMillan.

Smith, H. 2014. Meet the BART-stopping woman behind 'Black Lives Matter'. *Grist.* http://grist.org/politics/stopping-a-bart-train-in-michael-browns-name

Williams, M. T. 2013. Can racism cause PTSD? Implications of DSM-5. *Psychology Today.* https://www.psychologytoday.com/blog/culturally-speaking/201305/can-racism-cause-ptsd-implications-dsm-5

Yancy, G. 2012. *Look, a white! Philosophical essays on whiteness.* Philadelphia: Temple University Press.

CHAPTER 6

"Serving the Spirit of Goodness": Spiritual and Theological Responses to Affliction in the Writings of St. John of the Cross and Louise Erdrich

Wendy Farley

As long as the human species has wandered the earth, we may surmise that it has been exposed to sufferings so intense that they are impossible to metabolize in an individual or community's consciousness. Much of the profound beauty of the Bible lies in its wrestling with personal disasters, like those of Job and Tamara, and the communal turmoil of war, conquest, oppression, persecution, famine, slavery, and rape. While much classical theology focused on sin, post-Holocaust and liberation theologies have turned the spotlight on suffering. More recently, trauma theory, as this volume indicates, provides a powerful interpretative lens for Christian thought and practice.

Womanists and feminists are among those who have rightly criticized the valorization of suffering that has attended Christian theology and pastoral care.[1] But contemplative theology offers a different way of construing the relationship between suffering and Christian life. It does not perceive God as requiring suffering to appease God's anger, but it does

W. Farley (✉)
San Francisco Theological Seminary, San Anselmo, CA, USA

© The Editor(s) (if applicable) and The Author(s) 2016
S.N. Arel, S. Rambo (eds.), *Post-Traumatic Public Theology*,
DOI 10.1007/978-3-319-40660-2_6

conceive suffering as a potential pathway to God. It is not the case that because Jesus suffered, we must impose upon ourselves various sufferings in imitation of him. It is because we suffer that the Divine Mercy came to us in the form of one who suffers to manifest solidarity, not only with human nature in general, but also with the afflicted and brutalized human condition.

It would be more precise to say that Jesus's solidarity is forged through the experience of afflictive suffering. As Simone Weil argues, affliction (*malheur*) is a distinctive assault on the psyche of the human being in the face of a suffering that penetrates every aspect of personhood. "Affliction hardens and discourages us because, like a red hot iron, it stamps the soul to its very depths with the scorn, the disgust, and even the self-hatred and sense of guilt and defilement that crime logically should produce but actually does not."[2] In contrast to suffering, affliction "takes possession of the soul and marks it through and through with its own particular mark, the mark of slavery."[3] Affliction takes over the entire person "directly or indirectly, in all its parts, social, psychological, and physical."[4] Physical pain ties the mind to the body, chaining it so it cannot flee to thoughts or imagination. Social degradation destroys the sense of relationship and connection. Psychologically, one is filled with a sense of disgust and self-hatred. "If Job cries out that he is innocent in such despairing accents, it is because he himself is beginning not to believe in it; it is because his soul within him is taking the side of his friends."[5] This complicity of the mind in accepting the identity imposed by affliction is projected onto God, who "can be almost perfectly absent from us in extreme affliction."[6] The Romans imposed on Jesus the agony of suffering and the humiliating shame that affliction insists belongs to all of its victims. The solidarity of the divine with this condition reveals a power to transform even this most destructive experience.

Weil's analysis of affliction is pertinent because "in a time such as ours, where affliction is hanging over us all, help given to souls is effective only if it goes far enough to prepare them for affliction."[7] This is not a valorization of suffering but an acknowledgement that the human conditions subjects us, individually and collectively, to pain that unmakes us, body and soul, and which asserts itself with utter disregard for "just desserts." If Christianity cannot speak to this condition and it cannot tend to the wounds it produces, it is difficult to construe it as soteriologically relevant.

This essay will examine St John of the Cross's short work, "The Dark Night," together with Louise Erdrich's novel, *The Last Report of the*

Miracles at Little No Horse. Both of these provide evidence of the power of a certain kind of faith to enter into the land of affliction and return with news of the luminous goodness and compassion of divine reality. In both of these works, afflictive suffering reduces the mind and heart and religious belief to ash, and yet in this existential wasteland, an intense love is born. From a psychological point of view, healing of traumatic or afflictive suffering would enable someone to overcome their most devastating symptoms and live a functional life. When this happens, it is a great victory. But these spiritual teachers insist that we can hope for more than this. The Divine Beloved meets us precisely where absolutely everything and more than everything has been destroyed. In this meeting, direct connection with the Beloved opens the soul for a remaking in the image of compassionate love. The beauty of the world reappears. The heart's tenderness for humanity is awakened. The tasting of the intimate nearness of the Beloved becomes available. We need not seek affliction in hopes that we will share St. John's or Father Damien's religious experiences. But if we are struck by affliction, we can perceive in them witnesses that defilement is not the last word and that genuine transformation is possible.

The Heart of Darkness, the Heart of Compassion: John of the Cross

We began with the tender-hearted saint, John of the Cross, whose luminous vision of divine love is all the more striking for the difficult circumstances from which it emerged. John's life was composed of a chain of afflictive sufferings. His father married a woman disapproved by his family. When he died very young, his family abandoned his widow and children, leaving them partially homeless and devastated by poverty. John's brother starved to death. After a childhood mostly on the streets, John became a priest and a monk, joining Teresa of Avila's work to introduce more contemplative communities within the Carmelite order. The church to which he was dedicated was at the height of the Inquisition; split and divisive, its leaders were ruthless and power-hungry, its techniques violent and inhumane. Even the microcosm of his religious order was torn by these same impulses.

My next paragraph describes John's ordeal at the hands of his fellow monks. Those with sensitive constitutions may wish to skip it. I include it because this essay proposes to reflect on ways in which religious practice and theology can contribute healing specifically to the maiming caused by traumatic or afflictive suffering. John of the Cross is a guide in these reflections, not because he was one of the greatest of Christian mystics but because his theology arises from extremities of suffering that too often overthrows psyche and spirit. I am not sure we fully appreciate the significance of John's theology of divine goodness and spiritual transformation unless we have some picture of the suffering he experienced. In contrast to William of St. Thierry or other monastic contemplatives, John does not write of divine love from the relative security of an enclosed monastery. He writes in the immediate aftermath of cruelty that it is difficult to read about, let alone experience. His wisdom about the soul's transformation into love is an account of the stripping of mind and heart and spirit of everything to which they cling and by which they orient themselves. This is a spiritual dark night. But it is also a psychological dark night. His distinctive genius is to blend attention to ways in which melancholy and the path of spiritual perfection intertwine. Marguerite Porete and Meister Eckhart also describe the union with the divine that emerges from the annihilation of the soul emptied of its egocentric contents. But John of the Cross describes with great specificity the ravages of darkness on the mind. He attends to the power of divine love to heal and transform the entire person, even one severely afflicted.

During the struggle to reform the Carmelite order in sixteenth-century Spain, Teresa of Avila's younger associate, John of the Cross, was kidnapped by monks of his order and taken to their monastery. He was condemned as a rebel by those who rejected the reform movement and held in a small closet, six by ten feet. It was windowless, save for a slit in the wall high above him. First daily and later thrice weekly, he was taken to the refectory to eat while kneeling before the brothers. After dinner, he was stripped to the waist, and the monks took it in turn to lash him. This lasted as long as it took to recite Psalm 51 (the Miserere). The wounds were severe enough that it took years for them to heal. He was half-starved, denied the consolations of the sacraments, and given nothing to ameliorate the bleakness of his condition. After six months, a new warder permitted him a change of clothing and writing materials.[8] This last is significant for those who reflect on afflictive suffering, hope, and healing. It was during his time in prison that John began to compose some of the most beautiful love poems to the Divine Beloved ever penned.

After this litany of blows, one might expect someone to succumb to drink, despair, cynicism, or atheism. Many Christian theologians, who experienced violence or brutality, projected violence onto God in doctrines of double predestination, penal substitution, and the endless affliction of hell.[9] But John sank into the deepest darkness his brothers could devise and found there instead the infinite sweet tenderness of his Divine Beloved. He began his beautiful love poem, "Stanzas of the Soul," in prison. Soon afterward, he composed his commentary on the poem, "The Dark Night."

Affliction and the Spiritual Journey

John is a sixteenth century ascetic. His texts are directed to contemplative monks and nuns as they seek union with God. They include detailed accounts of how to purge the senses and soul of egocentric patterns of attachment. "The Dark Night" is one of the great jewels of contemplative theology. It also reads like a description of afflictive suffering: anxiety, the loss of meaning, forgetfulness and the inability to concentrate, alienation from community, a relentless feeling of worthlessness, the penetration of despair into an entire world-view. Though he is explicitly attending to the path toward transformation into divine love, he is aware that psychological and spiritual transformation can go hand in hand and that psychological difficulties will be healed either on the path or as a consequence of awakening.[10] His images of darkness, prison, dungeons, isolation, and despair provide a double entendre in which affliction and divine desire overlap.[11]

In the aftermath of John's sojourn in prison, he describes a psychological state resonant with Weil's analysis of affliction. But for John, not unlike Simone Weil herself, affliction can open the "marvelous dimension [in which] the soul, without leaving the place and the instant where the body to which it is united is situated can cross the totality of space and time and come into the very presence of God."[12]

As John describes the path through psychological disintegration toward union, he insists that it is crucial to remember at every point that God is always and only the Beloved. No evil or suffering comes from God, no punishment or harshness. "For the hand of God does not press down or weigh upon the soul, but only touches it; and this mercifully, for God's aim is to grant it favors and not chastise it."[13] God can only be sweet. But the soul in its anguish finds this extremely difficult to believe. This is the paradox of afflictive suffering. Ordinarily, if there is a wound or illness, we desire and accept healing ointments. But it is the distinctive power of affliction to adamantly reject the very thing it most needs. As Julian of

Norwich also argues, if we only could understand the nearness of God's love, our sufferings would be enormously diminished. But this is precisely what affliction makes impossible.[14]

John describes the soul abandoned to its own inner hell. "Everything becomes narrow for this soul: there is not room for it within itself, neither is there any room for it in heaven or on earth; and it is filled with sorrows unto darkness… This affliction the soul undergoes here is a suffering unaccompanied by the comfort of certain hope for some spiritual light and good."[15] In this comfortless prison cell of the mind, the soul's "spiritual substance" is stripped away, "absorbing it in a profound darkness- that the soul at the sight of its miseries feels that it is melting away and being undone by a cruel spiritual death; it feels as if it were swallowed by a beast and being digested in the dark belly, and it suffers an anguish comparable to Jonas's when in the belly of the whale."[16]

This his "sepulcher of dark death" is the precursor to resurrection.[17] The descent into hell plays havoc with one's mind, and the simplest tasks of concentration become impossible. "Consequently, a person can neither pray vocally nor be attentive to spiritual matters, nor still less attend to temporal affairs and business. Furthermore, he frequently experiences such absorption and profound forgetfulness in the memory that long periods pass without his knowing what he did or thought about, and he knows not what he is doing or about to do, nor can he concentrate on the task at hand, even though he desires to."[18] Such a person cannot do anything; they cannot think or believe or feel. "This is characteristic of the spirit purged and annihilated of all particular knowledge and affection: not finding satisfaction in anything nor understanding anything in particular, and remaining in its emptiness and darkness."[19]

John's affirmation that God is thoroughly good is difficult to preserve in this situation. The comforting knowledge of divine goodness has disintegrated. In the nadir of affliction, it seems that God has abandoned this soul. "He feels very vividly indeed the shadow of death, the sighs of death, and the sorrows of hell, all of which reflect the feeling of God's absence, of being chastised and rejected by Him, and of being unworthy of Him, as well as the object of His anger. The soul experiences all this and even more, for now it seems that this affliction will last forever."[20] The purgatorial suffering of affliction may last for years, and it constantly whispers that it is the only reality, suffering will never cease, and meaning will never be recovered. These despairing feelings will be intensified by the advice of unhelpful spiritual advisors, purveyors of the view that only the evil suffer, and therefore God must have rejected them.

But even if someone wise and compassionate were to offer aid, "a person in this state finds neither consolation nor support in any doctrine or spiritual director. Although his spiritual director may point out many reasons for being comforted on account of the blessings contained in these afflictions, he cannot believe this...[Such a person] resembles one who is imprisoned in a dark dungeon, bound hands and feet, and able neither to move, nor see, nor feel any favor from heaven or earth."[21] Such a person may pour out their spirit in love for God and yet "be unable to believe that God loves him. He believes that he neither has nor ever will have within himself anything deserving of God's love, but rather every reason for being abhorred not only by God but by every creature forever. He grieves to see within himself reasons for meriting rejection by Him Whom he so loves and longs for."[22]

These lost souls feel isolated, rejected by God, blameworthy, devoid of hope in any remedy. In fact, the inability to imagine a different future is intrinsic to the condition. In this anguish, former blessings are thought to be lost forever, and "this strong conviction is caused by the actual apprehension of the spirit which annihilates within itself everything contrary to this conviction."[23] If such a person could believe that these afflictions would end and that they may even carve open her or his soul for deeper communion, "he would be unconcerned about all these sufferings," but this is impossible, and the fear that God is forever lost is the soul's "greatest suffering."[24]

John is at such pains to describe the tyrannical power of the mind in these periods of psychological and spiritual stripping, because it is crucial to interpret them correctly. Many of those in this state suffer from spiritual directors who interpret these symptoms as signs of sin, and this only drives them deeper into despair. "If there is no one to understand these persons, they either turn back and abandon the road or lose courage, or at least they hinder their own progress because of their excessive diligence in threading the path of discursive meditation. They fatigue and overwork themselves, thinking that they are failing because of their negligences or sins."[25]

In our own time, symptoms similar to this are treated psychologically and, perhaps, pharmaceutically. John of the Cross adds to these a theological dimension that may speak more directly to the spiritual dimension of afflictive suffering. For John, if these symptoms are correctly interpreted, they can open onto the deepest joys of divine desire and love.

The Secret Ladder

As we have seen, in the dark night every aspect of the mind is marshaled against one. Darkness

> puts the sensory and spiritual appetites to sleep, deadens them, and deprives them of the ability to find pleasure in anything. It binds the imagination and impedes it from doing any good discursive work. It makes the memory cease, the intellect become dark and unable to understand anything, and hence it causes the will also to become arid and constrained, and all the faculties empty and useless. And over all this hands a dense and burdensome cloud which afflicts the soul and keeps it withdrawn from God.[26]

Memory, concentration, prayer, meditation, and—most of all—a sense of God's presence or love are stripped away. When every part of awareness conspires against us, and the church and its teachers have been the instrument of suffering and despair, where does one turn? But for John, this is precisely when a "secret ladder" appears.

"In this night the soul subtly escapes from its enemies, who are always opposed to its departure...it departs by a very secret ladder of which no one in the house knows."[27] Who are the enemies who strive so vigorously to block the soul's escape? One imagines in the background of John's writings the jailers themselves, the fellow monks who had imprisoned him. The "secret ladder" is the rope of sheets he had managed to weave and that—seemingly miraculously—lowered him to safety. But these enemies are also the interior ones that continually whisper defeat and despair. The mind has become an endlessly clacking propaganda machine from which there is no escape. But this is when a miraculous ladder drops into the deep dungeon of the mind. This ladder is "the living faith by which it departs in so concealed a way in order to carry out its plan successfully, and by which it cannot but escape very securely."[28]

For John, this "secret ladder" is a particular kind of faith. It cannot be faith in the sense of hope or belief; these have been blasted in this barren land. John describes well the impotence and *ennui* of affliction. He has indicated that neither memory, nor imagination, neither sense nor appetite, not self-confidence or a feeling of divine mercy remain. One's beliefs and familiar practices, one's sense of community with co-religionists have all been turned to ash. The mind is alone in the dark. For John, it is in this utter darkness when all of religion's familiar elements have been annihilated that the ladder of "living faith" appears.

We might identify two threads of meaning here. John is a spiritual director, and he is describing what happens when everything that is not God is stripped away from mind and heart. This is a work so intense and difficult, a person could never do it themselves. "Accordingly God makes the soul die to all that He is not, so that when it is stripped and flayed of its old skin, He may clothe it anew."[29] This language will be disconcerting to many readers. But St. John insists that God can do nothing harmful or even painful; it is not God, but the soul that makes this process so difficult. By way of analogy, we might think of a mother applying healing ointment to a baby's painful rash. She did not cause the rash and wishes only to heal it; but it is in the nature of rashes that they are pained by the application of soothing balm. John does not talk about suffering, whether caused by literal prisons or spiritual annihilation, as something God wishes. There is no hint that we must suffer because we are sinners. But God is able to use suffering to draw the heart into the utter nakedness of union.

As Marguerite Porete—among others—will also argue, it is only when reason and will have been reduced to nothing [*anientissement*] that the fullness of the Godhead floods awareness, displacing the structures of egocentric attachment and aversion with the divine emptiness, the flow of divine love. "Now this Soul, says Love, has her right name from the nothingness in which she rests...On account of such nothingness she has fallen into certainty of knowing nothing and into certainty of willing nothing...and she is surrounded by divine peace, without any movement in her interior and without any exterior work on her part...She has given all freely without a why for she is the lady of the Bridegroom of her youth."[30] Mental faculties become useless because no mental categories are adequate to divine reality; remaining tangled in thoughts and concepts creates a barrier against the purity of intimacy.

From a contemplative point of view, this purgation of thought and will is not penance, but the opening to the Divine Beloved. As one ascends the "secret ladder" step by step, boldness and ardor prepare the way until "love assimilates the soul to God completely because of the clear vision of God which a person possesses as soon as he reaches it...St. John [the Evangelist] says: We know that we shall be like him [1Jn3:2], not because the soul will have as much capacity as God – this is impossible – but because all that it is will become like God. Thus it will be called, and shall be, God through participation."[31] When everything has been reduced to nothing, a living faith appears from nowhere, a ladder leading out of prison and into the heart of the divine goodness.

John is evoking the sacred mystery that religion often obscures by relying so extensively on belief. In the depth of the heart, there remains a secret garden untouched and untouchable by anything other than the Beloved. Faith is the silver strand of awareness of this truth that survives, even when everything else testifies against it. It is an impossible, mysterious awareness that remains when the situation is so unbelievably awful the mind cannot take it in, when thought has collapsed, when imagination is so blasted nothing good remains to it; belief in church teachings merely mock the reality of experience, and memory is shattered into jagged fragments and haunting lacunae. So different from the fragility of relying on anything human, "living faith" is the ability to recognize the "Beloved in all things."[32] This faith, which becomes luminous even as belief and every faculty dies, is possible because "His Majesty dwells substantially in that part of the soul to which neither the angel nor the devil can gain access... the enemy cannot learn of the intimate and secret communications there between the soul and God."[33]

John's account of liberation from the dark night is all the more intriguing because of the uncanny insight with which he portrays the impossibility of hope. This paradoxical penetration of light into darkness, notwithstanding the mind's inability to entertain anything but its own debasement, derives from the anthropology he shares with other contemplatives. The human being is composed not only of thoughts, actions, emotion, and the unconscious or repressed elements of the psyche. In the dark night, all of these have become enemies. But from a contemplative point of view, there is this limitless spring within each person where the mind is constantly bathed and blessed, adored, and cherished by the Beloved. This invulnerable, sweet abyss is the source of deep psychological healing and spiritual transformation. It is the place where the human and divine are eternally united or, as Julian of Norwich puts it, "eternally knit and one-ed" with God.[34]

Any contemplative theologian will identify reconnection with this interior abyss of divine love as the heart and soul of their practice and theology. John is unusual in identifying this process of reconnection in connection to annihilating psychological and spiritual darkness. It is difficult to describe a faith that endures, when belief and hope are gone.

But there is in the deep heart of the human being a flame that will not be extinguished. St. John insists that it is precisely when all other lights have gone out when this one burns brightest. Not thought, or act, or hope, it is the raw vitality of the spirit in its unconquerable unity with divine reality.

Simone Weil also describes this persistent soul-force that remains in the very midst of affliction: the person "to whom such a thing happens has no part in the operation. He struggles like a butterfly pinned alive into an album. But through all the horror he can continue to want to love. There is nothing impossible in that, no obstacle, one might almost say no difficulty. For the greatest suffering, so long as it does not cause the soul to faint, does not touch the acquiescent part of the soul, consenting to the right direction. It is only necessary to know that love is a direction and not a state of the soul."[35] In case we were to so idealize John and believe the relief he describes is only for great saints, Simone Weil reminds us that it is possible to wish to love, and this wish alone is the thin ladder that can lead to safety, even if at any given moment we do not yet experience it.

Psychotherapists rightly, compassionately, and wisely direct psychological healing from afflictive suffering or trauma. But from a contemplative point of view, healing does not rest when one is able to survive or function. It presses on to release the spiritual greatness dwelling in every person: the deepest healing includes the enflaming capacity for love. This love flows to and from the Divine Beloved, but it includes everything beloved by the Beloved: all creatures, all beings, every enemy. This sense of a sacred unity with the divine does not belong to monks who dwell in caves for decades at a time or those whose superior holiness is the fruit of years of meditation. This intimacy with the divine is every person's heritage and birth-right. The troubled wisdom of contemplatives who have themselves undergone afflictive suffering, like John of the Cross or Simone Weil, is that suffering itself, for all of its destructive power, can be used to open the mind to the radical and sweet goodness of divine reality as present at the very heart of every human being.

St. John witnesses to a ladder that reaches from a cramped cell in the darkest dungeon to the brightness of the divine presence. John is described as someone filled not only with compassion but also with joy and equanimity. He was attentive to the physical needs of others; in the midst of his own poverty, he sought alms to pay for food for the hungry or pain-relieving medicine for the sick. He was alert to the particular suffering of sadness or depression. As a spiritual director, "he made his corrections with much gentleness and charity and always saw to it that the one being corrected would not leave his presence sad...'Who has ever seen men persuaded to love God by harshness,' he used to ask."[36] He was a loving guide to the educated and the simple, monks and nuns, lay people and street people. He had a lively sense of the beauty of the world. His poetry is steeped in this love, and he often took his fellow monks into the natural world for refreshment and contemplation. Notwithstanding his own history of suffering and his deep compassion for others, he is remembered as having a gift of making others laugh.[37]

This portrait of John is as important as his writings. He guides readers with wisdom on the path of afflictive suffering toward deep intimacy with the Beloved. This path opens onto psychological healing as well as spiritual health, in which capacities for humor, fun, beauty, mercy, compassion, and equanimity blend. Where trauma speaks to us only of despair, John's harsh descriptions of the dark night "describe these sufferings in their most intense form and thereby exclude no one. Everyone could take comfort in the thought that no matter how severe the purification, it is still the work of God's gentle hand...making room for the divine light."[38] Contemporary readers may not look on their suffering as purification, but they can nonetheless find council for working with the mind in its despair, working with a theology of divine goodness and love, and discovering contemporary contemplative practices that make this truth existentially real.

John's guidance alerts us to the secret garden within each soul and the possibility that every person can connect to it, becoming for themselves and others, a radiance in the midst of darkness.

> Oh guiding night!
> Oh night more lovely than the dawn!
> O night that has united
> The Lover and His beloved,
> Transforming the beloved in her Lover.[39]

THE INCOGNITO OF SAINTHOOD: AGNES AND FATHER DAMIEN

John of the Cross is a great saint. His testimony opens a path from misery and despair to fresh flowing joy and compassion. But when times are dark—personally or communally—it is easy, almost inevitable, that people become confused or disoriented. What is good and what is evil seem hopelessly veiled and counter-veiled. People do not act well in traumatic situations. The hero attracts our attention, but it is the ease with which individuals and communities acquiesce to anger or succumb to cruelty and violence that tend to govern history. Louise Erdrich offers us another portrait of a saint, but one whose incognito makes her difficult to recognize. Her fictional characters help us to disentangle destructive models of holiness from life-giving ones.

The narrative of *The Last Report of the Miracles of Little No Horse* is structured by the Vatican's investigation into reports of a saint at the impoverished Ojibwe reservation outpost, Little No Horse. A low-ranking priest has arrived to discern whether Sister Leopolda is a candidate for canonization. She is a saint certain corners of the church might honor: a mixed race Ojibwe, whose hatred of her people finds apt expression in cruelty to her charges in the Catholic residential school where she teaches; her extremes of asceticism shock and inspire, even if her miraculous penance was in truth, lock-jaw contracted from the barbed-wire rosary with which she strangled a man.

Her story emerges gradually, in parallel to another figure on the reservation—one that no Vatican investigator would recognize as a saint. Agnes DeWitt left a convent—her unbearably poignant piano playing proved intolerable to the sisters—and lived with Berndt Vogel, with love, tenderness and sexual adventure. She was shot by a robber disguised as a priest; Berndt dies in his effort to save her. These profound experiences of love, beauty, sexuality, and loss seem to end when a flood carries her far from home and drowns her. She awakens in the arms of a mysterious stranger feeding her soup with a bone spoon. "Kindness was there, sheer kindness, a radiance from within him fell upon her and it was like a pool of warm sunlight."[40] In the morning, the warm blanket and shelter are gone, the food, also gone but she understands she has been saved and nourished by the Divine Beloved. "As she stood there, she gradually came to understand what had happened. Through You, in You, with You. Aren't those beautiful words? For of course, she knew her husband long before she met Him, long before he rescued her, long before He fed her broth and held Agnes close to Him all through the quiet night."[41] And so, as she writes to a Pontiff who never reads her letters:

> Since then through the years, my love and wonder have steadily increased. Having met him just that once, having known Him in a man's body, how could I not love Him until death? How could I not follow Him? Be thou

like as me, were His words, and I took them literally to mean that I should attend Him as a loving woman follows her soldier into the battle of life, dressed as He is dressed, suffering the same hardships.[42]

Her battle-field is revealed to her almost immediately. As she walks away, she comes upon a priest hanging, like Judas, on a branch, drowned by the same flood that carried Agnes through death to her bridal chamber. He had been on his way to Little No Horse to be its mission priest. She buries him but takes his robes and few belongings. She cuts her hair and heads north, now as Father Damien.

During the course of his mission work, Father Damien is slowly converted to the religion of the Ojibwa's, or rather, he learns to integrate what is most beautiful about his Catholic faith into the world-view and practices of the Ojibwa. His mission is one of radical compassion, the same radiant, sheer kindness she encountered in her Beloved. This love and compassion prepares him to recognize goodness and wisdom wherever he sees it, even when it is at odds with his tradition. In his tough and unsentimental way, Father Damien simply loves people with incisive discernment, but without judgment or condescension. He appreciates creation in all of its excruciating beauty. He is the tireless advocate of the people on the reservation. When chided by a fellow priest for seeming to condone sexual indiscretions, he responds: "'I do not condone. It would be more accurate to say that I' – here he paused to choose the word – 'cherish. Yes, I cherish such occurrences, or help my charges to, at least. Unless they keep them safely in their hearts, how can they give them up...God will still be there when [they] are exhausted.'"[43] Repression and moralism do not figure into his imitation of the Beloved.

He rejects the notion that conversion to Christianity is necessary for salvation, instead recognizing the destruction the missions had caused. Asked by the same, bland priest who is investigating Leopolda why he continued if he had lost this faith, Father Damien replies:

Well, at first I didn't think we were wrong. Everything seemed clear. It was only after the epidemic that I knew. There was no doubt...' He trailed off. 'By then I was so knit into the fabric of the damage that to pull myself out would have left a great rift, a hole that would have been filled by...well, others perhaps less in sympathy...I believe even now that the void left in the passing of the sacred traditional knowledge was filled, quite simply, with the quick ease of alcohol. So I was forced by the end to clean up after the effects of what I had helped to destroy.[44]

Protecting his charges from the "mirthless trained puppets of dogma,"[45] he remains true to the dictates of great love and sacrifice, ministering to the "practical desperation of the situation...He'd put others above himself and lived in the abyss of doubt rather than forsake those in need."[46] Like St. John, Father Damien experiences the loss of faith and the overwhelming destruction of afflictive suffering, breaking like waves over and over on the reservation. In the midst of so much loss and destruction, Agnes prays "in exhausted fury, God the Father, God the Son, God the Son of a Bitch, God the Holy Ghost. But her prayers, said with increasing feverish despair, did not turn back the course of the disease."[47]

Agnes's robust compassion endures through epidemics, cultural devastation, loss of lovers and loved ones, poverty, isolation from the church and loss of faith. Devoted to her Beloved, even when left for decades in arid exile from Him, Father Damien bears the terrible anguish of the people. He recognizes the piercing beauty of a blue-bird's feather and holiness in the face of a poor woman with many children and a long string of rejected lovers. Prisoners, whores, drunks, the desperate, the mad, the starving, the lost, the recklessly mischievous, the joyously naughty all shine for Father Damien with a kind of divine light. Like Christ, he recognizes Christ in the world.

Her faith is nourished and watered by her joyous spirit of mercy. As a very aged priest, he remains in love with the sacrament of confession.

> More than any other blessed sacrament, Father Damien enjoyed hearing sins, chewing over people's stories, and then with a flourish absolving and erasing their wrongs, sending sinners out of the church clean and new. He forgave with exacting kindness, but completely, and prided himself on dispensing unusual penances that fit the sin. People appreciated his interest in their weakness as well as his sense of compassionate justice. Also, he knew when they lied to him. He read their hearts. He was a popular confessor.[48]

This compassion saves him, in the end, from the Black Dog who has haunted and cursed him throughout his ministry (if Christ can appear to her, why not the Devil?). As the wily hound sought out the vulnerable places in her heart, implying that her forgiveness "opened many a door to me, old friend," she finds sudden strength:

> It was then that Agnes was assured that her Father Damien had done the right thing in absolving all who asked forgiveness, and the realization filled her with a sudden and buoyant strength. Here it was – the reason she'd been

called here in the first place. The reason she'd endured and the reason she'd been searching for. This was why she continued to live. She shut the dog out and drew strength from the massive amounts of forgiveness her priest had dispensed in his life. She saw the forgiveness as a long, slow, soaking rain he had caused to fall on the dry hearts of sinners. Father Damien had forgiven everyone, right and left, of all mistakes and shameful sins.[49]

In all of this, the people of the reservation, those who became Catholic and those who did not, recognized "that the priest was in the service of the spirit of goodness, wherever that might evidence itself."[50] Father Damien lived for some 80 years as a woman disguised as a man—herself in disguise, he recognized Christ disguised in all the faces he saw.

Affliction and Holiness

Father Damien is important to include in the canon of great saints, not only because of her enduring love, her ever-flowing spring of mercy but because she recognized the great spirit of love in every circumstance and in every religious creed—as well as in the absence of any creed. Her faith was not in a church or doctrine, but in the Beloved and in the spirit of goodness that Christians claim is incarnate there. Amidst public lies and interior anguish, we may feel drawn to a saint like Leopolda; but we must refuse this temptation and, like Father Damien, remain lovers of the Spirit of Goodness.

We will face devastating loss, individually and communally. We cannot count on our beliefs to survive the blows of misfortune. But these two saints remind us that there is available to us a source which does not dry up and which is not contingent on our thoughts, our happiness or even our survival. John of the Cross "taught that trust in God should be so great that even if the whole world were to collapse and come to an end one should not become disturbed."[51] Father Damien teaches us that when "utter emptiness" opens, we can "trusting, yearning" put our arms "out into that emptiness. She reached as far as she could, farther than she was capable, held her hands out until at last a bigger, work-toughened hand grasped hold of hers. With a yank, she was pulled across."[52] The great abyss is the opening to undiluted Good.

However deeply despair and violence go, the great love goes deeper. It is our vocation, as humans, to send roots into this knowledge and share it with others. It is not enough—or even necessary—to believe in God. It is necessary to be pierced by the awareness of the cherishing love that flows from the divine into you, and through every dark and broken place—always, every day. Finding the practices that nourish this awareness—in and beyond what a familiar Christian denomination has offered—may enable each of us, like Father Damien, to minister to the "spirit of goodness, wherever that might evidence itself." In this, we seek healing from dark nights of the soul, of suffering, of social devastation: by not hating enemies or despising the vulnerable, by refusing despair, and by burning with radiant, compassionate joy even as night falls.

Notes

1. Many works exemplify this trend, including Marylyn McCord Adams (2006) *Christ and Horrors: The Coherence of Christology* (Cambridge: Cambridge University Press) or Emil Fackenheim (1982) *To Mend the World: Foundations of Post-Holocaust Jewish Thought* (New York: Schocken Books). The turn toward theologies of liberation (Latin American, African-American, Womanist, Feminist, Queer, Disability) have greatly enhanced this theological turn. John S. McClure and Nancy J. Ramsay (eds.) (1998) *Telling the Truth: Preaching about Sexual and Domestic Violence* (Cleveland, OH: United Church Press) is one example of this turn in practical theology.
2. Simone Weil (1951) *Waiting on God* (New York & London: Routledge), 121. See also her essay Simone Weil (1965) "The Iliad, or the Poem of Force," *Chicago Review*, vol. 18, no. 2, 5–30.
3. Weil, *Waiting on God*, 117.
4. Weil, *Waiting on God*, 119.
5. Weil, *Waiting on God*, 121.
6. Weil, *Waiting on God*, 127.
7. Weil, *Waiting on God*, 121. This point is echoed more recently in Marilyn McCord Adams (2006) *Christ and Horrors* (Oxford: University of Oxford Press) in which she argues that Christ could only be understood to be a savior if he is able to redeem us from horror: "Since this world is horror-infested, Divine love for created persons must mean that God know how and intends to be good to us even after the prima facie worst has already happened…not merely within the context of the cosmos as a whole, but within the framework of that individual horror-participant's own life," 45.

8. Much of this information is taken from the "General Introduction" to (1979) *The Collected Works of John of the Cross*, Kieran Kavanaugh (ed.) Otilio Rodriguez (trans.) (Washington, DC: Institute of Carmelite Studies, ICS Publications), though it is available in many places.
9. It is inappropriate to reduce theology to psychology. Nonetheless, material reality does find expression in knowledge and belief. Augustine suffered what we would now identify as child abuse. He wrote his brilliant and morally devastating *City of God* as he watched and waited for the Arian tribes to overwhelm northern Africa, subjecting church leaders like himself to torture and execution. Calvin also suffered an abusive childhood. His society was one torn by violent upheaval. His community in Geneva was populated by people remembering personal and collective suffering that had driven them from their home. In these contexts, it somehow made sense to envision God as eternally angry, judgmental, and in "his" way, as violent as those these theologians feared.
10. In *The Collected Works*, St. John mentions melancholy or "bad humors" several times, for example, Book I.4.3 or I.9.9.
11. He uses images that are associated with his imprisonment and with his escape at several important junctures of his text. He introduces the theme of the dark night of the spirit as a "liberation from a cramped prison cell" ("Dark Night," *The Collected Works*, II.1.1). He likens the desolation, isolation, and helplessness of the dark night to "one who is imprisoned in a dark dungeon, bound hands and feet, and able neither to move, nor see, nor feel any favor from heaven or earth" (II.7.3). Escape is likened to a secret ladder, not unlike the secretly woven ladder he contrived to make in his cell, by which one escapes at night from enemies opposed to one's departure (II.15.1).
12. St. John of the Cross, *The Collected Works*, 136.
13. St. John of the Cross, "Dark Night," *The Collected Works*, II.5.7, 337.
14. Julian of Norwich (1978) *Showings*, Edmunds College and James Walsh (trans.) (Mahwah, NJ: Paulist Press). This point is the central thesis of Julian's *Showings*, for example, "But in all this I saw truthfully that we are not dead in the sight of God, nor does He ever pass away from us, but He shall never enjoy His full bliss in us until we enjoy our full bliss in Him... [but] because of this dark-

ness, scarcely can we even believe and trust His great love and His faithful protection of us. That is why I say that we can never case mourning nor weeping," 72.
15. St. John of the Cross, *The Collected Works*, II.11.6, 354.
16. St. John of the Cross, *The Collected Works*, II.6.1, 337.
17. St. John of the Cross, *The Collected Works*, II.6.1, 337.
18. St. John of the Cross, *The Collected Works*, II. 8.1, 344
19. St. John of the Cross, *The Collected Works*, II.8.5, 345.
20. St. John of the Cross, *The Collected Works*, II.6.2, p 338.
21. St. John of the Cross, *The Collected Works*, 342.
22. St. John of the Cross, *The Collected Works*, 343.
23. St. John of the Cross, *The Collected Works*, II.7.6, 343.
24. St. John of the Cross, *The Collected Works*, II.13.5, 358.
25. St. John of the Cross, *The Collected Works*, I.10.2, 317.
26. St. John of the Cross, *The Collected Works*, II.16.1, 363.
27. St. John of the Cross, *The Collected Works*, II.15.1, 363.
28. St. John of the Cross, "Dark Night," *The Collected Works*, II.15.1
29. St. John of the Cross, "Dark Night," *The Collected Works*, II.13.11.
30. Marguerite Porete (1993) *Mirror of Simple Souls*, Ellen Babinsky (trans.) (Mahwah, NJ: Paulist Press), Chapter 81.
31. St. John of the Cross, "Dark Night," *The Collected Works*, II.20.5, 377.
32. St. John of the Cross, "Dark Night," *The Collected Works*, II.19.2. This point echoes Marguerite Porete: "But those are in good and profitable times who adore God not only in temples and monasteries, but adore Him in all places through union with the divine will…I find Him everywhere, says this Souls, and He is there. He is One Deity, One sole God in Three persons, and this God is everywhere. There, I find him," *Mirror of Simple Souls*, Ch. 69.
33. St. John of the Cross, "Dark Night," *The Collected Works*, II:23, 385.
34. "And when He wished, by full accord of all the Trinity, He created us all at once, and in our creation He knit us and one-ed us to Himself. By this one-ing we are kept as pure and as noble as we were created." Julian of Norwich, *Showings*, 58.
35. Weil, "The Love of God and Affliction," 135.
36. Kavanaugh, "General Introduction," 28.
37. Kavanaugh, "General Introduction," 28.
38. Kavanaugh, "General Introduction," 29.

39. St. John of the Cross, "Stanzas of the Soul," *Collected Works*, I.5, 296 (with the Spanish, 711).
40. Louise Erdrich (2001) *The Last Report of the Miracles at Little No Horse* (New York, NY: Harpercollins Publications), 42.
41. Erdrich, *The Last Report*, 43.
42. Erdrich, *The Last Report*, 43–44.
43. Erdrich, *The Last Report*, 134.
44. Erdrich, *The Last Report*, 239.
45. Erdrich, *The Last Report*, 276.
46. Erdrich, *The Last Report*, 239.
47. Erdrich, *The Last Report*, 121.
48. Erdrich, *The Last Report*, 5.
49. Erdrich, *The Last Report*, 309.
50. Erdrich, *The Last Report*, 276.
51. Kavanaugh, "General Introduction," 32.
52. Erdrich, *The Last Report*, 350.

Bibliography

Adams, M.M. 2006. *Christ and horrors: The coherence of Christology*. Cambridge: Cambridge University Press.

Erdrich, E. 2001. *The last report on the miracle at little no horse*. New York: Harper Perennial.

Fackenheim, E. 1982. *To mend the world: Foundations of post-holocaust Jewish thought*. New York: Schocken Books.

Julian of Norwich. 1978. *Showings*. Trans. E. College, and J. Walsh. Mahwah: Paulist Press.

McClure, J.S., and N.J. Ramsay (eds.). 1998. *Telling the truth: Preaching about sexual and domestic violence*. Cleveland: United Church Press.

Porete, M. 1993. *The mirror of simple souls*. Trans. E. Babinsky. New York: Paulist Press.

St. John of the Cross. 1991. *The collected work of St. John of the cross*, ed. K. Kavanaugh. Trans. O. Rodriguez. (Washington, DC: ICS Publications).

Weil, S. 1951. *Waiting on god*. New York/London: Routledge.

Weil, S. 1965. The *Iliad*, or the poem of force. *Chicago Review* 18(2): 5–30.

CHAPTER 7

Elegy for a Lost World

Mark Wallace

DESERT BOUQUET

During my childhood in Southern California, I slept under a window that opened out to a series of foothills covered with sagebrush. There is much I remember about those foothills and the wider natural world I encountered there—the scamper of road runners, the howl of coyotes, the red flash of prickly pears amidst the cactus. But what I remember most is the bittersweet fragrance of sagebrush wafting through my window at night, especially after a rare rainstorm.

Sagebrush is a woody, scrubby plant found throughout much of the Western USA, among other similar Mediterranean climates. It grows wild in arid grasslands and desert regions. It is cultivated for its ornamental flowers as well as its medicinal and herbal properties. I use sage in tea and in recipes, such as cornbread stuffing at Thanksgiving and paired with lemon in roasted chicken. It has long been considered one of the principal herbs for general cooking. Paul Simon and Art Garfunkel's 1966 ballad "Scarborough Fair" is a remake of an ages-old British melody that assigns special culinary status to sage as one of the four primary herbal spices used in traditional English recipes. In "Scarborough Fair," sage is highlighted

M. Wallace (✉)
Swarthmore College, Swarthmore, PA, USA

in a constant refrain that winds through the ballad: "Are you going to Scarborough Fair? / Parsley, sage, rosemary, and thyme."

Akin to its reoccurring role in the haunting chorus of the Simon and Garfunkel song, the sage of my youth was everywhere in the warm drafts and shifting winds of the California chaparral. Its peppery, pungent scent signaled the vitality of a robust ecosystem of Spanish oaks, horned toads and rattlesnakes, and wild Manzanita, poppy and lilac flowers. Not everyone likes the penetrating fragrance of sage—its strong smell can seem bitter to some—but I experienced sage as a distinctive mountain perfume that defined my boyhood foothills as a wild and untrammeled place. This was a place that had not yet been colonized by the shopping malls and freeway grids that characterized the rest of urbanized California. In my early life, my senses were quickened by a scrubland aromatherapy through my daily immersion in an atmospheric bath of fresh, alive, sweet-smelling sage. At night under my bedroom window, I enjoyed how the day's stress would drain from my body, and I felt relaxed as I took in the scented breezes coursing through my room.

My father still lives in the house where I was raised—a house that he and his friends built—but when I return to my early home, I can no longer take in great drafts of sagebrush-scented air. In childhood, the air was aromatically textured and nuanced, depending on which way the winds blew and whether there had been rain or fog that day or the day before. But now, regardless of the passing weather, the air is odorless and thin; it doesn't carry the sagey, zesty smell of wild plants like it used to. While sage plant is still abundant in the West, its habitat is increasingly threatened by overdevelopment and the widespread use of herbicides. Sage plants are shallow-rooted and easy to disturb. Once impacted, they struggle to re-establish themselves in soil that can no longer support fibrous root systems that lie close to the surface of the ground. I've heard that the sense of smell forms memories early in life that are the strongest recollections available to human beings. Many years later, my recall of the spicy fragrance of sage is still sharp and distinct. My memory is of a fragrant plant whose spiritual, medicinal and gustatory properties are woven together in a sensual experience of deep pleasure and reassuring comfort and joy. And my sadness is that the daily delight I experienced drinking in the pungent aroma of this healing herb has been largely attenuated, if not wiped out altogether, by the expansive sprawl of the California Southland.

Suffering Earth

My early immersion in pleasant-smelling sage taught me that the Earth is an all-encompassing gift with the potential to heal and restore all of its inhabitants.[1] My boyhood sage baths showed me that the world is an enchanted place, where natural forces can provide daily pleasure and renewal. The Genesis creation story's hymn-like refrain, "And God saw everything that God had made, and behold, it was very good,"[2] signals the buoyant grace and beauty within the natural world.[3] But this everyday splendor, in desert sage and across the planet, is under siege as human communities continue to lay waste to the goodness and bounty of creation.

Why are desert sage ecosystems, and most other planet-wide ecosystems, in danger of collapse in the current setting? Recent studies show that anthropogenic climate change is the primary driver of species loss worldwide today.[4] Human-caused global warming—the trapping in Earth's atmosphere of fossil fuel gases such as CO_2 and methane from car and power plant emissions—is propelling air and water temperatures to rise catastrophically, as much as three to ten degrees Fahrenheit this century. Climate change will produce melting Arctic ice and a corresponding rise in sea levels. Sea levels have already risen more than eight inches since the end of the industrial age and are predicted to continue to rise by three feet or more by the close of the twenty-first century. These changes are already generating a widespread loss of biodiversity and will continue to cause terrible flooding in low-level areas from Bangladesh to the Eastern Seaboard of the USA; cause the world's oceans to become more acidic and thereby lethal to coral reefs and fish stocks so that at this time, 90% of all large fish are gone from the oceans; and in general, a massive die-off of species similar to the last mass extinction event over 65 million years ago when the great dinosaurs were wiped out. Today's global wipe-out of plant and animal populations—what many scientists are calling the "Sixth Great Extinction"—is a biocidal runaway train, with biologists conservatively estimating that 30,000 plant and animal species are now driven to extinction every year—including, perhaps some day, the sweet-smelling sage fields that populated post-war Southern California.[5]

Our dependence on fossil fuels, then, is the source of Earth's suffering as Earth becomes hotter and waves of species-level extinctions are the result. This growing cataclysm stems from our shifting disposition toward Earth as a supply of energy and materials to be exploited rather than as a gift to be loved and protected accordingly. Earth, to use Martin

Heidegger's formulation, has become an extensive "standing-reserve" of raw power for modern industrial development.[6] Consider the "root metaphors" we use to describe the natural world.[7] Earth is no longer a "living being" or "feeling organism" who can undergo traumatic suffering – suffering that we could refer to as *ecocidal* insofar as we do harm, even lasting harm to our life-giving home. On the contrary, Earth is now a "resource," a commodity to be bought and sold in the financial marketplace, like toothpaste or pork futures. With this change of disposition, Earth has become a dead zone, an inert deposit of energy to fuel technological growth at all costs. The goal of my essay, therefore, is to *re-imagine* Earth as an animate being, a living soul, who feels joy and suffers sorrow and loss just as we do, and to empower our desire to *heal* Earth's suffering by re-kindling a religious vision of our biotic and abiotic kinfolk as revered members of a unified, blessed family. To paraphrase Stephen Jay Gould, once we forge an emotional bond between ourselves and nature—once we develop a sense of felt spiritual kinship between ourselves and all other beings as sacred members of a common household—then we will have the vision and energy to enter the public fray and win the battle to save our own and other species as well.[8]

To say that "Earth suffers," however, may seem to many of us to be an odd phrase. Many inhabitants of the natural order—rocks, bodies of water, trees and other plants—strike us a non-sentient and inanimate "matter." But from an ecosystems perspective, all members of the lifeweb are self-organizing beings with their own moods and traits. As well, all things possess value all their own as vital contributors to biological diversity. For example, large rocky landscapes, whose dispositional affects are rooted and stolid, support thickets of trees and shrubs which are necessary for the photosynthetic food chains that make all terrestrial life possible.[9] Scientifically speaking, this broader affirmation of the intrinsic value of all of Earth's residents has been advanced by paleontologist, James Lovelock, who regards the planet as a "superorganism," in which all of its biological, physical, and chemical components are "alive" and necessary for the life-supporting regulation of the atmosphere and climate.[10] Historically speaking, Christian theology has focused on *human* suffering in light of Jesus' saving death on behalf of humankind, but in this essay, I want to expand this horizon of concern to include the *more-than-human others* who also suffer, and often at the hands of their human oppressors. To cause these different beings to suffer is to do harm to the vital organisms and processes that make our common planetary system of life both generative and sustainable.

Religiously speaking, the model of Earth as an inherently valuable living organism with the capacity to feel and suffer is a green thread that ties together the biblical texts in the Jewish and Christian traditions.[11] An early example of this perspective is in the Book of Genesis, where God references Earth's innate agency and emotional life in response to Cain's murder of his brother Abel. In Genesis, Cain takes Abel to a nearby field in order to kill him, after which the Lord queries him:

> Then the Lord said to Cain, "Where is your brother Abel?" He said, "I do not know; am I my brother's keeper?" And the Lord said, "What have you done? Listen; your *brother's blood is crying out to me from the ground*, which has *opened its mouth to receive your brother's blood* from your hand. When you till the ground, *it will no longer yield to you its strength*; you will be a fugitive and a wanderer on the earth."[12]

Here Earth is not dead matter, an inanimate object with no capacity for feeling and response, but a vital living being that experiences the catastrophic loss of Abel's death. Aggrieved and bereaved, Earth weeps or shouts at the terrible harm Cain has done to his brother and, it seems, to the land as well. In this account, human violence causes Earth to suffer. Earth—a dynamic organism with dispositions and moods—is understood as profoundly agential with its own interior emotional life and innermost capacity for abjection and despair. Note the highly active and affective verbal constructions used to communicate Earth's heartfelt agony in this passage: the ground *cries out* over Abel's murder; the ground *opens its mouth* and *swallows* Abel's blood on the occasion of his death; and the ground *refuses* to assist Cain in the future ("it will no longer yield to you its strength")[13] as he tills it for purposes of food production.

The theme of the suffering Earth continues in other biblical texts as well. Throughout the writings of the Prophets, human sin causes the land to become polluted, desolate, waste and void. Sin causes time to run backwards and for Earth to return to the formlessness that characterized it at the dawn of creation in the opening verses of Genesis: "In the beginning God created the heavens and the Earth, and the Earth was formless and void."[14] In the Book of Jeremiah, the prophet's preachments against God's people—a people who have disobeyed God and now have been taken captive by their Babylonian enemies—emphasizes that Earth itself will mourn and suffer the agony God's people are suffering as well.

> I looked on the earth, and lo, it was waste and void; and to the heavens, and they had no light... For thus says the Lord: The whole land shall be a desolation, yet I will not make a full end. Because of this the earth shall mourn and the heavens above grow black; for I have spoken, I have purposed. I have not relented nor will I turn back (Jeremiah 4:21, 27–28).

The Book of Hosea makes the same point. Because people have turned away from God's ways, the land will feel pain. And the trauma is spelled out also in relation to all of the non-human animals who will languish and, in some instances, perish because humankind has abandoned the right way to live.

> Hear the word of the Lord, O people of Israel; for the Lord has an indictment against the inhabitants of the land.... Therefore, the land mourns, and all who live in it languish; together with the wild animals and the birds of the air, even the fish of the sea are perishing (Hosea 4:1, 3).

Similarly, in the Christian scriptures, Paul writes that the whole Earth groans in pain in anticipation of a final salvation. Drawing an analogy to a woman in labor, the created order of things, including, as Paul says, human beings as well, is in a protracted gestational state where painful groaning is an everyday reality. Literally, Paul writes that creation is Mother Earth who yearns to get beyond the pain of childbirth to a time of deliverance from suffering.

> I consider that the sufferings of this present time are not worth comparing with the glory about to be revealed to us. For the creation waits . . .in hope that [it] itself will be set from its bondage to decay and will obtain the freedom of the glory of the children of God. We know that the whole creation has been groaning in labor pains until now; and not only the creation, but we ourselves, who have the first fruits of the Spirit, groan inwardly while we wait for adoption, the redemption of our bodies (Romans 8:18–19a, 21–23).

What exactly the future redemption of the natural world, or the redemption of bodies, will consist of is not entirely clear in Paul. But that the created order of things, moaning and crying in pain over its present state of bondage is an echo of the weeping land in Genesis, and the mournful ground in the Prophets, seems abundantly clear. Earth in the Bible, like Lovelock's "Gaia," is a living, feeling being who suffers injury and despair from the depredation brought about by human malice.

In the present, one path toward healing the suffering ecosystems that make up our planetary home is by re-imagining these systems as *sacred communities of living, feeling beings*.[15] The first step, then, toward healing damaged ecosystems is to recognize them as vital life-forms capable of experiencing loss and trauma. Not only are these inherently worthwhile ecosystems alive with emotion and purpose because they have the capacity to experience depredation in a manner similar to how human beings experience pain. Moreover, these ecosystems comprise sacred kinship relationships wherein all beings—sentient and non-sentient, biotic and abiotic, organic and non-organic—share a common life together as equal and vital co-participants in the web of life.[16]

The biblical heritage consistently portrays the created order as saturated with God's presence and power. While many classical Christian thinkers avoided ascribing religious value to natural places and living things, and restricted terms such as *sacred, holy,* and *blessed* to God alone, the Bible, nevertheless, is suffused with images of sacred nature—God formed Adam and Eve from the dust of the ground; called to Moses through a burning bush; spoke through Balaam's donkey; arrested Job's attention in a whirlwind; used a great whale to send Jonah a message; and appeared alternately as a man, a lamb, and a dove throughout the New Testament—that challenge the erstwhile assumption that God is an invisible, heavenly being not of the same essence as plants, animals, rivers and mountains.

In the Christian scriptures, there are two primary constellations of sacred nature images: the stories about Jesus incarnating Godself in human flesh, rendering all flesh a source of sensual delight, on the one hand, and the accounts of the Holy Spirit coming down from heaven as a dovey pigeon at the occasion of Jesus' baptism, on the other.[17] Along with other instances of nature religion in scripture, these narratives of human divinity (Jesus) and divine animality (the Spirit) teach us to love and care for all things, because now we know that all things—humans, animals, and presumably everything else—are indwelled by God. If God became human flesh in Jesus, and animal flesh in the Spirit, is not all flesh—flesh that runs and crawls and flies and swims across and in Earth's land and sky and air—a bearer of God's presence? And if this is so, should not all things be venerated as holy and good, and thereby loved and protected accordingly?[18]

Mud and Spit

In my life, a sustaining force in forging this spiritual bond between myself and other life-forms is the Bible's stories about sacred Earth. My memory of aromatic sagebrush—living in the lap of creation's luxuriant pleasures—is for me a clue to understanding the medicinal powers of the natural world as set forth in one particular story about earth and flesh in the Gospel of John, namely, the story of Jesus' healing of the blind man with a poultice he makes out of the soil and his own spittle. Let me recount the highlights of the narrative:

> As [Jesus] passed by, he saw a man blind from his birth. And his disciples asked him, "Rabbi, who sinned, this man or his parents, that he was born blind?" Jesus answered, "It was not that this man sinned, or his parents, but that the works of God might be made manifest in him"... As he said this, he spat on the ground and made clay of the spittle and anointed the man's eyes with the clay, saying to him, "Go, wash in the pool of Siloam" (which means Sent). So he went and washed and came back seeing. The neighbors and those who had seen him before as a beggar said, "Is not this the man who used to sit and beg?" Some said, "It is he"; others said, "No, but he is like him." He said, "I am the man." They said to him, "Then how were your eyes opened?" He answered, "The man called Jesus made clay and anointed my eyes and said to me, 'Go to Siloam and wash'; so I went and washed and received my sight" (John 9:1, 6–11).

What arrests my attention in this story is Jesus' sacred mudpie ritual. Here Jesus actualizes God's power by mixing his saliva with the soil near the pool of Siloam, on the outskirts of Jerusalem, to form a clay-like compound that he then pastes onto the eyes of the blind man. Spitting on the ground, Jesus creates a wet salve that he applies to the man's face and then tells the blind man to wash his face in the Siloam pool, wherein the man experiences full sightedness for the first time in his life. Inhaling the calming aroma of wild sage as a child in California taught me that the ground itself is a quickening source of curative renewal and refreshment. I believe this exact dynamic is at play in Jesus' reliance on Jerusalem's ancient clay, now combined with his spit, to heal the sightless man in John's story. Whether as aromatic sage or a moist, earthy compress, sacred is the gift of the ground we inhabit, and its vital energies are essential to all beings' health and well-being.

Land is sacred in this story because it is the healing medium Jesus uses to perform his miracle. But also flesh—and, in this instance, one particular fleshly discharge, namely, spit—is singled out for its sacred, restorative capacities. But as readers of John 9, today, are we comfortable with Jesus going down into the dirt with his own spittle to heal the blind man? Or are we put on edge with the use of bodily fluids in this story of the blind man? On the one hand, we maintain that we are at ease with our bodies and their natural products. After Darwin, Freud, modern biology, and mass sex education, we think of ourselves as scientifically self-aware and accepting of our core bodily functions. As well, we say that we regard the many emissions that flow out of our everyday physical activities—blood, piss, feces, sweat, ejaculate, vaginal fluids, tears, and yes, saliva—to be the natural secretions of embodied, organic beings like ourselves. Our contention is that all of this is normal and healthy.

On the other hand, however, while we *say* we embrace our bodily excretions, our actual vocabulary for the body *betrays* us as feeling otherwise. Take the example of so-called sanitary napkins. Menstrual blood is a potent symbol of a woman's biological capacity, a marker of reproductive health and well-being, a sign that a girl or a woman, like the creator itself, is progenetrix, a Goddess. But contemporary societies have denigrated menstruation as a dirty, unclean activity that needs to be "sanitized." We claim to be enlightened about normal, healthy bodily functions, but our everyday language about hygiene and cleanliness belies such claims. The word sanitary is from the Latin *sanitas*, which means health. Etymologically, terms today that have their roots in *sanitas* stand for making something healthy or clean. These terms include, for example, *to sanitize*, the sterilization of an object free from filth and contamination; *sanitation*, the proper disposal of sewage and solid waste; and *sanitarium*, a hospital setting for the treatment of chronic disease. Filth, contamination, sewage, waste, disease—sanitary napkins function to "sanitize" female bodies, to protect girls and women from the "unhygienic" bleeding of their own bodies, sending the message that this outward sign of life itself is unclean and unsanitary.[19]

Anthropologist Mary Douglas writes that all cultures, including our own, are comfortable with the body when the body stays intact, its orifices and margins are secure, and nothing is seeping from the body or traversing the boundaries between the body and the outside world. We regard bodies as healthy and clean when they maintain their integrity and do not leak or discharge fluids, but when bodies break down and ooze at their margins, they are considered unhealthy and dirty. Douglas writes that

All margins are dangerous. If they are pulled this way or that the shape of fundamental experience is altered. Any structure of ideas is vulnerable at its margins. We should expect the orifices of the body to symbolize its especially vulnerable points. Matter issuing from them is marginal stuff of the most obvious kind. Spittle, blood, milk, urine, feces or tears by simply issuing forth have traversed the boundary of the body. So also have bodily pairings, skin, nail, hair clippings and sweat. The mistake is to treat bodily margins in isolation from all other margins.[20]

Bodily margins and openings are dangerous, Douglas argues, because they stand for a body out-of-control, a body that is pockmarked with orifices small and large that at any moment can crack open and threaten not only bodily integrity but the order of society as well. "Bodily margins," she writes, should not be seen "in isolation from all other margins,"[21] meaning that the body, like society as a whole, is healthy when intact and dangerous when its margins break down. Well-behaved, structurally whole bodies are a promise of physical and cultural cohesion as well. The breakdown of intact bodies is a dangerous sign of destabilizing forces outside of one's control that threaten both one's personal well-being along with the sense of unity and completeness social groups rely upon for ongoing stability. For this reason, Douglas writes, different societies have different rules for what constitutes dangerous, or in religious terms, polluting behavior. Anything that threatens the integrity of the body is experienced as hazardous to self and others, but social groups differ as to the particular events that cause social pollution and chaos. Douglas continues,

> In some, menstrual pollution is feared as a lethal danger; in others not at all. In some, death pollution is a daily preoccupation; in others not at all. In some, excreta are dangerous, in others it is only a joke. In India, cooked food and saliva are pollution-prone, but Bushmen collect melon seeds from their mouths for later roasting and eating.[22]

It is not clear, then, why particular activities—menstrual blood, in one case, or saliva in another—represent occasions for polluting behavior. Philosopher Julia Kristeva, commenting on Douglas's work, writes that there is nothing inherently dangerous or polluting about a particular boundary-violating discharge or event. She writes, "Taking a closer look at defilement, as Mary Douglas has done, one ascertains [that] filth is not a quality in itself, but it applies only to what relates to a *boundary*...The potency of pollution is therefore not an inherent one; it is proportional to the potency of the prohibition that founds it."[23] Instances, then, of chaos or defilement only have meaning as they relate to other elements within the symbolic system of "purity" and "filth" in a particular culture. Filth or pollution or defilement are what they are because of how these events relate to other features of a social system that are regarded as symbolically clean or pure.

Now returning to the topic of Jesus' mashing together dirt and spittle, we can see how likely it was that his mudpie behavior was offensive to his society, and how offensive it is in our own society as well. Jesus took two of the primary defiling elements within his and our own symbolic order—namely, mud and spit—and mixed them together to form, at least for some people, a "polluting" or "unsanitary" potion to heal the blind man in John's story. Note that I am not saying that Jesus performed a formal act of ritual impurity in terms of the Jewish purity laws of his time. This may be the case, but my interest here is on the ancient and contemporary experience of repugnance Jesus' action likely produced—and continues to produce. If Douglas and Kristeva are correct that bodily discharges are very often experienced as disgusting and degrading, then Jesus' spitting into the dirt most likely functioned then, and continues to function now, to shock and disrupt his audience. Kristeva writes that many bodily discharges are instances of what she calls "abjection." Abjection, she says, is

> [l]oathing an item of food, a piece of filth, waste, or dung. The spasms and vomiting that protect me. The repugnance, the retching that thrusts me to the side and turns me away from defilement, sewage, muck... I experience a gagging sensation and, still farther down, spasms in the stomach, the belly; and all the organs shrivel up the body, provoke tears and bile, increase heartbeat, cause forehead and hands to perspire.[24]

Is Jesus' dirt-and-spit miracle, therefore, a gagging instance of what Kristeva calls abjection? Could spitting onto the ground so much so that he could form a paste from the surplus of his spittle cause his audience to wretch? Did he bend down and spew a sizeable amount of foamy, phlegmy spit into the dirt to create his strange medicine? Was it merely spit he spewed onto the ground, or did he cough up something deeper, something more bilious and nauseating, something more like *sputum* than spit, with the aim of making a thick, wet plaster *out of the dirt*, no less, that he could then mold over the man's unseeing eyes? Is Jesus' healing action, ironically, an exercise in abjection?

We know Jesus often used more conventional means to perform healings. In Matthew 8, for example, he simply touches a man with leprosy and the man is healed; later, in the same chapter, he heals a centurion's servant by direct word without any physical touching or intervention. *But in John's story Jesus seems to want to drive home the point that the abject is holy.* He seems to want to say:

> You regard the earth and the body with disgust; you experience the soil as grimy and your body, and its normal functions and emissions, with anxiety, even loathing; but I want to show you that what you fear has been made by God and declared by God to be wholesome and blessed; nothing that is in the soil, or that your body emits, is filthy or degrading; indeed, the spit from my mouth, just like your own spit, and the dirt that I walk on, just like the dirt under your feet – all such things are sacred and beautiful. My message to you is to love, even worship, the ground you walk on, and your bodies given to you by God, and all that flows out of your bodies, because all that God has made, no matter how loathsome and unclean it may seem to you, is holy and good and worthy of your highest esteem and most heartfelt enjoyment – including, and especially, dirt and spit.

In this regard, let us not miss a final clue to the inestimably sacred value Jesus assigns to everyday embodied life—including soil and bodily emissions. Note the important word choices John uses to describe Jesus' action in applying to the man's eyes the wet earthen dressing he makes from saliva and clay. Here my emphasis throughout this essay about sacred earth—or to be more precise, sacred earth mixed with holy spit—emerges as the story's *leitmotif*. In v.6, Jesus "spat (*ptuo* in Greek, which may be an onomatopoeic use of a word sounding like its referent, perhaps the forerunner of *ptooey*, the English word for spitting) on the ground and made clay (*pelos*, which means clay or mud) out of the spittle, and put on (*epithesis*) the man's eyes the clay." Similarly, in v.11 we read, "He replied, 'The man they call Jesus made some mud and anointed (*epichrio*) my eyes. He told me to go to Siloam and wash. So I went and washed, and now I can see.'" What is sometimes missed in the English translation of this passage—but is obvious in the Greek of the original text—is the *liturgical* force of the verbs used to describe Jesus' smearing the man's eyes with saliva and dirt. Both of the verbs *epithesis* (v.6) and *epichrio* (v.11) that are used to describe how Jesus applied the muddy salve to the man's face denote a sacred ceremonial activity, such as the laying on of hands in an ordination ritual or the rubbing on of oil in a baptismal or healing service.

The verbs, *epithesis* and *epichrio,* can mean simply to put on, or to apply something, but throughout the New Testament, and in other ancient religious literature as well, the verbs more often stand for the sacred act of anointing somebody with transformative power by means of one's hands and/or through the application of natural elements such as water or oil.

The point of the passage is that Jesus' spit—now mixed into the soil to form a mucky paste—is the bodily discharge he uses to *anoint* the man's eyes and heal the man of his blindness. Like wine and bread in the Christian Eucharist, here saliva and earth are the holy elements Jesus uses to channel God's grace to his followers. Like the Eucharistic blood and body, here spit and dirt are the sacramental means of God's power and love. It is for this reason that Jesus says the man's blindness is not a result of sin, but the means by which God's work will be manifested (v.3). Ironically, then, spit is not mere spit, but the healing elixir Jesus uses to demonstrate divine power. Likewise, dirt is not simply dirt, but the life-giving soil Jesus further enlivens with his spit for healing and renewal. What we reject as dirty and unhygienic—as polluting and abject—God loves and persuades us to love. John 9, then, is a story of palpable holiness in which the sacred elements of dirt and spit—like bread and wine in traditional Christian liturgy—are God's holy means of grace and healing.[25] The story of the blind man in John 9 teaches us, most significantly, to worship as holy ground the dirt we walk on, and to regard our bodies and other's bodies—and all of the sticky, colorful, and aromatic fluids and secretions therein—with reverence and awe and love.

Sagebrush Again

My goal in this essay has been to demonstrate that all things are alive and sacred and suffused with God's power and wonder and to say that this attitudinal disposition toward Earth as holy ground is the basis for healing the suffering among ourselves and the wider community of living beings.[26] I have sought to show it is organic to Christianity that everyday life is saturated with divine presence – including, and especially, the abject elements within this common life, such as dirt and spit.

This conviction that God is with us in the here-and-now also entails the realization that there is no place else to look, there is no place else to go, there is nothing else to see or hear or taste or feel in order to find God. Correspondingly, there is no temple or holy man or sacred book that is required to traverse the boundary of heaven and earth, to make God come into this world, to actualize God's power through this or that religious ceremony or the agency of a special mediator. Why? Because, according to scripture, God is always-already here—present, tactile, enfleshed and enlivened by all that is around us. Jesus makes this point clear in his teaching about the kingdom of God even now being present in the everyday. When pressed by religious leaders in Luke's Gospel concerning the whereabouts of God's kingdom, we read,

> Now having been questioned by the Pharisees as to when the kingdom of God was coming, He answered them and said, "The kingdom of God is not coming with signs to be observed; nor will they say, 'Look, here it is!' or, 'There it is!' For behold, the kingdom of God is in your midst" (Luke 17:20–21).

The kingdom of God is here and available for all to enjoy: touch, taste, hear and see God in the wondrous hints of common grace always and everywhere present in ordinary time and the familiar of routine, often painful, but always-already enchanted existence.

In recent years, I have been fortunate to encounter intimations of pedestrian grace by spending summers at my in-laws' rustic cottage in Northern Spain; and there I have hiked, as a spiritual exercise, a peninsula at the foot of the Pyrenees Mountains called the "Cap de Creus." The Cap or Cape sits at the border between France and Spain and juts out into the Mediterranean Sea. It is a rugged, windswept landscape of spectacular vistas, violent windstorms and vibrant flora and fauna. The Cape's coastline is rocky and forbidding, and its name, "The Cape of the Crosses," stands for the many wooden ships that sank in its harbor, going straight down onto the seafloor, with their vertical masts and horizontal crosspieces extending straight up through the water, creating, as it were, a graveyard of underwater "crosses." Today, the Cape, surrounded by the clear turquoise water of the sea, is a beautiful chaparral of juniper and ash trees; wild rosemary, thyme, heather and rock roses; with many species of toads, lizards and geckos underfoot; and gulls, terns, falcons and eagles soaring though the sky overhead.

Culturally, the Cape of the Crosses is a union of ancient and medieval settlements. It is dotted with Neolithic "dolmens," small tables of standing stones, with large flat roof stones at their tops that were used for temporary shelters, or perhaps burial sites, for hunter-gatherer peoples many thousands of years ago. These pre-historic sites are nestled amidst the ruins of once-grand olive groves and grape orchards that covered the Cape roughly a thousand years ago. These groves and orchards were cultivated by Benedictine monks who settled the area in the ninth and tenth centuries CE. The monks built a spectacular monastery, Saint Peter of Rhodes, now a ruin, perched high on a ridge of the Pyrenees. Built around the same time, the monastery is complemented by a nearby hermitage named after Saint Onuphrius that is well-preserved and appears to have been chosen for its proximity to a still-flowing fresh-water spring. My hikes in these mountains often take me to this spring where I am reminded of creation's many gifts, including cool, clean water, which soothes my dry throat on a hot summer afternoon.

What stands out the most for me during these hikes is the wave after wave of pungent sagebrush fragrance that washes over the ragged outcroppings of rock and shrubs that make up the Cape. I walk the Cape intentionally and prayerfully, with my head slightly lowered, my gait deliberate, and my mind focused on the rhythm of my breath – in and out, in and out, in and out. My Cape hikes are a contemplative rite. They ground my existence in the good earth; they help me endure my own suffering and the suffering of others; they empower me to enter the public square with others and argue for sustainable policies that can pull our culture back from the brink of climate catastrophe.

This ritual hiking across the Cape returns me full-circle to my nighttime sleep and dream patterns in the bosom of the sagebrush hills of my boyhood. On the Cape of the Crosses, the sage is alive and fragrant. As a national park, the Cape is not to be disturbed, and so its many gifts—and in my case, the floral gift of wild sage—are proffered for pilgrims like me who hike its environs to find peace, to find strength, to find God. Through our addiction to fossil fuels in particular, and unsustainable consumption in general, we have wreaked havoc on our planet. Like Abel's blood at the hands of his murderous brother, Cain, the blood of our many victims cries out from the ground. As is lamented in Jeremiah, Hosea and Romans, as we saw, Earth mourns, the animals and plants continue to perish, and many of the less fortunate among us languish in squalor and desolation. We have laid waste to Earth, plundered its abundance and stripped bare its many gifts. But while the whole creation continues to groan in labor pains for a future deliverance about which we know very little, there are inklings of hope. There are still occasional droplets of grace within the tempest of encroaching ecocide in the biosphere. Even now, there are flickers of trust and faith amidst the darkness and despair of a world set afire by the fossil fuels extraction industries—a world that is *warming*, or to put this point more clearly, a world that is *dying* from our continuous burning of oil, gas, and coal. Our hope in living with, and perhaps at times in overcoming, this suffering that our global abuse has wrought, is to ritually re-discover our innermost relationships with the natural world—in my case, a re-awakening made possible by occasional hikes through the sagebrush rocklands of Northern Spain—and thereby find rest and security, and renewed energy, in the great bounty of creation God has made for our common life and common joy.

Notes

1. In this essay, I sometimes capitalize "Earth" when referring to the whole planet, as in the sense of "the natural world," while at other times I prefer "earth" in the sense of the "dirt" or "soil" that makes up the surface of the planet.
2. Gen. 1:31.
3. Anne Primavesi has written widely about Earth as an incalculably valuable wonder – a "gift event" that refuses to be quantified or commodified. See her (2000) *Sacred Gaia* (London: Routledge) and (2003) *Gaia's Gift* (London: Routledge). She compares Earth as pure gift to the song of a bird: "How could I pay a bird to teach me how to sing? What cash token corresponds to its freely given song?" (*Gaia's Gift*, 111).
4. See this analysis in Gerardo Ceballos, et al. (2015) "Accelerated Modern Human-Induced Species Losses: Entering the Sixth Mass Extinction," *Science Advances*, Vol. 1, no. 5 http://advances.sciencemag.org/content/1/5/e1400253.full. Also see Niles Eldredge (1998) *Life in the Balance: Humanity and the Biodiversity Crisis* (Princeton: Princeton University Press).
5. See Elisabeth Rosenthal and Andrew C. Revkin (2007) "Science Panel Says Global Warming is 'Unequivocal,'" *The New York Times*, February 3, 2007, http://www.nytimes.com/2007/02/03/science/earth/03climate.html?_r=0, A1, A5. Also see James Gustave Speth (2004) *Red Sky at Morning: America and the Crisis of the Global Environment* (New Haven: Yale University Press); and Elizabeth Kolber (2006) *Field Notes from a Catastrophe: Man, Nature, and Climate Change* (New York: Bloomsbury).
6. See Martin Heidegger (1977) "The Question Concerning Technology," in *The Question Concerning Technology and Other*

Essays, William Lovitt (trans.) (New York: Harper Colophon), 3–35.
7. The term "root metaphor" was coined by philosopher, Owen Barfield. Orienting metaphors are not mere figures of speech but expressions of the fundamental cognitive and emotional dispositions toward the world, within particular people and social groups. Root metaphors are indices to how people make sense of and participate in the world around them; they are founded in what Barfield calls humans' "original participation" in the worlds of nature and society. See Owen Barfield (1962) *Saving the Appearances: A Study in Idolatry* (New York: Harcourt Brace Jovanovich), 116–25.
8. Stephen Jay Gould (1993) *Eight Little Piggies: Reflections in Natural History* (New York: Norton). See also the excellent analysis of how the work of other natural and social scientists has been used to advance spiritual understandings of nature in Lucas F. Johnston (2014) *Religion and Sustainability: Social Movements and the Politics of the Environment* (Sheffield, UK: Equinox), 78–106.
9. See the argument for the intrinsic value of all species, independent of their utility to meet human needs, in Richard B. Primack (1995) *A Primer of Conservation Biology*, 2d ed. (Sunderland, Mass.: Sinauer Associates Inc.), 1–62.
10. James Lovelock (1988) *The Ages of Gaia* (New York: Norton).
11. See recent theologies of the land that emphasize Earth's suffering through human violence against living things in Ellen M. Ross (2007) "A Christian Vision of the Earth," *Friends Journal*, vol. 53, no. 4, 9–12; Eric Katz (2012) "Nature as Subject: Human Obligation and Natural Community," in Clifford Chalmers Cain (ed.) *Many Heavens, One Earth: Readings on Religion and the Environment* Cain (Lanham, MD: Lexington), 17–29; and Elizabeth Johnson (2007) *Quest for the Living God: Mapping Frontiers in the Theology of God* (New York: Continuum), 181–201.
12. Gen. 4:9-12; my emphases.
13. Gen. 4:12.
14. Gen. 1:1.
15. See the call to preserving a just and verdant Earth as sacred work in David Suzuki with Amanda McConnell (1997) *The Sacred Balance: Rediscovering Our Place in Nature* (Vancouver: Greystone Books).

16. Shelly Rambo writes that the task of theology in the midst of suffering is to engage in a "middle discourse" between religious triumphalism, on the one hand, and the loss of faith, on the other. To witness trauma using middle discourse is to account for ongoing fragmentation and despair vis-à-vis the broken promise of redemption and renewal. Today, we are on a collision course with ourselves. Beyond the loss of species and habitats, rising sea levels are destroying the lives of millions of human beings. Wealthy countries dump heat-trapping, ice-melting gases into the atmosphere causing rising sea levels and massive flooding in low-lying nations such as the Maldives, Fiji, Bangladesh, and here at home, in places such as New Orleans and New Jersey, where hurricanes and storms have killed and displaced thousands. In its witness to this unfolding global tragedy, middle discourse theology stumbles between the hopelessness of despair and the fractured possibility of new life. See Shelly Rambo (2010) *Spirit and Trauma: A Theology of Remaining* (Louisville, Kentucky: Westminster John Knox).
17. See Kate Rigby's exploration of Australian magpies and biblical animals in (2014) "Animal Calls," in Stephen D. Moore (ed.) *Divinanimality: Animal Theory, Creaturely Theology* (New York: Fordham University Press), 116–33, and similarly, regarding a variety of animals and the Bible, Laura Hobgood-Oster (2008) *Holy Dogs and Asses: Animals in the Christian Tradition* (Urbana: University of Illinois Press).
18. I have explored ecological readings of Jesus and the Spirit in (2010) *Green Christianity: Five Ways to a Sustainable Future* (Minneapolis: Fortress) and (2005) *Finding God in the Singing River: Christianity, Spirit, Nature* (Minneapolis: Fortress).
19. Other examples of how language for earth is a clue to deep thinking that earth is filth easily come to mind. To say that one has "soiled" oneself is to say that one has made oneself "dirty" by losing control of one's bowels and defecating on oneself.
20. Mary Douglas (1966) *Purity and Danger: An Analysis of the Concepts of Pollution and Taboo* (New York: Routledge Ark), 121.
21. Douglas, *Purity*, 121.
22. Douglas, *Purity*, 121.
23. Julia Kristeva (1982) *Powers of Horror: An Essay on Abjection*, Leon S. Roudiez (trans.) (New York: Columbia University Press), 69.
24. Kristeva, *Powers of Horror*, 3.

25. I am grateful to Shelly Rambo for proposing the phrase "palpable holiness" in this instance, and for her, and Stephanie Arel's, careful reading and suggestions regarding this essay.
26. Cynthia D. Moe-Lobeda analyzes the telling and inextricable link between our despoilment of Earth and destruction of human communities as an exercise in "moral oblivion," in (2013) *Resisting Structural Evil: Love as Ecological-Economic Vocation* (Minneapolis: Fortress).

Bibliography

Barfield, O. 1962. *Saving the appearances: A study in idolatry.* New York: Harcourt Brace Jovanovich.
Ceballos, G., P. R. Ehrlich, A. D. Barnosky, A. García, R. M. Pringle, and T. M. Palmer. 2015. Accelerated modern human-induced species losses: Entering the sixth mass extinction. *Science Advances* 1(5). http://advances.sciencemag.org/content/1/5/e1400253.full.pdf+html
Douglas, M. 1966. *Purity and danger: An analysis of the concepts of pollution and taboo.* New York: Routledge Ark.
Eldredge, N. 1998. *Life in the balance: Humanity and the biodiversity crisis.* Princeton: Princeton University Press.
Gould, S.J. 1993. *Eight little piggies: Reflections in natural history.* New York: Norton.
Heidegger, M. 1977. The question concerning technology. In *The question concerning technology and other essays.* Trans. W. Lovitt. New York: Harper Colophon.
Hobgood-Oster, L. 2008. *Holy dogs and asses: Animals in the Christian tradition.* Urbana: University of Illinois Press.
Johnson, E. 2007. *Quest for the living god: Mapping frontiers in the theology of god.* New York: Continuum.
Johnston, L.F. 2013. *Religion and sustainability: Social movements and the politics of the environment.* Sheffield: Equinox.
Katz, E. 2012. Nature as subject: Human obligation and natural community. In *Many heavens, one earth: Readings on religion and the environment*, ed. C.C. Cain. Lanham: Lexington.
Kolbert, E. 2006. *Field notes from a catastrophe: Man, nature, and climate change.* New York: Bloomsbury.
Kristeva, J. 1982. *Powers of horror: An essay on abjection.* Trans. L. S. Roudiez. New York: Columbia University Press.
Lovelock, J. 1988. *The ages of Gaia.* New York: Norton.
McConnell, A. 1997. *The sacred balance: Rediscovering our place in nature.* Vancouver: Greystone Books.

Moe-Lobeda, C.D. 2013. *Resisting structural evil: Love as ecological-economic vocation*. Minneapolis: Fortress.

Primack, R.B. 1995. *A primer of conservation biology*, 2nd ed. Sunderland: Sinauer Associates.

Primavesi, A. 2000. *Sacred Gaia*. London: Routledge.

Primavesi, A. 2003. *Gaia's gift*. London: Routledge.

Rambo, S. 2010. *Spirit and trauma: A theology of remaining*. Louisville: Westminster John Knox.

Rigby, K. 2014. Animal calls. In *Divinanimality: Animal theory, creaturely theology*, ed. S.D. Moore. New York: Fordham University Press.

Rosenthal, E., and A. C. Revkin. 2007. Science panel says global warming is 'unequivocal'. *The New York Times*. http://www.nytimes.com/2007/02/03/science/earth/03climate.html?_r=0

Ross, E.M. 2007. A Christian vision of the earth. *Friends Journal* 53(4): 9–12.

Speth, J.G. 2004. *Red sky at morning: America and the crisis of the global environment*. New Haven: Yale University Press.

Suzuki, D., and A. McConnell. 1997. *The sacred balance: Rediscovering our place in nature*. Vancouver: Greystone Books.

Wallace, M.I. 2005. *Finding god in the singing river: Christianity, spirit, nature*. Minneapolis: Fortress.

Wallace, M.I. 2010. *Green Christianity: Five ways to a sustainable future*. Minneapolis: Fortress.

CHAPTER 8

The Virtual Body of Christ and the Embrace of those Traumatized by Cancer

Deanna A. Thompson

VIRTUAL INTERRELATEDNESS AND THE BODY OF CHRIST

"Christ has no body but yours, No hands, no feet on earth but yours."[1] Widely attributed to St. Theresa of Avila (1515–1582), these words cast in stark, fleshy imagery, how followers of Christ are to *be* the body of Christ in a broken, hurting world. The poet riffs on biblical imagery offered by the Apostle Paul, who often refers to the church in bodily terms: "Now you are the body of Christ and individually members of it."[2] And just as it is the case in the medieval prayer, so it is for Paul: that members of the body of Christ are commissioned to attend especially to those who are broken, hurting. "[T]he members of the body that seem to be weaker are indispensable, and those members of the body we think less honorable we clothe with greater honor.... If one member suffers, we all suffer together with it."[3] Embodying Christ's love and care to those who suffer is, as the medieval prayer suggests, a thoroughgoing embodied, materially based task.

And yet, as pastor and writer Jason Byassee notes, even in its earliest incarnations, the body of Christ has always also been a virtual body.[4] The term originates with the Apostle Paul, founder of Christian churches in Asia Minor and Europe and author of many of the writings that appear in

D.A. Thompson (✉)
Hamline University, St. Paul, MN, USA

© The Editor(s) (if applicable) and The Author(s) 2016
S.N. Arel, S. Rambo (eds.), *Post-Traumatic Public Theology*,
DOI 10.1007/978-3-319-40660-2_8

the New Testament. In his letter to the church at Corinth, Paul describes his Corinthian brothers and sisters as members with him in Christ's body, even though his presence with them was primarily a virtual one, taking shape mainly through the letters he sent to each community. Byassee offers this intriguing view of Paul's relationship with the church communities he could only very occasionally visit:

> Paul so often longs to be with the congregations from whom he is absent in the body. But notice what he doesn't do: he doesn't wait to offer them his words until he can be with them. He sends them letters. Letters meant to be read corporately, perhaps even to lead worship or be part of it. Such letters allow him to engage personally without being present personally. They are a poor substitute in some ways. In others they are superior.[5]

Paul's connections with all the other members of the body of Christ are nurtured and maintained mostly through a virtual form of communication, which, as Byassee observes, has strengths as well as weaknesses. And these virtual communications were vital to the church's organization, practice, and growth.

Fast forward to the virtual realities of our contemporary twenty-first century world made possible through digital technology. Our world is saturated with the constant negotiation between the physical world and the worlds of Google, Twitter, Facebook, Instagram, and other quickly proliferating modes of virtual interaction. There is lively debate as to whether or not digital technology enhances or detracts from our ability to relate meaningfully to one another. Especially since the "Arab Spring" of 2011, scholars, journalists, and others have been debating the Internet's ability to foster social networks strong enough to support political and social reforms in places like the Middle East.[6] At the same time, social critics like Malcolm Gladwell remain skeptical of Web-based social media and their "weak-tie environments."[7] When assessing the capacity of social media to create strong ties among us, Gladwell argues: "The platforms of social media are built around weak ties. Twitter is a way of following (or being followed by) people you may never have met. Facebook is a tool for efficiently managing your acquaintances, for keeping up with people you would not otherwise be able to stay in touch with."[8] Sociologists have long pointed out that it is normal and healthy to have social networks made up of a combination of weak as well as strong ties.[9] Gladwell, however, gives voice to a widely held concern: that networks created through social media are primarily weak tie environments and, thus, incapable of instigating meaningful political change, or more to my purposes here, unable to build cultures of trust, support, and healing around the broken and hurting in our midst.

In this essay, I explore whether virtual worlds accessed through digital technology are capable of strong tie connections, that is, ties that are "built on trust and provide comfort in the face of uncertainty."[10] Following Gladwell, we might say that connections made virtually through digital technology are simply too weak to mediate trust or comfort—and thus Christ's hands and feet—to a suffering world. We need strong tie environments for that kind of work. Ethicist Stanley Hauerwas makes clear that when the church is being the church, it should be a strong tie environment, made up of people "who have learned how to be faithful to one another by our willingness to be present, with all our vulnerabilities, to one another."[11] If, then, the body of Christ is called to be present to one another in and out of pain, we are asking whether it is possible for Christ's hands and feet to be present in and through the virtual worlds made possible by digital technology.

Contrary to Gladwell, there are those who believe that strong tie environments can be created through the use of digital technology. Howard Rheingold, author of *The Virtual Community: Homesteading on the Electronic Frontier*, is willing to bet virtual networks can be as strong as "actual" ones. He suggests that, "The technology that makes virtual communities possible has the potential to bring enormous leverage to ordinary citizens at relatively little cost—intellectual leverage, social leverage, and most important, political leverage. But the technology will not in itself fulfill that potential; this latent technical power must be used intelligently and deliberatively by an informed population."[12] While there is much to lament about online interactions by seemingly uninformed populations, Rheingold's point is a vital one: it depends upon how the technology is used.

Cyberspace is changing our conceptions of the world and our place in it. Whether and how the body of Christ is and can be present virtually in the twenty-first century with those who suffer is a critical question inviting serious theological reflection. In what follows, I draw on my own experience of being supported by the virtual body of Christ while living with cancer to move toward a vision of the virtual body of Christ as a vital strong tie environment that has the potential to help the church be more present with those in pain than it has been in the past.

Cancer, Trauma, and the Embrace of the Virtual Body of Christ

Not many years ago, I had a dim view of the Internet's ability to create networks of trust and support. Living and working with others constantly connected to—and distracted by—digital tools left me skeptical that any new relational depth was being plumbed through our increasingly wired lives. I did not own a cell phone and was quick to judge others whose attention focused on their hand-held devices rather than on the human beings with whom they were in close physical proximity.

Then I got sick. Really sick. In a matter of months, I went from being a healthy 41-year-old religion professor, wife, and mother to a virtual invalid with a broken back, a stage IV cancer diagnosis, and a grim prognosis for the future.

To keep family and friends updated during the early days following the diagnosis, my brother created a CaringBridge site for me, a website dedicated to connecting people with serious illnesses with those who care about them.[13] News of my diagnosis spread quickly; just as quickly loved ones, friends, and even strangers signed up to receive my CaringBridge updates. From my narration of what stage IV cancer had done to my body to sharing the grief of having to resign from my very full and wonderful life, each of my posts was met with dozens of responses on the CaringBridge site, as well as additional emails, cards, packages, visits and calls from people from all corners of my life. It was startling to realize that through our connectedness via CaringBridge, I was being surrounded by a cloud of witnesses greater than any I could have previously imagined.

The theologians in this volume are all attending to experiences of trauma and to where and how theological work can contribute to greater understanding of such traumatic experiences and, hopefully, even to movements toward healing. When we talk about trauma, as Shelly Rambo describes in her powerful *Spirit and Trauma: A Theology of Remaining*, we are talking about the suffering that remains. "For those who survive trauma," Rambo writes, "the experience of trauma can be likened to a death. But the reality is that the death is not ended; instead, it persists. The experience of survival is one in which life, as it once was, cannot be retrieved. However, the promise of life ahead cannot be envisioned."[14] Rambo's description helps us appreciate that trauma involves a complex kind of suffering that is not easily understood. As we work to construct post-traumatic public theology around issues like the epidemic of cancer, then, it is crucial that we explore what "the suffering that remains" looks like through the lens of living with a life-threatening illness.

The majority of theological work on trauma, to date, tends to address the type of events that trauma theory most often focuses on: direct or indirect experience of violent acts that human beings do to one another, such as terrorism, war and combat, rape, or other violent personal assaults.[15] This is vital work. That at the heart of the Christian narrative stands a traumatic act of violence against an innocent person only heightens demand that such work on traumatic experiences of violence and their theological implications be done. At the same time, there are additional versions of trauma that are becoming more visible, such as the trauma related to living with life-threatening illnesses. It is important to note that it was only in the year 2000 that the category of "life-threatening illness" was added to the definition of "Post Traumatic Stress Disorder" (PTSD) in the American Psychiatric Association's Manual of Mental Disorders (DSM-IV-TR).[16] While those of us living with serious illness are now understood to be at risk of experiencing symptoms of PTSD (e.g. fear and anxiety regarding recurrence that manifest in hypervigilance and hyperarousal that affects sleep and mood),[17] the diagnosis remains somewhat controversial, as there are ways in which this particular version of trauma does not fit neatly into the PTSD category. Trauma associated with illness, typically, is not a singular traumatic event, but rather recurring events extending from diagnosis through treatment and beyond, possibly throughout the rest of a person's life.[18] Given this reality for people living with serious illness, researchers wonder whether those living with cancer can ever become "post-trauma."[19] In other words, the exact nature of the trauma can remain unclear, and subsequently, the PTSD condition of re-experiencing the trauma fails to adequately capture the ways in which "the suffering remains" for those living with cancer.[20] Especially as treatment progressively allows those of us with incurable cancers to live longer with the disease, more attention needs to be paid to these multi-pronged experiences of trauma persisting amid the ongoing uncertainty that living with cancer brings.

What is it that those who experience the trauma of living with serious illness need from those around them? Trauma theorist Cathy Caruth describes the challenging negotiation those who work with persons who've been traumatized face: "how to help relieve suffering, and how to understand the nature of the suffering, without eliminating the force and truth of the reality that trauma survivors face and quite often try to transmit to us."[21] An initial step in understanding the nature of the suffering for those living with advanced stage cancer might be to search for terms other than trauma or cancer *survivors*, a term that implies the traumatic event or cancer diagnosis has been endured, and that the question that needs to be answered is how to live in the aftermath. For those of us living with incurable diseases, living in the midst of the trauma and the diagnosis, the continuing treatments, the in-and-out of remission, the continuing scans, and so on, means living *with* the illness and its accompanying trauma. Survivor language does not adequately capture the ongoingness of the situation. In a recent piece for the New York Times, author Susan Gubar, who writes about living with ovarian cancer, explains her own problem with "survivor" language: "For years I have resisted the pervasive tag 'cancer survivor' because it erases or demeans patients who do not or suspect they cannot survive the disease."[22] In this post on "Coming to Terms" with cancer, Gubar advocates taking more care with the words we use, as language shapes how we "come to terms" with the ongoing trauma of living with an incurable illness. She writes, "Some of the vocabulary swirling around cancer leaves me feeling what I never wanted to feel or unable to think what I need to think."[23] What words, then, might we use instead of "survivor" language? Gubar reviews multiple options, from PLC (Person Living with Cancer) to "witty queer theorist," to Eve Sedgwick's preferred self-description as she struggled to live with metastatic breast cancer: "undead."[24] The jury is still out on appropriate replacements for "survivor" language. But just as Caruth argues, relief of suffering is closely linked to those who suffer being able to express the contours of their suffering as well as those who love and care for them understanding those same contours. Therefore, attending to the language those of us living with advanced stage cancer use to describe our condition is an important step in deepening our understanding of that condition and its enduring effects.

Beyond a shift in language, I want to suggest that virtual communication about a cancer diagnosis has some potentially significant advantages over face-to-face communication that allow for clearer articulations of the experiences of trauma that, in turn, can lead to deeper understanding of the trauma by those who want to care for the traumatized. My own experience of publically narrating my journey with stage IV cancer virtually on CaringBridge has become a powerful avenue for helping others understand the particularities of my cancer condition. In my case, the breast cancer was not detected through the annual mammogram; instead it metastasized to my bones, fracturing one and then two vertebrae in my back. It then was diagnosed through a biopsy on my spine. Immediate treatment included radiation to the bones where the cancer was most active: the spine, the pelvis, the hips. For those of us familiar with the breast cancer drill (finding a lump, biopsying the breast, undergoing a mastectomy, radiating the breast, undergoing chemotherapy), my story did not map the dominant breast cancer story. Neither did statistics of prognosis: at the time of my diagnosis in 2008, reports were that 80 percent of patients with metastatic breast cancer were dead within five years. My broken back coupled with the diagnosis altered every part of my world. And the ability to have the CaringBridge site, where I could begin to share the particularities of my story, proved a vital tool to help articulate the contours of the suffering I was experiencing.

It is necessary to point out that publically narrating an illness for hundreds to read and comment on is a risky endeavor. Moral philosopher Annette Baier's insight into possible risks of being vulnerable is applicable to my public sharing of my journey with cancer: "Where one depends on another's good will, one is necessarily vulnerable to the limits of that good will. One leaves others an opportunity to harm one when one trusts, and also shows one's confidence that they will not take it."[25] In the seven years I have been participating in these online conversations, there certainly have been responses I have found less-than-helpful. A couple even could be considered harmful. The much more common experience, however, is that others' online words of support have nurtured a powerful, healing culture that has been building since my diagnosis. I have found that sharing with hundreds of readers aspects of my grief, my struggles (physical, spiritual, psychological), my setbacks, and my progress better equips those who care for me and my family to offer tangible and specific care to me and my family.

Indeed, I have been awakened to a new—indeed, almost mystical—understanding of the church universal, mediated through what I am calling the virtual body of Christ; that is, the body of Christ incarnated in, with, and through virtual spaces like CaringBridge. What I'm talking about is a breathtakingly broad embodiment of Christ's hands and feet ministering to me and my family during our walk through the valley of the shadow of cancer. And similar to the virtual body of Christ of Paul's time, this emergent virtual incarnation of Christ's body via digital technology makes material differences in my life and in the lives of my family as we suffer at the hands of cancer. Taking risks of being vulnerable virtually has done much more to mitigate the trauma and suffering than to increase or compound it.

If the church is called to be a place where we can be vulnerable with one another, might it be possible to incarnate the body of Christ virtually in a way that permits and holds such vulnerability? While we can all generate examples of how the Internet enables people to behave more poorly online than they do in person, it is also the case that examples exist of how at times cyberspace allows us, as journalist Margaret Wertheim suggests, "to do better with the Net than we have done with the physical world."[26] For most of us struggling to live amid the suffering brought on by serious illness, capturing with words the upheaval we face is a continual struggle. It is almost always the case that it is less difficult for me to explain how I'm doing in an online post than in a face-to-face conversation. In virtual reality, my tears don't make my point unintelligible. Online, I can go back and edit out something that sounds more bitter or more optimistic than I want it to be. In cyberspace, my vulnerabilities often can be better managed than they are in face-to-face interactions. Being clearer about how I'm doing has allowed others to be clearer about how to be supportive.

Trauma, New Connections, and Vulnerability within the Expanding Virtual Body of Christ

As I struggled to find words that approximated the grief and disorientation brought on by my new life filled with cancer, I was surprised and humbled by the ties made possible by the virtual CaringBridge network. And in the process of being held and supported in many life-giving ways, the concept of the church universal moved from an abstract, intangible concept recited in a creed to a living body and a felt embrace. Posts about sleep problems yielded a host of helpful suggestions and a sleep machine in the mail. Prayer shawls from churches across the country arrived at our home. When I wrote about my uncertainty regarding whether I could continue tolerating the treatments I was getting, an email from a friend whose spouse is a physician helped me better understand the benefits and commit to continuing.

This experience of the virtual body of Christ has also gifted me with a fresh appreciation of the necessarily ecumenical character of church catholicity. Prompted by my entries on the Caring Bridge site, many of my friends from the Roman Catholic tradition—the church that holds most tightly to this notion of universality—have embodied Christ to me in stunning ways. Since news of my diagnosis spread via Caring Bridge, I have had Mass dedicated to me in India, Sri Lanka, California, and Minnesota;

I've received hundreds of cards from a California parish where Sunday School classes pray for me weekly; and I've been given a medallion blessed and sent on to me by a dear friend who is also a priest. These traditions of dedicating, blessing, and honoring—traditions that make rare appearances in Protestant expressions of church—have made their mark on my soul.

Perhaps the most poignant example of how a virtual community has encouraged vulnerability that leads to compassionate care and healing involves a colleague of mine at our university. In the decade she and I had worked together prior to the diagnosis, we had never had a substantive discussion about anything personal. Just a few months after I got sick, however, I received an email from this colleague, wherein she told me about growing up in Israel as an agnostic Jew and how she often felt on the outside of religious practices like prayer. Reading my postings about my own struggles to pray following the diagnosis, she told me that she became inspired to start praying. Not long after she began praying, she led a group of students to study in Israel. She told me about the group's day at the Western Wall in Jerusalem, that she and another Jewish colleague had placed prayers for me into the cracks in the wall. She wrote about how moved she was to see several of our students add their prayers for me to the wall as well. She then told me that in every church the group visited, she got down on her knees and prayed to Jesus for a favor: to heal her friend with cancer. Her message to me ended with this: "I hope I didn't offend Jesus–after all, I'm a Jew and I don't even pray regularly–and there I was, asking Jesus for a favor. I think he'll be ok with that, won't he?"

Words cannot adequately describe what these acts of care and compassion by my colleague have meant to me. That an agnostic Jew would get on her knees in churches throughout Israel to pray for her Christian colleague living with cancer also convinces me that the Internet is capable of strong tie connections that facilitate trust, comfort, even healing. It seems highly unlikely that without the virtual network we both participate in that either of us would have been able to risk the vulnerability that led to the gift of prayer for me in Jerusalem.

Moving this analysis into the theological realm, however, is where things get a bit more complicated. That my Jewish colleague's gifts were given and received by means of this virtual network raises the question of whether or not I can (or should) claim her as part of the virtual body of Christ. When I told another Jewish friend of mine about my colleague's request of Jesus, she looked at me incredulously and declared, "But she doesn't even know Jesus!" It is clear to anyone who knows my colleague—raised in Israel, steeped in Jewish tradition, regular attendee at synagogue—that she's a Jew and most definitely not a Christian, nor does she have any interest in becoming a Christian. And yet there was a crossing—however momentary—into the physical and theological space of the body of Christ. What, then, can be said about this religious boundary-crossing strong tie connection made possible through virtual reality?

I want to argue that strong tie connections formed via virtual networks push us theologically to rethink the boundaries of the church universal. But it's not as easy as simply declaring that my Jewish colleague is now part of the Christian church because she prayed to Jesus on my behalf. As theologian John Thatamanil notes, "When we speak about God, we are heard and overheard by a great cloud of witnesses, a cloud that includes persons of faith who are not part of the Christian community." Going even further, Thatamanil suggests that when Christians reflect on ways in which religious ideas, practices, and commitments intersect among Christians and those outside Christianity, we risk "bearing false witness" against our neighbors if we simply drop them into our already-determined Christian frameworks. Thatamanil writes, "Insofar as our affirmations either implicitly or explicitly challenge or even negate the conviction of others, we run the risk of misunderstanding and mischaracterizing them."[27] In order to avoid mischaracterizing my dear colleague, it is important for me to start where she started: with the Jewish practice of praying at the Western Wall, the holiest Jewish site in Jerusalem. The Midrash, an ancient Jewish commentary on Hebrew scriptures, quotes fourth century scholar Rav Acha who says that the Divine Presence has never moved away from the Western Wall.[28] The powerful gift she gave me of being prayed for came first of all out of her own Jewish tradition, in close proximity to Divine Presence as understood by that tradition.

But then my colleague took an additional step; she physically and theologically crossed into a tradition not her own (a tradition with a fraught relationship to her own, in fact) to address what Christians believe to be the incarnation of Divine Presence: Jesus. And this crossing, done in the name of compassion and hope for the healing of a friend, seems to be bound up somehow, someway, to God's universal community of saints. But how, exactly? To make such a claim means reconsidering the parameters of the body of Christ. This strong ties formed via a virtual network expands—even disrupts—conventional Christian notions of boundaries of the church universal. Her willing entry into that foreign space; her willing engagement with beliefs about Divine Presence very different from those in her own tradition; all of this was done out of compassion for the pain of someone she cared about. Her entrance into the physical and theological body of Christ was done because it's the space I inhabit, and she risked that crossing out of care and concern for me. That crossing links her hands and feet with the hands and feet of Christ, the first-century Jew whose Divine Presence, Christians believe, lives on in and through the church universal today.

Since my diagnosis, I've received a sage blessing from a Native American colleague, been prayed for in the synagogues and Hindu temples of friends and colleagues, had Buddhist meditation sessions dedicated to me, and Jesus has even been asked a favor by a Jewish friend who took a gamble on my behalf. When we willingly enter into space filled with another's story of trauma and respond with words and actions that facilitate hope for the one living the trauma, it's a gift—a gift that crosses and disrupts tidy theological frameworks. More work needs to be done on exploring the boundaries and parameters of the virtual body of Christ in a religiously diverse world. And yet I think it's possible to claim that these gifts have arisen from a virtual network, a network that mediates Christ's hands and feet in mysterious tandem with the hands and feet of practitioners of other traditions. All of these gifts enable me to keep walking through the valley of the shadow of cancer, even when the shadow being cast is frightfully long.

Virtual Strong Tie Environments and Incarnational Presence with the Traumatized

I'm arguing that the virtual world we access and inhabit through digital technology is capable of being a strong tie environment and bearing compassion and healing in the most awful of times. As my story suggests, there can be transformative, healing ramifications of the virtual embrace by others via technology. This is why I appreciate theologian Kathryn Reklis' challenge of conventional characterizations of virtual interactions and practices as disembodied and therefore less desirable while "actual" physical interactions and practices are embodied and therefore good.[29] Reklis points out that many embodied practices are neither healthy nor good. Feeding an addiction to drugs or alcohol, for instance, often leads to disregard for bodily safety. Addictions and their effects, then, are deeply *embodied*. Even as we cannot neglect cases of people so obsessed with participation in a virtual world that their neglect of the needs of the body is harmful,[30] Reklis' perspective is helpful in moving the conversation beyond "seeing the real vs. virtual divide in terms of embodied vs. disembodied" to thinking instead "about the new permutations of digital and virtual technology informing our lives as particular ways we are embodied."[31]

Returning to the Theresa of Avila prayer about how Christ has no hands, feet, body, today except for those who pattern their lives after his, it is imperative that Christian communities committed to addressing trauma in their midst see this call to incarnate Christ as extending into the virtual world as well. Particularly with respect to being Christ's hands and feet with and for those who are traumatized, we must acknowledge that such incarnational encounters are also being facilitated virtually, and that virtual connections might be in some ways superior to face-to-face interactions. Finally, it's also important to acknowledge that this expanding, expansive virtual body of Christ makes material, healing difference in the lives of the traumatized.

This emergent understanding of the virtual body of Christ has also opened the door for some communities of faith to experiment with a primarily virtual existence. *Extravagance*, an online church community of the United Church of Christ, started and continues with a fully online format.[32] Pastor Jo Hudson testifies to the strong tie environment that has been created with Extravagance. She "sees surprising honesty on social media. In the midst of the give-and-take of needing, caring, lamenting and hearing one another, bonds begin to form. People recognize names and hear each other's stories."[33] As the church universal commits to being the hands and feet of Christ with those who suffer, we who participate in the body of Christ must consider how Christ is incarnated in transformative ways in virtual as well as in face-to-face encounters.

Just as with the virtual presence of Paul at the time of the church's foundation, so it is with virtual presence now: there are ways such presence is inferior and ways it is superior to face-to-face interactions. Kathryn Reklis suggests that rather than pushing us to become disembodied, a major challenge with our current "augmented reality"[34] is the *dissipation* of our attention and energy. Rather than a disembodied lack of presence, the problem is that we're often *too present to too many people* at the same time.[35] If those who experience trauma are in desperate need of others who understand the nature of their suffering "without eliminating the force and truth of the reality,"[36] as trauma theorist Caruth argues, then deep, sustained attention to the needs (spoken and unspoken) of the traumatized is essential.

Attending to the Particular, Embodied Needs of the Traumatized

If Christian communities are going to be the hands and feet of Christ in the world (actual and virtual) today, calling us all to attend closely to the stories and the needs of those who suffer is a major task before us. In the gospel of Mark, we hear of Jesus making his way through the noisy, chaotic streets of Jericho. A man who is blind calls out to him saying, "Jesus, Son of David, have mercy of me!"[37] The disciples try and fend off the distraction, but Jesus "stands still"[38] and pays attention to the man at the margins. What follows is an encounter between Jesus and Bartimaeus, and Jesus' attentiveness to the needs of Bartimaeus leads to healing.

It is the case that attentiveness to the trauma of those living with serious illnesses is being forged in transformative ways through virtual networks of support. Before we conclude with that message, however, we must acknowledge that for all the ways cyberspace has the potential to reach further and more equitably than ever before, those with scarce resources likely will not experience strong tie connections via online social networks due to lack of their own virtual presence and connections. Meanwhile, those without strong virtual connections still get sick. The National Cancer Institute reports that urban poor are diagnosed with more advanced cancer and have lower rates of survival than those living in more affluent communities.[39] In a recent study on urban poor living with advanced cancer, oncology nurses report not just on frequent lack of supportive family structures but also on the prevalence of other traumas (violence against themselves or close family members, wartime military service, etc.) that compound the trauma of dealing with their life-threatening illness. The nurses insist that, "Understanding the everyday lives of patients is necessary to develop realistic and practical self-care plans and to identify needed community resources."[40] All of us need to attend to the shouts of the Bartimaeus' of our time; but even more, we are called to be attentive to those whose trauma is so great that their calls are not heard, virtually or actually.

In a world where millions live with the trauma associated with life-threatening illnesses, it is vital that scholars and practitioners of religion alike understand the virtual world as a strong tie environment capable of attending to the suffering and needs of the traumatized. As one who lives with cancer and has experienced the healing embrace of the virtual body of Christ and the bodies that work alongside Christ, I encourage us to direct attention toward other such networks of healing, both in the virtual and actual world. In a world saturated in trauma, we need all the space for attention, response, and healing we can get.

Notes

1. "Christ Has No Body," "Journey with Jesus," http://www.journeywithjesus.net/PoemsAndPrayers/Teresa_Of_Avila_Christ_Has_No_Body.shtml, accessed August 8, 2014.
2. I Cor. 12.27.
3. I Cor. 12.22-3a, 26a.
4. Jason Byassee (2011) "For Virtual Theological Education," *Faith and Leadership blog*, March 2, 2011, http://www.faithandleadership.com/blog/03-02-2011/jason-byassee-for-virtual-theological-education.
5. Byassee, "For Virtual."
6. See Parker J. Palmer (2010) *Healing the Heart of Democracy: The Courage to Create a Politics Worthy of the Human Spirit* (San Francisco: Jossey-Bass), 171.
7. See Malcolm Gladwell (2010) "Small Change: Why the Revolution Will Not Be Tweeted," *New Yorker*, Oct. 4, 2010, http://www.newyorker.com/magazine/2010/10/04/small-change-3.
8. Gladwell, "Small Change."
9. See for example Mark Granovetter (1973) "The Strength of Weak Ties," *American Journal of Sociology*, vol. 78, no. 6, 1360–1380.
10. See David Krackhardt (1992) "The Strength of Strong Ties: The Importance of Philos in Organizations," in N. Nohria & R. Eccles (eds.) *Networks and Organizations: Structure, Form, and Action* (Cambridge, MA: Harvard Business School Press), 216–239.
11. Stanley Hauerwas (2012) "Why Medicine Needs the Church," in M. Therese Lysaught, Joseph J. Kotva, Jr. (eds.) *On Moral Medicine: Theological Perspectives in Medical Ethics*, Third Edition, (Grand Rapids, MI: William B. Eerdmans), 50.
12. Howard Rheingold (2000) *The Virtual Community: Homesteading on the Electronic Frontier*, revised edition, (Cambridge: MIT Press), 4–5.
13. See the CaringBridge website, http://www.caringbridge.org/, and my personal site, http://www.caringbridge.org/visit/deannathompson.
14. Shelly Rambo (2010) *Spirit and Trauma: A Theology of Remaining* (Louisville: Westminster John Knox Press), 7.
15. In addition to Rambo's *Spirit and Trauma*, see for example Flora Keshgegian (2000) *Redeeming Memories: A Theology of Healing*

and Transformation (Nashville: Abingdon Press); Serene Jones (2009) *Trauma and Grace: Theology in a Ruptured World* (Louisville: Westminster John Knox); Dirk Lange (2010) *Trauma Recalled: Liturgy, Disruption, and Theology* (Minneapolis: Fortress Press).

16. American Psychiatric Association Diagnostic and Statistical Manual of Mental Disorders (2000) DSM-IV-TR, 4th revised edition, (Washington, D.C., American Psychiatric Association), 467–8.
17. As well as flashbacks and nightmares, avoidance of people, places, and things associated with the trauma, persistent fear, and feelings of isolation, and reactive symptoms, and a sense of a foreshortened future occur, see http://www.psychiatry.org/ptsd.
18. Meredith Y. Smith, William H. Redd, Caroline Peyser, and Dan Vogl (1999) "Post-traumatic stress disorder in cancer: a review," *Psychooncology*, Nov–Dec; Vol. 8, no. 6, 521–537.
19. Nancy Jo Bush (2009) "Post-Traumatic Stress Disorder Related to the Cancer Experience," *Oncology Nursing Forum*, vol. 36, no. 4, 395–400.
20. "Post Traumatic Stress Disorder: Diagnostic Criteria and Characteristics," National Cancer Institute Website, http://www.cancer.gov/cancertopics/pdq/supportivecare/post-traumatic-stress/HealthProfessional/page3.
21. Cathy Caruth (1995) "Preface," in *Trauma: Explorations in Memory* (Baltimore: The Johns Hopkins University Press), as quoted in Rambo, *Spirit and Trauma*, 3, footnote 2.
22. Susan Gubar (2015) "Living with Cancer: Coming to Terms," *New York Times* blog post, January 22, 2015, http://well.blogs.nytimes.com2015/01/22/living-with-cancer-coming-to-terms/?_r=0
23. Gubar, "Living with Cancer."
24. Gubar, "Living with Cancer."
25. Annette Baier (1986) "Trust and Antitrust," *Ethics*, vol. 96, no. 2, 235, as quoted in Martin E. Marty (2010) *Building Cultures of Trust* (Grand Rapids, MI: Wm. B. Eerdmans), 145.
26. Margaret Wertheim (2000) *The Pearly Gates of Cyberspace: A History of Space from Dante to the Internet* (New York: W. W. Norton & Co.), 285.
27. John Thatamanil (2006) *The Immanent Divine: God, Creation, and the Human Predicament* (Minneapolis: Fortress Press), xi–xii.

28. Bonna Devorah Haberman, "Terumah from a Feminist Point of View," accessed 20 May 2016, http://www.kolech.org.il/maamar/terumah-from-a-feminist-point-of-view/?lang=en.
29. Kathryn Reklis (2012) "X-Reality and the Incarnation," *New Media Project*, May 10, 2102 http://www.cpx.cts.edu/newmedia/findings/essays/x-reality-and-the-incarnation.
30. For stories on people who died because their obsession with video games led them to neglect their bodily needs, see Gillian Mohney (2013) "Video Game Leads to Life-Threatening Condition for Gamer," *ABC News*, December 12, 2013, http://abcnews.go.com/Health/video-game-leads-life-threatening-condition-gamer/story?id=21182106.
31. Reklis, "X-Reality and the Incarnation."
32. Extravagance United Church of Christ, http://www.extravaganceucc.org/.
33. Jo Hudson, as referenced by Carol Howard Merritt (2014) "Virtual Real Presence," *Christian Century*, vol. 131, no. 11, 43.
34. Reklis, X-Reality and the Incarnation," uses this term, one that suggests we no longer live in the "virtual world" while we're online and the "actual world" when we're not, but rather in a world that is constantly being augmented through our digital tools.
35. Reklis, X-Reality and the Incarnation."
36. Caruth, "Preface," vii.
37. Mark 10.47.
38. Mark 10: 39
39. As cited in Anne Hughes, Maria Gudnundsdottir, and Betty Davies (2007) "Everyday Struggling to Survive: Experiences of the Urban Poor Living with Advanced Cancer," *Oncology Nursing Forum*, vol. 34, no. 6, 1113–1118.
40. Hughes, Gudnundsdottir, and Davies, "Everyday Struggling," 1118.

Bibliography

American Psychiatric Association Diagnostic and Statistical Manuel of Mental Disorders. 2000. DSM-IV-TR. 4th rev. ed. Washington, DC: American Psychiatric Association.

Baier, A. 1986. Trust and antitrust. *Ethics* 96(2): 231–260.

Bush, N.J. 2009. Post-traumatic stress disorder related to the cancer experience. *Oncology Nursing Forum* 36(4): 395–400.

Byassee, J. 2011. For virtual theological education. *Faith and Leadership Blog.* http://www.faithandleadership.com/blog/03-02-2011/jason-byassee-for-virtual-theological-education

Caruth, C. 1995. Preface. In *Trauma: Exploration in memory*, ed. Cathy Caruth. Baltimore: The John Hopkins University Press.

"Christ has no body," "Journey with Jesus." http://www.journeywithjesus.net/PoemsAndPrayers/Teresa_Of_Avila_Christ_Has_No_Body.shtml

Extravagance United Church of Christ. http://www.extravaganceucc.org/

Gladwell, M. 2010. Small change: Why the revolution will not be tweeted. *New Yorker.* http://www.newyorker.com/magazine/2010/10/04/small-change-3

Granovetter, M. 1973. The strength of weak ties. *American Journal of Sociology* 78(6): 1360–1380.

Gubar, S. 2015. Living with cancer: Coming to terms. *New York Times* blog post. http://well.blogs.nytimes.com2015/01/22/living-with-cancer-coming-to-terms/?_r=0

Hauerwas, S. 2012. Why medicine needs the church. In *On moral medicine: Theological perspectives in medical ethics*, 3rd ed, ed. M.T. Lysaught and J.J. Kotva Jr.. Grand Rapids: William B. Eerdmans.

Help with posttraumatic stress disorder. American Psychiatric Association Website. https://www.psychiatry.org/patients-families/ptsd

Hughes, A., M. Gudnundsdottir, and B. Davies. 2007. Everyday struggling to survive: Experiences of the urban poor living with advanced cancer. *Oncology Nursing Forum* 34(6): 1113–1118.

Jones, S. 2009. *Trauma and grace: Theology in a ruptured world.* Louisville: Westminster John Knox.

Keshgegian, F. 2000. *Redeeming memories: A theology of healing and transformation.* Nashville: Abingdon Press.

Krackhardt, D. 1992. The strength of strong ties: The importance of philos in organizations. In *Networks and organizations: Structure, form, and action*, ed. N. Nohria and R. Eccles. Cambridge, MA: Harvard Business School Press.

Lange, D. 2010. *Trauma recalled: Liturgy, disruption, and theology.* Minneapolis: Fortress Press.

Merritt, C. H. 2014. Virtual real presence. *Christian Century* 131(11–11).

Mohney, G. 2013. Video game leads to life-threatening condition for gamer. *ABC News.* http://abcnews.go.com/Health/video-game-leads-life-threatening-condition-gamer/story?id=21182106

Palmer, P.J. 2010. *Healing the heart of democracy: The courage to create a politics worthy of the human spirit.* San Francisco: Jossey-Bass.

Post traumatic stress disorder: Diagnostic criteria and characteristics. National Cancer Institute. http://www.cancer.gov/cancertopics/pdq/supportivecare/post-traumatic-stress/HealthProfessional/page3

Rambo, S. 2010. *Spirit and trauma: A theology of remaining.* Louisville: Westminster John Knox.

Reklis, K. 2012. X-reality and the incarnation. New Media Project. http://www.cpx.cts.edu/newmedia/findings/essays/x-reality-and-the-incarnation

Rheingold, H. 2000. *The virtual community: Homesteading on the electronic frontier.* Rev. ed. Cambridge: MIT Press.

Smith, M.Y., W.H. Redd, C. Peyser, and D. Vogl. 1999. Post-traumatic stress disorder in cancer: A review. *Psychooncology* 8(6): 521–537.

Thatamanil, J. 2006. *Immanent divine: God, creation, and the human predicament.* Minneapolis: Fortress Press.

Thompson, D. *CaringBridge.* http://www.caringbridge.org/ and http://www.caringbridge.org/visit/deannathompson

Wertheim, M. 2000. *The pearly gates of cyberspace: A history of space from Dante to the internet.* New York: W. W. Norton.

CHAPTER 9

Examining Restorative Justice: Theology, Traumatic Narratives, and Affective Responsibility

Stephanie N. Arel

In the spring of 2014, a group of 20 theology students studying restorative justice in a class I was assisting, spent an evening at the Massachusetts Correctional Institute (MCI), a minimum-security prison in Norfolk, MA. The visit represented a practical encounter that broadened class examinations of the theological and secular interpretations of justice. It enabled students to see how restorative justice practices and values actually operate to change the lives of the incarcerated within the criminal justice system. However, the constructive intent of our presence in the prison did not insulate us from its entanglement with the jurisprudence of retributive justice. Restorative justice focuses on rehabilitation, while criminal justice focuses on punishment. The juxtaposition of these emerges in MCI's design: while the prison architecture and grounds mirror the layout of Harvard's campus, intentionally creating a communal feel, the high-security system entailing multiple sets of steel doors and various stages of inspection establishes a sense of powerlessness and intimidation. Thus, dual affective tensions of empathy and shame permeated the visit.

S.N. Arel (✉)
Boston University School of Theology, Boston, MA, USA

© The Editor(s) (if applicable) and The Author(s) 2016
S.N. Arel, S. Rambo (eds.), *Post-Traumatic Public Theology*,
DOI 10.1007/978-3-319-40660-2_9

After being frisk searched in a small room to the side of an enclosed entranceway, pulling up garments to ensure we possessed no hidden piercings or contraband, we walked across the MCI campus to a small auditorium and were greeted by nine or ten male inmates. At 7:00 pm, the 90-minute presentation began. The inmates revealed testimonies about committed acts of violence, tragic trauma histories, and failed efforts at integration upon release into life outside of the prison walls. Prosecuted primarily for sexual violence and murder, they also shared how their communities including restorative practices and education facilitated their own recoveries. Their stories reflected their own growth and healing through a variety of forms of rehabilitation available at MCI, while simultaneously divulging layers of personal abuse, victimization by the criminal justice system, and personal horror at their own acts.

At one point, an inmate directed three questions to students. "How many of you know someone who has been victimized by a crime?" Everyone in the room raised a hand. "How many of you have been victims of a crime?" Almost all of the women raised their hands. "How many of you would like to hear from your perpetrators?" No one in the room raised a hand. Without further comment, he continued to read from his letter, an apology to the family of the man he killed. Moving and heartfelt, his words reflected deep remorse. But neither he nor the moderators of the lecture addressed the unanswered question of whether victims would want to hear from their perpetrators. By disregarding the lack of response to the question, he evaded a moment for dialogue, an opportunity for reflection, and a possible connection with the students that might come by way of understanding the visceral reaction that interfered with their participation.

This inmate was one of many who shared heartfelt revelations about efforts at restoration and rehabilitation, including disclosures about histories of trauma and abuse. The students listened attentively throughout the evening. Even when the stories the inmates told were disturbing, they remained a gracious audience. Yet, I found myself distressed, at times disturbed, and continually wondering how many of them felt similarly.

Imprisoned for crimes of sexual violence and murder, the men's stories were affecting. But the reactions to the stories, the strong, affective bodily surges that evade language, went ignored. Still, witnessing accounts of trauma has a profound impact on the listener. The body responds to trauma, and the inmates' stories were imbued with such trauma. Hearing the traumatic realities of the incarcerated made up a significant portion of the lecture and added an important dimension to a theology class exploring the meaning of "justice," yet what is at stake when students are asked to listen but do not have an opportunity to process the affect they experience in response? Affects extend beyond cognitive capacities, happening faster than mental processing allows, and they materialized automatically in the student's participation that night. But affects, and their overwhelming impact, never made it to the foreground of discussion, not in the prison and not afterwards.

As untrained witnesses at MIC, students have little choice but to suspend their response to affect, or the articulation of it. This means that they manage the visceral emergence of negative affective experiences alone. If we subject students to episodes of trauma—through personal narratives or events like the prison visit—we have to be willing to, at the very least, help them be aware of what is happening at the affective level for their own safety. The prison visit, along with the accompanying disclosure of traumatic narratives, challenges facilitators and professors to be attuned to affect and trauma in all participants.

The class I assisted focused on the theological exploration of justice, which included an examination of how related narratives intertwine with trauma. In order for students to carefully distinguish the imbrication of theology, jurisprudence, and trauma, in language and praxis, the affect they experience as result of practical encounters must be negotiated. Thus, the issue at hand is dual: the importance of considering criminal and restorative justice through a theological lens, tempered by the risks of exposing the unprepared to trauma and heightened affect through such an examination. Restorative justice aims to provide for the incarcerated a way out of what scholars call "disintegrative shame."[1] This same respect afforded to students encourages a more robust and affectively responsible approach to restorative justice education.

Emergence of Affect

Affect theory with its attention to the body and its vicissitudes raises challenges for academic and theological explorations of justice. Not readily apparent or easily deciphered, affects precede language and often go unarticulated due to their rapidity in emergence. Normal classroom procedures might evade situations of high affect arousal, but with the introduction of trauma, here embedded in the prison environment, affects are more likely to make a negative impact. Emerging as the biological portion of emotions that lie outside of conscious or cognitive control, affects are sometimes difficult to identify.[2] Affects elude cognition and so easily escape understanding and awareness becoming what affect theorists call "dysregulated."[3] That is, when affects exceed a level of tolerance, they signal danger and provoke either heighted levels of arousal (hyper) or drastically reduced levels (hypo). In the case of fear, visceral signs include but are not limited to irregular breathing, tense muscles, wide eyes or enlarged pupils, sweaty palms, and even yawning as indicative of a tendency to dissociate, while shame manifests as downcast eyes, shrugged shoulders, warm body temperatures, nausea, hesitant speech or silence, and any attempts to remove the body from view, such as turning away the head or torso.

Whether regulated or not, affects are always present. When triggered, affects have a unique capacity to direct attention, highlighting what Kathleen Stewart calls, "the intimate impact of forces [as affect] in circulation," that have the capacity to "pull the subject into places it didn't exactly 'intend' to go."[4] This means that affects have a power to direct attention, thereby influencing cognitive control. At MCI, different aspects of the visit potentially triggered affects, "pulling" students into the depths of their own affective lives, places they may not have intended to go. Rather than extraordinary, this affective pull happened throughout the visit, starting when we arrived by car onto the heavily gated prison grounds.

Prisons appear anything but innocuous. The physical structure itself shapes affective responses. Intimidating from the first approach, prison walls elicit postures of reticence and caution, moderate indicators of affects like shame and fear. This physical space can neither be dissociated from affective space (what is experienced corporeally) nor from the social space of the prison's interior. In Henri Lefebvre's conception, types of place interact and merge rendering them "indistinguishable" from each other, and therefore affected.[5] Looming, concrete prison walls threaten and subdue. Authority figures support the ominous exterior, moderating security checks and body searches. The warden and guards indicate a secure and formidable hierarchy, conveying a sense of legitimacy that provokes interest, in the best case, and distress or fear, in the worst. Thus, affective stimuli emerge in the collision of space: the architecture of the prison, the security screening points, the prison hierarchy, and personal traumatic narratives. All of these provide opportunities for various types and levels of affective emergence.

To understand the visit to MCI through the lens of affect is to understand how these aspects of the evening may have made a serious and lasting affective impact. For instance, affects serve as a source of information about the world and include a visceral processing of stimuli that influences behavior and the capacity to act. Correspondingly, affects communicate to a body how to behave in the prison. This became immediately evident when we entered the building. Instinctively, our voices softened; our walking pace slowed, and the students continually looked to one another and myself for direction. They were mild in their responses to guards; nervous laughter and bowed heads during the body searches indicated discomfort and shame. Affects motivated these immediate responses, as the students were never briefed about what to expect or how to behave (only what to wear); instead, the experience itself shaped their behavior by stimulating particular affects.

The hierarchical structure within a prison limits students' capacity to move about freely in the name of safety. Yet it also inhibits self-control and decision-making. Thus, a trip to the prison as a part of any class changes the "normal" dynamics and ethos of the classroom from mutuality and cooperation to one of division and reproach. Lack of normalcy emerges when students are left trying to make sense of who is ultimately in control in the prison visit. In a classroom, stratification is understood, familiar, and sometimes even challenged, but a sense of safety, even if dubious, persists. Extending the classroom into a prison destabilizes feelings of security, instead highlighting vulnerability and danger. Safety emerges as a result of perceived protection from guards, rather than existing as a default. This protection, in the form of guards and locked doors, also serves to limit students' agency. Furthermore, teachers relegate the role of leader to the warden. In this construction, students and inmates seem to stand on common ground, each with their respective authority figure present. Until the students sit, when the inmates assume a certain control in the room, a potent power shift occurs eliciting another opportunity for the stimulation of affect.

Another and very personal dimension of the visit surfaces in the traumatic narratives the inmates present. Affects emerge naturally in response to such stories, but the reality that listening to stories about sexual violence and murder is, in a sense, required elicits its own affective response. The students have not been presented (as they would have in a classroom) an option to leave the auditorium. Students thus find themselves subjected to the scene. Certainly, this lack of power, even if simply perceived, leaves the body shuffling to make sense of fear (of leaving) and shame (of the desire to leave in the first place). To compound this, the students at varying degrees bring their own histories of trauma into the room. As James Gilligan aptly asserts, we all have a working theory of violence precipitated by our own experiences of it. Listening to others' stories of violence reminds us of our personal experiences, evoking the accompanying affect. The range of affective responses Gilligan indicates include, "horror, revulsion, outrage, fascination, arousal, and valorization."[6] When affective reactions of such intensity go unaddressed, their effects lodge themselves in the body and perpetuate negative affect. This situation is especially detrimental for those who have their own traumatic narratives.

Exposure to Trauma

Trauma and traumatic histories permeate the prison environment and revealed through the inmates' narratives of their own experiences, prior to, during, and after arrests, introduce the problem of childhood trauma. For instance, many of the inmates recount painful memories of abuse. Although reported numbers vary, in prisons nationwide the National Institute of Justice reports a 68% rate of some form of childhood victimization in male detainees prior to incarceration in the form of sexual abuse, physical abuse, or neglect.[7] These narratives of childhood abuse or struggle often precede accounts of violence that lead up to an arrest; the inmates at MCI corroborate this. Their stories also portray the arrest itself as a traumatic event. An added complication, although only alluded to during our visit at MCI, arises inside prison walls, as 10 % of the prison population report abuse while incarcerated, compounding the childhood trauma of inmates and the scenes of violence in their lives prior to and during the arrest.[8]

The affectivity the students experience in the prison visit intertwines with these traumatic narratives, revealed in detail by the inmates.[9] The students, attentive and captive listeners to these traumatic histories, have their own personal affective responses. In fact, confessions composed of violence, traumatic histories, and subsequent expressions of remorse belie the affective activation that undulates beneath the spoken word for both the speaker (the inmate) and the witness (the student). For those who bring their own narratives of trauma and personal scenes of violence to the room, the affective experience may be one of fear or anger. In any case, attending to narratives of murder and sexual violence, along with stories of pain, degradation, victimhood, survival, violence, and various levels of helplessness, elicits something highly affective. Subject to the stories and necessarily present to witness the revelation of traumatic narratives, the listener is susceptible to the dangers of unregulated affects. Traumatic stimuli are so dense that, in terms of affect, there is always "catching up" to do. That is, a struggle ensues when affects emerge in situations of high arousal—the body responds while cognitive processes try to make sense of the visceral signals that keep coming.

Being affected by trauma, even the narration of trauma, is not an unusual or rare occurrence. With or without a trauma history, studies show that those involved in working with the traumatized—for instance, first responders, social workers, and psychologists—inevitably experience some kind of "complex traumatic response" to traumatic material.[10] Studying restorative justice practices leaves participants just as susceptible to experiencing some level of traumatization. Social worker and Professor Madelyn Miller addresses at least two primary reactions that result from the witnessing of traumatic narratives in the classroom. The first is the experience of vicarious traumatization. Vicarious trauma, a secondary kind of traumatic stress, occurs as a result of deep empathetic engagement with the traumatized and their stories. Otherwise known as compassion fatigue, vicarious trauma happens as a result of caring when stories about fear, pain, and suffering are shared. The risk for vicarious traumatization is even more relevant for untrained witnesses like the students in the restorative justice class, who may or may not understand that the stories they hear can at once inspire compassion and fear, while also activating prior trauma.

The second response relates to the repetition of the traumatic scene when witnesses of the traumatic narrative have themselves been harmed. While talking about trauma may seem innocuous, simply recounting a traumatic narrative activates the area of brain where the trauma initially took place, thereby constituting a kind of repeat of the original traumatic experience as memories or flashbacks.[11] Flashbacks, or involuntary memory recall, are the sensory fragments of traumatic memory that slip into the present and are literally relived, provoking dissociation or hyper-arousal as affect dysregulation of anxiety, anger, or fear. These responses manifest as the fight or flight response characterized by rapid breathing, elevated heart rate, and increase in muscle tension to prepare the body for action.[12] Alternatively, dissociation, a depressed state generally indicative of shame and known as the freeze response, signals dysregulation as hypo-arousal: breathing becomes shallow or stops altogether, and muscles stiffen inhibiting the capacity to move.[13] Thus, trauma begets trauma, and neglecting this potential in situations, like the prison visit, can leave students and witnesses in affectively unsafe states. Further, the issue of secondary traumatization presents an especially precarious situation for students suffering from their own traumatic histories, as witnessing traumatic narratives can re-traumatize them.

With or without personal trauma, during the prison visit, students participated in situations where vicarious trauma is known to occur. Even though this visit marks a one-time event, or even more because of this, the repeated return to the traumatic narrative in restorative justice warrants awareness and a response to the potential of such vicarious trauma, along with associated fatigue, pressing the need for self-care. Students who visit prisons for educational purposes can experience vicarious trauma, which perpetuates the possibility for traumatic iterance, unless careful preparation and debriefing is part of the process. That the visit is brief and singular does not protect against its affective impact. In fact, the possibility for traumatic affect, and its suppression, increases when the exposure occurs once, as no real long-term involvement in the students' exploring and understanding their experiences occurs.

Restorative justice aims to offer a place for multiple voices to be heard in the effort toward justice, but in the class prison visit, lack of attention to the reactions of the students involved risks confusion and re-traumatization. For instance, while listening to an inmate speak, conscientious students might experience discomfort and wonder why they feel uncomfortable, or they may even encounter affect that stimulates a desire to stop listening and thus experience their own guilt or shame. Overwhelming affect might inspire an urge to leave the room, which in the prison is not a possibility, and has dangerously (insofar as affect regulation requires safety) not been made a possibility. The affective ramifications of enduring helplessness and vulnerability can be severe, fostering dissociation and the internal pain of shame.

Those who work within restorative justice, or similar movements that include the attention to traumatic narratives, can normalize the fact that people, especially those with traumatic histories, have intense and potentially negative affective responses to traumatic narratives. Miller suggests that providing a frame for these kinds of experiences in the classroom allows for an exploration of "the rich and complex issues of disclosure within the course content;" at the same time, it ensures that the student and the class have "a conscientious experience."[14] In fact, Miller reports that students feel a sense of relief and validation after they explore concepts about countertransference and vicarious traumatization, which allow careful distinctions to be made between the traumatic narrative and their own present day realities.[15] Talking about trauma and the confrontation of trauma in the theological classroom allows for attentiveness to the affective responses of the students, while discussing resulting experiences of aroused affect validates those experiences and communicates respect for all involved.

Attentiveness to affect and trauma begins to reveal what is at stake in community or educational involvement in the process of exploring traumatic narratives. Trauma is not just an event that happens at once and disappears. Instead, trauma resides in the body as affect and has residual effects at varying degrees. The challenge remains to negotiate the multiple layers, qualities, and experiences of trauma, especially when a traumatic event or events have not been assimilated, or integrated. Exploring the vicissitudes of trauma in the academic community, through classes like those in restorative justice, requires a greater sensitivity to affect and possible trauma histories in participants—in this case including inmates, victims, and the community.

Theo-logic of Criminal and Restorative Justice

While it reveals a range of affective experiences and presses the need for an affective responsibility within restorative justice education, the prison visit also exposes dual narratives of "justice." One is "retributive," and the other is "restorative." Embedded within both forms of justice are theological contexts which have distinct logical structures, and which elicit particular affects. Distinguishing the theological inheritance of each form of jurisprudence insists on an additional level of attention in the academic environment regarding how these intertwine with affect and trauma.

The current and predominant model of criminal justice has precise rules of procedure and evidence, strict statutory definitions, and narrow discretion for judges related to punishment for crimes. Recognized as an adversarial, retributive model, criminal justice assumes that punishment serves as the best response to crime. Established to redress wrongs, often at the expense of civil or human rights, criminal justice distinguishes a perpetrator and a victim, aiming to vindicate the victim (often interpreted as both the person harmed and the state) by inflicting pain and suffering on the perpetrator. With the power to punish the perpetrator for wrongdoing, the state also intervenes in retributive justice to rescue the victim from the perpetrator. Thus, the criminal justice model perpetuates and adjudicates a traumatic narrative, securing the ubiquity of the affects of fear and shame. Inherent to retributive justice is also a theological narrative. In this narrative, the state assumes the role of an all-powerful and punitive God, who avenges sins for wrong-doing and demands atonement. The possibility for forgiveness, or amelioration from pain, lies in the possibility of mercy from this God embodied as those who hold power within the prison system.

The theo-logic that emerges from this interpretation of God is one of rue and contrition, a logic that inspires and, as theorist Donald Nathanson argues, perpetuates shame. Nathanson describes how certain interpretations of the Christian tradition encourage the negative affect. According to Nathanson, the Edenic narrative fosters and underlies the Christian experience characterized by an awareness of "both of the nature of one's actions and the nature of the self who committed them," triggering the negative affect of shame; then fear of punishment for what one has done emerges followed by a sense of distress "produced by the constancy of one's shame."[16] Efforts to eliminate distress often dangerously emerge as violent acts. Nathanson names the pernicious shame cycle, obscured by narratives about guilt and sin in the Christian tradition, which Gilligan labels as a "guilt-ethic." Where certain theological assumptions label Adam and Eve as guilty of sinning, eating from the tree of knowledge despite God's order not to do so, Nathanson sees Adam and Eve in shame. They hide from God, fearing God, and experience anxiety because of what they dread comes next: their rejection from the Garden of Eden. According to Nathanson, this fear and anxiety of further punishment, rather than producing guilt and remorse, produces shame, and it is precisely this logic that drives rationale in the criminal justice system.

Scholars of the more progressive restorative model critique the narrative of rue and contrition that underlies the retributive model, arguing that it adds "harm to harm" by inflicting pain and suffering on those who have committed crimes; separates inmates from the world and from the ability to make amends; and perpetuates shame.[17] Understood affectively, shame leads to violence, instead of ameliorating it—undermining the stated goal of the criminal justice system. Furthermore, proponents of restorative justice argue that treatment and conditions in the prison compound the shame present prior to incarceration, which both results from trauma and motivates violence in the first place.

In support of restorative justice, Gilligan draws out the reality of prison as a kind of Dantesque "hell," which freezes the incarcerated in shame.[18] He presses the need to view violence in its epic or mythic dimensions, as a grand narrative that both reflects theological assumptions and takes affect to its extreme. Like Nathanson, he identifies a dynamic inherent in the Christian tradition that denies the tradition's participation in forms of punishment like prison. This dynamic emerges in the "guilt-ethic." Within this ethic, "the worst evil (the deadliest of the seven deadly sins) is pride, and the highest good is humility (self-humiliation, selflessness, altruism)."[19] One of the problems inherent in this construction emerges in the unnuanced notion of pride as a sin instead of, as Gilligan posits, a form of self-love that fosters dignity and esteem, combating shame. At the heart of the guilt-ethic, then, lies shame and fear, precisely the affective dimensions that Gilligan lays out in his critique of the prison system.

Furthermore, Gilligan argues that the guilt-ethic's binary (which places a negative value on self-love and a positive value on loving others) cannot solve the problem of violence. It cannot because it "does not dismantle the motivational structure that causes violence in the first place (namely, shame, and the shame-ethics that motivates it)."[20] Gilligan sees the perpetual guilt-ethic bind as sustaining the problem of violence because it directs violence toward the self, creating the image of the guilty, lonely sinner, facilitating, as Nathanson points out, shame instead of empathy.

Gilligan shows that in the effort to restore their own dignity, or ameliorate shame, violent men lash out and participate in crime or harm to others. The ability to enact violence on another derives from shame, which overwhelms other affective possibilities like empathy or joy and instead creates "a feeling of numbness and deadness."[21] Thus, shame from a lack of love beginning in childhood, a factor in cases of childhood abuse, motivates violence, and the prison system, instead of addressing this shame, perpetuates it.

In *The New Jim Crow*, Michelle Alexander corroborates Gilligan's critique of criminal justice from a different angle; she admonishes the prison system for being a unique form of social control. In her assessment that the USA has replaced one caste system (Jim Crow) with another (discipline and punishment in prison), she addresses the affects of fear and shame saturating the criminal justice system and imposed upon minorities. She explicitly mentions the fear of a lack of representation especially due to poverty, the fear of repercussions if inmates object to maltreatment and sentences, and the ultimate fear of a loss of selfhood removed from the all-powerful, God-like criminal justice system, which she states serves as "a *gateway* into a much larger system of racial stigmatization and permanent marginalization."[22] She also points out the social silence around the reality of incarceration in both the lives of those incarcerated and their families "driven by stigma and fear of shame."[23] Once branded a criminal or felon, inmates are stripped of civil rights and can no longer vote, serve on juries, and have access to housing, education, or equal employment. Thus, retributive justice practices, supported by a particular theo-ologic that uses stigmatization as a form of punishment, increases the affective experiences of shame and fear indicative of traumatic narratives. As a result, these narratives intensify affect, participating in what affect theorists understand as cycles or spirals of shame; that is, shame leads to rage which leads to more shame and thus more rage.[24]

Restorative Justice

Emerging theoretically from the historical context of the Truth and Reconciliation Commission (TRC) in South Africa instituted by Nelson Mandela and Desmond Tutu, restorative justice, especially in the USA and Canada, has become both a response to retributive justice and a social movement promoting positive affect and empathy as emollients to shame. Restorative justice proposes a more holistic approach than the retributive model, countering both the theo-logic inherent in the guilt-ethic's support of isolated pain and suffering and in the idea that the justice system somehow saves the inmate, presumably from further sin. Part of the theological shift in restorative justice includes Tutu's *Ubunto* theology, which constitutes a move away from punishment toward communal repair providing what Michael Jesse calls "a corrective hermeneutic for Western salvation theology that focuses on the individual," emphasizing instead of the solitary sinner, "the integrity of creation" and "the habitual recalling of our image of God (*imago Dei*) in the midst of human conflict."[25] As a result, restorative justice practices reflect a theology of mutuality and a compassion for both perpetrator and victim as loved by God.

Another component in the shift from retributive justice and the theo-logic of punishment for sins relates to restorative justice's emergence from a range of spiritual approaches. In addition to its *Ubuntu* roots, restorative justice principles and practices reflect influences from Aboriginal, Maori, Jewish, Christian, and First Nation Traditions in the US and Canada.[26] The varied theological roots offer an equally wide array of language and rituals, which promote healing and repair over retribution. Along with its multi-religious background, restorative justice reflects aspects of the Christian tradition including witnessing and forgiveness, insisting on accountability and community. One of the core approaches to healing in restorative justice is dialogue with the intention to foster relationships and empathy. Underlying this method is the belief that testimony facilitates restoration within relationship.

But while offering a counter narrative to that embedded in retributive justice, one that entails attention to rehabilitation and restoration, its own dedication to the idea of reparations among and amidst human relationships leaves it vulnerable at the level of affect and trauma.[27] In order for movements of restoration to hold constant to their missive of repair of harm for all parties, such movements must develop an affective responsibility and an awareness of the challenges that facing trauma present in the classroom.

For instance, a theme prevalent in restorative justice relates to the quote attributed to Gandhi but having roots in St. Augustine's theology, "Hate the sin but love the sinner."[28] Often used to reflect the sentiment inherent in restorative justice, this feature of the movement makes the theological claim that the sinner be attended to with love and that sin be met with resistance. While this quote uplifts the idea of mutuality and forgiveness, it also presents a threat. In the process of recovery from traumatic harm, compassion for the perpetrator (the sinner) may disturb or negatively affect victims or survivors. Judith Herman contends that many survivors of trauma do not want to hear from the perpetrator, or need any confirmation of his or her remorse, as was borne out by our classroom visit. Forcing the issue is tantamount to discounting the survivor's experience of trauma.

Furthermore, the statement projects the presence of positive affect (love), which is useful as long as the negative affects (anger, shame, and fear) that emerge as a result from trauma have been addressed. According to Herman's stages of recovery, anger and rage at perpetrators is not only perfectly normal but also necessary. In fact, she calls forgiveness during this stage a fantasy that impedes mourning.[29] That is, in an effort to assuage the pain of admission of being betrayed or wronged, a person claims to forgive, but not having grieved or processed through the affective anger perverts forgiveness. Traversing the affective bridge from anger and forgiveness happens over time as a part of a process.

Any program that attempts to connect victims, offenders, and the public, especially students, must try to ensure safety for all in order to do no harm and make known the limitations, for instance, in the case of time. This means paying attention not only to participants' present needs but also to understanding that processing violence and trauma happens in stages; hate the sin but not the sinner presents a theological claim that may indeed be true at last, but that in fact does not hold at every stage of recovery.

The affective responsibility that I press becomes even more critical when the shift from the theo-logic of the guilt-ethic that Gilligan critiques highlights the dynamics of shame. And if the shift from guilt to shame is right, then shame cannot be restricted to only the incarcerated.

As an affect, shame indicates a perceived failure or defect in the self that motivates a desire to withdraw. The body thus turns away, or the eyes fall downcast. The consequence of shame is diminishment, and the danger of shame is the increase of shame itself, which perpetuates violence. Gilligan affirms this when he reports that most of the violent men whom he meets attest to the fact that they committed violent acts as a way to ameliorate the shame of having been "dissed" or disregarded.[30] Committed acts of violence represent their attempts to reinstate pride. Violence fails to produce pride and, instead, generates additional shame.

Situating shame in this way allows a consideration of the students' experience of this affect. Shame adds another possibility to account for the students' failure to raise their hands when the inmate asked if they wanted to hear from a perpetrator. This presents an important question: does the lack of hand-raising mean that they did not want to hear from the perpetrator, or was shame at work to prevent their hand-raising? Shame causes a sinking back into the body, a wish to not be seen or heard, and silence is believed to be one of shame's greatest indicators.[31] The absence of raised hands accompanied by silence could indicate shame.

Thus, situating restorative justice education within the walls of a prison, a place that physically communicates to those within it that they have no power or capacity to choose, affectively imposes a sense of diminishment—shame. This lack of control, even if not actual but simply perceived, disempowers students and establishes the vulnerable foreground from which shame emerges. The added component of listening to traumatic narratives, many that featured young women and men as victims, could have also easily provoked shame. If Herman's association of shame with trauma—that shame motivates the desire to evade painful affect and evidences the stigma of having experienced trauma—then the traumatic narratives made shame ever more present.

The work of restorative justice is precarious work, as it not only situates itself as a progressive movement within a politically fraught and violent environment, but it also opens up a world of shame and trauma that necessarily needs attention. And while restorative justice promotes theological principles that facilitate mutuality, forgiveness, and even love, it does so at a great risk. The confrontation with trauma and shame poses affective challenges for all of those involved, especially for those who have experienced trauma.

Conclusion

In her book, *Unsayable: The Hidden Language of Trauma*, Annie Rogers reinforces the way that trauma can take over even the most basic capacity, the ability to speak. To emphasize this, she quotes poet Robert Pinsky: "What if I told you the truth? What if I could?"[32] Pinsky's question, and much of Rogers' discussion throughout her text, points to the nature of trauma to debilitate, to silence, to destroy lives, and to incur shame. Through the use of Pinsky, Rogers points to the inability to speak or language experience that trauma incurs, drawing attention to the students' silence when asked if they wanted to hear from their perpetrators. The quote also elicits the sense of shame that emerges when the capacity to speak is debilitated by trauma. Incapability as shame reaches into the heart to engender a feeling of worthlessness. It is this sense of inferiority that practices inherent in restorative justice attempt to repudiate. Theologically, this aim to restore dignity and counter shame emerges in the replacement of the image of the lonely sinner with that of mutuality, bringing people together to foster the idea that communities play a role in crime and violence. This theoretical move also rejects punishment, as it promotes the *imago dei*, especially for those incarcerated.

What if the students in the class answered "No" to the inmate's question regarding a desire to hear from one's perpetrator? Could they have said, "No" in the conditions of the prison visit? If trauma impedes language, and shame silences, then saying "No" presented another impossibility. Moreover, power structures overwhelmingly present in the auditorium instilled enough intimidation and affective fear and shame to make refusal unthinkable and subsequent withdrawal impractical. The students were not provided an option to leave the auditorium; they were thus subjected to narratives that they could withdraw from only affectively, with no place to go and with no preparation regarding the trauma that they would encounter. Students who found themselves triggered by the environment and the traumatic narratives they witnessed had only the choice to further internalize whatever affect they experienced. In any case, it is unlikely that a student would have voiced discomfort or refused to listen attentively at the risk of seeming indifferent or insensitive, or for the fear of being stigmatized. The inmate who read his letter was sincere, and the students' desire to support him as evident from their own participation in restorative justice may have allowed them to deny or question their own needs. This denial of self at the behest of another, as Gilligan points out inherent in the guilt-ethic, conjoins with the equal pressure to avoid the shame of calling attention to victim status and/or being a disruption to the process of testimony.

Trauma, theology, and jurisprudence combine in the classroom consideration of justice. This intense conglomeration demands an affective sensibility that would facilitate rather than hinder the study and practice of restorative justice, even by providing a more refined theological distance between retribution and restoration. Addressing affects normalizes the responses to trauma and continues to discount the theo-logic upholding the lonely sinner who deserves punishment, as it communicates to participants that experiencing affects like shame and fear is both normal and not always necessary. Contemporary understanding of trauma and affect thus presses restorative justice and movements of its kind, especially in education, to think about and address trauma and affect of the witnesses within all procedures and processes. In a program that is attempting to reconcile in the presence of the public, traumatic histories of all and accompanying affect must be considered. Attention to affects allows both an opportunity for their containment and a space for their expression. Ultimately, acknowledging trauma and discussing its affective impact on perpetrators, survivors, and communities allows for a regulation of affect, a necessary factor for enabling students to think and to participate fully in making changes in the interpretation of "justice."

NOTES

1. See Gerry Johnstone (2011) *Restorative Justice: Ideas, Values, and Debates* (New York: Routledge), 118–22.
2. Donald L. Nathanson (1992) *Shame and Pride: Affect, Sex, and the Birth of the Self* (New York: W. W. Norton & Company), 49.
3. See Alan Schore (2004) *Affect Regulation and Repair of the Self* (New York: W.W. Norton & Company).
4. Kathleen Stewart (2007) *Ordinary Affects* (Durham: Duke University Press), 40.
5. Henri Lefebrve (2000) *The Production of Space*, Donald Nicholson-Smith (trans.) (Oxford: Blackwell Publications), 19.
6. James Gilligan (1996) *Violence: Our Deadly Epidemic and Its Causes* (New York: G.P. Putnam's Sons), 29–30.
7. Robin Weeks and Cathy Spatz Widom (1998) "Early Childhood Victimization Among Incarcerated Adult Male Felons," National Institute of Justice, accessed April 9, 2015, https://www.ncjrs.gov/pdffiles/fs000204.pdf.

8. Terry Frieden (2012) "Study Finds Nearly 1 in 10 State Prisoners is Sexually Abused while Incarcerated," CNN, May 17, 2012, accessed April 1, 2015, http://www.cnn.com/2012/05/17/us/us-state-prisons-abuse/.
9. Melissa Gregg and Gregory J. Seigworth (eds.) (2010) *The Affect Theory Reader* (Durham: Duke University Press), 5.
10. Madelyn Miller (2008) "Creating a Safe Frame for Learning," *Journal of Teaching in Social Work*, vol. 21, no. 3–4, 161.
11. Bessel van der Kolk (2014) *The Body Keeps the Score: Brain, Mind, and the Body in the Healing of Trauma* (New York: Viking), 66.
12. van der Kolk, *The Body Keeps the Score*, 66.
13. Schore, *Affect Regulation and Repair of the Self*, 66 and 98.
14. Miller, "Creating a Safe Frame," 168.
15. Miller, "Creating a Safe Frame," 168.
16. Nathanson, *Shame and Pride*, 327.
17. Lode Walgrave (2007) "Integrating Criminal Justice and Restorative Justice," in Gerry Johnstone & Daniel W. Van Ness (eds.) *Handbook of Restorative Justice* (Devon: Willan Publishing), 559 and 569.
18. Gilligan, *Violence: Our Deadly Epidemic and its Causes*, 29–34.
19. James Gilligan (2009) "Shame, Guilt, and Violence," InternationalPsychoanalysis.Net, accessed February 21, 2015, http://internationalpsychoanalysis.net/wpcontent/uploads/2009/02/shamegilligan.pdf
20. James Gilligan (1996) *Violence: Reflections on a National Epidemic* (New York: G.P. Putnam's Sons), 235.
21. Gilligan, *Violence*, 47–48.
22. Michelle Alexander (2010) *The New Jim Crow: Mass Incarceration in the Age of Colorblindness* (New York: The New Press), 12.
23. Alexander, *The New Jim Crow*, 169.
24. Thomas J. Scheff (1987) "The Shame-Rage Spiral: A Case Study of an Interminable Quarrel," in Helen Block Lewis (ed.) *The Role of Shame in Symptom Formation* (London: Psychology Press), 109–149.
25. Michael Jesse Battle (2009) *Reconciliation: The Ubuntu Theology of Desmond Tutu* (New York: Pilgrim Press), 5.
26. Michael L. Hadley (2001) "Introduction: Multifaith Reflection on Criminal Justice," in Michael Hadley (ed.) *The Spiritual Roots of Restorative Justice* (Albany: State University of New York Press), 9.

27. See generally Susan Sharpe (2007) "The Idea of Reparation," in Gerry Johnstone & Daniel W. Van Ness (eds.) *Handbook of Restorative Justice* (Devon: Willan Publishing), 24.
28. Restorativejustice.org, accessed January 21, 2015, http://www.restorativejustice.org.
29. Judith Herman (1992) *Trauma and Recovery* (New York: Basic Books), 189–90.
30. Rebecca Aponte (2011) "James Gilligan on the Psychology and Treatment of Violent Behaviors," Psychotherapy.net, accessed April 20, 2015, https://www.psychotherapy.net/interview/gilligan-violence.
31. See Elspeth Probyn (2004) "Shame in the Habitus," in *The Editorial Board of the Sociological Review*, vol. 52, no. 2 (Malden: Blackwell Publishing) and Bernard Williams (1993, reprint 2008) *Shame and Necessity* (Berkeley: University of California Press).
32. Annie G. Rogers (2007) *The Unsayable: The Hidden Language of Trauma* (New York: Ballantine Trade Books), 30.

Bibliography

Alexander, M. 2010. *The new Jim crow: Mass incarceration in the age of colorblindness*. New York: The New Press.

Aponte, R. 2011. James Gilligan on the psychology and treatment of violent behaviors. Psychotherapy.net. https://www.psychotherapy.net/interview/gilligan-violence

Frieden, T. 2012. Study finds nearly 1 in 10 state prisoners is sexually abused while incarcerated. CNN. http://www.cnn.com/2012/05/17/us/us-state-prisons-abuse

Gilligan, J. 1996. *Violence: Our deadly epidemic and its causes*. New York: G.P. Putnam's Sons.

Gilligan, J. 2003. Shame, guilt, and violence. *Social Research* 70(4): 1149–1180.

Gregg, M., and G.J. Seigworth (eds.). 2010. *The affect theory reader*. Durham: Duke University Press.

Hadley, M.L. 2001. Introduction: Multifaith reflection on criminal justice. In *The spiritual roots of restorative justice*, ed. M. Hadley. Albany: State University of New York Press.

Herman, J. 1992. *Trauma and recovery*. New York: Basic Books.

Johnstone, G. 2011. *Restorative justice: Ideas, values, and debates*. New York: Routledge.

Lefebrve, H. 2000. *The production of space*. Trans. D. Nicholson-Smith. Oxford: Blackwell Publications.

Miller, M. 2008. Creating a safe frame for learning. *Journal of Teaching in Social Work* 21(3–4): 159–176.
Nathanson, D.L. 1992. *Shame and pride: Affect, sex, and the birth of the self.* New York: W.W. Norton.
Probyn, E. 2004. Shame in the habitus. *The Editorial Board of the Sociological Review* 52(2): 224–248. Malden: Blackwell Publishing.
Restorative Justice Website. http://www.restorativejustice.org
Rogers, A.G. 2007. *The unsayable: The hidden language of trauma.* New York: Ballantine Trade Books.
Scheff, T.J. 1987. The shame-rage spiral: A case study of an interminable quarrel. In *The role of shame in symptom formation*, ed. H.B. Lewis. London: Psychology Press.
Schore, A. 2004. *Affect regulation and repair of the self.* New York: W.W. Norton.
Sharpe, S. 2007. The idea of reparation. In *Handbook of restorative justice*, ed. G. Johnstone and D.W. Van Ness. Devon: Willan Publishing.
Stewart, K. 2007. *Ordinary affects.* Durham: Duke University Press.
Van der Kolk, B. 2014. *The body keeps the score: Brain, mind, and the body in the healing of trauma.* New York: Viking.
Walgrave, L. 2007. Integrating criminal justice and restorative justice. In *Handbook of restorative justice*, ed. G. Johnstone and D.W. Van Ness. Devon: Willan Publishing.
Weeks, R., and C. P. Widom. 1998. Early childhood victimization among incarcerated adult male felons. National Institute of Justice. https://www.ncjrs.gov/pdffiles/fs000204.pdf
Williams, B. 1993. *Shame and necessity.* Berkeley: University of California Press. Reprint 2008.

CHAPTER 10

9/11 Changed Things: The (Post-Traumatic) Religious Studies Classroom

Katherine Janiec Jones

September 11, 2001, changed the religious studies classroom. In the days and months that followed, people were disoriented, frightened, and not really sure what they were supposed to do next. Both public discourse and people's private understanding of themselves and of the world they lived in were shaken by the initial public trauma of 9/11 and its aftermath. One of the primary foci of public discussion was, of course, the subject of religion and the horrors to which it can lead; therefore, it wasn't at all surprising that the sadness, anger, insecurity, and confusion spurred by 9/11 affected the pedagogical tenor of the religious studies classroom.

The atmosphere of desperate and hyperbolic public discourse on religion characterized the landscape in which I began my first job as an assistant professor of religious studies in September of 2002. As I worked over the summer to plan my classes, I couldn't help but wonder what a post-traumatic religious studies classroom would look like and how I should approach my own role within that context. I wondered if the post-9/11 atmosphere would inhibit classroom discussion, or, alternatively, if it might make things so tense that people would have a hard time actually listening to each other and engaging ideas.

K.J. Jones (✉)
Wofford College, Spartanburg, SC, USA

I hoped that rather than letting the shadow of 9/11 shut down or straightjacket conversation, I could foster an atmosphere in which our shared sense of brokenness might allow us to shake off some of the cloaks of ego and insecurity that can hinder engagement with others and prohibit the type of vulnerability that often serves as a precursor to open-hearted listening and real learning. The question, of course, was how to do that.

As I have reflected on those early teaching days, I have realized that the trauma of 9/11 surfaced and brought into sharp relief three factors that were, and continue to be, at play in the religious studies classroom—factors that are crucial in shaping interactions between teachers and students, especially in a post-traumatic context. In retrospect, I don't think these factors were created by 9/11. They were already there, perhaps in nascent form, more deeply rooted beneath the surface of conversation. The trauma of 9/11 simply made them more active in the classroom, like molecules that move more quickly when heated up. The post-traumatic context also made it much harder for me to ignore their presence, even when I hadn't quite put my finger on what they were and what was going on.

Each factor had to do with identity formation and classification—specifically, with how we think of ourselves and how we think of others in relation to our sense of place in the world. The first had to do with how I classified myself, and it mapped onto what could best be described as the "religious studies/theology split" within the academy itself. This "split" affects how scholars think of themselves and think of what kind of pedagogical stance they should assume in the classroom. These self-classifications shape scholarly identity—how scholars envision themselves and how they want others to envision them. What I didn't realize at first, though, was the extent to which these self-identifications also shape our identities as teachers: they serve as the mold in which the heuristic lenses of our classrooms take shape.

The second factor that I think was already at play in 2002 (although it was not yet labeled as a sociological trend in the way that it has been recently) was the increase in the number of students who might, today, self-identify as a "none," as someone who is "spiritual but not religious," or as someone who finds resonance within more than one religious tradition. Recent data compiled by institutions such as the Pew Research Center and the Public Religion Research Institute show a marked shift in recent years, at least in the USA, in the ways people conceptualize their religious identities. Much of this shift seems to be generational; in other words, many of the people who seem to be identifying less with "traditional" religious institutions are in the undergraduate age bracket. Whether the escalation of this trend has been, in part, an unconscious response to 9/11, or whether the increase in numbers has merely been coincidental, I'm not sure. Either way, though, I think that whatever impetus has been leading more and more people away from identification with traditional religious (institutional) formations was already at play pre-9/11; perhaps the disorienting nature of 9/11 catalyzed it. It certainly made me more aware of the fact that something was going on in terms of what the word "religion" meant to my students.

The third factor also had to do with disorientation, but in a different way. College is a place to which many students come in a state of what might be thought of as "developmental disorientation." They are searching to figure out who they are, and so might feel like they are living "in between" various identities, partially self-identifying with several different categories of being, but not entirely assenting to any in particular. A sense of alienation often characterizes the coming to adulthood in college: as people grow up, they often face a period of disillusionment that accompanies the unseating of childhood perceptions about their families, their economic class, their ethnicity, their gender, and so on.

The Lay of the Land: The Religious Studies/ Theology Split, Hybrid Religiosities, and Identity Formation

It might seem that the concerns surrounding the religious studies/theology split constitute a discipline-specific, esoteric, oriented-toward-experts set of issues that wouldn't really have an impact on the concrete practicalities of the classroom. However, I couldn't help but wonder how my graduate school training, firmly planted on the religious studies side of the fence, had prepared me for the tenuous context of an undergraduate classroom studying religion in the aftermath of a public tragedy—one confusingly and painfully inflected with religious discourse. Issues of religious difference and similarity, of violence and healing, of societal cohesion and divisiveness, transformed my pedagogy post-9/11, making me think long and hard about the types of questions around which the learning outcomes of my courses might be conceptualized. The broader, meaning-of-life issues exploded into pressing, practical questions being posed to me, both implicitly and explicitly, by classrooms full of disillusioned, frightened, disoriented students. The world had changed for them overnight. Messages of fear and hatred peppered them everywhere they turned, but at the same time, these students were being told of the importance of healing and resilience. I realized they would be looking to me, their religion professor, for some sort of answers to the question of what had happened. What was the deal, really, with religion if it had been the very thing that had led to all of this pain?

The question that I faced as a teacher, then, was this: what practices might characterize the religious studies classroom, such that the vulnerable contexts of students could be treated with an ethic of care? Was there a way to provide the space for students to begin looking at their own wounds in a way that didn't exacerbate their sense of vulnerability, while at the same time, not creating an atmosphere of proselytization for a particular position or tradition?

My own academic training was oriented toward an effort to understand the philosophical claims that undergird various religious traditions and worldviews. I have been committed to the idea that my own place in the classroom, and in the institutions in which I have taught, has been one of trying to help students unearth their own presuppositions and value claims, in order to examine those value claims' coherence, validity, entailments, and implications. In short, I have seen myself as trying to help students learn *how* to think, rather than *what* to think. In retrospect, though, it occurs to me that the "big questions," the human questions, can engage students in a type of self-exploration that somehow allows them to move across the fragile landscape between what scholars think of when they juxtapose "religious studies" and "theology."[1]

And yet, it is in the very space of addressing "big questions" that issues of religious studies vs. theology perhaps become the most pertinent, especially in an era where more and more people are moving away from strict affiliation with a particular, institutionally inflected religious identity. To what extent does "thinking theologically" mean "thinking from within the normative claims of a particular, institutionally religious, category?" Might it be better to address "big questions" in a religious studies classroom in a way that is not explicitly theological, lest those who do not identify with a particular tradition feel left out of the conversation, as if their concerns are somehow invalidated by their lack of "membership" in a particular group?

These questions boil down to what we mean, exactly, when we use the word "theology." If, when people speak of theology, they are thinking of theological talk as being aimed at persons who feel that they have a clearly-delineated theological "home," then it becomes unclear whether theological talk is meant to be inclusive or exclusive. And in light of the fact that an increasing number of students seems to feel that they do not have a theological "home," if it is the case that big questions can only be addressed theologically, then a lot of people are going to feel excluded from vital conversations. Surely, making students feel excluded from questions of meaning cannot be the goal of higher education. Nor, it seems to me, can it be the proper goal of theology. If students who are "in between" identities understand, rightly or wrongly, theology to be something that excludes them, such perceptions would seem to obviate theology's healing potential by shutting people down and making them feel that they perhaps have no place in the classroom, except one of self-protective detachment.

It is certainly the case that many of the college students whom I have taught over the last 15 years, almost all of whom have been between the ages of 17 and 22, have expressed deep concerns—even anger and sadness—about theological exclusivity, even if they have not described their concerns in terms of their being explicitly "theological."[2]

In one course that I teach frequently, called "Introduction to Religion," for example, I ask students to write a brief essay during the first week of class in which they define the word "religion." I then ask them to write a paragraph in which they describe whether or not they consider themselves to be "religious," and why or why not. My goal, I explain, is to get them to begin the process of foregrounding their own presuppositions about what the words "religion" and "religious" mean before we embark on any of the reading.

The following excerpts, taken from essays written in the spring semester of 2014, highlight a fear that I have noticed, over the years, that is shared by many students. The fear revolves around an assumption that theological talk will be somehow punitive or dogmatic. One student wrote,

> I find [the term *religion*] very difficult to explain. I believe this is because religion can mean so many different things to different people … Because of this lack of clarity about what the term *religion* means, I am honestly not sure if I consider myself religious or not. I do not go to church every Sunday (although I am trying to be better about this), and I often find myself praying when I need something. However, I do feel that I am a *spiritual* person, meaning that although I do not know all of the doctrines and teachings of my faith, I believe in a higher power, and I absolutely believe in something beyond this world because I really cannot even fathom the possibility that this life is all there is. I have lost some loved ones in my life, and I believe in God and heaven because, if I'm completely honest, I do not have another choice.

I must believe that they are in a better place. So when people ask me if I am religious, I usually feel awkward and uncomfortable because I want to say 'yes,' but I am not quite sure what the term really means, and I feel that there is a pressure, especially in the South, to know it all when it comes to religion and I'm usually afraid that people will judge my answer as being wrong.[3]

Another wrote,

> At the risk of sounding like a west-coast housewife who experimented a little too much in college or every yoga instructor ever, I would have to say that I don't consider myself a religious person, but I do consider myself a spiritual person. And further, I find myself generally turned off by dogmatic ways of thinking. However, I do believe in something 'bigger' being out there or some 'telos'. Because of this I would say that I am still spiritual or if taken with a more liberal definition – religious.[4]

The lines between what falls under the rubric of "theology" and a more generic idea of "religion" can be difficult to discern in undergraduate student writing at the introductory level. Even so, while neither student talks about theological inquiry directly, theological concerns are clearly there in the subtext. Indeed, both excerpts express a distaste for dogmatic judgment. This distaste, along with the subtle lumping together of "religion" and "theology" reflect, I think, broader societal trends.

Whatever the myriad reasons might be for the stark line that religious studies scholars and theologians draw between their "territories" within the academy—and many of these are, I think, good reasons, and reasons that shape my thinking about what I do and don't do in the classroom—I can't help but wonder if this divide is helping students to make sense of their worlds. This division leaves the student in a tenuous position, caught between scholars' concerns about a pedagogical divide that projects ideas about what is proper to address in the classroom.

Identifying by Non-Identification: The "Spiritual but Not Religious," "Nones," and Other Religious Hybrids

One example of recent data parsing the increase in religious non-affiliation, compiled by the Pew Research Center, has shown that more and more Americans are describing their own religiousness as lying outside of traditional (institutional) categories, and even outside of categories (such as "atheist" and "agnostic") that are often defined in terms of the repudiation of traditional institutional categories. There is an upward trend in the number of people who self-identify as being either "spiritual but not religious" or as having "no particular religious affiliation." This latter, non-affiliated group is often referred to as the "nones."

A Pew Research study, published in 2012, states,

> The number of Americans who do not identify with any religion continues to grow at a rapid pace. One-fifth of the U.S. public – and a third of adults under 30 – are religiously unaffiliated today, the highest percentages ever in Pew Research Center polling...In the last five years alone, the unaffiliated have increased from just over 15% to just under 20% of all U.S. adults. Their ranks now include more than 13 million self-described atheists and agnostics (nearly 6% of the U.S. public), as well as nearly 33 million people who say they have no particular religious affiliation (14%).[5]

Indeed, as summarized by Linda Mercadante, "during the 1990s, the number of 'nones' began to rise exponentially until now it is considered the fastest growing 'religious group' in the nation."[6]

Not only are the ranks of the non-affiliated, the "spiritual but not religious," and what I think of as the "in-betweens" or the "multiples" growing; researchers are also realizing that within those ranks, there is a lot more variety than might appear at first blush. In other words, not all people who self-identify from the margins think the same things, or eschew traditional religious categories for the same reasons:

> In terms of their religious beliefs and practices, the unaffiliated are a diverse group, and far from uniformly secular. Just 5% say they attend worship services on a weekly basis. But one-third of the unaffiliated say religion is at least somewhat important in their lives. Two-thirds believe in God (though less than half say they are absolutely certain of God's existence). And although a substantial minority of the unaffiliated consider themselves neither religious nor spiritual (42%), the majority describe themselves either as a religious person (18%) or as spiritual but not religious (37%).[7]

In an effort to interpret what is going on, some scholars have read non-affiliation, religious hybridity and/or a sense of multiple belonging primarily in terms of representing an apparent threat to the health of religious institutions. Alternatively (and in some ways, similarly), some scholars have described self-identities that involve religious hybridity or feelings of multiple belonging as being a sign of a sort of spiritual or emotional immaturity, or as a kind of specifically-American hyper-individualism that misses the point about the importance of religious community. Many in this group of thinkers seem to worry that people who consider themselves "seekers" will never move out of the in-betweenness of a liminal state, never find a new, steady, theologically or ideologically coherent home.

Sometimes, these concerns seem to spring from presuppositions about the maturation and developmental soundness of the seekers; how can such seekers ever grow up if they make no clear decisions, have no coherent allegiances in which to ground themselves? Other times, concerns seem to spring from an inchoate worry that multiple belonging or "none"-ness represents some sort of zero-sum game: the fewer people there are finding allegiance in religious institutions, the weaker those institutions will be, this line of thinking suggests. And if religious institutions disappear or diminish in importance, what other institutions, if any, will rise up to take their place? What will "win" in terms of numbers of "members"? Or, alternatively, if this lack of affiliation suggests a lack of desire to affiliate with much of anything on the part of younger generations, then where will we be? Will everything else fall apart as well? And, of course, still others interpret the rejection of institutionally religious frameworks, a lack of willingness to claim "membership" in a given religious tradition, as a tacit rejection of their own values and existential claims. A person with this type of concern might be asking, unconsciously, "If so many people are saying 'no' to this thing upon which I've built my life, upon which my very identity and hope for the future depends, what does that say about *me*? Am I wrong, or deluded? Is the ground upon which I have stood, which I thought to be at least somewhat solid, disappearing around me, eroding and becoming a dangerous place to be?"

I would argue, however, that rather than indicating a passivity about or disinterest in the nature of meaning, of human suffering, or even a rejection of the idea of God, for many people, choosing to describe themselves as "spiritual but not religious" often suggests something much different. For those who grew up within a religious tradition, it sometimes suggests a desire to shed the easily-spoken but rarely-examined phraseology of their "home" traditions, and to seek out a raw, unmediated encounter with questions of meaning.

Theological Questions, Meaning Making, and Identity Formation

This desire for encounter brings me back to the undergraduates with whom I have interacted in my classes, especially within the last five to ten years. If I were to try to articulate one word or theme that seems to tie together what I hear in the voices of my students in terms of what they want, or what they feel their religious lives lack, it would be *authenticity*—a desire or craving for authentic, unmasked, honest encounter. Many students march into their searches for meaning during the college years, grasping a shield of quasi-theological phrases that they have absorbed and can parrot without much thought; they use them as a buffer, of sorts, like protective existential bubble wrap. However, eventually, these same students tend to want to shed that protective linguistic layer in favor of experienced authenticity—they are looking for something that they understand, for words that speak to their own experience, for words through which they hear their own voices.

What I see students experiencing reminds me of a phenomenon I have experienced in adulthood, when I have heard, after a long interval of time, some song that was popular when I was a teenager—one I used to listen to and sing along with, without really paying attention to what the song was saying. Sometimes, when I hear such a song again, I think, "Huh. I never really heard the words of that song. I never listened to what the song was about." And then I hear the song much differently. The college years, I think, present a similar experience, in that students begin to think through the value claims and worldviews they brought with them to college, really "hearing the words" for the first time, and think anew about what they mean.

In defining what she calls "post-traumatic public theology," Shelly Rambo says, "As religions offer frameworks of meaning for living in the world, theologians continually examine those frameworks with the aim of bringing them to life in the present moment."[8] This comment is especially helpful in thinking about teaching religion in today's undergraduate classroom. With reference to what theology can offer that is distinctive in the aftermath of tragedy, she describes "theology as a two worlds practice. It is the work of transfiguring the world – working between the *as is* and the *otherwise*."[9] This work of transfiguring the world—of trying to think through ways one might work to make it a better place, and of trying to find a way to be at home in the world—can occur, or at least begin, in the religious studies classroom as well as a theology classroom, especially in a post-traumatic era. If nothing else, the religious studies classroom can serve as a space for thought experiments, a place for students to stop and take a clear, unadulterated look at the "as is," and to think through what the "otherwise" might look like.

Rambo's description of a "two worlds practice" that works in the spaces between the "as is" and the "otherwise" resonates strongly with the work of personal identity formation with which I see many undergraduate students grappling. College, for them, is a sort of liminal space: students see themselves as being not-yet-entirely who they will be, but no-longer-entirely who they were before coming to college. For the time that they are living within the extended temporal parentheses that the college years can provide, students often find themselves both bracketing and then examining the matrix of value claims within which they have been formed during childhood—this, in an effort to figure out whether or not the things they have been taught to believe are really what they do believe. College is a testing ground: as students learn things within the classroom and have new types of interactions outside of the classroom—whether they be in the dorm, in service groups, in clubs, in internships, or even within extended research projects in the library—they often cannot help but begin asking questions about whether or not the things they have thought and believed up until now will provide a salutary staging ground for them to become the people they want to be, accomplishing the things they want to accomplish. College, in other words, is sort of like the "research and development" phase of personal identity development.

The image I have in mind for student development during the college years involves an Etch-a-Sketch toy: a red, rectangular, flat box with knobs at the bottom and a sort of drawing screen in the middle. I imagine each student bringing one of these Etch-a-Sketches to college. Each one already has lines drawn on the screen; these lines represent the value claims, beliefs, presuppositions, and overall worldview that have shaped the student, often without his or her being consciously aware of the lines' having done so. Over the course of the next several years, students will find themselves shaking up their Etch-a-Sketches so as to dismantle the pictures that were already there, and then trying to draw new pictures with the same sand to see what they look like. While it might be the case that the pictures they end up with will look very different from the original design, students might also end up with a picture that is very similar to the one with which they started. But what *will* be different is that the individuals holding their Etch-a-Sketches will end up with a picture that they have drawn themselves—ideally, with intention and careful thought. Their drawings will feel authentic to them, consciously created, rather than seeming like a drawing copied from someone else's design.

The college years comprise a time in which doubts that students have had—about their religious affiliation, about their sexuality, about their political commitments—often seem more pressing, and the freedom to explore them without the watchful eye of family and friends from home more capacious. They realize that if they are going to articulate a creed, for example, or proclaim allegiance to something, they want it to be something that they feel they have chosen for themselves, consciously, rather than something merely performed as an exercise in lip service, enacted like some sort of social theater just to escape censure.

Sketching the Lines of Self and the Desire for Authenticity in Identity Formation

Much of the Etch-a-Sketch shaking and tentative redrawing of identity formation occurs, unsurprisingly, in college religion and theology classes. A study published in 2007 by Barbara Walvoord called *Teaching and Learning in College Introductory Religion Courses* shows that students often come into their introductory religion and theology classes wanting to do this "shaking up," wanting to learn more about their own tradition and those of others, and wanting to explore their own ethical commitments and the contours of their spiritual lives. However, the study also shows that professors themselves generally do not take student-exploration-of-self to be one of the primary objectives of the class; rather, professors tend to think of the augmentation of critical thinking skills as being the primary desideratum of course work. Even so, the qualitative data from Walvoord's study point out that many professors often know that this type of inner work is going on among their students and try to create spaces (through writing, class discussion, etc.) in which such exploration can take place, if the student wants or needs it.[10]

I have inadvertently set up such an exploratory space through a writing assignment in one of my courses. I designed this assignment with the idea in mind of helping students understand the primary concerns of an author we were about to read. What they have ended up saying in their writing, though, is what has led to my conclusions regarding their desire for authentic encounter.

The text in conjunction with which I give the writing assignment is Mircea Eliade's *The Myth of the Eternal Return*, in which Eliade suggests that religious behavior springs from a human need to find cosmos out of chaos, to discover a point of orientation amidst a sea of existential options and paralyzing relativity. To help them sort through Eliade's argument, I ask students to write an essay on the following question before they get too far into the book: "When do you feel like you are most 'yourself'? Why?" I then follow up by suggesting that, if they are having trouble coming up with an answer, they might think about times or situations wherein they feel like they are *not* themselves. What are those situations like, and what it is about them that makes those situations feel that way?

While the essays all differ, there is a common theme that threads through each response: the students who respond to this essay say that they feel most like themselves when they are in situations that free them from the constraint of public performance—a type of public performance that makes them vulnerable to judgment, to rejection, to an ethos of "you aren't good enough" or "you don't belong." It's as simple as that. It's not so much being vulnerable that students seem to fear, that makes them feel alienated; it is a sense of being vulnerable without being truly *seen*. It is a fear that members of other groups will use an individual's vulnerability opportunistically, primarily to build up an unconscious sense of their own group's strength—that by making oneself vulnerable, he or she will be preyed upon.

For example, many students talk about feeling most like themselves when they are with family or friends, or when they're at home (however home is construed); the common idea here is that in such settings, they can be as silly or inappropriate or moody as they want to be, and the people around them will still love them *no matter what*. Family and friends, in this context, are those who know the person's stories, who share her experiences, who *know* her, and therefore, approach her with a hermeneutic of love and acceptance. They see *her*, no matter the form of her actions or speech.

Others write about feeling like they are the most themselves when they are alone, when they can stop trying to discern the tacit social script according to which they are expected to act. Still others talk about feeling the most like themselves when engaged in activity that, in a sense, takes them *out* of themselves—when they are riding horseback, or playing the piano, or playing a sport at which they excel. Others write about feeling the most themselves when performing—when singing or acting on a stage. While the idea of performing in an effort to get away from performativity might seem counterintuitive, the difference is that in this case, the fact of the song or play's already having a script in place allows the performer to tap into the depth of the feeling behind the words—to tap into the authenticity of the emotion. The security of the script or the music gives a person a sort of license to be vulnerable, a sanctuary in which to explore interiority.

On the other hand, while many students talk about feeling most themselves in situations of familiarity and comfort, still others talk about feeling most themselves in situations of anomaly or challenge, when they have to act without thinking too much: when jumping out of a plane, or traveling to a country they don't know, or challenging themselves to leave their own comfort zones in some way. Here again, there is a sense that freedom from the "normal," from the conventional, allows them to respond to the world with the deepest, truest, most authentic parts of themselves. They're not worried about what other people might think of them, because in these kinds of situations, they simply don't have time to worry. They just have to respond.

In sum, then, each of these essays tends to reflect an assertion that we feel the most ourselves when we are not trying to figure out what other people want from us, or trying to fit in; we are, paradoxically, the most ourselves when we are no longer-self conscious. The self-consciousness born of trying to fit in, of worrying about rejection, or of feeling fragmented from a wider context or lonely within a crowd is fundamentally self-alienating. It forces us to live in the past, fretting over past mistakes or miscues, or in the future, worrying about what consequences our actions or words will produce. A lack of self-consciousness, on the other hand, allows the possibility of being present in the moment. It allows us to engage, and be engaged, authentically and responsively.

It seems to me that, at its most basic, theology should be about just this: presence and authentic response. If theology is about imagining the possible "otherwise" in a non-harmful, compassionate way; and if, in order to facilitate this ability to imagine, theology must speak to people in their specific contexts; then theology should perhaps be something less self-consciously concerned with (exclusive) group identity—with getting or keeping people "in the fold" of a particular sociological group—and more concerned with authentically hearing and responding to the needs of conversation partners in all of their particularity. If we assent to the idea that theology is about meaning-making (rather than hegemony), and that its concerns are with making whole, or providing succor to, those who suffer gaping wounds from the sometimes traumatic realities of life (such as 9/11), and that its tone should be one of compassion and care, rather than legitimation of group identity, then it must speak with an ethic of care to those who are not "in the fold," and, in fact, do not necessarily see "being in a fold" as being their primary concern.

Seeing and Being Seen

Theology classrooms must provide a place that allows for the possibility of presence and authentic response without being prescriptive, normative, or exclusive, and religious studies classrooms must be a place where "big questions" can be addressed without jeopardizing objective inquiry. Since moments of authenticity also create moments in which deep learning can occur, and if we want to create pedagogical structures that enhance the possibility of such moments' occurring, teachers who see themselves as being theologians *and* those who see themselves as being scholars of religious studies must attend to how such structures can be created in ways that are pedagogically and ethically sound.

Of course, each student is different, and each classroom is different in terms of its ethos. Therefore, it's not entirely possible to come up with a fail-safe "prescription" for fostering a salutary environment. Instead, it seems that the professor has to figure out a way to invite authentic response while maintaining a pedagogical and heuristic framework that feels authentic to the corner of the discipline with which he or she identifies. Finding this invitational but pedagogically rigorous and ethical stance can be tricky, because the needs of an individual student or class can change from semester to semester, or even day to day. The professor, then, has to try to be as awake to the nuances and movements of the discussion as possible, and being awake and present to a room full of people day after day is very hard work. Even more so, it can be frightening work, because being present and inviting authenticity on the part of students necessitates authenticity on the part of the professor. When authenticity garners reciprocal response, there is nothing more fulfilling; but when it doesn't, few things can make a person feel more vulnerable. Putting one's self "out there" for a room full of students and not getting much of a response doesn't feel very good.

For me, the post-traumatic context of the religion classroom after 9/11 shifted the question from one of risking discomfort to one of responsibility;

I couldn't really afford *not* to at least try to be present to my students. But the kind of presence I felt that the situation demanded was not one of my own religious confession. Rather, it was one of my own willingness to admit that I didn't know all of the answers, that I was broken and disoriented, too, but that I could at least try to help my dialogue partners—in this case, my students—develop the tools to navigate a life lived in ambiguity.

In *I and Thou*, Martin Buber describes the act of speaking and being spoken to as an analogue for presence and authentic encounter. The framework he sets up is one in which authentic presence is represented by "being able to say You" to one's dialogue partner, rather than seeing one's partner only as an "It." He writes,

> the spirit is truly 'at home with itself' when it can confront the world that is opened up to it, give itself to the world, and redeem it and, through the world, also itself. But the spirituality that represents the spirit nowadays is so scattered, weakened, degenerate, and full of contradictions that it could not possibly do this until it had first returned to the essence of the spirit: being able to say You.[11]

Buber uses language and modes of speaking as analogies for the existential stance we take toward the world—the lens through which we see others, and, as a result, ourselves. Dialogue (the act of speaking), for Buber, can take two forms: speech can be characterized as "I-It" speech, or as "I-You" speech. When we "speak" to someone or something from the position of the "I-It" stance—when we speak the "I" of the "I-It"—we are seeing and approaching our dialogue partner as an object, as a fragment of himself. On the other hand, when we speak with the "I" of the "I-You," we are speaking to the whole of the other person, to his whole self. Moments of "I-You" dialogue, Buber argues, are what we all truly long for, because even though moments of "I-You" dialogue are transitory, they are life-giving. Why? Because in order to speak the "I" of the "I-You," to address the wholeness of the other, the speaker also has to present her whole self—unadorned, unfragmented, unprotected by masks of identity and ego, naked and vulnerable. So, in order to see the other fully, one has to allow oneself to be seen fully. Authentically.

Buber argues that the best chance any of us has of catching a glimpse of the Eternal, or of God, or the Transcendent, or of truth, for that matter, begins with cultivating an "I-You" relationship with another with whom we stand in relation. When a person confronts the other as an "It," she is fragmenting that other person from his wholeness, seeing that person primarily, and perhaps only, as being defined and determined by one of his costumes of identity—he is defined solely as a "liberal," "conservative," "Muslim," "Buddhist," "Marxist," or what have you. Seeing the other solely through the filter of one of these labels, the viewer assumes that she already knows what the other will say and think and do in every situation, and therefore does not allow him the flexibility that is inherent to being human. So, in essence, by seeing someone as a Buberian "It"—fragmenting him from his wholeness via linguistic and conceptual labels—she is denying that person his essential humanity.

What Buber describes as an "I-You" relationship is what I would describe as unsentimentalized, non-grasping love. I think it is fair to say that those we love, those with whom we are closest, are also often the people who can make us the most frustrated, the most angry, and the most incensed. And yet, it seems that this is part of what Buber is getting at: being oriented toward someone as a "You" prevents one from seeing that Other as being exhaustively defined by her annoying habits (or political leanings or religious commitments). One realizes that there is more to that person than her annoying habit or political stance or theological position and loves that other person *in the face of* all the stuff that she doesn't agree with or like. This is what I mean by unsentimental, non-grasping love. It is not solely the stuff of diffused lighting, clouds, and fields of flowers. It is the stuff of bills to be paid, laundry to be folded, and commitments to be remembered. It is hard work. It is being *present* to the other, and to oneself, *in the moment of dialogue*. It is seeing and being seen. It is authentic being, a shelter from the alienation and insecurity of performance.

Buber's emphasis on the salvific ability to say "You" presses religious studies and theology professors to consider making students' needs—their positionality as hearers—a primary hermeneutic concern, every bit as important as the lens of their own scholarly identity. Otherwise, one runs the risk of making the classroom a realm of "I-It," thereby precluding the possibility that students will feel safe enough—clearly seen enough—to respond as a You. A classroom that shuts off the possibility of authentic encounter cannot be life-giving. The dialogue partner (the student) has to trust the intentions of the speaker (the professor) to be a seer and hearer, rather than an ego-driven pedant, an ideologue, or a fear-driven membership organizer.

In an age of religious pluralism,[12] it is perhaps even more incumbent upon educators to make sure that the classroom does not become an antiseptic space of "I-It" language games. David Tracy portrays theological pluralism as presenting a potentially inviting situation that can, if handled with care, allow individuals to maintain their particularity, difference, and the integrity of their commitments without devolving into "coercive theological nonsense."[13] Rather than fomenting a hermeneutic of "Us vs. Them,"

> The global culture which the present suggests and the future demands impels everyone – every individual, every group, every culture, every religious and theological tradition – to recognize the plurality within each self … Our present situation demands that *each come to the dialogue with a genuine self-respect in her or his particularity as well as a willingness to expose oneself as oneself to the other as really other.* Self-exposure is merely the reverse side of the self-respect demanded by this pluralistic moment.[14]

Combining Buber's (and Tracy's) ideas regarding a dialogical willingness to expose oneself as oneself to the other with Tracy's ideas about internal and external pluralism, it seems that a necessary precondition for the religious studies or theology classroom's being non-alienating depends upon those who enter the classrooms being able to assume a hermeneutic of openness to "I-You" dialogue on the part of the professor. Put more simply, the hearer in the dialogue needs to trust the intentions of the speaker in the dialogue. Both the speaker and the listener must be fully who they are and trust the other enough that he or she is willing to expose, to reveal, a true, particular, and specific self.[15]

However, professors must not fall into the trap of assuming that those without religious affiliation have no theological concerns, or, conversely, that those who do have a religious affiliation have fully formed, coherent theologies. In her book, *Belief Without Borders: Inside the Minds of the Spiritual but not Religious*, Linda Mercadante expresses misgivings about the assumption that those who self-identify as "spiritual but not religious" are just "commitment phobic, overly self-focused, or salad-bar spiritualists."[16] What, she wonders, are the "belief issues playing into the decrease in religious affiliation"?[17] Couldn't it be the case that even those who eschew traditional categories still have "both a spiritual and a theological thirst?"[18] In other words, does a person's identifying as "spiritual but not religious" or "none" or as religiously hybrid *necessarily* indicate a lack of interest in theological questions? While Mercadante doesn't present her idea of theological "thirst" as being inflected through the specific lens of a post-9/11 context of disillusion, her analysis provides a useful jumping-off point to think about those who are "religiously liminal," or, at least, institutionally or religious traditionally liminal, in the post-9/11 classroom.[19]

Mercadante concludes that in fact, there is no reason to assume that one's not seeing herself as a "member" of a religious institution, or seeing herself as existing somewhere between or beside institutions, indicates a lack of interest in theological questions—*if* we are defining "theological questions" as being related primarily to "big questions" of the meaning of human life, the nature of suffering, and attention to existential unrest, or even trauma.

While it might seem self-evident to professional theologians that theology is about asking those big questions, I do not think that this is always evident or clear to students: that theology is not *just* about creeds, or doctrines, or that one doesn't necessarily have to be a "member" of a given tradition to have permission to think theologically. Nor do I think it is always clear to students that theology isn't necessarily, inherently judgmental or exclusivist. In sum, it doesn't seem to be clear to many students that theology can provide breathing space, a pause in the tumult of life—that it can provide the ground for genuine encounter. The "religious studies" type of classroom, on the other hand, might seem to be more welcoming to students who are in a liminal phase, or multiply, differently religious, perhaps because of its self-presentation (often erroneous) of objectivity, or, at least, of not having a "membership check" bar in front of its door.

If the theologian finds that her own pedagogical imperative is in accord with the physician's oath to first, do no harm, then the theologian must give serious, empathetic, non-acquisitive thought to the needs of those with no theological home, and to those who know and love others whose theological homes are different from their own. The religious studies professor must do the same. A religious studies scholar and teacher might assert that her primary role is to help students learn how to think critically, and how to understand the role that religion has played in the histories and self-understandings of people who have come before. In so doing, however, the teacher in the religious studies classroom cannot forget that religion (and learning about religion) is also playing a role in the self-understanding of students in the classroom *at that moment*, while they are in the very process of learning. Theological formation might not—perhaps should not—be the religious studies professor's primary concern. But the religious studies professor would be wise also to consider the imperative to "do no harm" or, at least, be aware of the fact that a sense of harm could be operative in the room and informing any learning that might be taking place.

While the specific, on-the-ground needs of students in their everyday lives will, of course, vary, one thing seems safe to assume: the context in which people exist today involves an increasing awareness of religious pluralism. Rare is the person who does not have a friend who was raised within the context of a different religio-theological tradition. If a person were to understand a religion professor to be saying that his or her friend who comes from a position of "otherness" is, in some fundamental way, flawed, simply by virtue of his or her otherness, this assertion simply would not ring true on some level; the friendship would, in all likelihood, provide too much good evidence to the contrary. And then, everything else the professor said would probably be cast into doubt as well.

Given the sheer number of people who now self-identify as "spiritual but not religious" or "none," perhaps because of a distrust of what they take theology to be; and given the fact that most people either have or will someday have people with differing religious commitments as friends; and given that today's younger generations have grown up in a post-9/11 world where religion is often portrayed as an "Us vs. Them" enterprise in various public arenas and media outlets — given all of these factors, professors of theology and religion must, somehow, try to come to terms with religious pluralism and various shades of commitment and of "none-ness," if those professors truly want to engage students, to talk *to* them rather than *at* them. Similarly, the theologian must ask whether or not it is her very theological commitments themselves that demand a more spacious and open-hearted understanding of her dialogue partners.

Notes

1. I am grateful to Shelly Rambo for her careful reading of a draft of this essay – one that helped me unearth and explicitly articulate this insight.
2. Students often do not describe their concerns by using the word "theological" for a variety of reasons, I think. One has to do with the fact that the questions I pose to them are generally not phrased using that specific term. Even so, what they say in response to my prompts clearly has theological resonances. Second, as suggested by Linda Mercadante (2014) *Belief Without Borders: Inside the Minds of the Spiritual but not Religious* (New York: Oxford University Press), many undergraduate students do not come into the classroom well-versed in theological language. Mercadante

interviewed many people who self-identified as "spiritual but not religious," and who were also asking existential and theological questions. Of this group of people who were, in a sense, asking conceptually-theological questions without necessarily realizing it, she writes, many "had not been given tools adequate for the task. For them, theology did not mean a systematic or consistent set of beliefs. It did not mean leaning on a catechism learned in childhood. It did not mean a permanent theological thought world which, once accepted, guides the rest of life ... But theology was happening, nevertheless," 228. On this point, see also Christian Smith, Kari Christoffersen, Hilary Davidson, and Patricia Snell Herzog (2011) *Lost in Transition: The Dark Side of Emerging Adulthood* (New York: Oxford University Press), cited in Mercandante, 296 n. 2. The third reason I would argue that students often do not characterize their concerns as being "theological" has to do with the fact that most students do not enter the classroom with a clear understanding of how academic skills oriented around critical thinking might be applicable to theological thought, or, truthfully, to religious life in general. The link between critical thinking skills and religious life is not, for many people, readily apparent. On this point, see Barbara Walvoord's findings on what she calls "the great divide" between the learning goals of students taking college introductory courses in theology and religious studies and the learning goals of their professors. Walvoord found that students generally lacked "a nuanced vision of how critical thinking can relate to belief and commitment" – at least, *before* taking the college courses themselves. Barbara E. Walvoord (2007) *Teaching and Learning in College Introductory Religion Courses* (Malden, MA: Wiley-Blackwell), 6–7 and 13–15.
3. Alana Ling, paper written for Introduction to Religion (REL 260), Wofford College, Spring 2014. Permission granted.
4. Michael Shedd, paper written for Introduction to Religion (REL 260), Wofford College, Spring 2014. Permission granted.
5. "Nones' on the Rise" (2012) Pew Research Religion and Public Life Project, October 9, 2012, http://www.pewforum.org/2012/10/09/nones-on-the-rise/.
6. "Nones"—those who do not claim any particular communal faith identity—are on the rise. Although the term "none" may sound pejorative, it is simply a shorthand used by sociologists to designate

those who might check "none" on a survey when asked to what particular faith group they belong. This phenomenon is increasing so rapidly that worldwide "unbelief" now represents the world's third largest "religion." See Mercadante, *Belief Without Borders*, 2. As Mercadante explains, the estimates regarding the number of "nones" in the U.S. vary widely; scholars have estimated the percentages as lying somewhere between 19% to 25% of Americans. For a detailed and helpful list of research in this area, see pp. 272–273, note 5. Media outlets, research organizations, and scholars who have worked on this subject include the American Religious Identification Survey (ARIS 2008), Barry A. Kosmin and Ariele Keysar, Trinity College; the Pew Forum on Religion & Public Life, *Faith in Flux: Changes in Religious Affiliation in the U.S.*, 2009; *Newsweek*, *Parade*, *The Christian Century*, *The New York Times*, National Public Radio, and "Religion and Ethics Newsweekly"; Robert Putnam in (2012) *American Grace: How Religion Divides and Unites Us* (New York: Simon and Schuster). See also Christian Smith and Melina L. Denton's (2009) *Soul Searching: The Religious and Spiritual Lives of American Teenagers* (New York: Oxford University Press); Smith et al. (2011) *Lost in Transition: The Dark Side of Emerging Adulthood* (New York: Oxford University Press); and Christian Smith and Patricia Snell (2009) *Souls in Transition: The Religious and Spiritual Lives of Emerging Adults* (New York: Oxford University Press). Other sources include **"Spirituality in Higher Education: Students' Search for Meaning and Purpose" out of UCLA's Higher Education Research Institute (HERI)**, a "seven-year study examining the role that college plays in facilitating the development of students' spiritual qualities," http://spirituality.ucla.edu/, and Alexander W. Astin, Helen S. Astin, and Jennifer A. Lindholm (2010) *Cultivating the Spirit: How College Can Enhance Students' Inner Lives* (San Francisco: Jossey-Bass). An overview of *Cultivating the Spirit* and the study that produced is provided at http://spirituality.ucla.edu/book/. Still another collection of data dealing with religious identity and affiliation among college-aged students has been compiled by The Interfaith Youth Core (IFYC) out of Chicago. Over the last few years, IFYC has been working with an instrument called the Campus Religious and Spiritual Life Survey (CRSCS), created by Matthew Mayhew (New

York University) and Alyssa Bryant Rockenbach (North Carolina State University). Information about this survey is available at http://www.ifyc.org/content/campus-religious-and-spiritual-climate-survey.
7. "'Nones' on the Rise."
8. See the introductory essay of this volume, 2.
9. See the introductory essay of this volume, 3.
10. Walvoord, *Teaching and Learning in College Introductory Religion Courses*.
11. Martin Buber (1970) *I and Thou*, Walter Kaufmann (trans.) (New York: Simon and Schuster), 99–100.
12. Here I am thinking specifically of Diana Eck's definition of religious pluralism, outlined in chapter seven of (1993) *Encountering God: A Spiritual Journey from Bozeman to Banares* (Boston: Beacon Press) as well as at http://www.pluralism.org/pluralism/what_is_pluralism.
13. "Can these really be our only choices: the pathos of privateness or coercive theological nonsense? For ethicists, philosophers, artists and theologians, both alternatives should be unacceptable." David Tracy (1981) "Defending the Public Character of Theology," in James M. Wall (ed.) *Theologians in Transition*, The Christian Century "How My Mind Has Changed" Series (New York: Crossroad), 118.
14. Tracy, "Defending the Public Character of Theology," 122–123, italics my own. At the time of this writing, I am currently co-teaching a new course called, "Interfaith Engagement and Religious Pluralism." The students in the course seem amply convinced of the necessity for a more pluralistic outlook, and of the necessity of being able to engage the religious "other" on real, human, engaged, three-dimensional terms. These students' lives, punctuated by experiences wrought through religious conflict, have made such needs clear and pressing in more than just intellectual terms. And yet, the questions brought up here by Tracy—those revolving around what one can and should do with her own theological commitments in the face of disagreement, what the appropriate dispositions of mind and heart should be—are the questions with which many of them are struggling. How, many of them wonder, can they be true to themselves and true to their dialogue partners at the same time? Is it possible to open up one's heart without losing a part of oneself? And if one does open oneself

up to the "other," does this mean that she is no longer a good "member" of her own tradition? Is the specificity of self threatened by encounter?
15. Tracy, *Theologians in Transition*, asserts that "in an ambiguous world, an ambiguous self can still find trust." He also asserts, though, that such trust depends upon the integrity of both dialogue partners' particularity, 120.
16. Linda Mercadante (2014) *Belief Without Borders: Inside the Minds of the Spiritual but not Religious* (New York: Oxford University Press), 192.
17. Mercadante, *Belief Without Borders*, 227.
18. Mercadante, *Belief Without Borders*, xiv.
19. In fact, it is not even necessarily the case that *only* students without a sense of belonging within a specific theological/traditional religious framework experience a sense of disillusion or liminality when trying honestly to engage with the religious "other." Those with a strong theological identity struggle experience it as well. For example, time and time again, I have seen students struggle to adjudicate their assumptions about and understandings of their own theological/religious heritage with new learning about their own tradition's history—its role in colonialist hegemony, for example, or the ways in which theological justifications have buttressed people's doing harm to others in the name of religion. Seeing students learn about the darker sides of traditions they have come to love is analogous to seeing someone learn some dark fact about a beloved family member's past. In such a situation, one cannot help but wonder how he can still love his family member while still recognizing facets of that family member's less-than-admirable past.

Bibliography

Astin, A.W., H.S. Astin, and J.A. Lindholm. 2010. *Cultivating the spirit: How college can enhance students' inner lives*. San Francisco: Jossey-Bass.

Buber, M. 1970. *I and thou*. Trans. Walter Kaufmann. New York: Simon and Schuster.

Eck, D. 1993. *Encountering god: A spiritual journey from Bozeman to Banares*. Boston: Beacon.

Ling, A. 2014. Paper written for Introduction to Religion (REL 260), Wofford College, Spring 2014. Permission granted.

Mercadante, L. 2014. *Belief without borders: Inside the minds of the spiritual but not religious*. New York: Oxford University Press.
'Nones' on the Rise. 2012. Pew research religion and public life project, October 9, 2012. http://www.pewforum.org/2012/10/09/nones-on-the-rise/
Putnam, R. 2012. *American grace: How religion divides and unites us*. New York: Simon and Schuster.
Shedd, M. 2014. Paper written for Introduction to Religion (REL 260), Wofford College, Spring 2014. Permission granted.
Smith, C., and M.L. Denton. 2009. *Soul searching: The religious and spiritual lives of American teenagers*. New York: Oxford University Press.
Smith, C., and P. Snell. 2009. *Souls in transition: The religious and spiritual lives of emerging adults*. New York: Oxford University Press.
Smith, C., K. Christofferson, H. Davidson, and P.S. Herzog. 2011. *Lost in transition: The dark side of emerging adulthood*. New York: Oxford University Press.
"Spirituality in higher education: Students' search for meaning and purpose" out of UCLA's Higher Education Research Institute (HERI). UCLA Spirituality Website. http://spirituality.ucla.edu
Tracy, D. 1981. Defending the public character of theology. In *Theologians in transition*, The Christian century "how my mind has changed", ed. J.M. Wall. New York: Crossword.
Walvoord, B.E. 2007. *Teaching and learning in college introductory religion courses*. Malden: Wiley-Blackwell.

CHAPTER 11

"La Mano Zurda with a Heart in Its Palm": Mystical Activism as a Response to the Trauma of Immigration Detention

Susanna Snyder

We're gonna just love the detention center until it closes, but with real – I mean with sort of a tough love. Loving the people who are in detention. Loving the people who are perpetuating the detention system, but loving in such a way that we also feel a real call to action, and a call to stand up and to protest, and to make a positive change (Martin)[1]

[God's] presence deep within me just permeates everything. I think those are sisters and brothers who sit in that jail and there is God (Ethel)

INTRODUCTION

Mysticism has often been regarded as an esoteric, elite phenomenon—a lofty occupation for the religiously earnest and those with much spare time on their hands, the specialist activity of nuns and monks. Associated with gazing upwards and inwards, few have considered that it might also turn us outwards.[2] In this chapter, I suggest that mysticism can open up possibilities for creative individual and communal responses to trauma—particularly collective trauma—and that it has the potential to bolster resilience and

S. Snyder (✉)
University of Roehampton, London, SW, UK

spur political and social resistance to the causes of pain. Drawing on the work of two contemporary feminist mystics, Dorothee Soelle and Gloria Anzaldúa, I explore ways in which a mystical path might support both the oppressed and their privileged allies, as they seek to engage with trauma profoundly and hopefully. I ground my reflections in the experiences of activists responding to immigration detention—a context imbued with trauma both for detainees and for those seeking to stand alongside them.

IMMIGRATION DETENTION AS TRAUMATIC CONTEXT FOR ACTIVISM

In 2013, there were approximately 232 million migrants across the globe, with around 45.8 million living in the USA.[3] These numbers include privileged migrants who have relocated for work and students living overseas for study, as well as refugees, asylum seekers and people who have crossed borders without authorization—the "alternately documented" or those popularly called "illegals."[4] For many less privileged migrants, immigration can generate what Rose Marie Perez Foster terms "traumatogenic experiences"—experiences that can potentially produce trauma—and the USA turns out not to be the "Promised Land" that they had hoped it would be.[5] Many experience poverty, hardship, hostility, isolation and fear. Often hounded from their homes by violence or economic desperation, most then face new hardships in the countries to which they travel.

Immigrants in detention are among those who face particularly traumatic experiences, and this trauma infuses the experience of people seeking to support them. It colors the milieu within which immigrant and non-immigrant activists work and affects many involved in pastoral support and advocacy at the emotional, spiritual and psychological levels. So, what is it about immigration detention that generates such trauma? In 2012, ICE detained approximately 33,000 immigrants per night in around 250 detention centers across the USA and conditions in these centers are often abysmal.[6] Human rights groups and journalists have challenged "substantial and pervasive violations" of government standards.[7] People often have to wait a long time for decisions on their cases or for deportation, and 84% lack legal counsel.[8] Isolation is intense. Families of detainees are often unable to visit, as many live far away, or their own alternately documented status prevents them from entering a facility. Frequent transfer of detainees across the country makes it hard for families to locate loved ones and disrupts attorney-client relationships that do exist. Phone calls can be prohibitively expensive, costing up to $5 per minute. For those who do not speak English or Spanish, challenges are only deepened. Medical care and mental health provision are routinely inadequate, and 115 deaths occurred in detention between 2003 and 2010 alone.[9] On any given day, about 300 immigrants are held in solitary confinement and nearly half of these for 15 days or more, at which point they become at risk for severe mental harm.[10] LGBTQI detainees are often sent to "the hole" supposedly for their own protection. Food is poor, and boredom is rife, and some report verbal, physical and sexual assault and unfair disciplinary procedures. Every day, about 5500 detained immigrants are exploitatively hired to provide essential labor, such as cooking or cleaning, for a meager $1 a day or less.[11]

Activists can experience guilt and shame as they come to realize the complicity of their country or religious tradition in this trauma. Most, for instance, reel at the substantial profits that are being made from detainees' misery. Many detention facilities are operated by private companies, such as Geo and Corrections Corporation of America, and since 2009, ICE has received a "bed mandate" from Congress—stimulated by millions of dollars lobbying by private prison corporations—obliging them to fill 34,000 beds nightly. The estimated $164 a day it costs to detain an individual goes directly to the company or county housing the detainee.[12] What is more, it can be difficult to realize that religious practices and beliefs that inspire you to work for social justice can in fact compound the stresses experienced by those incarcerated. A Catholic Haitian detainee held in a county jail told me that he had felt disappointed because the chaplain rarely came to their immigration wing: mass was held in the main part of the jail, and a sister was sent over to them with consecrated wafers. He felt that it was not proper mass without a priest. I discovered that in another detention facility, only Christian worship was organized: no services were provided for detainees who practiced Islam or other religious traditions.

Ultimately, detained immigrants often end up being deported. Indeed, deportations have increased during the Obama administration, with 392,000 "removals" taking place in 2010.[13] On arrival in their destination—sometimes a country of which they have no memory and do not speak the language, as they left when very young—deportees can face imprisonment, poverty, gang violence and unemployment along with grief, depression and isolation.[14] Kanstroom paints a troubling portrait: "the sadness never seems to go away; the hope of a possible return—a flickering, ephemeral evanescence—mixes with guilt and shame and haunts deportees for the rest of their lives."[15] Deportees' children who are often citizens become, in the words of Luis Zayas and Mollie Bradlee, the "collateral damage of immigration enforcement." Parents are forced to choose whether to take them as "exiles" to a country they may never have been to or leave them behind in the care of others as "orphans."[16] Although not wishing to pathologize immigrant detainees as victims—many are resilient, extra/ordinary human beings who manage their situations skillfully and build fulfilling lives—the potential for trauma is clearly significant. Particularly concerning is the reality that, as Perez Foster notes, for many, time in detention can arouse "disturbing memories of their earlier trauma" and re-awaken "trauma symptoms."[17] What she claims of immigrants, more generally, is even more true for detainees: "anxiety, depression, posttraumatic stress disorder (PTSD), substance abuse, and higher prevalence of serious psychiatric disorders have all been associated with multiple immigrant populations both in and outside of the United States."[18] In addition, the suffering that detention causes for the families and friends of those detained as well as for immigrant communities who live in constant fear of detention and deportation should not be underestimated.

Activists participate in this trauma. In witnessing such pain and injustice and in empathizing—feeling with—those they wish to support, few escape without being profoundly affected. Activists experience anger, shock, frustration, vicarious suffering, heartbreak and burnout, in addition to a sense of guilt that it is their country that maintains such a damaging and exploitative system. It is hard to inhabit spaces where so many are in pain without noticing that wounds and scars are simultaneously developing within the self.

"LA MANO ZURDA WITH A HEART IN ITS PALM": INHABITING AND PRACTICING MYSTICAL ACTIVISM

What, then, can mysticism contribute to post-traumatic responses? How could it help activists engage with contexts such as immigration detention? Many in the helping professions today, from medicine to social work, are suspicious of religion and Christian theology, in particular, and may fear that encouraging mystical practice would simply be a way of placating detainees—a means of enticing them into accepting their oppression. And they are right to be suspicious. I have heard of chaplains describing detention facilities as mission fields full of potential for evangelism or places where detainees are gifted with an opportunity to turn their lives around for the better. In this section, however, I hope to demonstrate that mysticism can, in fact, do the opposite: it can act as a powerful source of endurance for individuals, as well as providing a subversive stimulus to resistance and the fight against injustice. Mysticism provides a way of attending fully and respectfully to trauma while also resisting oppression. Two feminist mystic activists who grappled in different ways with the trauma that immigrants face in their writing and praxis have been instrumental in developing my thinking.

Gloria Anzaldúa (1942–2004), an American cultural theorist and activist who described herself as a *"third world lesbian feminist with Marxist and mystic leanings"* and alienated from institutional religion, spoke out of "la communidad latina" —a community with intimate experience of immigration and the suffering that can result.[19] In a provocative and personal essay, "now let us shift" (2002), Anzaldúa articulated seven stages on the "path to conocimiento [intuitive knowledge]" culminating in a stance she described as "la mano zurda [the left hand] with a heart in its palm."[20] She revealed how mystical spirituality helped to facilitate her journey from internalized oppression due to race, ethnicity, gender and sexual orientation toward resistance. Dorothee Soelle (1929–2003), a German Lutheran theologian, similarly wrote about the role mysticism played in her struggles for justice. Soelle supported the Sanctuary Movement in the 1980s seeking to assist Central Americans seeking refuge in the USA while she was teaching at Union Theological Seminary in New York City. In *The Silent Cry: Mysticism and Resistance* (2001), she outlined three stages of a mystical journey—being amazed, letting go and healing/resisting.[21] She identified primarily as a person of privilege and focused on how the privileged might stand alongside those who are marginalized.[22] Both scholars understood mysticism to be an everyday experience accessible to all, and both believed that mysticism and the transformation of suffering were intimately connected.[23] The stages they explore are messily interwoven rather than linear.[24]

In what follows, I explore how inhabiting a mystical way of being may enhance our own engagement with trauma, whether we are the one experiencing pain or supporting someone who is. I explore three stages of a mystical journey—waking up to suffering, letting go and resisting in solidarity—and interweave the insights of Soelle and Anzaldúa with the voices of immigration detention activists as a means of bringing alive what could otherwise seem abstract.[25] During my conversations with activists, I discerned the presence of mystical journeys, and what I seek to do here is build on their experience to suggest what mysticism might offer other activists. I also suggest that mysticism has the potential to be a valuable resource for those who are oppressed. My reflections emerge largely from gratitude for the enriching effect the writings of these two women have had on my own immigration activism and experiences of pain. So, to the first mystical stage.

Stage One: Waking Up to Suffering

Mystical engagement with trauma first involves facing it head on. This stage is about waking up to the pain of the world and dwelling with it until it permeates your very being—an unusual approach in a society that encourages us to think positive and to believe that we can be happy if only we try hard enough (not least with the assistance of the self-help industry). Anzaldúa describes this first step as "awakening consciousness" and sees Cihuacoatl (serpent woman) who represents "instinctual knowledge and other alternative ways of knowing that fuel transformation" as its symbol.[26] For those among us experiencing oppression, she suggests, there are moments when an instinctual understanding wells up and forces recognition of forced exclusion and marginalization, causing searing pain.[27] She writes,

> every arrebato – a violent attack, rift with a loved one, illness, death in the family, betrayal, systematic racism and marginalization – rips you from your familiar "home" ... resulting in a great sense of loss, grief, and emptiness, leaving behind dreams, hopes, and goals. You are no longer who you used to be ... Exposed, naked, disoriented, wounded, uncertain, confused, and conflicted, you're forced to live en la orilla – a razor-sharp edge that fragments you.[28]

Waking up to the reality of oppression, it is as if your soul has been knocked out of your body.[29] "*La facultad*"—"the capacity to see in surface phenomena the meaning of deeper realities"—makes you "excruciatingly alive to the world" as it really is.[30] Following this initial jolt, Anzaldúa describes a second step—Nepantla (the space of the middle)—where you feel torn between different interpretations of the world, causing you to swing "between elation and despair, anger and forgiveness."[31] Even more painful is the third step, where you try to resist this new, more real understanding of the world you have glimpsed: "You close your eyes to the ravening light waiting to burst through the cracks. Once again you embrace desconocimiento's comfort in willful unawareness ... You wallow in the ruins of your life – pobre de ti – until you can't stand the stench that's yourself."[32] For Anzaldúa, then, facing the extent and depth of your trauma is the essential starting place for transformation. A conversation I had with a detention activist, an immigrant himself, struck me as resonant. He talked of his painful awakening to the treatment of immigrants, having arrived in the USA from El Salvador without papers. When seeking to enroll at Community College, he discovered that his tuition would be $2000 instead of $500 because he did not have a social security number. He said, "It was so hard for me to cross the border ... [and this] really hit my heart. It made me think like, 'This is not what I thought it was.'... I never went back."

Soelle, from her more privileged perspective, depicts this first stage of the mystical journey as amazement, characterized by wonder, gratitude and praise. Amazement can be provoked through experiences of nature, joy, sex, beauty or community, and represents the *via positiva*: it is when a "discovery of the world plunges us into jubilation, a radical amazement that tears apart the veil of triviality."[33] Most of the time, Soelle notes, human beings are preoccupied with owning or succeeding, or hopelessly accept the way things are as inevitable: we fail to recognize wonders happening around us. Amazement is about seeing with "wide-open eyes."[34] Soelle recognizes that it is often, though, suffering or the "bleak side of terror and hopelessness that renders one mute" that helps us to do this.[35] Pain—"the senseless, spiritless suffering that separates humans from all that makes for life"—can connect us with the divine.[36] She is not suggesting that the privileged pursue "dolorousness"—masochistic asceticism that Christianity has frequently encouraged—but rather that we seek to be compassionate and stand in solidarity with those who suffer innocently.[37] While natural to try and avoid suffering, we need to *choose* to experience "anguish about unliberated life" and make this into a habit. Agony felt in compassion is better than numbness.[38] Suffering, along with other sources of amazement, helps to free us from our "self-imposed and imagined limits,"[39] and we desperately need "repeated liberation from customs, viewpoints, and convictions, which, like layers of fat that make us untouchable and insensitive, accumulate around us" if suffering in the world is going to be ameliorated.[40] Anaesthetization and inaction are all too easy for those of us who are privileged.

Many of the more privileged activists I interviewed seemed to indicate that they had had just such an awakening moment in relation to detainees' pain. Simon narrated the journey home from his first visit to a detention facility: "I remember coming back and almost having this kind of almost nauseated feeling ... It was almost like an awakening moment: Oh my

God, this is happening and I had no clue." Lisa talked of how heartbreaking and "shocking" she found her work on detention. Those of us with privilege need to expose ourselves to the suffering experienced by so many immigrant detainees—standing alongside people personally and choosing to be emotionally affected by relationships—as well as learning about the system and its implications, or writing a check. Proactively countering the compassion fatigue that can cause a "catatonic state" is crucial.[41]

Both Soelle and Anzaldúa stress that waking up involves recognizing that trauma is a collective and social rather than simply an individual phenomenon.[42] Suffering is not just faced randomly by individuals in isolated ways, but is more often *caused* by structural, systemic violence at economic, political and social levels. Or as Nancy Pineda-Madrid puts it, we need to link "personal accounts of extreme suffering to the social matrix that precipitates them."[43] Soelle distinguishes between those living "in the center of the fragmented world," who can produce, buy and possess anything, and those living at "the periphery." As she puts it,

> the minority in the rich countries has rendered the majority in the poor countries dependent in every sense of the word: economically, politically, technologically, ecologically, and culturally ... the few rob the many and plunder, disenfranchise, and kill them.[44]

Trauma is also experienced collectively, as communities in fact only come to see themselves as traumatized, as they together define injuries that have taken place, name the victims, delineate consequences and call out the perpetrator/s.[45] Waking up together to the collective nature of trauma can be liberating for those oppressed, because you realize that the suffering you are experiencing is not of your own doing. In terms of immigration detention, this involves naming the ways in which racism, ethnocentrism and xenophobia, along with the legacy of colonialism, neo-imperialism and neo-liberalism, are actively creating pain. Bob, along with a number of other activists, articulated the link between detention and racism: "The flip side of immigration enforcement is the attack on the Black community." Others talked of the effects of NAFTA in creating unstable and underperforming economies in Latin America, which benefited the USA while forcing more people to migrate north for survival. Acknowledging these causalities is difficult for those of us who are privileged, as we would prefer not to know that our lifestyle is maintained at the expense of the wellbeing of people from majority world countries and those forced to inhabit the substrata of Western societies.⁴⁶ Yet, as both scholars suggest, waking up in these ways is like breaking out of a prison. Soelle talks of being "a prisoner in the huge machine" of globalization, individualism and consumerism, and she believes that amazement can enable us to step out beyond the bars—the bars that we, as a society, have erected around ourselves.⁴⁷ Anzaldúa similarly articulates her first step as "Breaking out of your mental and emotional prison and deepening the range of perception."⁴⁸

Religious and spiritual practices, and in particular contemplation, can help both the privileged and oppressed to wake up and see suffering clearly. Contemplation is an intrinsic part of the mystical path. According to Soelle, "Listening, being still, at rest, contemplating, and praying are all there to make room for amazement," and while we contemplate without hope of achieving a particular goal, it can create space within us to be more attentive and to notice what is occurring within ourselves and in the world.⁴⁹ Anzaldúa witnesses how challenging this being still or listening "with both outer ear and inner ear" can be: "it's hard for me to listen and look because there are so many things demanded of me. I need to simplify my life and slow it down so that I have these moments of connection."⁵⁰ Through contemplation, we can create a space in which the painful realities of the world and the trauma of so many people can well up and be beheld in all their raw ugliness. A number of immigration detention activists, interestingly, mentioned the importance of the practice in helping them to wake up to suffering. One practiced Zen Buddhism, another spoke of her photography as contemplative, and Arturo was part of a group of detention facility visitors and activists that gathered regularly for prayer. He articulated,

> Part of the nourishment, it precisely comes from an attitude of contemplation, contemplation being able to see, right, to see and to really appreciate and to be able to – *como se dice?* – to feel, touch, sense, to have our senses be awake and with each other, and to recognize that none of us can do anything alone, but rather by supporting each other we can transform not just our personal life, but the lives around it.

Stage Two: Letting Go

Having awoken, the second stage of the mystical journey that helps us to respond to trauma is letting go. According to Soelle, in the Christian tradition this stage represents the *via negativa* or dark night of the soul. We need to relinquish all that keeps us trapped our prisons, and particularly false desires relating to the ego, possessions and violence—three preoccupations that Soelle believes define this era of globalization. "Mysticism," she claims, "relativizes them, frees us from their spell, and prepares us for freedom."[51] The privileged need to become empty or "homeless," losing their moorings, and give up "success as the ultimate criterion."[52] Far from advocating withdrawal into an escapist other worldliness, this is about being "un-formed" and then reformed as a "new being" who can enter into the messy, flesh-and-blood world in fresh ways.[53] Self-forgetting on the part of the privileged can liberate those who are marginalized as well as those who are letting go: giving up pursuit of money, status and security at the expense of others' wellbeing allows all human beings to step out of their prisons.

Anzaldúa describes a comparable process of letting go in her fourth and fifth stages on the mystical road toward conocimiento and la mano zurda with a heart in its palm. It is vital that those experiencing oppression also let go, but in a different way: she suggests that those marginalized and excluded need to shed damaging images of the self that have been absorbed from the oppressor, and this involves discovering a new energy (Stage 4) and reconstructing the self (Stage 5). She suggests, "It feels like you've given birth to a huge stone. Something pops out … Soon energy zings up to cuerpo (body) in an ecstasy so intense it can't be contained. You twirl around, hugging yourself, picking up speed and kicking the walls … [you have a] new perception of yourself and the world … You begin to define yourself in terms of who you are becoming, not who you have been."[54] As you open yourself to the unconscious self, you become aware of the sacredness of life, nature and humanity.[55] Anzaldúa uses the language of death to portray the extent of this letting go. She writes that something in a person must die before something new can be born, and employs the evocative image of a snake shedding its skin for this process of letting go: you "shed your former bodymind and its outworn story like a snake its skin," rethinking yourself in "global-spiritual terms" rather than constricted "conventional categories of color, class, career."[56] You name oppression and rewrite the story of your life that you have always assumed to be true. For Anzaldúa, surrendering diminished images of the self and a sense of powerlessness are crucial steps that those who are marginalized need to take toward addressing their suffering.

How have I glimpsed this stage in terms of responses to the trauma of immigration detention? A number of the activists I spoke with talked of letting go. For a few, there had been material sacrifices: Laura had given up her job, house and car in order to establish a hospitality house to support family members coming to visit detainees. She struggled to pay the rent and utility bills and hadn't bought new clothes or shoes in a year. James talked of losing friends who disagreed with his political stance on this issue. More pervasively, activists talked about a letting go of their (for the privileged, usual) sense of power and efficacy: they were having to accept that they could not just change the system and that their ability to transform suffering was limited. Carmen found it "very frustrating" that nothing was changing in the detention system, and Karen said, "all I can do is pray." There was a letting go even of having to succeed at activism, with most doing the work for its own sake. There was something of the *sunder warumbe*—"the absence of all purpose, all calculation, every *quid pro quo*, every tit for tat"—that Soelle, drawing on Meister Eckhart, suggests is the essence of mysticism.[57] Acting for the sake of acting is important. For some, there was also a letting go of an image of the USA that they had held dear. Lisa pointed out that visitors can suddenly realize, "it's just unbelievable: how could this country, that we all think is predicated on ideals of liberty, freedom, and justice – could be so unjust to deny civil liberties for immigrants?" For Ernesto, though, letting go had looked somewhat different: his experience once again made me think of that described by Anzaldúa. After finally enrolling at community college, he seemed to let go of accepting that oppression of immigrants was acceptable: "I was like, 'I am happy. I'm going to school. I'm doing what I want to do. What happens with so many other students that are undocumented that are not able to go to college?' ... I said, 'I think we gotta do something'." He talked of finding his voice in the Student Immigrant Movement.

Letting go of privilege and power (false inflated images of the self) and/or powerlessness (false diminished images of the self), then, is a crucial second step on the mystical journey—a step that enables keener and deeper responses to our own and others' trauma. Contemplative practices can again facilitate the process in this stage. Soelle viewed contemplative silence as an "ascetic practice of preparation," and Anzaldúa valued meditation and "dropping down" into the place "where your soul is ballast," as a means of letting go.[58] One detention activist talked of yoga practice in this way: she found that having to sit in uncomfortable poses and just breathe in and out helped her to process and let go of the sadness and powerlessness she experienced in her work with detainees.

Stage Three: Resisting in Solidarity

Mystical engagement with suffering does not end with these two stages, however. It culminates in the oppressed and privileged standing together in solidarity—in a deep oneness—to resist the root causes of trauma. For the marginalized, this stage is highly complex. Anzaldúa recognizes an "us-versus-them" point (stage six) where the oppressed feel pitted against their privileged allies, making it hard to stay in connection: the privileged are still unwittingly oppressing, and there are misunderstandings. However, this eases into a deep knowing that "beneath individual separateness lies a deeper interrelatedness"—a time when "you feel love, peace, happiness, and the desire to grow" (stage seven).[59] An "alchemy of connection provides the knowledge, strength, and energy to persist and be resilient in pursuing goals."[60] Anzaldúa offers a vivid, evocative symbol for this final stage—"un milagro, a tiny silver hand with a heart in its palm" given to her by her mother. She sees this "mano zurda [left hand] with a heart in its palm" as being about "engaging with self, others, world," and it resonates with another concept of hers—that of el mundo zurdo [the left-handed world]—meaning a world that is turned upside down. The hand symbolizes implementing a vision, and the heart within it has

> intelligence, passion, and purpose, a "mindfull" heart with ears for listening, eyes for seeing, a mouth with tongue narrowing to a pen tip for speaking/writing. The left hand is not a fist pero una mano abierta raised with others in struggle, celebration, and song.

Fostering connection between those who are oppressed and their allies involves negotiating "racial contradictions" and developing "a spiritual-imaginal-political vision together." For Anzaldúa, oneness—a sense of interrelatedness and connection—defines spiritual activism (or what I am calling mystical activism): "You form an intimate connection that fosters the empowerment of both (nos/otras) to transform conflict into an opportunity to resolve an issue, to change negativities into strengths, and to heal the traumas of racism and other systemic desconocimientos."[61] With regards to immigration, as Céspedes notes, this implies "loving those who risk their lives to enter US boundaries as well as those who create painful borders in the name of securing their own safety."[62]

Soelle names the third stage of mysticism as resistance, or the *via transformativa*, and as for Anzaldúa, she understands it to be rooted in union, connecting and interrelationship.[63] Inhabiting the mystical path involves connecting with the divine "Other," and through that, connecting with the human "other". Being "one with what was intended in creation" necessitates active resistance against all injustice that causes division and inhibits oneness.[64] Or, in other words, the "inner light of being at one with every living thing and the resistance against the machine of death" go together.[65] What constitutes resistance varies and can include "small actions, simple education, and mere symbolic acts" as well as more dramatic actions.[66] This stage is about saying, "surely, this is not all there is to it; it wasn't meant to be like this."[67] For Soelle, resistance *is* mysticism, and mysticism has to involve the pursuit of social justice if it is to be authentic.[68] Or in other words, mysticism is by definition mystical activism. While the relationship between the inner and outer life has been a topic of debate within the Christian tradition, she concludes firmly, "The point is neither to practice an introverted mysticism nor to engage in an extroverted critique of the age alone, but to find one's *vita mixta* in this sense between contemplation and activity."[69] Mysticism is a spiritual path that seeks transformation of traumatic suffering in the here and now.

For most of the immigration detention activists I spoke with—immigrant and non-immigrant alike—practices of resistance were what they lived for and were undergirded and infused by a deeply spiritual sense of connection and union. They practiced the *vita mixta* of which Soelle talks. Bob contrasted a reunion he witnessed with what he saw as the "divide and conquer" approach of the "ruling elite." At a vigil he attended, a mother glimpsed her son being held in the facility for the first time and broke down in tears. He pointed out, "We do the vigil to have that communication with the people inside so they know that we're here – we're there on the outside supporting them." Simon saw "unlikely friendships" between new and existing residents of the USA as crucial to transforming the hostility surrounding the exclusion of immigrants, and Bethany explicitly stated that "we are all one." This sense of oneness as the ground of and reason for resistance went beyond just connection with detainees, however. Hannah spoke about the importance of connecting with the humanity and the image of God in ICE and facility staff, and Martin saw advocacy and protesting as acts of connecting too. As he said in the quotation with which this chapter began, "We're gonna just love the detention center until it closes, but with real – I mean with sort of a tough love … Loving in such a way that we also feel a real call to action, and a call to stand up and to protest, to make a positive change." Connecting with detainees in ways that resist their dehumanization—through visiting, for example—can provoke connection with the divine. For Ethel, God's "presence deep within me permeates everything; I think those are sisters and brothers who sit in that jail and there is God."

Engaging with trauma through resistance in solidarity affirms the resilience of migrants rather than pathologizing them as vulnerable victims. In other words, mystical spirituality fosters a sense of agency. It recognizes the importance of detainees leading and shaping resistance, as they have been doing through collective hunger strikes and individual challenging of bureaucratic obstacles, and it affirms that oneness and equality rather than paternalism underlie action. This path honors people's trauma *and* their strength, and actively seeks to transform trauma—to relieve it—rather than to accept it as inevitable, or to wallow in it, masochistically or voyeuristically. At the same time, spiritual growth and the experience of encounter with the numinous that can emerge during this journey can be life-changing for the privileged: Simon stated explicitly that the detention center was where God came alive for him. As Cesepdes puts it, "Those who enact spiritual activism simultaneously engage in a movement for complete social, economic and political justice and a profound spiritual journey toward a consciousness that will bring about an end to internal and external wars."[70]

Conclusion: Mystical Activism as a Practice of Hope

This mystical path could enrich responses to collective trauma—those of privileged allies and, perhaps also, those of people directly experiencing suffering and oppression. In an environment where religion is often viewed with suspicion, and many in the helping professions (including those supporting immigration detainees) are uncertain as to how to engage with faith or spirituality, theologies and spiritualities of mysticism have something important to offer. Not only do they give expression to the spiritual dimensions of persons, offering ways of thinking about how trauma impacts and evokes connection to the numinous or divine, but they can also offer a broader diagnosis of trauma that goes beyond understanding it as an individual-by-individual issue.

What mysticism or the "*mistica revoluncionaria*" as outlined by Soelle and Anzaldúa offers is, in fact, hope. Hope, unlike wishful thinking or superficial positivity, requires us to stare pain in the face while simultaneously straining toward freedom, joy and delight. Or as Ellen Ott Marshall puts it, responsible hope "unearths beauty and faces tragedy"; it "celebrates goodness and knows cruelty." It is both "a spiritual discipline and an ethical endeavor": hope is enacted and practiced.[71] Hope, being dependent on our ability to awaken fully to pain, is all too often absent in our contemporary efforts to respond to trauma. We tend to see the experience of trauma as a pathology to be eliminated as quickly as possible, rather than as a space through which meaning and new life can emerge. Soelle, by contrast, affirms its meaning and possible value "for growth, for learning, for leading to God, for motivating change, for making us human."[72] Trauma needs to be "approached rather than avoided."[73]

Many responding to suffering— be they Christian, spiritual, religious or none of the above, and be that suffering their own or that of others— are already walking this hopeful mystical path without recognizing that their awakening moments, letting go, and resistance in solidarity can be a place of connection with others and personal, spiritual growth. While not wishing to impose this framework on those who find it unhelpful, understanding their responses in terms of this journey—as mystical activism—could offer some strength through having a sense of being part of something larger than themselves. Approaching suffering mystically forms us, shaping our *habitus* or way of being, so that "our own pain and the pain of the other are taken on as actions of love, discipleship, and resistance."[74] Responding to suffering hopefully is, for many, a mystical and life-enhancing process.[75]

The way of "la mano zurda with a heart in its palm" offers a deeper, more hopeful way of engaging with social trauma—including the suffering of immigration detainees—than is often found today. It requires that we stare pain in the face, let go of some of our habitual ways of being in the world, and strive for the liberation of all. The mystical journey outlined by Anzaldúa and Soelle is transformational, promoting "growth, empowerment, and justice in ways that challenge an existing status quo,"[76] and as a result, it can ignite hope. For, as Soelle says,

> Mysticism wants nothing else but to love life, even where analysis has run its course and all that is left is to count the victims. To love life also where it has long been condemned to death, even from its very beginning, is an old human ability to go beyond what is. That ability is called transcendence or faith or hope – or listening to the silent cry. It is the most important movement that human beings can learn in their lives.[77]

Notes

1. Parts of this essay were first published in Susanna Snyder (2015) "Looking Through the Bars: Immigration Detention and the Ethics of Mysticism," *Journal of the Society of Christian Ethics*, vol. 35, no. 1, 167–187. These words were spoken by faith-based detention activists: their names have been changed to protect anonymity.
2. Exceptions include Matthew T. Eggemeier (2012) "A Mysticism of Open Eyes: Compassion for a Suffering World and the *Askesis* of Contemplative Prayer," *Spiritus*, vol. 12, 43–62; Johann B. Metz (1998) *A Passion for God: The Mystical-Political Dimension of Christianity*, M. Ashley (ed. & trans.) (New York: Paulist Press); Leonardo Boff (1980) "The Need for Political Saints: From a Spirituality of Liberation to the Practice of Liberation," *Cross Currents*, vol. 30, no. 4, 369–376; Thomas Merton (1998) *Contemplation in a World of Action*, 2nd edition, (Notre Dame: Notre Dame University Press); Susan Rakoczy (2006) *Great Mystics and Social Justice: Walking on the Two Feet of Love* (New York: Paulist Press); Janet Ruffing (ed.) (2001) *Mysticism and Social Transformation* (Syracuse, NY: Syracuse University Press); Luther Smith (2007) *Howard Thurman: The Mystic as Prophet*, 3rd edition, (Richmond, IN: Friends United Press).
3. UN, Press Release, accessed May 26, 2014, http://esa.un.org/unmigration/wallchart2013.htm.
4. Carmen Nanko-Fernandez (2013) "Alternately Documented Theologies: Mapping Border, Exile and Diaspora," in Sarah Azaransky (ed.) *Religion and Politics in America's Borderlands* (Lanham, MD: Lexington), 33–55.
5. R. Perez Foster (2001) "When Immigration is Trauma: Guidelines for the Individual and Family Clinician," *American Journal of Orthopsychiatry*, vol. 71, no. 2, 155. Salman Akhtar similarly talks of "the trauma of geographical dislocation." See Salman Akhtar (2011) *Immigration and Acculturation: Mourning, Adaptation, and the Next Generation* (Lanham, MD: Jason Aronson), 3.
6. Detention Watch Network (2013) *One Year Later: The Absence of Accountability in Immigration Detention* (Washington, DC: DWN), 1; Tanya M. Golash-Boza (2012) *Immigration Nation: Raids, Detentions, and Deportations in Post-9/11 America*

(Boudler, CO: Paradigm Publishers), 64–65. Most detainees are unauthorized immigrants and legal residents who have committed a minor crime, though people applying for asylum at the border and those suspected of being a threat to national security can also face detention.

7. Karen Tumlin, Linton Joaquin, and Ranjana Natarajan (2009) *A Broken System: Confidential Reports Reveal Failures in U.S. Immigration Detention Centers* (Los Angeles, CA: NILC), 7. Community Initiatives for Visiting Immigrants in Confinement [CIVIC] (2013), *Detention in the Desert: A Look Inside the California City Correctional Center* (San Francisco, CA: CIVIC); Seattle University School of Law International Human Rights Clinic (2008) *Voices from Detention: A Report on Human Rights Violations at the Northwest Detention Center in Tacoma, Washington* (Seattle, WA: Seattle University School of Law).

8. Alison Mountz (2012) "Mapping Remote Detention: Dis/Location Through Isolation" in J. Lloyd, M. Mitchelson, and A. Burridge (eds.) *Beyond Walls and Cages: Prisons, Borders, and Global Crisis* (Athens, GA: University of Georgia Press), 91; Geoffrey Heeren (2010) "Pulling Teeth: The state of Mandatory Detention," *Harvard Civil Rights-Civil Liberties Review*, vol. 45, no. 2, 604.

9. D. Ackerman and R. Furman (2013) "The criminalization of immigration and the privatization of the immigration detention: implications for justice," *Contemporary Justice Review*, vol. 16, no. 2, 251–263; K. Ochoa, G. Pleasants, J. Penn & D. Stone (2010) "Disparities in Justice and Care: Persons with Severe Mental Illnesses in the U.S. Immigration Detention System," *Journal of the American Academy of Psychiatry and Law*, vol. 38, no. 3, 395; Detention Watch Network, "List of Deaths in ICE Custody: October 2003–December 2, 2013," https://www.ice.gov/doclib/foia/reports/detaineedeaths2003-present.pdf

10. I. Urbina and C. Rentz (2013) "Immigrants Held in Solitary Cells, Often for Weeks," *New York Times*, March 23 2013, http://www.nytimes.com/2013/03/24/us/immigrants-held-in-solitary-cells-often-for-weeks.html?_r=0. On the effects of solitary confinement as an "assault on the human spirit," see Derek S. Jeffreys (2013) *Spirituality in Dark Places: The Ethics of Solitary Confinement* (New York: Palgrave Macmillan), 57.

11. Ian Urbina (2014) "Using Jailed Immigrants as a Pool of Cheap Labor," *New York Times*, May 24, 2014, http://www.nytimes.com/2014/05/25/us/using-jailed-migrants-as-a-pool-of-cheap-labor.html?hpw&rref=us&_r=0&referrer.
12. See "The Math of Immigration Detention: Runaway Costs for Immigration Detention Do Not Add Up to Sensible Policies" (2013) National Immigration Forum website, https://immigrationforum.org/blog/themathofimmigrationdetention, 3; Golash-Boza, *Immigration Nation*, 152–154. See also Renee Feltz and Stokely Baksh, "Business of Detention," in J. Lloyd, M. Mitchelson and A. Burridge (eds.) *Beyond Walls and Cages: Prisons, Borders and Global Crisis* (Athens, GA: University of Georgia Press), 143–151.
13. Daniel Kanstroom (2012) *Aftermath: Deportation Law and the New American Diaspora* (New York: Oxford University Press), 12.
14. Golash-Boza, *Immigration Nation*, 101–104. See also Kanstroom, *Aftermath*.
15. Kanstroom, *Aftermath*, 156.
16. Luis H. Zayas and Mollie H. Bradlee (2014) "Exiling Children, Creating Orphans: When Immigration Policies Hurt Citizens," *Social Work*, vol. 59, no. 2, 167. See also Joanna Dreby (2014) "The Modern Deportation Regime and Mexican Families: The Indirect Consequences for Children in New Destination Communities," in C. Menjívar and D. Kanstroom (eds.) *Constructing Immigrant "Illegality": Critiques, Experiences, and Responses* (New York: Cambridge University Press), 181–202.
17. R. Perez Foster (2001) "When Immigration Is Trauma: Guidelines for the Individual and Family Clinician," *American Journal of Orthopsychiatry*, vol. 71, no. 2, 156.
18. Foster, "When Immigration is Trauma," 156 and 154.
19. See AnaLouise Keating (ed.) (2009) *The Gloria Anzaldúa Reader* (Durham: Duke University Press), 45.
20. Gloria Anzaldúa (2002) "now let us shift … the path of conocimiento … inner work, public acts," in G. Anzaldúa and A. Keating (eds.) *this bridge we call home: radical visions for transformation* (New York: Routledge), 540–578.
21. Dorothee Soelle (2001) *The Silent Cry: Mysticism and Resistance* (Minneapolis: Fortress Press).
22. Flora A. Keshgegian (2003) "Witnessing Trauma: Dorothee Soelle's Theology of Suffering in a World of Victimization," in

S. Pinnock (ed.) *The Theology of Dorothee Soelle* (Harrisburg, PA: Trinity Press International), 99.
23. Soelle, *Silent Cry*, 14–15 and 19–20.
24. As Kelli Zaytoun suggests, each stage "informs and influences the others," (2011) "Shifting," in AnaLouise Keating and Gloria Gonzalez-Lopez (eds.) *Bridging: How Gloria Anzaldúa's Life and Work Transformed Our Own* (University of Texas Press), 206.
25. In 2013, I undertook a qualitative study that explored faith-based engagement with immigration detention in the U.S. This involved interviewing 20 immigration detention activists, and the study was approved by the Institutional Review Board of the University of Texas at Austin. Details of research methods and findings can be found in Susanna Snyder (2015) "Looking Through the Bars: Immigration Detention and the Ethics of Mysticism," *Journal of the Society of Christian Ethics*, vol. 35, no. 1, 167–187; Susanna Snyder, Holly Bell, and Noel Busch-Armendariz (2015) "Immigration Detention and Faith-Based Organizations," *Social Work*, vol. 60, no. 2, 165–173.
26. Anzaldúa, 'now let us shift,' 543.
27. I honor the choice of pronouns the two authors make. Anzaldúa uses "you" as if talking personally to a fellow human being who is oppressed, while Soelle employs "we" and "us."
28. Anzaldúa, 'now let us shift,' 547.
29. Anzaldúa, 'now let us shift,' 547.
30. Gloria Anzaldúa (2012) *Borderlands/La Frontera: The New Mestiza*. 25th Anniversary 4th Edition (San Francisco, CA: Aunt Lute Books), 60–61.
31. Anzaldúa, 'now let us shift', 548–549.
32. Anzaldúa, 'now let us shift,' 551.
33. Soelle, *Silent Cry*, 89–90. Anzaldúa talks both of nature and orgasm as places of connection and energy. See Keating, *The Gloria Anzaldúa Reader*, 74 and 85.
34. Soelle, *Silent Cry*, 284.
35. Soelle, *Silent Cry*, 90.
36. Soelle, *Silent Cry*, 90.
37. Soelle, *Silent Cry*, 138–139.
38. Soelle, *Silent Cry*, 140. As Vento suggests reading Soelle, this is not "a series of isolated events but a way of suffering": it is a *habitus* chosen by agents. See Johann M. Vento (2011) "Formation(s) of the Mystical-Political in the Age of Globalization: Suffering as

Agentive Choice in Dorothee Soelle and Talal Asad," in L. Cassidy and M. H. O'Connel (eds.) *Religion, Economics, and Culture in Conflict and Conversation*, College Theology Society Annual Volume 56 (Maryknoll: Orbis Press), 123.
39. Soelle, *Silent Cry*, 27; Dorothee Soelle (1975) *Suffering*, translated by Everett R. Kalin (Philadelphia, PA: Fortess), 170.
40. Soelle, *Silent Cry*, 90.
41. Nancy Pineda-Madrid (2011) *Suffering and Salvation in Ciudad Juárez*, (Minneapolis, MN: Fortress), 20.
42. Sarah K. Pinnock (ed.) (2003) *The Theology of Dorothee Soelle* (New York: Trinity Press International), 132; Soelle, *Suffering*, 106.
43. Pineda-Madrid suggests adopting a "*social-suffering hermeneutic*" and explores suffering as a "social reality." See *Suffering and Salvation*, 9 and 19. She draws on Arthur Kleinman, Veena Das and Margaret Lock (eds.) (1997) *Social Suffering* (Berkeley: University of California Press), x–xi. On social suffering, see also P. Bourdieu et al. (1999) *The Weight of the World: Social Suffering in Contemporary Society*, Priscilla Parkhurst Ferguson et al. (trans.) (Cambridge: Polity Press); Iain Wilkinson (2005) *Suffering: A Sociological Introduction* (Cambridge: Polity Press); and Diana Cheyenne Harvey (2012) "A Quiet Suffering: Some Notes on the Sociology of Suffering," *Sociological Forum*, vol. 27, no.2, 527–533.
44. Soelle, *Silent Cry*, 279–280.
45. Jeffrey Alexander (2012) *Trauma: A Social Theory* (Cambridge: Polity Press), 26.
46. Pineda-Madrid, *Suffering and Salvation*, 22 and 25. See also Wilkinson, *Suffering*, 93.
47. Soelle, *Silent Cry*, 1 and 5.
48. Anzaldúa, 'now let us shift', 542.
49. Soelle, *Silent Cry*, 91 and 294.
50. Keating, *The Gloria Anzaldúa Reader*, 75.
51. Soelle, *Silent Cry*, 259.
52. Soelle, *Silent Cry*, 196 and 231.
53. Soelle, *Silent Cry*, 91 and 218.
54. Anzaldúa, 'now let us shift', 555–556.
55. Anzaldúa, 'now let us shift', 558.
56. Anzaldúa, 'now let us shift', 561.
57. Soelle, *Silent Cry*, 60.

58. Soelle, *Silent Cry*, 74; Anzaldúa, 'now let us shift', 572.
59. Anzaldúa, 'now let us shift', 569.
60. Anzaldúa, 'now let us shift', 571.
61. Anzaldúa, 'now let us shift', 572; Zaytoun, 'Shifting', 208.
62. Karina L. Céspedes (2011) "A Call to Action: Spiritual Activism ... An Inevitable Unfolding," in A. Keating and G. Gonzales-Lopez, *How Gloria Anzaldúa's Life and Work Transformed Our Own* (Austin: University of Texas Press), 78.
63. Soelle, *Silent Cry*, 93.
64. Soelle, *Silent Cry*, 93.
65. Soelle, *Silent Cry*, 5.
66. Soelle, *Silent Cry*, 276.
67. Soelle, *Silent Cry*, 3 and 197.
68. Soelle, *Silent Cry*, 54 and 199.
69. Soelle, *Silent Cry*, 201. Wendy Farley, recognizing the importance of compassion and resistance as a response to suffering, similarly recognizes, "Resistance is the holy ground wherein divine presence is known and experienced." See Wendy Farley (1990) *Tragic Vision and Divine Compassion: A Contemporary Theodicy* (Louisville: Westminster John Knox), 127 and 132–134.
70. Céspedes, "A Call to Action," 76–77.
71. Ellen Ott Marshall (2006) *Though the Fig Tree Does Not Blossom: Toward a Responsible Theology of Christian Hope* (Nashville: Abingdon), xvi.
72. Soelle, *Silent Cry*, 133 and 137.
73. Richard G. Tedeschi and Lawrence G. Calhoun (1995) *Trauma and Transformation: Growing in the Aftermath of Suffering* (Thousand Oaks, CA: Sage Publications), 8; Pineda-Madrid, *Suffering and Salvation*, 22. For more debate concerning whether suffering can be "productive" or meaningful, see Liza J. Rankow (2006) "The Transformation of Suffering," *Pastoral Psychology*, vol. 55, no. 1, 93–97; and Soelle, *Suffering*, 170.
74. Vento, "Formation(s) of the Mystical-Political," 131–132.
75. Tedeschi and Calhoun, *Trauma and Transformation*, 13.
76. Edward Canda and Leola D. Furman (2010) *Spiritual Diversity in Social Work Practice: The Heart of Helping*, 2nd edition, (New York: Oxford University Press), 314–315.
77. Soelle, *Silent Cry*, 282.

Bibliography

Ackerman, D., and R. Furman. 2013. The criminalization of immigration and the privatization of the immigration detention: Implications for justice. *Contemporary Justice Review* 16(2): 251–263.

Akhtar, S. 2011. *Immigration and acculturation: Mourning, adaption, and the next generation.* Lanham: Jason Aronson.

Alexander, J. 2012. *Trauma: A social theory.* Cambridge: Polity Press.

Anzaldúa, G. 2002. Now let us shift ... the path of conocimiento ... inner work, public acts. In *This bridge we call home: Radical visions for transformation*, ed. G. Anzaludúa and A. Keating. New York: Routledge.

Anzaldúa, G. 2012. *Borderlands/La frontera: The new mestiza*, 25th anniversary and 4th ed. San Francisco: Aunt lute Books.

Boff, L. 1980. The need for political saints: From a spirituality of liberation to the practice of liberation. *Cross Currents* 30(4): 369–376.

Bourdieu, P., et al. 1999. *The weight of the world: Social suffering in contemporary society.* Trans. P. P. Ferguson et al. Cambridge: Polity Press.

Canda, E.R., and L.D. Furman. 2010. *Spiritual diversity in social work practice: The heart of helping*, 2nd ed. New York: Oxford University Press.

Céspedes, K.L. 2011. A call to action: Spiritual activism... an inevitable unfolding. In *Bridging: How Gloria Anzaldúa's life and work transformed our own*, ed. A. Keating and G. Gonzalez-Lopez. Austin: University of Texas Press.

Community Initiatives for Visiting Immigrants in Confinement [CIVIC]. 2013. *Detention in the desert: A look inside the California city correctional center.* San Francisco: CIVIC.

Detention Watch Network. 2010. List of deaths in ICE custody: October 2003–December 2, 2013. https://www.ice.gov/doclib/foia/reports/detaineedeaths2003-present.pdf

Detention Watch Network. 2013. *One year later: The absence of accountability in immigration detention.* Washington, DC: DWN.

Dreby, J. 2014. The modern deportation regime and Mexican families: The indirect consequences for children in new destination communities. In *Constructing immigrant "illegality": Critiques, experiences, and responses*, ed. C. Menjívar and D. Danstroom. New York: Cambridge University Press.

Eggemeier, M.T. 2012. A mysticism of open eyes: Compassion for a suffering world and the *askesis* of contemplative prayer. *Spiritus* 12: 43–62.

Farley, W. 1990. *Tragic vision and divine compassion: A contemporary theodicy.* Louisville: Westminster John Knox.

Feltz, R., and S. Baksh. 2012. Business of detention. In *Beyond walls and cages: Prisons, borders and global crisis*, ed. J. Lloyd, M. Mitchelson, and A. Burridge. Athens: University of Georgia Press.

Foster, R.P. 2001. When immigration is trauma: Guidelines for the individual and family clinician. *American Journal of Orthopsychiatry* 71(2): 153–170.

Golash-Boza, T.M. 2012. *Immigration nation: Raids, detentions, and deportations in post-9/11 America.* Boulder: Paradigm Publishers.
Harvey, D.C. 2012. A quiet suffering: Some notes on the sociology of suffering. *Sociological Forum* 27(2): 527–533.
Heeren, G. 2010. Pulling teeth: The state of mandatory detention. *Harvard Civil Rights-Civil Liberties Review* 45(2): 601–634.
Jeffreys, D.S. 2013. *Spirituality in dark places: The ethics of solitary confinement.* New York: Palgrave Macmillan.
Kanstroom, D. 2012. *Aftermath: Deportation law and the new American Diaspora.* New York: Oxford University Press.
Keating, A. (ed.). 2009. *The Gloria Anzaldúa reader.* Durham: Duke University Press.
Keshgegian, F.A. 2003. Witnessing trauma: Dorothee Soelle's theology of suffering in a world of victimization. In *The theology of Dorothee Soelle,* ed. S. Pinnock. Harrisburg: Trinity Press International.
Kleinman, A., V. Das, and M. Lock (eds.). 1997. *Social suffering.* Berkeley: University of California Press.
Marshall, E.O. 2006. *Though the fig tree does not blossom: Toward a responsible theology of Christian hope.* Nashville: Abingdon.
Merton, T. 1998. *Contemplation in a world of action,* 2nd ed. Notre Dame: Notre Dame University Press.
Metz, J.B. 1998. *A passion for god: The mystical-political dimension of Christianity.* Ed. & trans. M. Ashley. New York: Paulist Press.
Mountz, A. 2012. Mapping remote detention: Dis/location through isolation. In *Beyond walls and cages: Prisons, borders, and global crisis,* ed. J. Lloyd, M. Mitchelson, and A. Burridge. Athens: University of Georgia Press.
Nanko-Fernandez, C. 2013. Alternately documented theologies: Mapping border, exile and Diaspora. In *Religion and politics in America's borderlands,* ed. S. Azaransky. Lanham: Lexington.
Ochoa, K., G. Pleasants, J. Penn, and D. Stone. 2010. Disparities in justice and care: Persons with severe mental illness in the U.S. immigration detention system. *Journal of the American Academy of Psychiatry and Law* 28(3): 392–399.
Pineda-Madrid, N. 2011. *Suffering and salvation in Ciudad Juárez.* Minneapolis: Fortress.
Pinnock, S.K. (ed.). 2003. *The theology of Dorothee Soelle.* New York: Trinity Press International.
Rakoczy, S. 2006. *Great mystics and social justice: Walking on the two feet of love.* New York: Paulist Press.
Rankow, L.J. 2006. The transformation of suffering. *Pastoral Psychology* 55(1): 93–97.
Ruffing, J. (ed.). 2001. *Mysticism and social transformation.* Syracuse: Syracuse University Press.

Seattle University School of Law International Human Rights Correctional Center. 2008. *Voices from detention: A report of human rights violations at the Northwest Detention Center in Tacoma, Washington.* Seattle: Seattle University School of Law.

Smith, L. 2007. *Howard Thurman: The mystic as prophet*, 3rd ed. Richmond: Friends United Press.

Snyder, S. 2015. Looking through the bars: Immigration detention and the ethics of mysticism. *Journal of the Society of Christian Ethics* 35(1): 167–187.

Snyder, S., H. Bell, and N. Busch-Armendariz. 2015. Immigration detention and faith-based organizations. *Social Work* 60(2): 165–173.

Soelle, D. 1975. *Suffering*. Trans. E. R. Kalin. Philadelphia: Fortress.

Soelle, D. 2001. *The silent cry: Mysticism and resistance.* Minneapolis: Fortress Press.

Tedeschi, R.G., and L.G. Calhoun. 1995. *Trauma and transformation: Growing in the aftermath of suffering.* Thousand Oaks: Sage.

The math of immigration detention: Runaway costs for immigration detention do not add up to sensible policies. 2013. National Immigration Forum website. https://immigrationforum.org/blog/themathofimmigrationdetention/

Tumlin, K., L. Joaquin, and R. Natarajan. 2009. *A broken system: Confidential reports reveal failure in U.S. immigration detention centers.* Los Angeles: NILC.

UN. 2013. Press Release. http://esa.un.org/unmigration/wallchart2013.htm

Urbina, I. 2014. Using jailed immigrants as a pool of cheap labor. *New York Times*. http://www.nytimes.com/2014/05/25/us/using-jailed-migrants-as-a-pool-of-cheap-labor.html?hpw&rref=us&_r=0&referrer

Urbina, I., and C. Rentz. 2013. Immigrants held in solitary cells, often for weeks. *New York Times*. http://www.nytimes.com/2013/03/24/us/immigrants-held-in-solitary-cells-often-for-weeks.html?_r=0

Vento, J.M. 2011. Formation(s) of the mystical-political in the age of globalization: Suffering as agentive choice in Dorothee Soelle and Talal Asad. In *Religion, economics, and culture in conflict conversation*, College theology society annual, vol. 56, ed. L. Cassidy and M.H. O'Connel. Maryknoll: Orbis Press.

Wilkinson, I. 2005. *Suffering: A sociological introduction.* Cambridge: Polity Press.

Zayas, L.H., and M.H. Bradlee. 2014. Exiling children, creating orphans: When immigration policies hurt citizens. *Social Work* 59(2): 167–175.

Zaytoun, K. 2011. Shifting. In *Bridging: How Gloria Anzaldúa's life and work transformed our own*, ed. A. Keating and G. Gonzalez-Lopez. Austin: University of Texas Press.

CHAPTER 12

Taking Matter *Seriously*: Material Theopoetics in the Aftermath of Communal Violence

Michelle A. Walsh

She wears a small button pin with the photograph of her murdered cousin on it. It is hard to miss. She sits across from me and begins to tell me about it, "I always have my button on me just to have him with me... If it's not on my jacket then I have it on my bag... I just bring it along so he wouldn't be left out of nothing that's going on." Even though I've been working as a lay youth minister and clinical social worker in her community for nearly two decades, I am hearing "something more" that increases my attention. She goes on earnestly to tell me, "Even when we go to parties, I wear my button... If it's a family function or something and somebody has on his button, he'll be all right...he'll be here; he won't be left out..." This is not my usual cultural association to putting a picture of a deceased loved one on a shelf as a form of memory. Instead, her murdered cousin is alive and present with us through her testimony.

M.A. Walsh (✉)
Boston University School of Social Work, Boston, MA, USA

© The Editor(s) (if applicable) and The Author(s) 2016
S.N. Arel, S. Rambo (eds.), *Post-Traumatic Public Theology*,
DOI 10.1007/978-3-319-40660-2_12

She tells me this felt connection is magnified when more people wear their buttons or t-shirts with the loved one's picture at family events. She is testifying to a *living presence* in the material button. This presence remains with her and witnesses to the family's ongoing lives. He will not be "left out." I now see and hear with transformed eyes and ears the annual Mother's Day march for peace by family survivors of homicide in Boston. By the hundreds, their chants of "What do we want? Peace! When do we want it? Now!" rise through the Dorchester neighborhood streets as they carry images of their murdered loved ones on banners, button pins, and t-shirts. I take this phenomenon seriously as prophetic spiritual testimony in material form—a "theopoetics"[1] of public testimony in material form—warning both of the costs of violence and the ongoing visceral presence of the deceased and of a fierce love. As witness, I too am awakened by her testimony and transformed at a deeper level of consciousness in my connection to her. I am awakened to our common human connection across our respective cultures and to our shared spiritual desires and needs for solidarity, love, peace, and justice.

Transforming Pain and Anger Into Power and Action

In the aftermath of her 15-year-old son's murder, when the black mother who founded the Louis D. Brown Peace Institute in Dorchester inherited a hand-held button-making machine from a white peace activist, she did not realize what a powerful, prophetic, and transformational material tool these buttons would become for families in Boston. Initially, she simply felt a drive to connect with other families who had lost loved ones to murder. She clipped pictures and words from newspaper reports, created a button, and asked a reporter to forward it onto the family. Gradually, this grew into a Traveling Memorial Button Project and part of the ongoing work of the Peace Institute with survivor families. The Traveling Memorial Button Project is described on the Peace Institute website as giving prophetic testimony by survivor families: "As survivors of homicide victims we have a unique understanding of the impact violence has on individuals, families, friends and communities. We must use this painful understanding to provide leadership to our society in its quest to find true and lasting peace."[2]

Young people began to put the image of their lost loved one on t-shirts and banners for marches as well. The founder describes her original motivation in creating the buttons:

> I...wanted the larger community to see that violence touches all of us... whether it's inner city gang violence, domestic, sexual abuse, whatever it is, violence touches everybody, and I wanted the photos to be more than just a number... I wanted people to see the faces are real, the names are real and the impact that it has on the community...more than the homicide statistics...take off this myth that it's only gang related in a concentrated area...

In the hands of surviving family members, a simple button pin-making machine became a channeling mechanism for the ongoing viscerally experienced living presence of their murdered loved ones and a means, along with t-shirts and banners, to magnify the fierce prophetic moral call to communal peace and justice. The buttons, banners, and t-shirts became a means to testify publically to the value of black lives and all lives—that violent loss should unify prophetic protest across lines of race, class, and gender. The motto of the Peace Institute would become "transforming pain and anger into power and action"—a linking of pastoral spiritual care and the moral call to prophetic justice through the combined use of the "healing" power of the arts in their Holistic Healing Center and a comprehensive anti-oppression and leadership education program. Many of the founders and organizers of the later developing *Mothers for Justice and Equality*[3] were trained first through the Peace Institute's Leadership Academy, which became a means of facilitating resilience and "posttraumatic growth" for homicide survivors (Fig. 12.1).[4]

Such post-traumatic growth is *a process that takes time*, however, in the face of complex trauma from violent communal loss in already marginalized communities—and lays incomplete for some. There is a process by which what is material becomes a living testimony to "the pact that the living have with the dead,"[5] as well as to a moral call for peace and justice in the streets of Boston. As Rubem Alves writes, "Politics begins not with the administration of the dead but with the resurrection of the dead."[6] Such "politics" recognizes a pre-existing power imbalance and need to challenge institutional and cultural structures of power and oppression, calling forth "dangerous memories"[7] of the dead made living in the creative hands of survivors. I call this living testimony of the spirit in and through the material – *material theopoetics*.

Fig. 12.1 The Louis D. Brown Peace Institute's Traveling Memorial Button Project, bottom reads: "When Hands Reach Out In Friendship, Hearts Are Touched With Joy"

Material Theopoetics in the Hands of Survivors

Rebecca Chopp conceptualizes theopoetics as a form of testifying and witnessing to the movement of Spirit in the moral call to imagination, hope, and transfiguration.[8] In the aftermath of communal violence, how do the above phenomena give expressive poetic testimony and witness, beyond the discursive, to spiritual resilience, political resistance, and the transformation of our relationship to one another and the Divine in and through the material made sacred? Such phenomena call witnesses to take matter *seriously* in human creative hands. Theopoetics in material form represent first-order expressions of our *felt* relationship to hope, grace, transcendent connection, transformation, and the divine. Such performative material creations cannot be dismissed or minimized as "merely" material religion.[9] In human hands made in the *Imago Dei*, matter becomes fiercely living and transformative as theopoetic testimony and witness to life after violent trauma. In giving normative priority to the experiences of "survivors as experts,"[10] I call attention to educators, therapists, healers, and social science researchers, among others, of our mutual need to account for and language these phenomena in post-traumatic care.

As an example of this type of phenomenon in need of interdisciplinary attention, in the initial aftermath of communal violent loss, survivor families experience a need to testify to their personal stories and *"continuing bond"*[11] with the dead, and the community also needs guidance on response. Meeting this need can take material artistic form in post-traumatic care. For example, the Peace Institute's Survivor Outreach Services assists families in designing a uniquely personal eight-to-ten-page funeral order of service that contains pictures of, letters to, and poetry about their murdered loved one, illustrating not only their past relationship but also communication to the dead in the present. Each page is tied to the Peace Institute's Seven Principles of Peace—love, unity, faith, hope, courage, justice, and forgiveness. Additionally, the Peace Institute includes information about trauma reactions, symptoms, recommendations, and resources as a pastoral spiritual guide for the broader community in how to support the family in the coming years. At the end of these specialized funeral orders of service, the Peace Institute requests members of the community to commit to a Peace Prayer, spiritual peace practices, and the creation of neighborhood and school Peace Zones.

This material legacy functions as a creative and performative work of material art by the family, with therapeutic, educational, and public theological implications. The pain of the loved one's violent loss is transformed spiritually through the family's visual and written testimony to the precious and present vividness of the loved one's life, rather than overtly to the traumatic circumstances of their death. But importantly, this transformation also serves a prophetic function in educating the larger witnessing community to the pastoral spiritual needs of the family in the aftermath of the overt violent trauma, while also motivating the larger community to commit to and advocate for peace and justice through particular practices. The pastoral and prophetic— a family's personal spiritual "healing" and a public moral call to social justice—become intertwined and living in the family's material creation of poetic testimony and witness.

Recognizing that such transformation of violent loss also is complex and takes time, particularly for politically marginalized and oppressed communities, post-traumatic care needs to engage a *"kaleidoscope of practices"* while recognizing that "one size does not fit all."[12] Practices illuminated in the study of the Peace Institute include play with other forms of material art, such as collages, drawings, quilts, photography, and most particularly, a unique art form known as sandplay. In sandplay, or sand tray/world play, a survivor places miniature objects into a tray of sand (other elements such as fire and water also may be present) to create a story about a world, often a world that has symbolic and metaphoric meaning for their lived experiences.[13]

Ideally, this play is witnessed by a trained Peace Institute staff member to facilitate the survivor's processing of their personal trauma and story. In play, this world is created and transformed solely under the control and vision of the survivor, with the witness only taking notes or asking questions. A Peace Institute staff member expresses the usefulness of this type of play with our material world in relationship to the neurophysiological experience of trauma:

> I think that it's so hard to talk about [the trauma] that you have to provide different ways to express [it]… Trauma…can't always be explained in words. You have to feel it, and one way that you can feel it is through art and music and literature and sand tray… When you play in the sand and just touch it, it opens up that part of your brain that the trauma affected. And…[in] the process of playing in the sand and…creating [with] the figures…a world allows for the trauma to…kind of come to the front of the brain to be processed.

Embodied material play using the senses provides direct access to the limbic system where trauma might be frozen in affect without narrative. Such physical play activates movement in the brain between the sensory base of memory in the limbic system and the frontal lobes of language and reason. This allows affect to be slowly reconnected to language through play with material symbols in the sand, symbols that point to the "something more" remaining in the aftermath of the trauma through their metaphoric excess of poetic and affective associations (Fig. 12.2).[14]

Languaging in the aftermath of neurophysiological and cognitive disruption from trauma is significant for spiritual and/or religious meaning-making as well. Some survivors interviewed specifically linked their material play with objects in the sand to their experience of God moving through their play, the theopoetic movement of Spirit in the world play, drawing from their Christian interpretative linguistic frame. Their experiences included testifying and being witnessed, being surprised and challenged, and yet desiring "something more." Listen to the voice of this survivor of a family homicide as she creates, moves, and transforms her world, all the while experiencing a mysterious guiding of her process:

Fig. 12.2 *A Peace Institute Survivor's Sandplay Example.* Sandplay performed by a participant following a visit with her son's murderer in jail. In the picture, the participant indicates she is reflecting on self through the figure placed by the mirror. She also indicates she is reflecting on reconciling the perpetrator's innocent child self with the horrific action in which he had later engaged through her placement of other figures in the tray. Struggles with experiences of anger, "evil" or "othering," suffering, and trauma in tension with the survivor's belief in the Peace Institute's peace principles of forgiveness and justice are expressed in material theopoetic form through her play with material objects in the sand and the metaphoric excess of poetic and affective meaning suggested

> It just took me somewhere spiritually. I just went somewhere, and I began to just put things in the sand tray… I would pick up the pieces and say, 'This is my family,' and…I put the house in, and I could remember I felt like I needed to protect my family. I can remember…'Okay, if I put up this wall, I could protect my family.' Then I would move stuff because it didn't represent this, and…I was like, "You have to experience it personally to even understand it 'cause, I'm tellin' you, I felt like something else took over me." But it was a feeling that I wouldn't mind feeling again over and over again. When I left there, I kept thinking about, "Wow, how did that happen? Okay, God, what's really going on?" I wasn't scared, but it was *different*.

Another young adult survivor would say: "... it's like taking a leap of faith... You're going somewhere that you might not necessarily want to go and then once the world comes to you, then you can either shut down or you can explain where you fit in there... It's just a real deep spiritual moment that happens in sandplay... I mean that God's working through me and...really trying to show me something."

The use of material artistic play in the pastoral "healing" care of survivors often would go hand in hand with the survivor's *post-traumatic growth and increased capacity* to perform prophetic testimony for peace and justice in the public square. An example is Peaceville, a city constructed of cardboard, paint, and other objects by youth that theopoetically expressed an eschatological public vision of peace and subsequently was placed on display at the Massachusetts State House in Boston. This material theopoetic became another tool of empowerment for the youth in particular, as expressed by one survivor parent:

> I have a younger son, so he attends the youth program during the year when there's a particular project, like they did Peaceville...and they did an appearance at the State House... He spoke to different people that were there about his project, and the news reporters...had questions for him... He's now 13. And he's able to articulate what he feels and expresses himself, whether it's with his hands or verbally.

The *place and space* in which post-traumatic care occurs can be as important as the kaleidoscope of practices offered. For example, nearly all Peace Institute participants referred to their material surroundings at the place and space of the Peace Institute as testifying to a theopoetic sensibility—a "spiritual aura" and a "culture of peace" and safety. Walls are decorated with survivor artwork, peace quotes, and general attention to the beauty of the space. One staff person stressed, "this *space* is healing in itself," while an institutional supporter of the Peace Institute said, "It is sort of a touchstone...It's solid, it's in the community...There's a welcoming sort of aura there *and I* often use it as a place where I'll stop by." The *materiality* of the place and space of the Peace Institute come alive theopoetically in testimony and witness to a larger culture of peace, one that also holds the ambiguities of *the process* of pain and anger being transformed into power and action in its place and space.

Play and Transfiguration in Material Theopoetics

On the theopoetics of story and testimony, Chopp writes: "The telling of these stories is for life, for the mending of life, the healing of life, the ability of life to live and survive and thus conquer...extremity... If one is not authorized to live, then surviving is both resistance and hope. These testimonies are discourses of survival for hope and of hope for survival."[15] There is a theopoetic realm of resistance, hope, and survival, of testimony and witness, beyond the discursive, however, as seen in the pastoral and prophetic material work of the Peace Institute.[16] This essay suggests that our material world is *transfigured*[17] and made vividly living as sacred, holy testimony in the hands of human play and performance. I identify such human play with transfiguring matter, "godly (or holy or divine) transfiguring play."[18]

The use of the term "transfiguration" has Christian roots in the New Testament's witness to the transfiguration of Jesus Christ into the Son of God before his disciples, Peter, James, and John. This vision takes place on a "high mountain," with references to Jesus' face shining "like the sun" and his clothes becoming "dazzling white" and to the appearance of Moses and Elijah in their "glory." Transfiguration impacts both Jesus and the witnesses—all are enveloped by a "bright cloud overshadow[ing]" them and from which the presumed voice of God speaks to them, with temptation to fear or slumber by the disciples. Yet, all still are touched and awakened in the aftermath by this embodied experience of the divine in flesh and made new in awareness of God. In this essay, I metaphorically expand the idea of transfiguration to include the human capacity to channel sacred energy into material creations, such that testifiers and witnesses are transfixed, enveloped, and awakened together in a sudden and new awareness of the holy.

In the case of the Peace Institute, such play and performance include personal and public material theopoetic responses to communal violence, responses demonstrating experiences of resilience, grace, resistance, connection, faith, transformation, and hope. World play witnessed with small figures in a tray of sand becomes an opportunity for a survivor of family homicide to engage a leap of faith into the mysterious unknown and for the Spirit of God to reveal a new path to her through the story she narrates. Memorial buttons become vehicles for the dead to be a living presence and witnessing at family events. Matter in the hands of the *Imago Dei* becomes a source of "godly transfiguring play," with creative possibilities for transformation and transcendence of violent trauma, including when performed prophetically in the public square of witness, as in the Mother's Day march for peace.[19]

"Play" as a response to trauma may appear to be an odd category for a theologian to employ due to its typical association with frivolity and childhood. Such a focus attends only to the most limited dimensions of play in human life, however, ignoring the vital and serious role of play for creativity, learning, transformation, and the experiences of freedom, choice, resilience, and the opening of imaginative possibilities. This biological capacity for play is a characteristic humans share with other mammals, though greatly expanded in human hands.[20] The restoration of possibilities in imagination through the facilitation of choice, control, and opportunities for meaning-making, are recognized as core "healing" components by many who specialize in the social science and therapy of trauma.[21]

Expressive, poetic, and metaphorical play with our material world can be integral to such serious work on both pastoral and prophetic levels for adults, children, families, and groups.[22] Beyond this pastoral therapeutic value, however, survivors themselves *interpreted* their play in religious language—as God's Spirit moving mysteriously, guiding and leaving desire for more in the aftermath. Play becomes serious, powerful, and deep when viewed through a religious lens. Play becomes enticing and persuasive—and through this, awakening to the possibilities of the social imagination of new worlds, connections, and relationships in its prophetic function.[23]

Material play *invites* this godly position of performing expressive acts of creation, destruction, and re-creation, a playing in the dark and with the deep in transformation and possibilities of resurrection.[24] Through sandplay, a survivor mother can play with confronting her traumatic loss as well as her efforts to reconnect with images of and the hope still for innocence in the aftermath of encountering horror or "evil." Her sand tray/world play is in movement, reflecting the *process* of transformation in her actual lived world—both on a personal pastoral level and on a public prophetic level. The pastoral "healing" movement of internal transformation extends her capacity for later prophetic moral movement toward transforming the external lived world. Destruction of prior worlds and re-creation of new worlds is precisely the material theopoetic experience suggested when living in the aftermath of communal violence.

What remains of the prior world in this transformation of the new? Survivor voices suggest that it is not "merely" spirit, love, and memories in a wistful, fragile connection to the past. Spirit, love, and memories are embodied and enlivened in and through our material world, with visceral, fierce, and sacred testifying power. Here, there is no easy separation between the material, the spiritual, and the corporeal, as Patricia Cox

Miller discovered in her work with relics: "...when a martyr's dust, bone, or body becomes the center of cultic activity and reverence, it loses its character as a natural body and begins to function as a site of religious contact. No longer a mere object, it becomes a...locus and mediator of spiritual presence and power."[25] The material is made divine through the hands of survivors, and when a material theopoetic is performed in testimony before witnesses, "something more" has the potential to happen beyond survivor's personal testimony and transformation. Testifier and witness both have the potential to be *transfigured with the material* in this fuller visceral engagement of the body's senses through the material theopoetic performance—whether as testifier and witness to the building of a personal sand tray world or as testifiers and witnesses on public streets in a march for peace. Both have the potential to be touched in that moment by the "something more" of the holy, enveloping their senses and pointing to *something new* in their shared awakening.

This potential awakening is dependent, however. Given that human beings are created in the image of the divine in *particular cultures*, a culturally specific material theopoetic that *transfigures* trauma, both personally and socially, within and across cultures, is the potential of material play in the aftermath of communal violence. Rita Nakashima Brock and Rebecca Ann Parker write of the power and value placed on the role of icons in making the world beautiful and new again in the Eastern Orthodox cultural tradition: "To this day, theologians of the Eastern church speak of 'the transfiguration of the world.' They define salvation as an awakening to the whole world illumined by the brilliance of divine presence. Sacred art and ritual initiate people into this life-changing knowledge..."[26] The Eastern Orthodox tradition represents a different cultural lens than typically employed in the Western Christian context, arising out of a particular cultural context and heritage. Yet, because we share a common human experience of being embodied players in a material world, the possibility exists for connecting and being transfigured into awakening by icons and sacred art of the Eastern tradition in cross-cultural exposure.

Similarly, the black mother who founded the Peace Institute in the aftermath of her son's murder speaks from an intense desire to disrupt dominant cultural norms of separation and slumbering numbness, to transfigure cross-cultural awareness: "I didn't want people to forget the names...violence touches everybody...I wanted people to see the faces are real, the names are real and the impact that it has on the community...I mean more than the homicide statistics that they show in the inner city." This black mother fiercely testifies to "awaken the world" in her material theopoetic creation, first of memorial buttons and then of a Peace Institute named for her murdered son, as well as a Traveling Button Memorial witnessing to all the murdered. Through the hands and testifying material works of survivors, and as witnessed by a cross-cultural community, violent death and the world itself is *transfigured* and awakened into a powerful visceral experience of ongoing life and beauty and of resistance and hope and new possibilities. The *tools of transfiguration* enveloping testifier and witness are a *culturally specific* material theopoetics—sand trays, memorial buttons, t-shirts, funeral orders of service, the place and space of the Peace Institute, and banners in marches for peace on the streets of Boston.

Taking Matter Seriously Through Intercultural Encounter

Across cultural differences of race and class, human beings express their continuing bonds with the dead. In the aftermath of violent trauma in culturally specific contexts, human beings often feel called to transform their traumatic loss through holy or divine transfigurational play and performance with their material and expressive worlds. When public theologians and others pay attention to this material theopoetic of transfiguration, the interdependence of human beings with our material expressions across cultures, and the differences in cultural meaning-making possibilities, are witnessed more clearly. Through intercultural encounter with material theopoetics, deeper levels of human awakening to transfiguring the wounds of our shared world become transformational possibilities.

When public theologians *of trauma* pay attention particularly to survivors, and those who serve them, treating survivors as "experts" or "primary theologians,"[27] we learn how materials become living in the hands of human beings, and through that living, how our bonds with the dead continue in new, often surprising, powerfully sacred forms. In the aftermath of communal violence, indeed, "these bones live again,"[28] and their public performance in material form creates a prophetic theopoetic moral call to the divine transfiguration of the world through the testifier(s) to the witness(es).[29] When such public testifying and witnessing occurs across the lines of race, class, gender, and culture, there can be a particular shining and compelling brilliance (a persuasive divine allure) in the encounter with difference in material expressive forms.[30] Intercultural theology[31] derived from such encounters holds a potential to forge an awakening to new awareness of common human desires for and paths of love, peace, and justice.

Yet, this intercultural encounter must be received as different, intriguing, beautiful, and enticing, rather than alien or frightening and terrifying and thus inducing of feelings of being overwhelmed, indifferent, or repelled and desiring to slumber or to flee, similar to the disciples' experience of the transfiguration of Jesus. The sanctity of life must be received in witness to the material artistic cultural form expressed. In the religious response to communal violence, what resonates as theologically beautiful and with potential for transfiguration of the world differs by cultural context, including by lived experiences of oppression.[32] Who or what has the power to normalize and lift up an aesthetic of transfigured beauty after trauma—to lift up such a material aesthetic from a pastoral need for "healing" to a prophetic challenge for a new vision of the world? This often is contested public terrain when considering a material theopoetic after communal violence.[33] The public post-traumatic theological voice contends with a multiplicity of these cultural publics. Latina intercultural theologians recognize the need for a "polyphony of voices"[34] to be heard in forging a common path of love, peace, and justice. But *which voices* gain access to prophetic power across cultural public divides to testify and be witnessed, particularly in the aftermath of communal violence?

A *power analysis* entails understanding how institutional and cultural dominance is shaped by who or what has the power to *define reality* (including what will or will not be considered a "problem" deserving of regular attention) by virtue of *access to resources, decision-making capacity*, and the ability to *establish cultural norms and standards* through social institutions and systems.[35] Engaging in such a power analysis of institutional oppression for liberation is a crucial component of the Peace Institute's Leadership Academy. The black mother who founded the Peace Institute in her murdered son's name has labored for over two decades empowering other mothers and fathers to testify in the public arena as "Peace Warriors." Her hope remains to create zones of peace in Boston and beyond—yet it is the Boston Marathon bombing that garners significant national attention and a ritual annual marking, not the daily labor of the Peace Institute.

Additional voices from survivors of family homicide continue to illuminate these power dynamics, particularly the impact of dominant cultural norms of mental health and healing. Young adults interviewed in Boston repeatedly shared, often in hushed voices with worries that this made them seem "crazy," that they sought to preserve the bloodstained clothing or actual blood from the ground where their murdered loved one lay, simultaneously demonstrating their resistance to mental health norms through these actions. Similarly, survivors of homicide often contested their comfort with the "normalized" language of "healing." Such language suggested to them that they were to be restored to a former sense of wholeness through a therapeutic process that meant loss of connection to their murdered loved one. Instead, survivors consistently spoke of finding the ability *to move* again. One spoke of having "1,000,001 pieces wounded," but of knowing that they would not "shatter again," though they might "lose pieces" at times and need to "replace them."

These experiences of being judged and limited in their expressions by a dominant culture, read as a white culture by black survivors, compounds their pain and struggle in the aftermath of communal violence. Peace Institute leaders firmly state that there is a need for a "kaleidoscope" of cultural practices for survivors in the aftermath of violence—that "one size does not fit all."[36] Perhaps the same is true of our public theologies of trauma. Perhaps there is no perfect public theology of trauma for all cultural contexts, and one must remain open and attentive to the lived experiences of survivors for the unexpected expression that might be divine transfiguring allure in new form. To search for a universal, "one size fits all" public theology of trauma is perhaps to engage in the Western theological tradition of imposing Spirit as an agent of "Final Perfection" rather than experiencing Spirit "on the slant," as Sharon Betcher writes.[37]

Using the lens of an institutional power analysis, these survivor voices lead me to ask whether a dominant culture, intentionally or unintentionally, including through our academic institutions and research, mutes the fiercest material theopoetic expressions of survivors of violent trauma. For example, when Emmett Till's mother chose to leave the casket of her brutally beaten son open for viewing to a larger media—a theopoetic material performance—who was most uncomfortable, his mother as testifier or the "respectable public" in witness?[38] Survivor voices suggest that those witnesses privileged and separated by race, class, and gender need to be "haunted" by the allure of the divine in new and different forms, while survivors oppressed by race, class, and gender need to be recognized and empowered as the fierce and testifying advocates for life.[39] There always is a socio-cultural and political context to public theologies of trauma, as well as to social policies and cultural standards for healing, art, and education. These need clearer and more explicit illustration through a richer and deeper conversation, using ethnographically grounded cross-cultural research. Across all academic disciplines, including practical and constructive theology, working from a power analysis and anti-oppression lens is foundational to an authentic intercultural encounter that will result in public prophetic theologies, as well as educational and social policies, with transformational potential for the world.[40] To be awakened and transformed first requires *transfigurational* access to the *unwitnessed realities*. In fuller intercultural encounters, public theologies of trauma may begin to lay bare the cross-cultural dimensions of the sacred.

Conclusion

The Peace Institute has been witnessing to peace in the aftermath of violence on Boston streets for decades. The current rash of public massacres—including desecration on and destruction of the sacred material ground and space of religious institutions—requires our witness to the wisdom offered by groups, such as the Peace Institute and others.[41] These tragedies continue a public confrontation in different respects with the fact that the USA is a country founded on violence, where violence is woven into every chapter of its history and contemporary institutions.[42] While the Boston Marathon bombing, like 9/11, calls forth a sustained annual public ritual marking, the expressive focus limits to a particular injury rather than expanding inclusively to all impacted by violence, thus serving to reinforce national or religious narratives justifying retaliation and retribution. The "routine" slaughter of children in our inner cities, particularly young black men and children, as well as the massacre of children at Newtown, does not elicit a sustained, organized, unifying, and meaningful response on a national scale by *religious communities* in their public theologies of violence and trauma.

We are a country of wounded "pieces," of shattered pieces, of oppressed and privileged communities holding these different pieces. None of us are untouched. Each community holds its own piece of the historical legacy of violent trauma, ruptured relationships, and dangerous memories, as currently testified to by the powerful Black Lives Matter public movement. Each community has been shaped in its cultural identity by relationships to patterns of violent conquest across time, lands, and peoples. Only intercultural theological and religious work, grounded in an anti-oppression lens, can create a countercultural public theology serving the divine impulse to transfigure all the wounded pieces of our world. Trauma bears a register that calls for a fuller range of cultural expressions and practices than the spoken or written word, so that each of the wounded pieces is embraced rather than rejected or repressed. This entails a willingness to recognize and be with our own "vulnerable personhood" and an ability to live together in "vulnerable communion" through a multiplicity of expressive cultural practices.[43] It entails our capacity to be open to the illusions of perfection and privilege that mark us as falsely defective or separate by a dominant white Western culture.

Aesthetic theologies of music, art, drama, and material play respond to and resonate with these wounded and shattered pieces. They risk playing with the depths, playing with the dark unknowing, playing with soulful blues or creative jazz, playing with tentative movements, playing with fierce resistance, and playing with "sacred ambiguity," and "holy humor" that mark our shared human vulnerabilities and knit our imperfections into creative new patterns.[44] As we open possibilities for a public theology of aesthetics and power in relation to trauma and prophetic pastoral care, we widen our own capacity to encompass the broadest intercultural range of relational and material theopoetic testimony. We witness more fully to our shared humanity as *Imago Dei*. This is the serious prophetic task of aesthetic theological play in supporting the improvisational movement of the divine across cultures toward the transfiguration and ultimate transformation of the world with a greater love, peace, and justice.

Notes

1. Rebecca S. Chopp (1998) "Theology and the Poetics of Testimony," *Criterion*, vol. 37, no. 1, 2–12.
2. See the Peace Institute website, accessed October 7, 2014, http://ldbpeaceinstitute.org/content/traveling-memorial-button-project.
3. See http://www.mothersforjusticeandequality.org, accessed March 12, 2015.
4. See Lawrence G. Calhoun and Richard G. Tedeschi (2005) "Posttraumatic Growth: The Positive Lessons of Loss," in Robert A. Neimeyer (ed.) *Meaning Reconstruction and the Experience of Loss*, 4th edition, (Washington, D.C.: American Psychological Association), 157–172.
5. A paraphrase from Ysaye Maria Barnwell's (1980) "Breaths," lyrics By Birago Diop/Musical Setting By Ysaÿe M. Barnwell, (Washington, D.C.: Barnwell's Notes Publishing, Inc.) in which she sings: "The dead have a pact with the living."

6. Rubem A. Alves (1992) "Theopoetics: Longing and Liberation," in Lorine M. Getz and Ruy O. Costa (eds.) *Struggles for Solidarity: Liberation Theologies in Tension* (Minneapolis: Fortress Press), 159–171.
7. Here I draw on Sharon Welch's expanded metaphorical use of Johann Baptist Metz' term, "dangerous memories," to describe survivor use of images to testify to their "pact with the dead," in a way that Welch also would describe as revealing an implicit "theology of resistance and hope." See *A Feminist Ethic of Risk*, revised edition, (Minneapolis: Fortress Press, 1990), 153–155.
8. Chopp, "Theology and the Poetics of Testimony." In my dissertation, combining analytic perspectives from material religion with theopoetics, I argue that such a moral call to imagination, hope, and transfiguration also takes material form in prophetic performance beyond the purely discursive. See *Prophetic Pastoral Care in the Aftermath of Trauma: Forging a Constructive Practical Theology of Lived Religion From Organized Trauma Response Ministries* (PhD diss., Boston University, 2014, ProQuest AAT 3610856).
9. Daniel J. Louw calls practical theologians to take the expressive dimensions of human life and the human capacity for aesthetic reasoning more seriously in our work. See (2001) "Creative Hope and Imagination in a Practical Theology of Aesthetic (Artistic) Reason" in Paul Ballard and Pamela Couture (eds.) *Creativity, Imagination and Criticism: The Expressive Dimension in Practical Theology* (Fairwater, Cardiff: Cardiff Academic Press), 91–104. See also E. Frances King (2010) *Material Religion and Popular Culture* (New York: Routledge).
10. See this discussed in Michelle Walsh (Forthcoming 2016) *Violent Trauma, Culture, and Power: An Interdisciplinary Exploration in Lived Religion* (New York: Palgrave Macmillan).
11. "Continuing bonds" is a concept utilized in my dissertation and forthcoming book and is drawn from psychological grief work theory that normalizes human desires for continued relationships with the dead. This theory challenges traditional Western psychoanalytic conceptions that pathologize ongoing connections. See Dennis Klass, Phyllis R. Silverman, and Steven L. Nickman (eds.) (1996) *Continuing Bonds: New Understandings of Grief* (New York: Routledge).
12. Walsh, *Violent Trauma, Culture, and Power*.

13. Sandplay, as a therapeutic technique originally used with children, is traced back to the work of Margaret Lowenfeld in England and later was developed further by Dora Kalff, including uses with adults. Peace Institute staff have trained in the Sand Tray/World Play technique of Gisela Schubach De Domenico (1995) *Sand Tray World Play: A Comprehensive Guide to the Use of the Sand Tray in Psychotherapeutic and Transformational Settings* (Oakland, CA: Vision Quest Images). For general information and history, see also Katherine Bradway (ed.) (1981) *Sandplay Studies: Origins, Theory, and Practice*, collected by the C.G. Jung Institute of San Francisco (Boston: Sigo Press) and Kay Bradway and Barbara McCoard (1997) *Sandplay – Silent Workshop of the Psyche* (New York: Routledge).
14. The neurophysiological and cognitive impact of trauma is well known. See Judith Herman (1992) *Trauma and Recovery* (New York: Basic Books); Ronnie Janoff-Bulman (1992) *Shattered Assumptions: Toward a New Psychology of Trauma* (New York: The Free Press); Babette Rothschild (2000) *The Body Remembers: The Psychophysiology of Trauma and Trauma Treatment* (New York: W.W. Norton and Company); and Bessel van der Kolk, Alexander C. McFarlane, and Lars Weisaeth (eds.) (1996) *Traumatic Stress: The Effects of Overwhelming Experience on Mind, Body, and Society* (New York: The Guilford Press).
15. Chopp, "Theology and the Poetics of Testimony," 7.
16. Welch also calls attention to implicit theologies of "resistance and hope" in *A Feminist Ethic of Risk*. Such implicit theologies can be recognized in material expressions as well.
17. See Matthew 17:1–7, Mark 9:2–8, and Luke 9:28–36.
18. The language of "godly play" is drawn from the work of Jerome W. Berryman (1991) *Godly Play: An Imaginative Approach to Religious Education* (Minneapolis: Augsburg Fortress). "Godly play is the playing of a game that can awaken us to new ways of seeing ourselves as human beings. It is the way to discover our deep identity as Godly creatures, created in the image of God… Godly play is a way to know God… The place for play is at the edge of knowing and being. The time has a very clear limit. It is our lifetime," 7–8. "The edge of knowing and being" is pointed to through poetic metaphors suggested in the material play.

19. Jack Santino's work has long noted the political performative dimensions of works of art in the public space. See his (2001) *Signs of War and Peace: Social Conflict and the Uses of Symbols in Public in Northern Ireland* (New York: Palgrave Macmillan) as well as his edited volume (2006) *Spontaneous Shrines and the Public Memorialization of Death* (New York: Palgrave Macmillan).
20. Stuart Brown (2009) *Play: How It Shapes the Brain, Opens the Imagination, and Invigorates the Soul* (New York: Avery).
21. See, for example, early classics in the field. Herman, *Trauma and Recovery* and Janoff-Bulman, *Shattered Assumptions*. I place "healing" in quotations because the use of this word was challenged by survivor voices in my dissertation, *Prophetic Pastoral Care in the Aftermath of Trauma*. "Healing" often implied a closure and forced disconnection from the survivor's ongoing bond to their lost loved, an implication that was overtly rejected in favor of a language that more closely paralleled finding the ability to "move" again.
22. Therapists have long pointed to the power of expressive art and play therapy for personal "healing" in their work with traumatized children and adults. See for example Cathy A. Malchiodi (ed.) (2008) *Creative Interventions with Traumatized Children* (New York: The Guilford Press) and Nancy Boyd Webb (ed.) (2007) *Play Therapy with Children in Crisis: Individual, Group, and Family Treatment* (New York: The Guilford Press).
23. Process theologians often find resonance in this experience of God's movement and persuasive power. See for example Catherine Keller (2003) *Face of the Deep: A Theology of Becoming* (New York: Routledge).
24. Drawing on Toni Morrison's text of the same name, (1992) *Playing in the Dark: Whiteness and the Literary Imagination* (Cambridge: Harvard University Press), and focusing on the American historical trauma of race and racism, James H. Evans, Jr. (2010) *Playing: Christian Explorations of Daily Living* (Minneapolis: Fortress Press) writes of "playing in the dark" as "attempt[ing] to construct a livable world in which the realities of race and racism continue to hold sway," 18 – for "race and racism," one also might substitute the words "violent trauma." Evans asks: "What does it mean…to play in the dark as a radical, revolutionary act of resistance and re-creation?" 15. Attending similarly to con-

frontations with danger and evil, Diane Ackerman, a poet and naturalist, writes of deep play as "the ecstatic form of play...[that] involves the sacred and the holy," 12–13, in (1999) *Deep Play* (New York: Vintage Books). She points to the forms of deep play that can pit the forces of good and evil against each other, where danger, risk, and the social order are at stake.
25. Patricia Cox Miller (2009) *The Corporeal Imagination: Signifying the Holy in Late Ancient Christianity* (Philadelphia: University of Pennsylvania Press), 2. Miller's work parallels my own, while my focus is on the power of performance between testifier and witness and Miller's focus is shaped by literary analysis.
26. Rita Nakashima Brock and Rebecca Ann Parker (2008) *Saving Paradise: How Christianity Traded Love of This World for Crucifixion and Empire* (Boston: Beacon Press), 155.
27. Mary Clark Moschella (2012) "Ethnography," in *The Wiley-Blackwell Companion to Practical Theology* Bonnie J. Miller-McLemore (ed.) (Malden, MA; Blackwell Publishing Limited), 224–233. Peace Institute staff also point to the need to consider "survivors as experts."
28. Ezekiel 37:3.
29. See Chopp, "Theology and the Poetics of Testimony." Chopp calls for theologians to become responsive witnesses to the Spirit's revelation in community, "to the moral summons in testimonies," in order to "refigure and reimagine the social imaginary," 9–10. "Testimonies invoke a moral claim: it is from someone to someone about something. A decision is called for, a change in reality is required. This responsibility is a social reality," 7.
30. Here, I am nuancing Shelly Rambo's significant contributions in (2010) *Spirit and Trauma: A Theology of Remaining* (Louisville: Westminster John Knox Press) by distinguishing the roles and experiences of witness and testifier in the movement of Spirit. In my dissertation, I also critique the failure of public theologians of trauma, consciously and explicitly, to consider their racial and socioeconomic cultural context when theorizing for their audiences. For a critique of the universalization of "public," see Janet R. Jakobsen (1997) "The Body Politic vs. Lesbian Bodies: Publics, Counterpublics, and the Use of Norms," in Rebecca S. Chopp and S.G. Davaney (eds.) (1994) *Horizons in Feminist Theology: Identity, Tradition and Norms* (Minneapolis: Fortress Press), 116–136.

31. Olga Consuelo Velez Caro (2007) "Toward a Feminist Intercultural Theology," in *Feminist Intercultural Theology: Latina Explorations for a Just World* Maria Pilar Aquino and Maria Jose Rosado-Nunes (eds.) (Maryknoll: Orbis Books), 248–264.
32. See James H. Cone (2007) "Strange Fruit: The Cross and the Lynching Tree," *Harvard Divinity Bulletin*, vol. 35, no. 1, 47–56. Drawing from the Billie Holiday song of the same name, this essay finds theopoetic and transfigurational power in images of black lynchings in the American South to challenge, prophetically, the dominant white cultural power structure that continues to oppress African American men today. Depending on one's cultural identity, appreciating the "strange beauty" in such images for their prophetic power can become an enormous intercultural task, requiring a significant shift in worldview and stance. See also the work of M. Shawn Copeland in this area (2010) *Enfleshing Freedom: Body, Race, and Being* (Minneapolis: Fortress Press).
33. The public memorialization of death, particularly after social traumas such as the Vietnam War or the AIDS epidemic, witnesses to these contested terrains of cultural publics. See for example Marita Sturken (2007) *Tangled Memories: The Vietnam War, the AIDS Epidemic, and the Politics of Remembering* (Berkeley: University of California Press). See also James E. Young (1993) *The Texture of Memory: Holocaust Memorials and Meaning* (New Haven: Yale University Press).
34. Velez Caro, "Toward a Feminist Intercultural Theology," 225.
35. I am indebted to the Women's Theological Center of Boston for this understanding of a power analysis. See www.thewtc.org, accessed March 15, 2015.
36. For different approaches to clinical care sensitive to culture and liberation, see Judith Jordan (2010) *Relational-Cultural Therapy* (Washington, D.C.: American Psychological Association); Dawn Belkin Martinez and Ann Fleck-Henderson (eds.) (2014) *Social Justice in Clinical Practice: A liberation health framework for social justice* (New York: Routledge); and Sheryl A. Kujawa-Holbrook and Karen B. Montagno (eds.) (2009) *Injustice and the Care of Souls: Taking Oppression Seriously in Pastoral Care* (Minneapolis: Fortress Press).
37. See Sharon V. Betcher (2007) *Spirit and the Politics of Disablement* (Minneapolis: Fortress Press), vii. Betcher seeks to deconstruct the

binary "hermeneutic of brokenness versus wholeness" in the Western theological and philosophical traditions, where conceptions of wholeness imply freedom from chaos, risk, impurity, limits, wounds, or suffering, a "freedom" that ultimately comes at political costs by normalizing empire and colonialism in history.

38. See again the work of Copeland, *Enfleshing Freedom*, in her attention to Emmett Till's mother's choice to leave the casket open as a prophetic gesture of challenge. Copeland works with this image and historical event through the theological lens of the Eucharist and transfiguration, while mine is through the material theopoetic.

39. See the brilliant work of sociologist, Avery F. Gordon, on the power of the past to "haunt" the imagination of the present in (2008) *Ghostly Matters: Haunting and the Sociological Imagination* (Minneapolis: University of Minnesota Press). "Haunted" appears suitable language to the role of witness to such testifiers, who are stirred from the slumber of amnesia or apathy by the "call for accountability," 187.

40. Within theology, many are incorporating this understanding and attempting to construct theologies from intercultural encounters. See, in particular, the work of Mary McClintock Fulkerson (2007) *Places of Redemption: Theology for a Worldly Church* (Oxford: Oxford University Press). See also the works of James W. Perkinson (2004) *White Supremacy: Outing Supremacy in Modernity* (New York: Palgrave Macmillan); and Dwight N. Hopkins (2005) *Being Human: Race, Culture, and Religion* (Minneapolis: Fortress Press).

41. See Walsh, *Prophetic Pastoral Care in the Aftermath of Trauma* for my separate case study of a shooting in a church in 2008 and the response of the Unitarian Universalist Trauma Response Ministry and practices of the church for re-sacralizing their material space. See also Walsh (forthcoming), *Violent Trauma, Culture, and Power*.

42. As much as being a country founded on slavery, the USA also is a country founded on the colonial genocide of indigenous peoples. See most recently Roxanne Dunbar-Ortiz (2014) *An Indigenous Peoples' History of the United States* (Boston: Beacon Press).

43. Thomas E. Reynolds' work with this ecclesial concept holds useful promise for public theologies of trauma, as argued in my disserta-

tion. See (2008) *Vulnerable Communion: A Theology of Disability and Hospitality* (Grand Rapids, MI: Brazos Press), 105. The mythical illusion of perfection and wholeness as challenged by Betcher's work, *Spirit and the Politics of Disablement*, needs to be laid down, and cultural privileges that maintain that illusion need to be given up, in favor of a larger freedom that comes from resting and sharing in our innate vulnerabilities.

44. I am again influenced by Sharon Welch's attention to the aesthetic and theological power of musical analogies in these remarks, as well as by participants in my dissertation interviews, such as the UU Trauma Response Ministry leaders, from my second case study, who spoke of concepts they termed as holding "sacred ambiguity" and developing "holy humor," while working in the aftermath of trauma.

Bibliography

Ackerman, D. 1999. *Deep play*. New York: Vintage Books.
Alves, R.A. 1992. Theopoetics: Longing and liberation. In *Struggles for solidarity: Liberation theologies in tension*, ed. L.M. Getz and R.O. Costa. Minneapolis: Fortress Press.
Barnwell, Y.M. 1980. *Breaths*. Washington, DC: Barnwell's Notes Publishing.
Berryman, J.W. 1991. *Godly play: An imaginative approach to religious education*. Minneapolis: Augsburg Fortress.
Betcher, S.V. 2007. *Spirit and the politics of disablement*. Minneapolis: Fortress Press.
Bradway, K. (ed.). 1981. *Sandplay studies: Origins, theory, and practice*, collected by the C.G. Jung Institute of San Francisco. Boston: Sigo Press.
Bradway, K., and B. McCoard. 1997. *Sandplay-silent workshop of the psyche*. New York: Routledge.
Brock, R.N., and R.A. Parker. 2008. *Saving paradise: How Christianity traded love of this world for crucifixion and empire*. Boston: Beacon.
Brown, S. 2009. *Play: How it shapes the brain, opens the imagination, and invigorates the soul*. New York: Avery.
Calhoun, L.G., and R.G. Tedeschi. 2005. Posttraumatic growth: The positive lessons of loss. In *Meaning reconstruction and the experience of loss*, 4th ed, ed. R.A. Neimeyer. Washington, DC: Psychological Association.
Caro, O.C.V. 2007. Toward a feminist intercultural theology. In *Feminist intercultural theology: Latina explorations for a just world*, ed. M.P. Aquino and M.J. Rosado-Nunes. Maryknoll: Orbis Books.

Chopp, R.S. 1998. Theology and the poetics of testimony. *Criterion* 37(1): 2–12.
Cone, J.H. 2007. Strange fruit: The cross and the lynching tree. *Harvard Divinity Bulletin* 35(1): 47–56.
Copeland, M.S. 2010. *Enfleshing freedom: Body, race, and being*. Minneapolis: Fortress Press.
De Domenico, G.S. 1995. *Sand tray world play: A comprehensive guide to the use of the sand tray in psychotherapeutic and transformational settings*. Oakland, CA: Vision Quest Images.
Dunbar-Ortiz, R. 2014. *An indigenous peoples' history of the United States*. Boston: Beacon.
Evans, J.H. 2010. *Playing: Christian explorations of daily living*. Minneapolis: Fortress Press.
Fulkerson, M.M. 2007. *Places of redemption: Theology for a worldly church*. Oxford: Oxford University Press.
Gordon, A.F. 2008. *Ghostly matters: Haunting and the sociological imagination*. Minneapolis: University of Minnesota Press.
Herman, J. 1992. *Trauma and recovery*. New York: Basic Books.
Hopkins, D.N. 2005. *Being human: Race, culture, and religion*. Minneapolis: Fortress Press.
Jakobsen, J.R. 1997. The body politic vs. lesbian bodies: Publics, counterpublics, and the use of norms. In *Horizons in feminist theology: Identity, tradition and norms*, ed. R.S. Chopp and S.G. Davaney. Minneapolis: Fortress Press.
Janoff-Bulman, R. 1992. *Shattered assumptions: Toward a new psychology of trauma*. New York: Free Press.
Jordan, J. 2010. *Relational-cultural therapy*. Washington, DC: American Psychological Association.
Keller, K. 2003. *Face of the deep: A theology of becoming*. New York: Routledge.
King, E.F. 2010. *Material religion and popular culture*. New York: Routledge.
Klass, D., P.R. Silverman, and S.L. Nickman (eds.). 1996. *Continuing bonds: New understandings of grief*. New York: Routledge.
Kujawa-Holbrook, A., and K.B. Montagno (eds.). 2009. *Injustice and the care of souls: Taking oppression seriously in pastoral care*. Minneapolis: Fortress Press.
Louw, D.J. 2001. Creative hope and imagination in a practical theology of aesthetic (artistic) reason. In *Creativity, imagination and criticism: The expressive dimension in practical theology*, ed. P. Ballard and P. Couture. Cardiff: Cardiff Academic Press.
Malchiodi, C.A. (ed.). 2008. *Creative interventions with traumatized children*. New York: The Guildord Press.
Martinez, D.B., and A. Fleck-Henderson (eds.). 2014. *Social justice in clinical practice: A liberation health framework for social justice*. New York: Routledge.
Miller, P.C. 2009. *The corporeal imagination: Signifying the holy in late ancient Christianity*. Philadelphia: University of Pennsylvania Press.

Morrison, T. 1992. *Playing in the dark: Whiteness and the literary imagination.* Cambridge: Harvard University Press.
Moschella, M.C. 2012. Ethnography. In *The Wiley-Blackwell companion to practical theology*, ed. B.J. Miller-McLemore. Malden: Blackwell.
Mothers for Justice & Equality website. http://www.mothersforjusticeandequality.org
Perkinson, J.W. 2004. *White supremacy: Outing supremacy in modernity.* New York: Palgrave Macmillan.
Rambo, S. 2010. *Spirit and trauma: A theology of remaining.* Louisville: Westminster John Knox Press.
Reynolds, T.E. 2008. *Vulnerable communion: A theology of disability and hospitality.* Grand Rapids: Brazos Press.
Rothschild, B. 2000. *The body remembers: The psychophysiology of trauma and trauma treatment.* New York: W.W. Norton.
Santino, J. 2001. *Signs of war and peace: Social conflict and the uses of symbols in public northern Ireland.* New York: Palgrave Macmillan.
Santino, J. (ed.). 2006. *Spontaneous shrines and the public memorialization of death.* New York: Palgrave Macmillan.
Sturken, M. 1997. *Tangled memories: The Vietnam war, the AIDS epidemic, and the politics of remembering.* Berkeley: University of California Press.
"Traveling Memorial Button Project" Peace Institute. http://ldbpeaceinstitute.org/content/traveling-memorial-button-project
der Kolk, Van, B.A.C. McFarlane, and L. Weisaeth (eds.). 1996. *Traumatic stress: The effects of overwhelming experience on mind, body, and society.* New York: The Guilford Press.
Walsh, M.A. 2014. *Prophetic pastoral care in the aftermath of trauma: Forging a constructive practical theology of lived religion from organized trauma response ministries.* PhD diss., Boston University, ProQuest AAT 3610856.
Walsh, Michelle. Forthcoming 2016. *Violent Trauma, Culture, and Power: An Interdisciplinary Exploration in Lived Religion.* New York: Palgrave Macmillan.
Webb, N.B. (ed.). 2007. *Play therapy with children in crisis: Individual, group, and family treatment.* New York: The Guilford Press.
Welch, S. 2000. *A feminist ethic of risk*, 2nd ed. Minneapolis: Fortress Press.
"Women's Theological Center of Boston," website. http://www.thewtc.org/
Young, J.E. 1993. *The texture of memory: Holocaust memorials and meaning.* New Haven: Yale University Press.

CHAPTER 13

Traumas of Belonging: Imagined Communities of Nation, Religion, and Gender in Modernity

Susan Abraham

Europe and North America are not the only sites of violence and trauma. A global view of political trauma and violence will go far in envisioning a decolonial, posttraumatic theology. To that end, I assert that Trauma Studies take into serious consideration some of the histories arising out of non-Western contexts. "Nation" and "Citizenship," as the essays in the volume have demonstrated, are contexts ripe for theological reflection. Modern nationhood and citizenship, however, are contested sites of continuing violence, especially against women, racial, and religious others and to immigrants. The USA is not exceptional in the kind of violence it sanctions and regulates as part of its nation building exercises. Thus, Trauma Studies can only be enriched by the reflections on modern trauma from other parts of the world. Theological reflection that considers the contexts and consequences of historical trauma from other parts of the world is both relativized and rooted by those narratives. Consequently, I track the traumatic context of the emergence of modern India and Pakistan, arguing that its most vulnerable citizens—women and the religiously different

S. Abraham (✉)
Loyola Marymount University, Los Angeles, CA, USA

others—are the subjects for reflection in postcolonial Trauma Studies. In a volume such as this one that explores what posttraumatic theology may mean in the USA, this essay argues that US subject positions and US history cannot remain oblivious to the ways in which European colonial history affected and continues to affect contexts of trauma elsewhere. It is not simply the US nation-state that is a site for trauma analyses; all nation-states and their emergence in alliance with European colonialism are contexts for reflection by posttraumatic theology. Trauma Studies that avoid examining its complicity with European Colonial history and contemporary neo-colonial relations between the Euro-American academy and its "peripheries" results in continuing trauma for global citizens. What ought to be the imagined contexts of Trauma Studies? decolonizing Trauma Studies demands a global and comparative perspective which is also simultaneously interdisciplinary.

The modern nation-state emerged in a bloodbath. This assertion is true of both India and the USA. The historical record of the Partition of India 1947 reads like a horrific account of physical, sexual, psychological, and emotional trauma. It also reads like an account of social suffering on a scale comparable to the Jewish Holocaust. Colonialism, militaristic nationalism and religious identity politics which emphasize difference: of language, bodies, and technologies of memory, all together contribute to an ongoing trauma of belonging. It is traumatic to belong to nation. Students and colleagues from South Asia recount generational traumas and debilitating anxiety disorders that have their roots in the now 60-some-years old Partition of India. One particularly evocative historical source presents the Partition as traumatic:

> One should not forget the emotional suffering of the refugees, forced to quit all of a sudden and forever the familiar scenes of childhood and youth… [Refugees enroute from India to Karachi] were squatting disconsolately along the railway line for several hundred yards on either side of the station and seemed so stunned by their misfortunes as to be incapable of speech or movement. As we were strolling about among them, trying to reassure them and cheer them up, a long train of open trucks drew into the station from the West, crammed with Hindu refugees from Multan who were being evacuated to India. Thus the two sets of refugees, driven in opposite direction by the same impalpable forces…gazed at each other in lugubrious silence. Not a word was exchanged and the sense of cumulated misery was overpowering… all alike had been driven from their homes by the exigencies not of war but of freedom.[1]

What may an account of postcolonial trauma offer to trauma theory? I ask this question precisely because trauma theory in its current form is a western and also in many ways a Western *Christian* discourse. Western trauma theory, however, has only recently begun to account for the trauma arising out of colonial contexts even as it emerges in the West's own emergence as a cultural identity forged within a colonial history. Thus, on the one hand, deepening Trauma Studies' theological commitments to include a nuanced postcolonial critique of identity is balanced on the other by a constructive and intellectual theological enterprise that turns on the authority of the suffering of others. Trauma Studies, therefore, cannot "speak" for global trauma, without acknowledging its social location and its limited scope, even as it simultaneously carves a space for a theology of suffering across the globe. Such a theological enterprise will go far in decolonizing the secular frame of contemporary Trauma Studies.

As an example of what I mean by the Western and Christian context of Trauma Studies, I point to Cathy Caruth's influential anthology on trauma. The volume situates the study of trauma squarely in the West's twentieth century, its secular political, academic, and cultural contexts, but does not acknowledge the West's colonial history explicitly.[2] Caruth's introduction to the volume opens with these words: "In the years since Vietnam, the fields of psychiatry, psychoanalysis, and sociology have taken a renewed interest in the problem of trauma," implicating trauma theory in a colonial history, but hardly developing the implication.[3] That is, she points towards the Vietnam War as a historical marker, but ignores the Western religious, political, and economic stakes that framed that war and its aftermath. Critical reviews of Caruth's work by a number of scholars challenge the Eurocentric context of western trauma theory. Further, trauma theory is only just beginning to grapple with the ethics and politics of its own disciplinary contexts, which deepen the charge of Eurocentrism. Decolonizing trauma theory is the goal of postcolonial Trauma Studies. Such decolonizing, as I will show, requires assiduous attention to the categories and contexts of knowledge production.

Decolonizing Trauma Studies

How can we decolonize Trauma Theory? Stef Craps in *Postcolonial Witnessing: Trauma Out of Bounds*[4] seeks to challenge what he terms "The Empire of Trauma" and Caruth's elision of the colonial frame for trauma theory. Significant in his work and other critical evaluations of Western trauma theory is the broad acceptance of postcoloniality[5] as an interrogation of Western knowledge systems. In this chapter, and the previous one entitled "The Trauma of Empire," Craps sets the stage for a postcolonial critique of trauma theory by affirming the methods of deconstruction and psychoanalysis employed by postcolonial thinkers. However, as Craps points out, deconstruction as a method has been castigated as Western academic textualism, even as postcolonial theorists have demonstrated that deconstruction is a way to counter "intellectual colonization."[6] Craps himself situates deconstruction in a non-European frame: "many pioneers and key theorists of poststructuralism—Derrida, Hélène Cixous, Jean-François Lyotard and Jean-Paul Sartre among others came from Algeria or were personally involved in the (Algerian) war of Independence."[7]

Psychoanalysis, the other methodological mainstay in postcolonial theory, is also uncoupled from colonial frames.[8] Postcolonial trauma theory in emphasizing the cultural context of modern trauma identifies a non-therapeutic use of psychoanalysis in postcolonial contexts, shifting attention from individualized psychological experiences to a larger context: "Since Fanon, focusing on subjectivity, identity or the relational dynamic between colonizers and colonized, through psychoanalytic language, has allowed postcolonial criticism to insist and demonstrate that there are devastating cultural and personal manifestations of colonialism that strictly economic and political accounts have not been able or willing to reveal."[9] A postcolonial exploration of trauma, recovery, and survival use both of these methods by drawing together multiple disciplines that explore historical trauma.

Caruth's anthology initially carved its academic and intellectual niche in association with North American secular culture's understanding of psychiatry as a science unfettered by cultural, religious, ethnic, nationalist, or gendered issues.[10] But the inadequacy of the anthology is captured in Stef Craps' critique that the anthology does not consider the extent to which colonial and imperial forms of knowledge-making continue to create trauma. He points to the work of Didier Fassin and Richard Rechtman in the book entitled *The Empire of Trauma: An Inquiry into the Condition of Victimhood*, as indicative of the myopia of trauma theory: "Trauma—or rather, the social process of the recognition of persons as traumatized—effectively chooses its victims. Although those who promote the concept assert that it is universal, since it is the mark left by an event, study reveals tragic disparities in its use."[11] Thus, the ethical context of trauma theory as limited reveals a larger context than the relationship of the individual to the political, which often devolves into a victimology of identity. In other words, the disciplinary boundaries marking trauma theory have been negatively scrutinized recently.

Another critical voice examining the politics of knowledge and Trauma Studies, Susannah Radstone, offers a critique of much of trauma theory's models of subjectivity and self-referentiality, arising as it does in the context of Humanities research in the West: "books [such as Cathy Caruth's *Trauma: Explorations in Memory*] do not make their mark in a vacuum."[12] In her reading, the cultural context of academia itself retraumatizes because it is Eurocentric, buttressed as it is by rather particular interpretations of Western law on the one hand and individualistic psychoanalysis on the other. The context of legality is further heightened by a "neuro-scientific approach to memory disorders" that sidelines traditional Freudian psychoanalysis. Radstone's work has been characterized as an "outright and hostile rejection of trauma theory," even as she provides an evaluation of academic fields and disciplines in the mode of postcolonial criticism. Postcolonial theorists face much the same struggle when attempting to rethink the boundaries and borders of their respective fields: the attempt to decolonize is fraught when individualist experiential, identity, and subjectivity models saturate liberal political agendas.

For instance, she evaluates the effects of trauma theory on critiques of subjectivity, referentiality, testimony, and history. In much of the literature on trauma, the traumatized subject is one that "does not know or remember."[13] Thus, argues Radstone, a theory of subjectivity is implicit in trauma theory. Following the US-identified postmodernization of Freudian psychoanalysis, the neuro-scientific emphasis of traumatic memory separates memory from the actions and intentions of the subject: "Though the Subject of trauma theory cannot be restored to coherence through acts of remembrance, a *belated* acknowledgement of that which has been forgotten is a possibility."[14] Like a number of other postcolonial theorists, Radstone is critical of the reinscription of the autonomous, though passive subject. She argues for a return to traditional psychoanalysis for trauma theory which may seem contradictory to the decolonizing emphasis in this essay. That is, one may wonder how a critique of Western modernity, conceived and sustained in the West could function as a critical and postcolonial framework. I see parallels in Radstone's argument to similar arguments for the *judicious* use of psychoanalysis: "If we can begin to specify the ways in which the apparently universal ideas of Self and Other that are at the heart of psychoanalysis were formed by colonial influences and encounters, we may be able to construct and act upon new ways of thinking about the relations between identity, difference, dissent and solidarity."[15] The postcolonial use of psychoanalysis, as we can conclude from Radstone's analysis, reveals a more complex subjectivity not just of the victim, but also that of the aggressor. Victimology, which reinscribes colonial forms of subject making, presents the colonized as being passive and helpless. Radstone's postcolonial challenge is that it is rare that a "Manichean" perspective consistently operates in the dynamics of victim and aggressor in colonial contexts. Consequently, for Radstone, trauma theory and its methodologies fail to incorporate the very insights of psychoanalysis and deconstruction: "Trauma theory's topography of the inner world dispenses with the layering of conscious/subconscious and unconscious, substituting for them a conscious mind in which past experiences are accessible, and a dissociated area of the mind from which traumatic past experiences cannot be accessed."[16] The event of trauma thus remains "unexperienced." In this way, the subject and her sovereignty remain intact. Postcolonial trauma theory that decolonizes will find such a critique of contemporary trauma theory important.

Identifying a "Manichaean" framework operating in contemporary trauma theory, Radstone provides postcolonial Trauma Studies with a more constructive and decolonial perspective than Caruth and many Western scholars of trauma. She writes:

> What I am suggesting then, is that notwithstanding the sophistication of trauma theory's underpinnings in De Manian or Derridean deconstruction, it nevertheless offers a theory of the subject which retreats from psychoanalysis' rejection of a black-and-white vision of psychical life to produce a theory which establishes clear, not to say Manichean binaries of 'inside' and 'outside,' 'trauma' and 'normality' and 'victims' and 'perpetrators.'[17]

Radstone's caution that trauma theory not dissolve into a form of Manichaean description of victim and oppressor outlines the current ethical imperative for trauma theory. How does memory function in relation to a significant event of trauma? What complex subjectivities are forged by historical trauma? Who is a victim? Who is the aggressor? These questions begin with a reflection on the central event refracting trauma theory in the West, the Shoah.

For Radstone, Craps and other postcolonial theorists of trauma, the Shoah offers an ambivalent moment for decolonial Trauma Studies. On the one hand, the primacy of the event of the Shoah cannot be downplayed. On the other, the insistence on narrating the trauma of the Holocaust in exclusion to other forms of historical and cultural trauma points to a myopia of Trauma Studies. Further, categories that evolved in the colonial context such as "religion" and "nation" continue to function in certain narratives of the Shoah in ways that perpetuate colonial knowledge. Consider for example, a recent report on how the history of the Jewish Holocaust is "taught" in cultural contexts other than the West (India and China). The report tracks how anti-Semitism is manifested in school curricula teaching history to young students.

> The five textbooks, published between 1995 and 2006, show much disparity in descriptions of the holocaust and the treatment of the Second World War. Most of the lessons in these textbooks attempt to relate the events of the war to local happenings in India. Some refer to Mahatma Gandhi's letters to Adolf Hitler appealing for peace while others imply comparisons between the German persecution of people of color with colonialism in India.[18]

That the report is presented as evidence of anti-Semitism by arguing for a *sui generis* status for the Jewish Holocaust is significant. I do not see evidence of anti-Semitism in the selective presentation of the Shoah in Indian and Chinese history books. Instead, the histories are implying that the Shoah is continuous with Europe's colonial and racial history, producing gruesome manifestations of "religion" and "nation."

In addition to the event of the Shoah, I suggest that "religion" for trauma theory cannot be grasped outside of ongoing nationalist rhetoric and narratives of nationalist remembering. Consequently, thinking of the trauma of the Shoah as fundamentally a trauma incited by narratives of national and religious purity brings the categories "religion" and "nation" to crisis, an urgent decolonizing task. Similarly, one can see how these categories can be brought to crisis in other than European contexts of political trauma. Thus, the Partition of India, like the Shoah, remains a living reality for Indians and Pakistanis today, both because of the horrific violence perpetrated against particular religious groups by others in the nation and also because Western liberal ideas of citizenship and sovereignty are confounded in the postcolonial context.

The Partition of India is a fundamental postcolonial moment which signals the idea of a nation emerging out of a colonial history as a moment of birth. Yet, the history of the Partition is also one that signaled a death and in many ways, a continuing death for some in the newly minted nation. The actual plan of the Partition was traumatic, harshly and abruptly executed, leaving utter chaos in its wake. Yasmin Khan, for example, argues that once the plan was announced on June 3, 1947, it was met with a mixture of "joy, horror, bewilderment and fury."[19] She writes:

> For all its superficial complexity and fine detail, (the Plan)—was wafer thin and left numerous critical aspects unexamined and unclear. Where was India and where was Pakistan? Who was now an Indian or Pakistani? Was citizenship underpinned by a shared religious faith, or was it a universal right, guaranteed by a state that promised equality and freedom to all? Were people expected to move into the state where their co-religionists resided in majority? The tragedy of the Partition was that by the time people started to ask and try answering these questions, unimaginable violence had escalated to the point of ethnic cleansing.[20]

The horror, grief and trauma of the Partition have fostered bitter and intractable relations between India and Pakistan over the past 60 years, not in the least expressed as fraught relations between religiously different communities. Belonging to the postcolonial nations of India or Pakistan is traumatic, because national identity is structured by religious difference.

Thinking of this reality alongside Cathy Caruth's argument that trauma induces a "new ignorance"[21] of the impact of the experience, as well as its impact on the construction of history, it seems clear to me that the emergence of postcolonial nations in the twentieth century adds an important layer of complexity to Trauma Studies. As Caruth argues, trauma induces a crisis of truth: "It is not having too little or indirect access to an experience that places the truth in question...but paradoxically, its very overwhelming immediacy that produces its belated uncertainty."[22] What then, does it mean to remember a historical event such as the Partition of India and its trauma, even as one identifies as Indian or Pakistani 60 years removed? Moreover, for Caruth, it must be said, the site of trauma also offers the possibility of survival. While it is traumatic to repeatedly suffer through the memory of the actual event, it is "also the continual leaving of the site (of trauma)."[23] However, as I hope to show, this is impossible for those who claim the identity of "Indian" and "Pakistani." Thus, narrating nationalist history, which is *also* now a narrative of modern religious identity, is the occasion for postcolonial trauma.

Contemporary critical studies in South Asia, such as the work of Gyanendra Pandey and Veena Das, demonstrate how religious identity as it meshes with nationalist narratives continues to traumatize. I show in what follows, that decolonizing Trauma Studies, the basis for postcolonial posttraumatic theology, engages multiple disciplinary perspectives that bring "religion" and "nation" into crisis.

Gyanendra Pandey: History, Religion, and the Trauma of Remembering

Remembering is traumatic, as South Asian historian Gyanendra Pandey's history of the Partition reveals. Decolonizing history is critical historiography.[24] The entanglement of event and interpretation is the focus of critical history. Interpreting the traumatic event of history therefore aligns itself with the goals of postcolonial posttraumatic theology, because it ascertains how interpretation arises from colonial systems of knowledge, history, technologies of difference, and the suffering of (different) bodies. Two relevant issues make the case. First, "religion" as a category focuses Pandey's analysis of how history can be critical. He shows how traditionalist Indian histories in an older Orientalist key minimize the influence of religion even as the assumptions made about religion are far reaching. Second, Pandey's analysis suggests that "religion" in the colonial aftermath emerges in a disciplinary matrix in which gendered bodies intensify religious identity in relation to national identity.

Pandey, a Professor of Anthropology and History at Johns Hopkins University, emphasizes that historical accounts of the Partition do not adequately assess how religious identity was created in its aftermath. He writes:

> Sikhs, Muslims and Hindus were all redefined by the process of Partition: as butchers, or as devious others; as untrustworthy and anti-national; but perhaps most fundamentally as Sikhs and Muslims and Hindus alone.[25]

But his critique is even more pointed. It is not only that the emergence of a postcolonial religious identity emerges out of the Partition, but also that history as a discipline creates colonial knowledge and subjectivities in the academy as well. "History" therefore has a history. In the chapter entitled, "Historian's History," he asserts that the history of historians works to produce the "truth of the traumatic, genocidal violence of the Partition," while simultaneously eliding the complex "eventuality of the Partition."[26] That is, in my reading, for Pandey the "eventuality" of the Partition is the violent development of antithetical religious identity emerging as it does out of antithetical and competing national identities, which represents the postcolonial problem for critical studies. Pandey's critical historiography has more relevance for decolonizing Trauma Studies than the earlier history of Indian historians, because it does not freeze the event of the Partition in a narrated past, even though he does not articulate the decolonizing potential of his critical historiography.

The freezing maneuver in Indian history is the result of a combination of theoretical problems. For example, the inability to theorize on religiously and nationalistically motivated violence as related to the emergence of a colonial form of identity is based in the idea of "nation" as progress. Pandey is critical of this maneuver. He writes of an "interesting convergence" between three different accounts of a particularly important instance of Partition violence in the town of Garhmukteshwar in November 1946.[27] Recent historical accounts minimize the far reaching effect the incident had. Garhmukteshwar is treated as a "local" incident:

> ...something that appears as a bit of a distraction. Here, again, history is equated with the 'national,' the 'rational,' the 'progressive'—the programmed. This history is recognizable, traceable, and of course, *relevant*. It has other names as well, 'Europe' being one of these, as we have noted. In this perspective the national/universal/historical is that which can be narrativized, and theorized, as the road to the future—the Indian variant of capital and Enlightenment so to speak. The 'local' is none of these things: it is by contrast, of little consequence, mere particularity, and sometimes literally unnamable.[28]

Declaring such violence to be intractably resistant to narration because it was a "local" incident, making of the history of the Partition a history of causes or a narrative of origins and finally as a "freak occurrence," one which requires no historical explanation at all, marks history oriented to the narrative of progress of nation. Thus, "the writing of history—in each and every case—is implicated in a political project, whether consciously or unselfconsciously."[29] There is an indelible nation-history connection where "private memories and individual histories continue to feed on the memory-histories of states, parties and pressure groups representing communities and nations."[30]

Pandey implicitly is making the same argument here as Craps and Radstone—the trauma of the Partition is not grasped unless its continuing effects are tracked. Thus, "when History is written as a history of struggle, it tends to exclude the dimensions of force, uncertainty, domination and disdain, loss and confusion, by normalizing the struggle, evacuating it of its messiness and making it part of a narrative of assured advance towards specified resolutions,"[31] revealing the Manichaean organization of modern Indian histories. It is such a history of us vs. them that also creates the conditions for the right-wing, religious-community based politics of the 1970s. Pandey's presentation of the History of the Partition is therefore questioning of the very manner in which historical trauma is remembered. Cathy Caruth's own intuition that "historical listening" is a task that is layered multiply because it is a "crisis that is not yet over"[32] and is given a particular sharpness in Pandey's remembering of the Partition.

Some contemporary Indian histories also continue the Western, European, and Christian conviction that "religion" implies rigid boundaries between different religious groups, a point that Pandey notes as problematic. In pre-Independence India, such a rigid drawing of boundaries was never the case; religious identities and cultural identities flowed into each other. The eventuality of the Partition is also dependent on particular assumptions made about "religion" as a category. Religion, Pandey points out, is assumed in Indian histories to be a backward and atavistic reality, one not worthy of theorization. Hence, the violence of the Partition is treated symptomatically,[33] when historical evidence points to the intertwined nature of religious and nationalistic violence:

> The result is to consign religion to oblivion in the best general histories of pre-modern India. Much the same thing happens to the question of violence and here the criteria seen to be making for self-respect, rationality and progress are very much more widely shared. In its most common representation (or self-representation), modern civilization has been equated with a state of non-violence, where mature adult human beings negotiate with one another and determine their rights and duties through rational argument.[34]

A critical evaluation of Indian history reveals how religious identity undergirds national identity, conveniently identifying the treasonous enemy of the nation as the religiously different other. Pandey is suggesting in his analysis of Indian history and its elision of religion that the eventfulness of the trauma of the Partition continues in the current emergence of right-wing political attitudes in India and Pakistan and a growing social tolerance of brutal violence towards the religiously different other. This move in his work is the decolonizing moment. That is, if Posttraumatic theology takes into consideration the political contexts in which histories are remembered, like Pandey does with History, then it too will uncouple from its colonial frames.

Nationalist thinking furthered such a sense of distinctiveness with its form of religious jingoism, only Hindus belonged in India and Muslims belonged in Pakistan. Further, the rigid separation of religious identity is most clearly demonstrated by the gendered body. The *bindi* and saree, both adornment and clothing worn by women all over South Asia, in the wake of nationalized religious identity, came to be identified exclusively with Hindu women's dress. Such a "socialization of the body," asserts Pandey, led to the further "disciplining of difference" of gendered bodies, religious identities, and national identities. The idea therefore of a "one-nation" nation, in which women, their bodies and how they dress their bodies, create the conditions for religious belonging is an idea that depends on a particular imagination about national identity as sameness. In such a context, neo-colonial nativism, a particularly violent form of narrating identity and belonging, defines Muslims as "naturally" belonging to Pakistan and Hindus as "naturally" belonging to India. Pandey asserts that the argument of natural belonging led to the most tragic consequences, especially for women:

> If the Hindus and Sikhs were 'naturally' ours, and Muslims 'naturally' theirs, as in the circumstances of the Partition they were commonly declared to be, the hostile conditions of the time also raised the demand that these natural possessions be restored to their natural homes. The poignant history of abducted women caught on the wrong side of the new international border illustrates some of the tragic consequences of this curious collapsing of the religious community into natural nation.[35]

Women and their bodies, consequently, remain unnatural citizens, especially if marked by religious identity: Hindu in Pakistan and Muslim in India. Decolonial and critical trauma theory, therefore, must attend to critical historians like Pandey who do not shy away from the aggressions being perpetrated by the former victims of European colonialism. Or, to think with Susannah Radstone, the unconscious at the heart of remembering is not devoid of distortions of desire and fantasy. Nationalist remembering of the Partition "forgets" that rigid religious boundaries emerged in the colonial context of European modernity and enacts a parallel form of violence on those who are religiously different.

In what follows, I sketch explorations of trauma from another disciplinary perspective that tracks the specific case of gendered violence in the nation-state and its relationship to religion, intensifying Pandey's observation that bodies matter in significant ways when remembering the Partition.

Veena Das: Women, Nation-State, and the Trauma of Report

Recent scholarly interest in political theology emphasizes that the postsecular in contemporary politics is animated in great part by religious violence. Religious violence and the trauma it creates is a renewed focus of contemporary political theologies. Additionally, as argued in his Introduction to *Political Theologies: Public Religions in a Post-Secular World*, Hent de Vries asserts that India's communal violence has to be theorized as a form of gendered violence which calls into question sovereignty, citizenship, and natural rights.[36] Sovereignty, citizenship, and natural rights are the mainstay of Western liberal political theologies. Interdisciplinary interventions that challenge these assumptions are refocusing the concerns of political theology. For example, Veena Das' contribution in De Vries' influential volume analyses the role the "abducted woman" (women who were kidnapped or forcibly converted to the "other" religious identity in India and Pakistan at the time of the Partition) played and plays in nationalist rhetoric. If contemporary political theology can hardly afford to ignore her analysis that "nation" is constituted by sovereignty, citizenship, and natural right, posttraumatic theology will have to also consider the gendered context of historical trauma as well as the trauma of gendered testimony. That is, in contrast to Western trauma theory where testimony plays an affirmative role, Das' anthropological research reveals that a "tonality of rumor" swirled around the testimonies of and by the women. Das' analysis, therefore, implies some amount of skepticism with regard to the role of testimony. An important insight for trauma theory, therefore, is the move in reflective South Asian historiography that tracks "how hearsay and rumor tainted government fact-finding missions....and how elements of myth and popular narrative circulated in an imaginary of social and sexual disorders."[37] Many of the women who were the victims of both colonialism as well as the Partition of India were "disappeared" by gendered narratives (engaged in by masculinist political and legal structures) that reveal the gendered and sexed nature of sovereignty, citizenship, and natural rights.

The event of the Partition exposes the legal-political context which decides whether a woman can be a citizen of the nation. Das asserts:

> First, in order to be a citizen of the state you must be a head of the household; the second is that you must know for whom you ought to die. For the woman, the duty of a citizen is confounded with her duty to her husband.

> A woman's comportment must be such that not only her husband but also his neighbors and friends must believe in her fidelity. When she gives her husband children who are not his own, we are told, she is false both to him and to them and her crime is "*not infidelity but treason.*"[38]

It is noteworthy that the state is imagined in the language of purity and honor, religious idioms that are played out on the bodies of women. Unlike the feminist historian's retelling of the history of the partition, Das focuses on those discourses that in the telling effected and deepened the trauma experienced by these women. For example, the testimonies of the women who were abducted by one or the other side included testimonies of mass rape and murder. The kind of violence that were used against women of the "other" side were not the kind of violence that could be put on trial or memorialized, because violence towards women of the "other" side is rationalized as collateral damage. Violence done to women of one's own side in contrast is presented as aggression on national honor. Rape in this situation is interpreted as a violence of the sexual contract between the men of warring groups, instead of a violence perpetrated at women for being women. Since the testimonies of the abducted women are recounted with no possibility of memorialization (unlike the Holocaust), Das argues that the testimonies take on the "tonality of a rumor." [39] Further, because these stories do not validate the women and their experience; the stories paradoxically "reinstate the nation as a pure and masculine space."[40]

Das' essay emphasizes an important concern for trauma theory.[41] Testimony, the attempt to include speech, certainly folded the stories and experiences of individual women into the narrative of the Partition. The caution here is one that explicitly contravenes strategies of telling in trauma theory, that of subjective and personal experience. As Susannah Radstone reminded us, the stage of telling, or the reception of testimony, requires particular kinds of recognition. The rape and abduction of Hindu and Muslim women by the opposing side was enabled as an account for the horror inflicted on them by the horrible "others." That is, the accounts provided by these women had no validity other than as testimony of the depravity of the male others of the other side. The narrating of their experiences take on the cast of a story of national identity instead of the concretization of experience and validation of personal subjectivity as is assumed in Western contexts. Telling, by these violated women is not the same telling presumed in Western contexts. The gendered suffering endured by these non-citizens of India and Pakistan is the basis of the nationalist and masculinist discourse of the modern nation-state. Rather than emphasize the experiential as a number of contemporary feminist South Asian historians do, Das provides a different theoretical context that specifically addresses how the figure of the abducted woman functioned (and, continues to function) in the imaginary of the masculine Nation.

As Hent De Vries pointed out in the "Introduction," the question that the figure of the abducted woman, the rumors swirling around her, the horrific violence perpetuated against her, and the legislation that enforced the forcible return of these women, challenges Political theology because the assumptions of Western political theology are based in the liberal assumptions of the West. Nation in his view is a "technology of life." [42] Any political theology that assumes the autonomy, neutrality, and homogeneity of national mechanisms ignores the ethical and juridical consequences such a "technology of life" has on women. National identity, for women, is a highly unstable and even deadly category for women, because, as Das' essay argues, "the figure of the abducted woman allowed the state to construct 'order' as essentially an attribute of the masculine nation, so that the counterpart of the social contract becomes the sexual contract, in which women as sexual and reproductive beings are placed within the domestic sphere, under the control of the 'right' kinds of men."[43] National identity is irrelevant to women in such a view, because her value as woman lies in her reproductive capacity for the family and for the state.

In another essay[44] that deals more closely with violence and the formation of subjectivity, Das presents an even more nuanced argument for postcolonial subjectivity after the trauma of the Partition. Similar to Pandey, Das is interested in tracking the eventuality of the Partition rather than freezing the historical moment of violence. As she argues, the violence of the Partition was more even than the brutalities endured by women. It also included the "betrayal coded in their everyday relations."[45] The focus of continuing trauma into the everyday is a better map of gendered subjectivity in the wake of political trauma like the Partition:

> How does one bear witness to the criminality of societal rule, which consigns the uniqueness of being to eternal forgetfulness, not through an act of dramatic transgression but through a descent into everyday life? Thus, how does one not simply articulate loss through a dramatic gesture of defiance but lean to inhabit the world, or, inhabit it again, in a gesture of mourning? …How you make such a space of destruction your own not through an ascent into transcendence but through a descent into the everyday is what I shall describe…[46]

The eventuality of trauma, for gendered subjects, is not only related to the experience of the trauma or the subjugation by aggressors (in the case of the victims of the Partition). The women also took these "noxious signs of violation" and occupied them differently through the work of "domestication, ritualization and re-narration."[47] Das' work therefore, is mapping a nuanced path towards a posttraumatic and postcolonial subjectivity that Craps and Radstone will find useful. That is, as more than a narrative of victimhood, Das articulates "a more complex agency made up of divided and fractured subject positions" because of women's recognition that violence really is the shattering of relationships.[48]

Das' ethnographic anthropological study is of a widow Asha, whose conjugal family "turns" from being a safe and accepting one to one that revictimizes her in the aftermath of the Partition. When the family escaped from Lahore to Amritsar (Pakistan to India), they arrived empty-handed, but as Punjabis, accepted as citizens of India. Asha's natal family who were in Amritsar were unwilling or unable to help. Das points out that before the Partition, Asha did not experience despair with her widowed condition as much as she did after: "she was slowly being pushed into being the scapegoat."[49] Not only that, but her elder brother-in-law now began to make sexual advances towards her. Eventually, Asha remarried outside the conjugal family, which also occasioned great stress because of religious and cultural sanctions against widows remarrying. Nevertheless, Asha strove mightily to retain her relationships with the conjugal family, especially with her sisters-in-law, a point that Das explores at length. Asha reoccupies a site of trauma by assiduously maintaining her association with a community of women even though it was a community that is framed primarily through a patriarchal family system. Das' complex argument therefore, unlike Caruth's,[50] is not how "the events of the Partition were present to consciousness as past events but how they came to be incorporated into the temporal structure of relationships."[51]

Asha's "divided and fractured subject position"[52] is unlikely to find a home in the "Empire of Trauma" as Steve Craps had argued. The Western notion of trauma enshrined in Western Trauma Studies cannot be exported elsewhere and could even be understood as a form of cultural imperialism. Das' attempt to complicate the picture of psychic universalism that trauma theory depends on is better understood in the postcolonial context where "nation," "gender," and "religion" as analytical concepts reveal their colonial origins. Similarly, Radstone's plea that Trauma Studies engage the ethics and politics of trauma analysis is answered in Das' work. For example, in asking for a renewed attention to the ethics of representing trauma, Radstone asks who decides "which events, experiences and texts are to be classed as traumatic."[53] In the case of Asha, as Das chronicles, the trauma of the Partition is equivalent to the trauma of being unwanted by her natal family and being sexually harassed in her conjugal one post-Partition, even as she "belongs" to the newly minted nation of India.

Mapping a Postcolonial, Posttraumatic Theology

This essay attempts an intervention in Western Trauma Studies. While it began with the assertion that it is traumatic to belong to a nation, it has also presented the possibility that the historical amnesia and intercultural analyses that ignore other-than-Western-trauma is in itself trauma inducing. Implicit in the notion of traumatic belonging is the idea that the relation between nation and violence is construed through forms of identity construction in modernity, dependent on how communities are imagined. The postcolonial is therefore to be grasped as the continuing of a critique of modernity (rather than the facile hope of postmodern subjectivity accorded to the postcolonial by some). The violence of the postcolonial nation-state is perpetuated by its mechanisms and technologies of belonging, which includes the academy and its occlusions. Political theology, informed by trauma theory, consequently expands the event of trauma to examine its eventfulness as Gyanendra Pandey argues, symbolized by the manner in which "religion" and "nation" transform into exclusive identity claims. Further, as Veena Das' anthropological argument that the Partition be considered a form of gendered violence to women by the newly minted nation-state tenders that theological reflections on political trauma engage the rhetorical space of women in nationalist discourse. Each in their own way also throws light on the limits of the secular modern and the trauma enacted by that discursive field. In India, the "secular" not only deepened and extended religious differences, but its colonial frame created two antithetical nation-states, perpetually hostile to each other *because* of religion. Religion and its theological apparatus of belonging, identity, purity, shame, and dishonor creates the conditions for nation and nationalism.

Even keener is the trauma experienced by the disenfranchised women of India and Pakistan. Belonging to religious groups led to the horrific violence enacted on their bodies, but the trauma of the Partition is more than even this violence. The continuing betrayal by the nation, by one's family, and by one's religious community marks the eventuality of the Partition. The "postcolonial secular" therefore remains a site of gendered violence. That is, the trauma of postcolonial nation creation, hitherto unrecognized as a site of global trauma and continuing agony, reveals a "post-Auschwitz" and non-subjectivist frame to examine trauma in other-than-Western contexts. Trauma for postcolonial political theology is not only about the event of the Partition, but in the way that women's bodies function as non-citizens in the nation. As Susannah Radstone argues, the referentiality of the trauma to the event may be limited: "for is it that theories of trauma are taken to illuminate the relation between actuality and representation in general, or is that actuality is beginning to be taken as traumatic in and of itself?"[54] The Partition's effect, for example, is more than the eyewitness accounts or even the accounts of women who were victims of horrific sexual and emotional violence. I take Radstone's question to illuminate Das (and Pandey's) plea that the very frame of modernity, its technologies of life and belonging, the understanding of religion and secular, all remain traumatic for women. The theological task for a posttraumatic public theology is a movement between the coercive restrictions of traditionalist religious identity as well as patriarchal nationalist identity. A theology of citizenship for women that is not circumscribed by religious belonging is a destiny in abeyance for the women in the nations of India and Pakistan.

Decolonial Posttraumatic theology moreover, attends to reflection on trauma from an interdisciplinary and comparative frame. From a different disciplinary perspective than political Trauma Studies, Stef Craps in *Postcolonial Witnessing* presents an analysis of relational trauma in Anita Desai's *Baumgartner's Bombay* (1988). Decolonizing Trauma Studies requires that theological analyses range further than the study of religion. Craps' perspective that advances a literary analysis enlarges the context for Trauma Studies. Again, the emphasis here is on a relational understanding of trauma, in which the imagined community of nation, gender, and religion are explored through Desai's presentation of "camp-thinking." "Indians," "Germans," "Jews," "Hindus," and "Muslims" are unthought categories in the novel. Thus, what citizenship means in the chaotic worlds of late 1930s Europe and pre-Partition India is examined through the eyes of Hugo Baumgartner, a Jew who escapes the Holocaust in Germany and flees to Bombay from a British internment camp. Eventually, Baumgartner dies in Bombay, elderly and impoverished, after he is stabbed to death by a young German drug addict. Desai's novel, as Craps points out is a postcolonial novel examining trauma in the wake of cultural chauvinism and extremist nationalism. An Indian view of the Holocaust is not experiential, but draws on the experience of trauma to expose what existential suffering might mean in the context of nation making. Europe's linkages to its peripheries, explored deftly by Desai, can go very far in delinking the study of trauma to the historical event of the Holocaust as a solely European story.

As Craps points out, the story is an indictment against what he identifies as "camp thinking." Camp thinking is a term borrowed from Paul Gilroy's work *Between Camps*[55] in which literal camps like refugee and concentration camps and metaphorical camps like "Indian" and "American" totalizes and essentializes identity. To see the Holocaust as a solely Euro-American history of trauma is to engage in "camp thinking," which ignores the continuity of Europe's colonial history across the globe. For Craps, one of the features of colonial frames for trauma theory is what he terms "cross-cultural incomprehension" which is brilliantly explored in the novel by the manner in which Baumgartner is treated by Indians as a representative of a group of people: sometimes Jew, sometimes German and always a firanghi (foreigner). Indian characters in the novel seem to have no understanding of the Holocaust, replicated by Baumgartner's own incomprehension of India: "Habibullah had no more conception of Baumgartner's war, of Europe's war than Baumgartner had of affairs in Bengal, in India."[56]

The novel challenges the idea that the Holocaust has a global and universal significance. It does so in the manner that the characters in the novel seem to have no understanding of each other as individuals. For Baumgartner, Indians are just that and when they fight, they fight as Hindus and Muslims. That Muslims are not safe in India is revealed in Habibullah's assertion that Hindus are driving Muslims out. Subtle connections are drawn between German Nazi nationalism and modern Indian nationalism in figures like Sushil, Baumgartner's neighbor, who has renounced religion for politics, is a determined Hindu nationalist, and will brook no criticism of Germany. Craps points out that a number of scholars have pointed out parallels between India's Muslims and Germany's Jews in Baumgartner's Bombay: "exploring the complex interrelations between European and Asian traumatic histories, Baumgartner's Bombay suggests the need for a productive and dynamic cross-culturalism which could help break what it portrays as a global cycle of violence."[57]

Comparative perspectives engaging more than Western colonial frames for trauma ought to be the emphasis of posttraumatic theology. Theologies of trauma that exhibit a "camp" mentality as has been argued, whether of geographical context, or historical trauma context, or of disciplinary contexts are inadequate for decolonizing Trauma Studies. "India" and "United States" as imagined communities are connected to both Europe's colonial past and a neo-colonial present. A future for its citizens: women and minoritized others will be a reality only when we reimagine the ways in which we speak about trauma.

Notes

1. Sir Penderel Moon (1998) *Divide and Quit: An Eyewitness Account of the Partition of India* (Delhi and Mumbai, India: Oxford University Press in India), 259–260.
2. Cathy Caruth (1995) "Introduction" in Cathy Caruth (ed.) *Trauma: Explorations in Memory* (Baltimore: Johns Hopkins University Press), 3.
3. Caruth, "Introduction," 3.
4. Stef Craps (2013) *Postcolonial Witnessing: Trauma Out of Bounds* (New York, NY: Palgrave MacMillan).
5. Narasingha P. Sil (2008) "Postcolonialism and Postcoloniality: A *Premortem* Prognosis," *Alternatives: Turkish Journal of International Relations*, vol. 7, no. 4, 20–33.
6. Sil, "Postcolonialism and Postcoloniality," 36.
7. Sil, "Postcolonialism and Postcoloniality," 36.
8. See for example, Mrinalini Greedharry (2008) *Postcolonial Theory and Psychoanalysis: From Uneasy Engagements to Effective Critique* (Basingstoke, United Kingdom; New York, NY: Palgrave MacMillan). See also a very early and prescient study of the "Psychology of Colonialism" in Ashis Nandy (1983) *The Intimate Enemy: Loss and Recovery of Self Under Colonialism* (New Delhi: Oxford University Press), 1–63.
9. Greedharry, *Postcolonial Theory and Psychoanalysis*, 6.
10. See in particular Shoshana Felman (1995) "Education and Crisis, or the Vicissitudes of Teaching," and Laura S. Brown (1995) "Not Outside the Range: One Feminist Perspective on Psychic Trauma" in Cathy Caruth (ed.) *Trauma: Explorations in Memory* (Baltimore: The John Hopkins University Press).

11. As quoted by Craps, *Postcolonial Witnessing*, 12.
12. Susannah Radstone (2007) "Trauma Theory: Contexts, Politics, Ethics," *Paragraph*, vol. 30, no. 1, 9.
13. Radstone, "Trauma Theory," 20. Thus "trauma" itself seems related and relatable to individualist modes of being.
14. Radstone, "Trauma Theory," 20, emphasis in the original.
15. Greedharry, *Postcolonial Theory and Psychoanalysis*, 157.
16. Radstone, "Trauma Theory," 16.
17. Radstone, "Trauma Theory," 19.
18. Quarts Holocaust-Germany-India-China (2015) "Monitoring, Exposing & Fighting Against Anti-Semitism and Racism," accessed February 8, 2015, http://www.anti-semitism.net/holocaust/how-india-and-china-explain-the-holocaust-to-school-kids.php.
19. Yasmin Khan (2007) "Introduction," *The Great Partition* (New Haven, CT and London, UK: Yale University Press), 4.
20. Khan, *The Great Partition*, 4.
21. Caruth, *Trauma: Explorations in Memory*, 4.
22. Caruth, *Trauma: Explorations in Memory*, 6.
23. Caruth, *Trauma: Explorations in Memory*, 10.
24. Gyanendra Pandey (2001) *Remembering Partition*, (New York: Cambridge University Press). Historiography in his argument is the "history of history," 10.
25. Pandey, *Remembering Partition*, 16.
26. Pandey, *Remembering Partition*, 45–66.
27. See Pandey, "Garhmukteshwar, November 1946" in *Remembering Partition*, 92–120. He provides an extraordinary reading of this particular incident through which he refracts colonialist historiography. The actual statistics on the numbers killed are sobering, but hardly comparable to the nationalist accounts in Pakistan and India on the same which depended on rumor rather than report. Neither are they comparable to a record of the incident compiled a few years later by a British official, see page 96. What is of interest to me, of course, is Pandey's analysis of contemporary histories which tend to minimize the significance of this particular incidence of violence, see pages 114–120.
28. Pandey, *Remembering Partition*, 119, emphasis in the original.
29. Pandey, *Remembering Partition*, 10.
30. Pandey, *Remembering Partition*, 11.
31. Pandey, *Remembering Partition*, 5.

32. Caruth, *Trauma: Explorations in Memory*, 156.
33. Pandey, *Remembering Partition*, 52.
34. Pandey, *Remembering Partition*, 54.
35. Pandey, *Remembering Partition*, 164.
36. Hent De Vries (2006) "Introduction," in Hent De Vries and Lawrence R. Sullivan (eds.) *Political Theologies: Public Religions in a Post-Secular World*, (New York: Fordham University Press), 65.
37. De Vries, "Introduction," 65.
38. Veena Das (2006) "The Figure of the Abducted Woman" in Hent De Vries and Lawrence R. Sullivan (eds.) *Political Theologies: Public Religions in a Post-Secular World* (New York: Fordham University Press), 441, emphasis in the original.
39. Das, "The Figure of the Abducted Woman," 428.
40. Das, "The Figure of the Abducted Woman," 427.
41. Das' work in Anthropology has variously dealt with Trauma Studies, especially in her association with Arthur Kleinman. The triptych of volumes (1997) *Social Suffering* (Berkeley: University of California Press), (2000) *Violence and Subjectivity* (Berkeley: University of California Press) and (2001) *Remaking a World: Violence, Social Suffering and Recovery* (Berkeley: University of California Press) contribute to Trauma Studies as anthropological investigations of social trauma.
42. De Vries, "Introduction," 75.
43. Das, "The Figure of the Abducted Woman," 428.
44. Veena Das (2000) "The Act of Witnessing: Violence, Poisonous Knowledge and Subjectivity" in Veena Das, Arthur Kleinman, Mamphela Ramphele and Pamela Reynolds (eds.) *Violence and Subjectivity* (Berkeley and Los Angeles, CA: University of California Press), 205–225.
45. Das, "The Act of Witnessing," 218.
46. Das, "The Act of Witnessing," 208.
47. Das, "The Act of Witnessing," 205.
48. Das, "The Act of Witnessing," 222.
49. Das, "The Act of Witnessing," 215.
50. See especially Caruth, *Trauma: Explorations in Memory*: "Perhaps the most striking feature of traumatic recollection is the fact that it is not a simple memory. Beginning with the earliest work on trauma, a perplexing contradiction has formed the basis of its many definitions and descriptions: while the images of traumatic reenact-

ment remain absolutely accurate and precise, they are largely inaccessible to recall and control," 151. That is, for Caruth, the memory of trauma remains as a violent trace in the subjectivity of the victims of trauma. Her exploration of the work of trauma and memory do not extend to what Das describes as the "descent into the everyday."
51. Das, "The Act of Witnessing," 220.
52. Das, "The Act of Witnessing," 218.
53. Radstone, "Trauma Theory," 24.
54. Radstone, "Trauma Theory," 13.
55. Paul Gilroy (2000) *Between Camps: Nations, Cultures and the Allures of Race*, (London: Routledge).
56. As quoted in Craps, *Postcolonial Witnessing*, 116.
57. Craps, *Postcolonial Witnessing*, 123.

Bibliography

Brown, L.S. 1995. Not outside the range: One feminist perspective on psychic trauma. In *Trauma: Explorations in memory*, ed. C. Caruth. Baltimore: The John Hopkins University Press.

Caruth, C. 1995. Introduction. In *Trauma: Explorations in memory*, ed. C. Caruth. Baltimore: The John Hopkins University Press.

Craps, S. 2013. *Postcolonial witnessing: Trauma out of bounds*. New York: Palgrave MacMillan.

Das, V. 2000. The act of witnessing: Violence, poisonous knowledge and subjectivity. In *Violence and subjectivity*, ed. V. Das, A. Kleinman, M. Ramphele, and P. Reynolds. Berkeley/Los Angeles: University of California Press.

Das, V. 2006. The figure of the abducted woman. In *Political theologies: Public religions in a post-secular world*, ed. H. De Vries and L.R. Sullivan. New York: Fordham University Press.

Felman, S. 1995. Education and crisis, or the vicissitudes of teaching. In *Trauma: Explorations in memory*, ed. C. Caruth. Baltimore: The John Hopkins University Press.

Gilroy, P. 2000. *Between camps: Nations, cultures and the allures of race*. London: Routledge.

Greedharry, M. 2008. *Postcolonial theory and psychoanalysis: From uneasy engagements to effective critique*. Basingstoke/New York: Palgrave MacMillan.

"How India and China explain the Holocaust to school Kids," Monitoring, Exposing & Fighting Against Anit-Semitism and Racism website. http://www.anti-semitism.net/holocaust/how-india-and-china-explain-the-holocaust-to-school-kids.php

Kleinman, A. 1997. *Social suffering.* Berkeley: University of California Press.
Kleinman, A. 2000. *Violence and subjectivity.* Berkeley: University of California Press.
Kleinman, A. 2001. *Remaking a world: Violence, social suffering and recovery.* Berkeley: University of California Press.
Moon, P. 1998. *Divide and quit: An eyewitness account of the partition of India.* Delhi/Mumbai: Oxford University Press.
Nandy, A. 1983. *The intimate enemy: Loss and recovery of self under colonialism.* New Delhi: Oxford University Press.
Pandey, G. 2001. *Remembering partition.* New York: Cambridge University Press.
Radstone, S. 2007. Trauma theory: Contexts, politics, ethics. *Paragraph* 30(1): 9–29.
Sil, N.P. 2008. Postcolonialism and postcoloniality: A *premortem* prognosis. *Alternatives: Turkish Journal of International Relations* 7(4): 20–33.
Vries, H.D. 2006. Introduction. In *Political theologies: Public religions in a postsecular world*, ed. H. De Vries and L.R. Sullivan. New York: Fordham University Press.

Afterword

In this collection, we have invited readers to think about what we are calling "post-traumatic public theology." The authors have explored the ways that theology informs responses to the aftermath of trauma, featuring how these play out in the public sphere. Although the theological complexities and responses to trauma are varied and multi-dimensional, we wanted to welcome readers to think further about what it means to *do* theology in the aftermath. In order to explore future trajectories and contexts for post-traumatic public theology, we invited four eminent theologians whose scholarship expands to publicly engage contexts of trauma. Each in turn responds from their particular perspectives.

We are grateful for their contributions and introduce them here. Phillis Isabella Sheppard is Associate Professor of Religion, Psychology and Culture at Vanderbilt University. She approaches trauma through an intrapersonal, interpersonal, and social analytic lens. Interlacing the social and intrapsychic, she emphasizes that theology must be "*of* those who live with trauma." Andrea Bieler is chair in Practical Theology at Basel Divinity School in Switzerland who engages trauma from the perspective of liturgical theology. Her work recognizes human vulnerability as a theological subject, advancing intercultural perspectives in theological praxis that responds to the aftermath of trauma. Warren Kinghorn is Associate Professor of Psychiatry at Duke University Medical Center; Associate Research Professor of Pastoral and Moral Theology at Duke Divinity School; and Staff Psychiatrist at the Durham VA Medical Center.

He explores the moral and theological dimensions of combat-related post-traumatic stress disorder, aiming in his interconnection of psychiatry and theology to enhance human flourishing. Storm Swain is Associate Professor of Pastoral Care and Theology and Director of Anglican Studies at the Lutheran Theological Seminary at Philadelphia. She encounters theological responses to trauma on the ground as a minister, hospital chaplain, and clinical pastoral education supervisor.

> **Question** *Why is theology important in reflecting on and responding to trauma? What role might theologians play in the public sphere to address traumatic aftermath?*
>
> **Phillis Isabella Sheppard** I would first say that trauma is important in theological reflection. Directing our attention to the brutal realities and traumata that are, very often, integral in some communities and people's lives, makes theology worth the paper on which it is written. Trauma demands that our theology and commitments begin on the ground, in the blood, sweat, and tears, and the pain-induced lesions that are carved into our bodies and psyches, and in the intersubjective realm. Historically, theology has often taken its categories or doctrines as the lens from which reflection embarks. The efficacy and result of this theological reflection is in the service of rationality over experience and thinking about theology, rather than those who should be the epistemological basis of theological reflection. If our theology is not *of* those who live with trauma and, I might add, subject to their reflection, it is dangerous talk *about* theology, and its danger lies in its power in theological discourse and theological practices to reproduce trauma. I am reminded of a woman who, in a course titled "Experiences of the Body and Pastoral Ministry," responded "I don't care what you say, God is a God of love" after we read the Judges text about the concubine who was raped, murdered, and then cut into 12 pieces. Her theology began with her doctrine of God. Delores Williams would remind us that "Rape is defilement, and defilement means wanton desecration."[1] She would also remind us that God-talk forms and informs what we see and believe about ourselves, the wielding of power (and trauma is so very

(continued)

> (continued)
>
> often induced in the ungodly and unjust wielding of power) and the culture that makes up our surroundings. As my student offered her god-talk of love, the narrative of violation and misogyny was rendered impotent—it could not tell us about a God on the ground; it could not dismiss a God who was ineffective; it could not challenge the ways in which misogyny and the violation of women's bodies was and is sustained by theological rhetoric.

In a strange paradox, this student also revealed why theology is important for reflecting on and responding to trauma. Theology that takes trauma into its core—its methodology, epistemology, aims, and hopes for practices that have the potential to resist what the psychoanalyst Alice Miller has referred to as "poisonous pedagogy" of trauma and theology. The response or reaction to trauma teaches the lessons, at least to those upon whom trauma is inscribed and therefore those most effected, that trauma is individual in terms of its impact; that trauma is limited to the interpersonal in its infliction, and that trauma is finite in terms of its duration. These are theological mistruths that have dire consequences for theology and for the lives of the traumatized.

Thus, trauma in theological reflection must be/come, albeit contested, a public theological matter. Of course, this means that theology, as a discipline, must allow itself to be a contested site and disciplinary matter. This requires a radical shift in and where theology/theological reflection take place. The shift is one where theological reflection is understood to begin in public with publics and communities; methodologically, theology would begin and end in the same place: in communities where trauma is inflicted upon those most vulnerable to the capricious and predictable wielding of injustice, as well as those who resist the denial of trauma, the pedagogies of silence, the theologies of violence. Theologians and theology have been sustained by rationality and abstract discourse; thus, the role of theologians, in the effort to respond to trauma, is to relinquish their status and power, and to unshackle theology from the power of the guilds, and to construct its work in the horror and muck that trauma enacts and embodies. The role of the theologian is to help make sense of trauma without claiming to be *the one* who is able to make sense.

> **Question** *Some of the authors turn to resources within the Christian tradition to respond to trauma. Where do—or would—you turn?*
>
> **Andrea Bieler** As a Christian theologian, I turn to the traumatic center of the Christian faith that moves around the edges of a wound that cannot be fully grasped in its significance. The New Testament offers at least nine different attempts to give words and meaning to the violent death of Jesus of Nazareth as well as to the uncanny, scary, beautiful, and unstable encounter with the risen Christ. A theologically grounded trauma response will unfold approaches to the cross that defy a victorious theology that sanitizes the trace of violence when it speaks about resurrection, reconciliation, or redemption. Instead, it will be inspired by the wisdom the passion stories unfold. If, for instance, we engage the gospel of Matthew, we can learn a lot about the banality of evil, how perpetrators and bystanders relate to inhumane humiliation that is at the heart of practices of torture, how the one who has to suffer through the violence loses his voice, and how the perpetrators and bystanders enter into a process of dehumanization as well. This trauma scene reveals at the same time what it truly means to be a child of God.

A Christian spirituality that situates itself in the context of trauma response will reject a bourgeois cynicism about the seemingly unchangeable nature of particular political circumstances. It engages a vision that makes itself known in glimpses and fragments that testify to the transformation of violence. A public Christian trauma theology will hold up this hope with a restless heart in the public square in the midst of injustice and the precariousness of life.

I would also turn to the Hebrew Bible. The Jewish and Christian sacred scriptures offer manifold reflections on how to reorder the world and the relationship with God and among humans in the aftermath of atrocious collective violence. Experiences of war against civilians, forced migration and deportation, the destruction of Jerusalem and the temple as sacred places in which God is believed to reside became major impulses for the creation and the re-shaping of sacred texts. Picturing divine pathos and action in relation to such experiences—as well as the future of involved communities and individuals—are key issues of theological reflection. Probably many communities of faith in the USA as well as in Europe have lost the ability to interpret the biblical witness along these lines. Being entrenched in a biblically informed theology will be one pivotal piece that helps theologians to regain a voice in the public square in the aftermath of collective violence.

Furthermore, careful consideration needs to be given to actual practices that attend to acts of truth telling, remembering and release, empathy, witnessing, and confession in the framework of restorative justice. An impressive example that comes to mind that has been developed within a Christian framework is the work of the Institute for Healing of Memories in Cape Town South Africa. Since 1998, this initiative brings together people from different ethnic groups that seek to attend to the wounds of Apartheid.

Question *Most of the essays focus on trauma within the USA. Is there a particular way in which you think trauma is worked out/expressed within this country?*

Warren Kinghorn The US Department of Veterans Affairs Medical Center in Durham, North Carolina, is not known for its artwork. Unlike the university hospital across the street, there are no marble fountains or Alexander Calder sculptures. But the poster-framed wall hangings of the Durham VA testify to the politics of traumatic forgetting and remembering. The oldest prints, faded from years of fluorescent glare, are comforting Monets, Winslow Homers, and other European and early American works showing natural beauty and peaceful (white) faces. A more recent installation showcases iconic scenes of North Carolina: The Blue Ridge Mountains, quaint coastal towns, the reconstructed Moravian village of Old Salem. And then, in a heavily traveled basement corridor leading to the "Patriot Café," an array of prints from the Second World War shows warplanes, naval vessels, and the smiling servicemen who operated them.

The art of the Durham VA was selected, no doubt, in order to promote a calming and healing environment for veterans, and to honor veterans' service. But within these healing and honoring intentions, a particular politics is displayed: *This is the culture you fought to protect. This is the homeland that remains at peace because of your service. These are the victorious American soldiers in whose long shadow you follow.* Such messages are overtly reinforced by the "Thank You For Your Service" banner that greets veterans when they arrive from the parking garage. But any representation of the grimness and brutality of war is missing. Indeed, purposefully so: when a recent display of Vietnam-era photos meant to honor Vietnam veterans included scenes of carnage, it provoked outcry and was removed within a day.

The art of the Durham VA, on the whole, displays a politics of traumatic forgetting. But the bodies of the veterans who pass by this art—sometimes briskly, sometimes slowly and painfully, sometimes pushed by others, often wearing veteran insignia—enact a politics of traumatic remembering. Trauma is engraved in many of these bodies. Sometimes, the engraving is discrete and overt: a facial scar, an above-the-knee amputation, a prosthetic arm. But more often, the traumatic inscription is displayed not in visible injury but in chronic illness, both psychological and somatic. Childhood sexual abuse, childhood physical abuse, intimate partner violence, wartime trauma, military sexual trauma, rape: these traumas inscribe themselves not only in "mental disorders" like PTSD and depression but in hypertension, diabetes, obesity, and low back pain. And these traumatic events themselves emerge within a broader cultural traumatic context: a racial order born in violence and maintained with violence, an industrialized economy that uses bodies and then discards them, a civil-religious order that renders homage to the American veteran as a "GI Messiah" who bears the sins of the people, whose life is offered as ultimate sacrifice, and whose death continues to secure the salvation of the chosen people.[2]

VA clinicians, of which I am one, are privileged to care for the remarkable human beings entrusted to us. But medical progress and billions of dollars of federal appropriations will not overcome the politics of traumatic forgetting. They may even perpetuate and reify it, assuaging a nation's guilty conscience that because we are serving those who served; nothing else is required. Even trauma-focused psychotherapy can perpetuate traumatic forgetting by abstracting post-traumatic stress, as a clinical phenomenon, from its originating sociopolitical contexts.[3] Indeed, there is no clinical language available to the VA by which the VA can narrate its own complex relationship to the shaping of traumatic experience in our culture. How essential, then, that clinical language be supplemented by non-clinical language—including theological language—that resists the evasions of traumatic forgetting and enables those touched by trauma to go on, alive and open-eyed.

> **Question** *Working in the area of trauma, where do you find hope?*
>
> **Storm Swain** Hope is grounded in the divine spark, the Trinitarian image of God in the human person.

When I think of hope in relation to trauma my mind goes to at least three places: a hospital room on a psychiatric ward, a street corner near the site of a mass shooting, and a Christmas tree standing next to the towering rubble of the World Trade Center. These places ground me in a hope that is light years away from a Hallmark card that is stitched on a sampler, or inscribed on a fridge magnet, but the kind of hope that is birthed in the places where suffering is known intimately. Having worked as a psychiatric chaplain, a pastoral psychotherapist, a spiritual care counselor responding to disasters, I have seen trauma up close and personal. Yet, I also believe I have been privileged to see some of the best of the human spirit even in and through brokenness. These spaces we could describe, along with Shelly Rambo, as Holy Saturday spaces. Intrapsychic, interpersonal, and sometimes institutional places where a traumatic event, or series of such, have happened, and there is no obvious sign of reconciliation, redemption, or resurrection in sight. Externally, nothing can 'make right' a brutal gang rape, one's mother beating a child mercilessly with a golf club, the slaughter of one's children, or the command to kill innocent others. The annihilation of life or self at the heart of such trauma is real and not fantasized. Pastoral theology, when it speaks of such trauma, has to face into that often brutal and violent Good Friday reality. Yet, hope emerges in how we face such realities.

It was in the psychiatric wards, where I began to hear and hold the stories of those almost or literally driven crazy by the actions of others, that the resilience of the human spirit began to impress itself upon me. Some mental illnesses seemed indeed to have a major genetic component and were often helped through discerning psychopharmacological intervention. Other illnesses were an in-working of traumatic experiences and, therefore, needed a different kind of working through. In the face of such traumas, hope could be as basic as the ability to hold on the idea that one will not be destroyed by that which has happened to you.

David Allison, a hospital chaplain, writing in the Journal of Pastoral Care, in 1992, outlined a model of spiritual assessment that had hope as one of its four key components. On one axis, he noted two relational dimensions, God, and the person's support system, and on the other axis were two existential dimensions, hope, and the meaning of the present situation. God and hope were seen as transcendent dimensions, the other two as immanent. (On these two axes, one was to plot the assessment of each of the four components, which radiated from a central position of strength, to widening circles of concern, distress, and despair.). This is a helpful way to think of hope, as a transcendent existential dimension of life, but intimately related to the meaning of a particular situation, how one is held in relationship throughout, and how or where we see God (or what we hold as ultimate concerns) in relation to such.

The hope that I have come to see has, for me, an intimate connection with trauma. Despite the choice of the diagnosticians who revised the Diagnostic and Statistical Manual of Mental Disorders to leave the experience of feeling hopeless, helpless, and/or horrified out of the criteria for PTSD in the DSM V, I think this is often the case. Those suffering from a trauma are often consciously hopeless. However, as a chaplain and therapist, I think I have experienced an unconscious hopefulness that arises in the therapeutic alliance. Those in the Object Relations field, rather than working from a theoretical perspective that sees 'repetition compulsion' as a continual negative reenactment associated with an instinctual drive toward death, see a purposiveness in the repeated ripples of traumatic experience in a person's life, where a trauma continues to be experienced and enacted in various ways. Whether we see it as experience that is held in the amygdala and has yet to process through hippocampal pathways, or see it as the unconscious driving for expression against the repressive forces of the ego, in practice, traumatic experience doesn't go away until it is attended to. Hope is often expressed as the courage to form such healing relationships that may make that possible. Yet, for those who are traumatized, it may not be consciously felt. Often, their hope may be in others, not themselves, and in the therapeutic transference. It may be the other that carries the hope for those that are broken by the action of others in this "sinful and broken world." Nevertheless, I have experienced time and again, this palpable drive for healing when there is a therapeutic relationship strong enough to hold the brokenness. Psychologists may describe this as a desire to master the original trauma; however, I would describe it as the movement of the spirit in the human person toward wholeness, which requires working through and integrating the suffering, to find that which is life-giving. Such transformation is not easy, as one fees the risk of annihilation all over again; yet when faced in sustainable ways, we can move through and begin to grieve the multiplicity of losses and find our way to a new normal, even a new sense of self.

Unfortunately, not all of us get that opportunity. Sometimes the trauma is too big, the losses too great, the sense of self too fragmented. Some don't get to experience Easter Sunday moments in their lives. Those that do, realize that this new reality is not an "everything is alright again" state of being. The resurrected body is a scarred one. It is one that has literally or metaphorically been brought back from the dead. This reality has taken relational intervention from outside the self. For those that don't get the opportunity, resources, and relational support to work through their trauma, our hope is that their story is not the end of the story. Our hope is that God's story will be the end of our story, in life and death. For those that cannot work through the trauma, those whom evil has touched too closely, those for whom forgiveness is not a reality they can live into, whose isolation is too constant, and when the call to love and prayer for those who persecute us is not attainable, hope has to rest in the one who can attain that, the one in whom brokenness is wholeness, and death can lead to a life beyond. God can forgive when I can't; God can see me as whole when I can only experience myself as broken; God can forgive even my lack of forgiveness; God sees and knows the evil, even when no one else does, and God weeps. Signs of the divine burst through, despite that evil, despite that brokenness, despite the suffering. Some of us are privileged enough to see such signs.

I will close by sharing one such moment. On the fourth anniversary of the shooting of 26 children and teachers at Sandyhook Elementary School, after all the memorial services were over, two people stood on the corner of the intersection at the bottom of the hill down the road from the site of the now demolished school and the construction of a new one. Further up the road, the roof of the firehouse was decorated with 26 light-up stars that shone out as a memorial in the December night.

Snow was falling, as these two individuals, just down the road from the Christmas trees, one dressed in a snowman's costume, the other in a gingerbread man's costume, waved their homemade corrugated cardboard sign at passing motorists, who honked affirmatively in return. The sign said, simply, "Love Wins." In the midst of a still grieving community, on the anniversary of an undeniably traumatizing event for so many, hope was expressed in that simple sign, "Love Wins."

Notes

1. Delores S. Williams (1993) *Sisters in the Wilderness: The Challenge of Womanist God-Talk* (Maryknoll, NY: Orbis), 148.
2. Jonathan H. Ebel (2015) *GI Messiahs: Soldiering, War, and American Civil Religion* (New Haven: Yale University Press).
3. David J. Morris, "The VA Treated My PTSD All Wrong," *Washington Post*, 11 Nov 2015, https://www.washingtonpost.com/posteverything/wp/2015/11/11/the-va-treated-my-ptsd-all-wrong/.

Bibliography

Ebel, J.H. 2015. *GI Messiahs: Soldiering, war, and American civil religion*. New Haven: Yale University Press.

Morris, D. J. 2015. The VA treated my PTSD all wrong. *Washington Post*. https://www.washingtonpost.com/posteverything/wp/2015/11/11/the-va-treated-my-ptsd-all-wrong/

Williams, D.S. 1993. *Sisters in the wilderness: The challenge of womanist god-talk*. Maryknoll: Orbis.

Appendix: Images

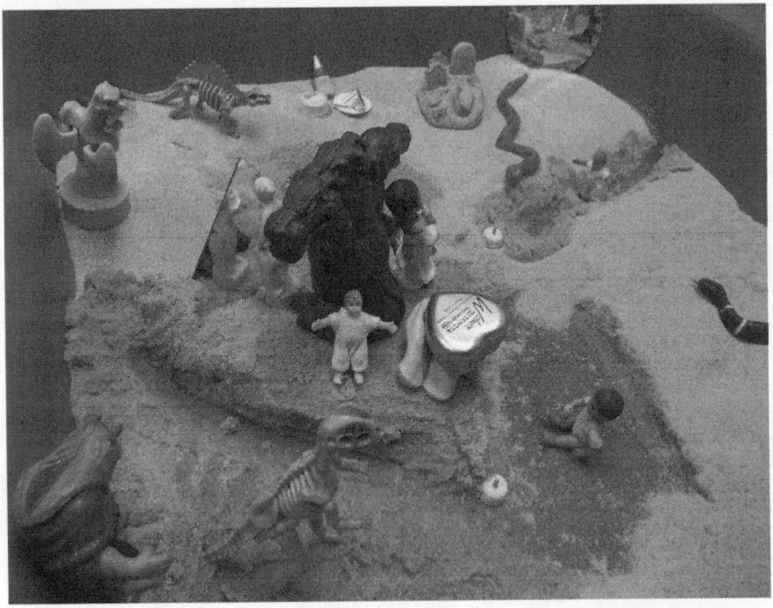

Index[1]

A

abjection, 139, 145
Abraham, Susan, 13, 17, 267–89
activism, 16, 222, 227
   mystical activism, 228–9, 231
   relationship to spirituality, 230
aesthetics, 9, 54, 79, 256
affect, 27, 65–6, 70, 73, 80, 138, 175–88, 206, 246, 266
   political affect, 65, 69
   regulation, 180, 188
   theory, 6, 175
affliction, 15, 115–17, 119–22, 125
agency, 26, 105, 108, 139, 148, 230, 280
   moral agency, 24
Ahmed, Sara, 83n15, 106–8
Alexander, Michelle, 183
Andrejevic, Mark, 39–42
anti-Semitism, 73, 271
Anzaldua, Gloria, 16, 22–31, 218
Arel, Stephanie N., 16, 153n25, 173–90
asceticism, 77, 127, 223
Augustine, Saint, 55, 132n9, 185

B

Baier, Annette, 161
Barth, Karl, 27–8
Betcher, Sharon, 86n87, 254
Bieler, Andrea, 17, 291, 294
Black Lives Matter, 12, 90, 255
Blanchot, Maurice, 79–80
body, 65, 69–71, 74, 78–80, 99, 116, 119, 143–4, 251
   body of Christ, 16, 54–5, 57, 155–7, 158–63, 165
   disabled bodies, 15, 65, 67–9
   flesh, 55, 64, 66, 68, 72, 77–9, 81, 82, 141–3, 249
   gendered bodies, 276
   Jesus' body, 13, 30–2, 77, 127
   relationship to trauma, 6, 46, 174, 179, 181
   shared or social, 33, 55
   virtual body, 155, 157–68
Boston Marathon bombings, 1, 10, 17, 63, 73, 253, 255

---

[1] Note: Page numbers with "n" denote notes.

© The Editor(s) (if applicable) and The Author(s) 2016
S.N. Arel, S. Rambo (eds.), *Post-Traumatic Public Theology*,
DOI 10.1007/978-3-319-40660-2

Brock, Rita Nakashima, 34n5, 69, 81, 251
Buber, Martin, 207–8
Burrus, Virginia, 66, 76, 77
Butler, Judith, 5, 11, 19n8, 68, 73, 79

C
Cain and Abel, 7, 139, 149
cancer, 16, 78, 158, 161
  diagnosis of, 158, 160
  relationship to trauma, 158, 161
Carter, Robert T., 94–6
Caruth, Cathy
  critiques of, 267, 270, 272, 275, 280 (*see also* (trauma theory))
  defining trauma, 4, 46, 159
  Trauma: Explorations in Memory, 19n7
Charcot, Jean-Martin, 4
Chopp, Rebecca, 244, 249, 259n29
Christianity, 47, 66, 73, 74, 77–8, 116, 128, 147
  the Christian tradition, 5, 69, 77, 99, 139, 182–3, 184, 225, 229
  faith, 130
  history of Christianity, 155, 249, 251
  identity, 53
  liturgy, 147
  narrative, 26, 27, 159
  practice/practices, 14, 38, 53, 115
  theology, 9, 14, 15, 48, 53, 77, 99, 115, 138, 220
  worship, 219
citizenship, 2, 17, 78, 219, 265, 271, 277, 282
Civil Rights Movement, 98–9
climate change, 137
Cole, Darrell, 29, 32

colonialism, 224, 260n37, 266, 267, 271, 276–7
  and Christianity, 9
  colonial practices, 98, 266, 276
compassion, 3, 11, 15, 31, 126, 128–9, 164, 205
  divine compassion, 117
  fatigue, 179, 224
  and justice, 129
  and love, 117
  orientation to others, 126, 164
Cone, James, 99–103, 260n32
confession, 32, 38, 49–51, 178
  culture of confession, 46
  practice of confession, 29, 129
Connerton, Paul, 26
contemplation, 29
  practices of, 16, 126, 225
  relationship to activism, 225, 229
Craps, Stef, 267–8, 270, 274, 280, 282–3
Crawford, Neta, 6, 7
creation, 90, 184
  account in Genesis, 137, 141
  God's creation, 32, 102, 128, 141, 149, 150, 229
  theopoetic creative process, 244–5, 249, 251–2
criminal justice, 16, 173–4, 181–3
crucifixion, 38, 48, 53, 73–5, 80, 81
  event in Christian teachings, 48, 53, 73, 75
cyberspace, 157, 162, 167

D
Das, Veena, 235n43, 272, 277–81, 282
detainees, 218–24
diagnosis, 9, 14, 34n4, 94, 97, 102, 109, 230
  cancer diagnosis, 158–61, 163, 165

Diagnostic and Statistical Manual of Mental Disorders, 168n16, 296
DSM-3, 4
DSM-4, 94
DSM-5, 94, 111n13, 296
dignity, 67, 75, 77, 99, 103, 183, 187
　indignity, 63–4, 68, 76, 91, 92, 95, 104
disability, 64–9, 74–6, 79, 131n1
　crip, 63–5, 68–70, 73
　disabled bodies, 65 (*see also* (body))
dissociation, 179, 180
Douglas, Mary, 143–5

E

Eaglestone, Robert, 5–6, 8, 19n10
Easter, 48, 57, 74, 81, 297
Eckhart, Meister, 118, 227
ecosystem, 136–8, 141
Erdrich, Louise, 116, 127
eschatology, 8
ethics, 183, 267, 280
Eucharist, 38, 53–7, 147, 261n38
Eurocentrism, 267, 269

F

Farley, Wendy, 236n69
Father Damien, 15, 117, 126, 128–31
forgetting, 11, 226
forgiveness, 30, 31, 182, 186, 222
　divine forgiveness, 297
　nature of forgiveness, 8
　process of forgiveness, 8, 29, 107, 185
　relationship to healing, 32, 129
Foucault, Michel, 29
Freud, Sigmund, 4, 143, 269
Fulkerson, Mary McClintock, 56–7, 261n40

G

Garland, Robert, 68–9, 74
Genesis
　Genesis 1:1, 1:26-28, 1:31, 4:9-12, 1:1, 102, 137, 139–40
Gilligan, James, 7, 178, 182–3, 186, 187
Gladwell, Malcolm, 156–7
globalization, 78, 225–6
God, 55, 77, 100, 109, 164, 230
　beloved, 117–19, 123–30
　God's Memory, 26, 31
　humiliated God, 15, 81
　image of God, 69, 74, 92, 102, 184, 187, 229 (*see also* (imago *dei*))
　of Israel, 31
　kingdom of, 148
　people of, 30, 139
　power and presence in trauma, 1, 141, 147, 217, 230
　Son of God, 249
　Spirit of God, 249
Good Friday, 48, 57
Gopin, Marc, 3
grief, 80, 158, 161, 162, 219
　grief work, 28, 257n11
　from trauma, 182, 185, 246

H

Hauge, Daniel, 15, 89–113
Herman, Judith, 11, 48, 185, 257n14
Hindu, 165, 266, 282
　nationalism, 276, 283
　relationship to Islam, 273, 278, 283
Holocaust, 45, 115, 266, 271, 278, 282–3
Holy Saturday, 48, 53, 80. *See also* Rambo, shelly
Holy Spirit, 31, 32, 54, 141
homicide, 242–3, 246, 249, 251, 253

hope, 13, 48, 57, 73, 107, 120, 149, 165, 219
  Christian conceptions of, 122, 124, 141, 295–8
  relationship to trauma healing, 117, 118
  and resistance, 231, 249, 252
Hosea, 140, 149
  Hosea 4:1, 3, 140
humiliation, 7, 49, 183
  politics of humiliation, 15
humility, 73–81, 109, 183
  as counterpoint to humiliation, 72–3
  as way of communal living, 75–8, 81
Hurricane Katrina, 10

I

identity, 24, 32, 77, 100, 116, 205
  cultural identity, 255, 267
  formation of, 194–5, 202–3, 281
  national identity, 13, 67, 272–3, 275–6, 279
  religious identity, 2, 53, 102, 196, 226, 231n6, 272–3, 275–7, 288
imago dei, 103, 184, 187, 244, 249, 256
immigration, 2, 16, 217–37
  detention, 16, 217–37
incarceration, 104, 178, 182, 183, 219
incarnation, 73–4, 77, 161, 164
India, 13, 64, 144, 162, 265–6, 271–2, 275–8, 280–4
  Muslim–Hindu relations, 273, 276, 278, 282–3
individualism, 13, 30, 52, 101, 200, 225, 268
intercultural, 17, 252–6, 281
interfaith service, 1, 2

J

Jennings, Willie James, 9, 101
Jeremiah, 139–40, 149
  Jeremiah 4:21, 27–28, 140
Jesus, 33, 76, 81, 109
  baptism of, 80, 141
  body of Jesus, 14, 32
  crucifixion of, 73, 80
  as healer, 15, 142–6, 167
  humiliation of, 66, 73, 75
  incarnation, 141, 164 (*see also* (incarnation))
  ministry of, 9, 30–1, 148
  resurrection of, 9, 30, 31, 53, 66, 75, 76, 81, 138
  suffering of, 13, 115–16
  transfiguration of, 249, 253
John, Gospel of, 73, 142, 167
  John 20:19-29, John 9:1, 6–11, 31, 142
John of the Cross, Saint, 115–33
Jones, Katherine Janiec, 193–215
Julian of Norwich, 119–20, 124
justice, 129, 221, 227, 231
  criminal justice, 173, 181, 183
  injustice, 32, 52, 69, 75, 91, 93, 95, 98, 104, 105, 108, 220–1, 229
  justice system, 7, 173–4, 182–4
  prophetic justice, 243
  racial justice, 99, 108
  restorative justice, 16, 173–88
  retributive justice, 173, 181–2, 184, 185
  social justice, 219, 229, 245

K

kingdom of God, 148
Kinghorn, Warren, 17, 24, 29, 32
King, Martin Luther, Jr., 73
Kleinman, Arthur, 9, 20n21, 235n43, 286n41
Koestenbaum, Wayne, 71
Kristeva, Julia, 144–5

L

Lacan, Jacques, 39
Lange, Dirk, 53–4, 168n15
liberation, 98–100, 109, 115, 124, 223, 231, 253
  black liberation theology, 92, 99
  liberation theology, 115
limbic system, 6, 246
Louis D. Brown Peace Institute, 242–4
love, 48, 53, 57, 81, 146, 155, 185–6, 231
  beloved, 117–19, 123–30
  divine love, 55, 117–19, 123–7
  great Love, 15, 81, 129, 130, 132n14
  redemptive love, 48
  self-love, 183
Lowney, Kathleen, 50–1
Luke, Gospel of, 148
  Luke 17:20–21, Luke 9:28-36, 258n17
Luther, Martin, 54

M

Mandela, Nelson, 73, 184
marginalization, 183, 222
  marginalized peoples, 66, 99, 103, 109, 221, 226, 228, 243, 245
  Mark 10:47, Mark 9:2-8, 167, 258n17
martyr(s), 77, 251
Mary, mother of Jesus, 75, 76, 81
Matthew, gospel of, 292
  Matthew 8, Matthew 17:1–7, 146, 258n17
media, 1, 10, 40, 41, 43, 44, 46, 47, 97
  media coverage, 11, 254
  relationship to trauma, 90, 211
  social media, 12, 39, 156, 166

medical model, 9, 34n4
meditation, 121, 122, 125, 165, 227
memorials, 2
  Traveling Memorial Button Project, 244
memory, 9, 46, 63, 66, 67, 95, 120, 122, 124
  God's memory, 26, 31
  memory work, 14, 24, 27, 28, 30–2
  problems of memory, 11, 25, 46, 266
  remembrance, 241
  trauma and memory, 52, 56, 57, 179, 246, 269, 270, 272 (*see also* (traumatic memories))
Mercadante, Linda, 199, 209, 211n2
migrant(s), 218, 230
Miller, Madelyn, 179, 180
Miller, William Ian, 68, 71
Mollica, Richard, 9, 20n22
moral injury, 14, 25, 26, 28, 31–3
morality, 25, 28, 51, 71, 72, 108
  moral calling, 243–5, 252
mourning, 2, 139, 140, 149, 185, 279
mystic, 161
  Christian mystics, 118
  mystical activism, 217–37
  mystical journey, 221, 223, 225, 227, 231
  mysticism, 217, 220, 221, 228–31

N

Nathanson, Donald, 182, 183
nationalism, 266, 281, 283
  "ablenationalism", 64, 70
neoliberalism, 78, 224
"9/11", 2, 7, 12, 16, 193–5, 206, 255
  "post-9/11", 12, 193, 195, 210, 211
"nones", 198–200

O

oppression, 91, 115, 220, 222, 226, 227, 230
   race and, 10, 15, 92, 93, 96, 98, 100, 102–5, 108
   resistance to, 220, 226, 243, 254–5
   structures of, 51, 243

P

Pakistan, 17, 265, 271, 272, 275–8, 280–2
Pandey, Gyanendra, 272–6, 279, 281, 282
Parker, Rebecca, 81, 251
partition of India, 13, 266, 271–82
pastoral care, 26, 28–30, 33, 115, 218, 243, 245, 248, 250, 256
patriotism, 25
Paul, Saint, 74, 140, 155, 156, 161, 166
peace, 3, 31, 123, 149, 228
   peace and justice, 104, 243, 245, 248
   Peace Institute (*see* (Louis D. Brown Peace Institute))
   peace march, 242, 249, 251, 252
penance
   relationship to therapeutic, 29, 30, 123, 127, 129
   religious practice, 29, 30, 32, 33
perpetrators, 47, 247
   relationship to victims, 24, 174, 181, 184–8
Pew Research Center, 194, 198
Philippians, 74
   Philippians 2:5-8, 85n53
Pierce, Yolanda, 99, 103–5, 107
Pinsky, Robert, 187
play, 17, 245
   concept of play, 246, 249–52, 256
   sandplay, 245–8, 250
pluralism, 209, 211
political theology, 14, 277, 279, 281. *See also* theology
politics, 243, 266, 267, 269, 277, 283
   politics of humiliation, 280
   politics of trauma, 63–8, 71, 74–5, 77–9
popular culture, 46, 52, 53
Porete, Marguerite, 118, 123
postcolonialism, 224, 269, 271–3
   critiques of trauma, 266, 268–71, 279–83
postmodernism, 78
   postmodern culture, 39, 46
post-traumatic care, 245, 248
post-traumatic growth, 248
post-traumatic stress disorder (PTSD), 2, 4, 34n4, 94
prayer, 122, 129
   eucharistic, 54
   Peace Prayer, 245
   practice of prayer, 155, 163, 225
prison(s), 16, 173, 175–7, 225, 226
   imprisonment (*see* (incarceration))
   prison system and trauma, 178, 180, 182, 183, 219
prophetic, 17, 92, 252
   justice, 243 (*see also* (justice))
   pastoral care, 249, 250
   power, 253
   testimony, 241, 242, 248, 256
Psalm
   Psalm 51; Pslam 103:14, 31, 34n16, 118
psychiatric disorder, 220
psychoanalysis, 4, 98, 267–70
PTSD. *See* post-traumatic stress disorder (PTSD)

public, 47, 55, 76, 138, 188
  discourse, 160, 161, 193
  humiliation, 75–7 (*see also* (politics))
  performance, 204, 252
  vs. private, 38, 43, 45, 46, 49, 54
  square, 149, 248, 249, 253
  theology, 158, 201, 252, 254, 256, 282
punishment, 69, 74
  institutions/systems, 7, 30, 173, 181, 183
  and theology, 124, 184, 185, 188

R

racism, 10, 68, 92, 94, 97, 107
  connection to other forms of oppression, 102
  institutional racism, 91, 92, 221
  and mental health, 93, 94, 96, 99–101
  and policing, 89
  structural racism, 15, 91, 94, 96, 102, 106, 107, 109
  systemic racism, 90, 107, 109, 222, 228
Radstone, Susannah 49, 291–293, 298, 300, 302, 304–307
Rambo, Shelly
  conception of the "middle", 38, 169n16
  defining trauma, 46, 48, 201, 202
  integrating theology and trauma, 50–4
  Spirit and Trauma, 158, 285n30
reality TV, 14, 37–50, 52–6
reconciliation, 92, 107, 109
  process of reconciliation, 29
  racial reconciliation, 99, 101, 104

Truth and Reconciliation Commission (TRC), 184
recovery, 33, 44, 50, 56, 67
  movements, 38, 51
  from trauma, 11, 45, 48, 105, 108, 185, 268
redemption, 47–52, 109
  as healing, 141
  in popular media, 38, 43, 47, 50, 51
  religious conceptions, 53, 56
Reklis, Kathryn, 165, 166
religious identity, 196, 236n6, 272
  relationship to nation, 266, 272, 273, 275–7, 282
religious studies, 193–214
resilience, 3, 10, 12, 68, 73, 196, 217, 230, 243, 244, 249, 250
restorative justice, 173–90. See also justice
resurrection, 66, 77, 120, 243
  event in Christian teachings, 9, 38, 48, 53, 81
  relationship to healing, 66, 76, 81, 250
retributive justice, 173, 181, 184
Rogers, Annie, 187
Romans, 116, 149
  Romans 8:18-19a, 21–23, 140
Root, Maria, 10
Roth, Anne, 44, 45, 47, 51

S

sacraments, 14, 53, 55, 118
sacred texts, 1, 7, 15
sacrifice, 25, 28–30, 48, 129
salvation, 8, 51, 184
  Christian understandings of, 48, 53, 81, 128, 140, 251
scars, 57, 66, 74, 220

"secret ladder", 122–6, 132n11
shame, 6, 7, 31, 281
   relationship to guilt, 180, 183, 186, 219
   relationship to trauma, 24, 186–8 (*see also* (trauma))
   shame and affect, 176, 182, 185–8
   shame and humiliation, 64, 66, 71, 77, 116
Shay, Jonathan, 23
Sheppard, Phillis, 98, 103
Shoah, 270, 271
Shoop, Marcia, 56, 57
Sirach
   in early Christianity, 74, 116
   history in the United States, 98, 104, 108, 261n42
   Sirach 11:1, 2:1-3a, 4b-5, 76
Snyder, Susanna, 16–17, 217–37
social justice. *See* justice
Soelle, Dorothe, 16, 218, 221, 223–9
soul repair, 25, 29, 30, 32
sovereignty, 270, 271, 277
spiritual, 221, 230
   care, 1, 243
   journey, 14
   narratives, 103, 242
   practices, 184
   "spiritual but not religious", 199, 207, 211n2
   teachers, 117, 120, 121, 123, 125, 245
   transformation, 118, 119, 124
Stone, Bryan P., 14, 37–61
strong tie environment, 156, 157, 163–7
suffering, 25, 38, 44, 49–52, 91, 115, 179
   afflictive, 116–19, 125, 126, 129
   collective suffering, 266, 273
   nature and meaning of, 2, 3, 200, 210
   psychological suffering, 46, 102, 104

   suffering of the Earth, 137–40, 149, 151n11
   traumatic suffering, 46, 48, 53, 64, 138, 158, 180, 229
   witnessing suffering, 46, 57, 220, 224
Swain, Storm, 17, 292, 297

T
technology, 67, 166, 279
   digital technology, 156, 157, 161, 165
   technology of the self, 29, 33
Teresa of Avila, Saint, 117, 118
terrorism, 1, 2, 67, 73, 159
testimony, 46, 59n42, 89, 90, 95, 107, 126, 269. *See also* witness
   role of testimony in trauma, 53, 185, 187, 241, 242, 249, 277, 278
Thatamanil, John, 164
theology, 56, 194–8, 205, 210
   of atonement, 53
   black, 92, 99, 105
   Christian, 9, 48, 115, 138, 220
   classical, 5, 115
   contemplative, 15, 115, 119
   pastoral, 297
   political, 4, 277, 279, 281
   post-traumatic, 201, 265, 273, 275, 277, 282, 284
   public, 158, 201, 254–6
   systematic, 77
theopoetics, 241–61
therapeutic, 25, 44, 46, 50, 250, 257n13
   conventions, 44, 47, 50, 52, 57
   framing of trauma, 94, 97, 106, 109, 268
   practices, 26, 29, 30, 92, 105–10, 254
   relationship, 28, 92

INDEX   311

Thompson, Deanna, 16, 155–70
Timberg, Robert, 67–9
Tombs, David, 66, 75
torture, 66, 70, 75–7, 80
transcendence, 57, 100, 105, 231, 249, 279
transfiguration, 3, 244, 249–53, 256
transformation, 8, 14, 56, 110, 242, 244
  spiritual transformation, 118–19, 124
  transformation and reality TV, 37, 42, 43, 48–50, 52–3 (*see also* (popular culture))
  transformation of trauma, 245, 250–1
trauma, 31–60, 117–18, 139–40, 159
  collective trauma, 107, 194, 243, 265–6
  impact on the body, 6 (*see also* (body))
  individual trauma/personal trauma, 4, 38, 52, 246
  insidious, 10
  and language, 159–60, 186–7
  racially motivated, 91–4, 96, 100–5, 107–9
  re-traumatization, 94, 97, 106, 109, 180
  and shame, 81, 180, 186–7
  study of trauma, 50, 265–7
  vicarious, 179–80
  war trauma, 11, 13
trauma theory, 5, 17, 46, 115, 268–70
  critiques of, 17, 159, 266–7, 270, 277–81, 283
traumatic memories, 11, 56–7, 270

V
Van der Kolk, Bessel, 189n11, 258n14
Veterans, 14, 23–33, 45, 293, 294
  military culture, 23, 30
  Veterans Administration (VA), 293, 294
  wounded veterans, 23, 26, 29
Victim, 44–7, 51–2, 75, 96–7, 116, 242
  relationship to perpetrator, 24, 149, 181, 184–5, 270
  victimization, 44, 47, 51, 174, 178, 277–8, 282
Violence, 32, 45, 46, 76, 90, 103, 118, 139, 159
  aftermath of, 4, 31, 69, 241–61, 267
  communal, 241–61, 277
  of the cross, 54, 567
  domestic, 95
  gang-related, 10
  gendered, 277, 282, 291
  nonviolence, 73, 79
  police, 90–1, 97, 109
  psychic, 91
  racial, 94
  sexual, 174, 177–8, 266, 281–2
  war, 26–8, 31
virtual community, 16, 157, 163

W
Wallace, Mark I., 15, 135–53
Walsh, Michelle, 17, 241–63
Weak tie environment, 157
Weil, Simone, 116, 119, 125
Wesley, John, 54
Western, 65–6, 69, 184, 251, 254, 256, 267, 271, 277–8, 280–1
whiteness, 15, 93, 105–6, 108
wholeness, 15, 69, 78, 99, 207–8, 254

Williams, Delores, 290, 300n1
witness, 31, 90, 242
   Christian witness, 53, 165, 184, 256
   "cloud of witnesses", 158, 164
   role of witnessing in trauma, 38, 43, 46–9, 51–2, 77, 151n16, 188, 246
   and testimony, 178–80, 244–5, 248–9, 251–3, 279
wounds, 28, 32, 57, 116, 196
   of racism, 93, 107
   as religious image, 31, 252
   traumatic wounds, 17–18, 67, 108, 118, 206

Z

Zephaniah
   Zephaniah 2:3, 85n76
Zizek, Slavoj, 41

CPI Antony Rowe
Eastbourne, UK
December 07, 2019